D1497799

The Autobiography of John Hays Hammond

TAFT AND MYSELF

THE AUTOBIOGRAPHY OF

JOHN HAYS HAMMOND

Illustrated with Photographs

VOLUME

2

FARRAR & RINEHART · INCORPORATED

On Murray Hill, New York

Contents Volume Two

List of Illustrations

The Autobiography of John Hays Hammond

CHAPTER TWENTY

In Pretoria Gaol

THE DEATH CELL—SENTENCE COMMUTED—FRIENDS
IN NEED—SMUGGLED SAUSAGES—SUICIDE OF A
FELLOW PRISONER—TWO HUNDRED MILLION BIG
BUGS—THE MISPLACED HUMOR OF MARK TWAIN—
"MAGNANIMITY BY INCHES"—THE BARGAINING
BEGINS—SOUTH AFRICA DEMANDS OUR RELEASE TO
RESTORE PROSPERITY—PRICED AT $125,000—
WELCOMED BY JOHANNESBURG—THE SELECT
COMMITTEE OF THE CAPE OF GOOD HOPE—A NOVICE IN
INTERNATIONAL LAW—"REVOLUTIONS ARE EXPENSIVE"

As I stepped from the dock, the spectators were so emotionally stirred that an old man collapsed directly in front of me. I stooped to lift him and was reminded of my status by a swift blow from the rifle butt of a guard.

Du Plessis, the head jailer, seated himself beside me in a closed carriage, and we started off at a quick pace for the jail. As we neared the gates, a delivery wagon carrying a coffin passed and entered the prison gate just ahead of us. My nervous tension was so great that the most macabre circumstance would have seemed funny. I pointed out the coffin and asked Du Plessis, "Is that for Phillips or for me? It looks as though it would fit either of us."

Du Plessis made no comment. The English claimed he was gross and brutal, and were resentful of his methods. I, on the contrary,

388 The Autobiography of John Hays Hammond

considered that only the characteristics of a jailer should be looked for in a jailer. We were in prison and not at a party. Du Plessis and I respected each other's position and got along without friction.

News of our sentence had preceded us. Even the guards were visibly moved. The other prisoners, who had been given a sentence of two years and a fine of $10,000 each, were marched through the streets. As they filed within the prison gates, Dr. Leyds stood smiling at them, unable to suppress his evident satisfaction. The sinister character of Kruger's chief counselor was at this moment truthfully revealed. Leyds hated the Uitlanders more keenly than did the bitterest Boer. It was the Uitlanders who thwarted the large-scale grafting schemes of Leyds and his associates.

Phillips, Farrar, Frank Rhodes, and I were at once placed in the death cell, and the customary formalities for those about to die were observed. The death watch was maintained for twenty hours. The silence of the night was disturbed only by the occasional subdued guttural voice of the guard and the steady hammer strokes of the carpenters erecting the gallows outside.

I was so utterly worn out with fatigue and illness that I threw myself on the nearest dirty cot and passed the night tossing restlessly from side to side.

When daylight finally came I sat up and all four of us looked disconsolately at one another.

"What sort of night did you pass, Jack?" asked Frank Rhodes.

"I'm afraid I didn't sleep much," I replied. "How about you, Frank?"

"The same," Colonel Rhodes sighed.

At this moment the door was thrown open to admit a messenger. He announced that he had been sent by Dr. Leyds who had interceded with Kruger in our behalf.

"Gentlemen, I have the honor to inform you that the death sentence has been commuted."

I had risen to my feet at his entrance. As soon as he finished speaking, I asked quickly, "To what?"

"Life imprisonment."

"Oh, hell!" I exclaimed disgustedly and turned on my heel.

Leyds's emissary seemed taken aback by our reception of his news.

He had evidently been told to bring back an accurate report of our joyous excitement and expressions of gratitude. But Leyds was not a good psychologist. He had underestimated the moral stamina of the leaders and had felt sure that they would be deeply grateful for his intervention, so that he might appear before the world in the role of one who is generous to a defeated enemy.

The messenger asked rather stiffly, "Is there any message you would like me to convey to Dr. Leyds?"

"Not so far as I am concerned," I said shortly, and asked the others, "How do you feel about it?"

They agreed that thanks were uncalled for.

It had suited the Boer purposes to keep us on the rack as long as possible and then, by proclaiming an act of clemency, to impress the world with Boer magnanimity. After several days in the death cell, we were moved back to the Jameson cottage, and then informed for the first time that on the very afternoon of the trial our sentence had been commuted to fifteen years' imprisonment. So even the message Leyds sent us under the guise of mercy was a cruel lie.

The decision as to the commutation of our sentences had not been arrived at without extended argument. The Executive Council had taken several votes. At each ballot two recalcitrant Boers had insisted they would be satisfied with nothing less than having us hang as high as Haman.

Kruger himself favored milder punishment—he hated the idea of blood guilt. He was astute enough to realize the effect on the world at large if so drastic a revenge were taken. He was fully aware that there were definite bounds beyond which he could not pass without precipitating intervention by the British government.

Finally, he won over his opponents by telling them the leaders would become martyrs if they were hanged, but that as hostages they might prove of considerable commercial value to the Boers. The virtual certainty of ultimately being able to extort large fines was so enticing that the Council voted unanimously not to hang us.

Many of my friends in the United States and Europe assured me later that they had had no fears for my life, but the Uitlanders had been far from convinced that the matter would end happily. There was no telling what might happen. Because of their limited knowledge of circumstances, it was natural for outsiders to be confident of our safety, but we were living in the midst of a Boer populace inflamed by race hatred to a point where the possibility of foreign complications was stubbornly ignored.

The news of our conviction, cabled all over the world, brought an immediate reaction. Messages were received from all quarters urging the exercise of the presidential pardoning power.

One of the most generous responses to my need did not come to my attention until I returned to America some years later. Harry Davis, a mining promoter, asked me, "Have you been to see John W. Mackay yet?"

"Why, no, why should I? I hardly know him."

"Hasn't anyone told you of his efforts on your behalf when you were in Pretoria Gaol?"

"What did he do?"

"He offered me $100,000 to use in any way I saw fit that might help you and said he'd add another $100,000 when that was gone."

This generous gesture certainly merited acknowledgment. The next morning I called on Mackay, who was then head of the Mackay cable system. When I tried to thank him for his kindness, Mackay interrupted, "Let's not talk about it."

"But," I protested, "I have to talk about it. I'd have done it long ago if I had known anything about it before yesterday."

"Look here, Hammond. I'm an older man than you, but I bet I can lick you and I'll do it right here if you mention the matter again."

Mackay was truly beloved by miners of the West. After his death I met many of his old friends and from them learned of his innumerable kindnesses and his great generosity. When his estate was settled it transpired that Mackay had given hundreds of thousands of dollars to old chums of his, and had always done it so quietly that no one but the recipient knew it.

The report of my plight brought Robert W. Chapin and his wife from Cape Town to Pretoria. Chapin was acting American consul in the absence of Consul Manion, and Mr. and Mrs. Chapin were old-time friends of my wife and myself; indeed, "Bob," as well as three of Mrs. Chapin's brothers, and I had been intimate friends during our Yale schooldays. Mr. and Mrs. Chapin went to see Paul Kruger the morning after the trial. They found him in one of his prophetic moods, awaiting divine inspiration. To their appeals for mercy he said, "I tell my generals to show mercy on the battlefield; but the penalty of murder is bloodshed."

Barney Barnato, whose reactions were always immediate and unrestrained, called at once upon my wife and told her not to worry: he would stay in Pretoria just so long as the prisoners were in jail. When I repeated this remark, the almost universal response was that Barney was bluffing as usual. I maintained that he would keep his word, and he did. He became active on our behalf immediately.

With his innate love of theatricality he put a mourning band around his hat and crape on his sleeve and went to the Pretoria Club. There he happened on Gregorowski. Barney planted himself in front of the judge and began to denounce him roundly for his conduct of the trial.

Gregorowski responded in Dutch: "Mr. Barnato, you are not a gentleman. I was appointed to put down rebellion, and I have done so to the best of my ability."

Barney could not understand him, and countered with, "Maybe you're right, but still you're a damn rotten judge!"

For a time Gregorowski was exceedingly unpopular; when he returned to Bloemfontein there was a demonstration against him.

My last news of him came just after the Boer War. James Barnes, war correspondent, writer, and big game hunter, brought me a message from Gregorowski to the effect that, if the judge had known about Paul Kruger at the time of the Reform Committee's trial what he found out later, he would have condemned Kruger to death instead of the four leaders.

Some of the more cool-headed residents of the Rand were made uneasy by anti-Boer demonstrations, which tended to perpetuate the race antagonism it was to our interest to subdue. They rightly believed that our cause would be injured by too violent condemnation of the Boers. George Farrar's brother, Percy, had notices posted throughout South Africa urging the Uitlanders to be moderate in their expressions of opinion while negotiations on our behalf were going forward.

Barnato, whose threat to close his mines had caused widespread concern, was persuaded to confine himself to more temperate efforts. Nevertheless, he worked night and day for our release. He gave $25,000 to the Boer government to alleviate the distress caused by the Raid, and told Kruger that this donation ought to warrant the release of his nephew, Solly Joel.

When Kruger refused even to discuss the subject of prisoners, Barney adopted a new mode of procedure. He ordered two great marble lions as a gift for the president, to be presented on his birthday in October. Oom Paul pretended not to know what lay hidden under the tarpaulins on his front porch, and the pleasure evinced by these two grown-up children over the secret helped to bring a spirit of amity into the dealings between Boer and Uitlander. On Kruger's birthday, a religious service was held in the parlor, and then the two lions were unveiled in all their gleaming majesty. In a halo of whiskers, these three monarchs of the veldt confronted the camera.

Immediately after adjournment of the court that convicted us, a petition for commutation of sentence had been drawn up and circulated among the Boers themselves. We knew nothing of this. Botha was one of the signers. Even the chairman of the First Raad, Schalk Burger, expressed keen sympathy for many of the convicted men, and said they would be well advised to leave the decision to the government.

The opinion of the liberal Boers as to "this grim judicial farce" was well summarized in a letter to the Johannesburg *Star:*

> . . . the resolute and fearless demeanour under the trying ordeals through which they [the Reform Committee] have passed has gained for them increased respect and honour from the many thousands here and elsewhere in South Africa, who make common cause with them in striving for those just and righteous reforms which are the inalienable heritage of every free-born citizen—a cause which must eventually succeed, however mighty the opposition may be . . . Johannesburg has been asked to suppress all demonstrative excitement lest the interest and safety of its leaders be prejudiced,

and it has loyally responded to the request, although the feelings of its citizens have been strained to breaking point . . . I am a son of the soil, with not a strain of English descent, and by choice a Republican, but I have the Englishmen's love for fair play; and admire their sense of honour and love of liberty; hence it is a keen humiliation to feel that an indelible blot has been cast upon the escutcheon of this Republic by the events of this week.

Immediately upon our arrival at the jail, the prisoners were searched and all our money, jewelry, tobacco, matches, and pipes were taken away. Tobacco was always contraband and had to be smuggled in.

Jail regulations were ultimately relaxed in respect to visitors, books, and papers. Except for spasmodic censorship, we could write and receive letters freely. The most unpleasant aspect of our treatment was that we were once more put on Kaffir rations, but soon most of the Reformers' wives arrived in Pretoria and were moving heaven and earth to improve conditions for their husbands.

Mrs. Solly Joel used to come into the prison with the crown of her hat filled with cigars, a bottle of cream under her skirt, and a brace of ducks (too well broiled to quack) concealed in her bustle. Mrs. Clement wore a huge sausage around her waist. In the big sleeves of the period the ladies were able to conceal tins of sardines, beef essence, condensed milk, and other delicacies. After a short while, however, the rules were again modified so that food could be sent in from the Pretoria Club, as had been done during our first imprisonment.

I used to obtain an additional tidbit from Sullivan, a trusty employed in the prison hospital kitchen. One evening he brought me a chop; while I was devouring it, he asked, "Want to know how I got in here, Mr. Hammond?"

"Why, yes, Sullivan; as a matter of fact I've been wondering, but I didn't like to seem curious."

"Could you stand a hard-luck story?"

After receiving a sentence of fifteen years' imprisonment, I felt sure a regulation hard-luck story would cheer me up.

Sullivan needed no encouragement. "I was working for a Boer who had a store near Pretoria. He went out one night, and forgot to lock the safe—the damn careless cuss. I could see all the coin just begging to be used, and I'd had a hot tip on the market that very day. I thought I could make a quick cleanup and put the money back before the stingy old Boer found out I'd borrowed it. Just as I'd taken it from the safe, damned if the old fellow didn't come back. He thought I was stealing, when I was only borrowing.

"The judge asked me whether I'd taken the money and I said I had, but I told him the Boer had no right to leave his money around like that. He wouldn't listen to me. He said five years was the penalty for my kind of borrowing. So I said to him, 'I'll make you a sporting proposition, Judge, I'll toss you double or quits.'

"He didn't see the joke. He gave me a nasty look and said, 'Five years more for contempt of court.'

"I had a chance at him later. I was working on the road gang when he went by one day. I dodged the guard, made a quick dive, and would have finished him proper if I hadn't been dragged off. They gave me some more time for that, but it was worth it."

I agreed with Sullivan that the punishment does not always fit the crime.

I should like to tell another story about Sullivan, which I am sure will amuse the younger generation, who blush very little at such things—the older generation may skip if they find it indelicate. One of the cockney English prisoners was talking with Sullivan one day, and protesting against the treatment he was receiving. "Sullivan, these Boers can't put an Englishman in stocks like this and get away with it, can they?"

Sullivan said: "The hell they can't. They are doing it, aren't they, and they are getting away with it. Just look around you and see all the Englishmen and how they are being treated.

"Let me tell you something," continued Sullivan, "these Boers can do anything they want to with you, except one thing."

Sullivan's friend was all ears by now and he asked eagerly what that one thing was.

"They can't put you in the family way," said Sullivan.

Several years later, on one of those dreary days that characterize the London winter, my secretary said there was a man waiting to see me.

"What sort of fellow is he?"

"Well, he doesn't look much like a gentleman, sir."

"That's fine, show him right in. I'm sick of Bond Street haberdashery and Oxford accents."

My visitor was Sullivan, and I was doubly pleased.

"Well, if it isn't Sullivan!" I greeted him. "How did you get here? The last time I saw you, you had several years ahead of you yet. How'd you manage it? Over the wall?"

"No, sir. Right through the gate like the rest of you gentlemen. I bought my way out with the money you and the other Reformers gave me when you left. I'm trying now to get back to my family in Ireland, but I hate to go looking like this!"

I could understand that, for he was a bedraggled-looking object.

"Surely it didn't take all your money to get this far! Why don't you buy yourself a decent suit of clothes?"

"Would you believe it, Mr. Hammond," he replied ingenuously, "I was robbed last night on the dock at Southampton."

"No, Sullivan, to be quite frank with you, I wouldn't believe it."

I started to reach in my pocket but thought better of it. "I'll go with you right now and get you a suit and buy you a ticket. That is the only way you'll ever get to Ireland."

I fed and clothed him and saw him safely on the train. At the last moment, I relented and provided him with cash for tips, though I suspect it was promptly diverted into the till of some tempting pub.

I did not begrudge him this; in the jail at Pretoria I had luckily found a substitute for a pub myself. Among the prisoners were two I remember with special gratitude: A. L. Lawley, an Englishman who had helped build South African railways, and F. R. Lingham, an American who had spent many years on the western cattle ranches of the United States. They had no social graces, but no fault could be found with the quality of their friendship.

All prisoners were, of course, deprived of liquor in any form. Occasionally, at what seemed to us exceedingly long intervals, Lawley and Lingham would manage to have a bottle of whisky smuggled into their cells. I had a standing invitation to attend on these gala occasions.

They would bribe a friendly guard to unlock the door of my cell. I would follow him stealthily, keeping to the shadows, until we reached the haven of the Lingham and Lawley quarters. There I would remain until anxiety for the safety of my guard would drive me back to my cell.

After their release, these men did not forget the friendship formed in prison. They returned as visitors with much the same ideas for my escape as had been presented on two previous occasions.

"Look here, Hammond," Lingham burst forth eagerly as soon as we were alone. "We've got everything fixed up. All you have to do is to get over the wall; we'll throw a rope over for you and will have horses hidden near by. In two days we'll be over the Natal border. Before any extradition papers can be served, we'll be safe in Rhodesia. What about it?"

Their offer warmed my heart. But they admitted the impossibility of taking Phillips, Frank Rhodes, and Farrar along with us. One prisoner might escape unnoticed, but it would hardly be possible for the inmates to walk out in any numbers without the Boer guards becoming "slightly aware." Since I still hoped for release and exoneration, I told them I was grateful but could not accept their friendly offer.

My cell mates had one favorite diversion. All three were accomplished whist players. For some inscrutable reason they considered a fourth indispensable to their game. They would carefully pin blankets around the cell so that no ray of light would betray them. Then they would crouch like gnomes over a small candle end stuck on an old wooden box.

Since I was neither an enthusiast nor a good player, they would draw lots to see who would be the unfortunate one to get me for a partner. The "Oh, hell, I drew Jack" was distinctly uncomplimentary to me. Not only was I pressed into service, but the stakes were higher than I could afford. I was always relieved when the bit of candle guttered to a smelly death in a pool of grease. The

IOUs often had to be gathered up in the dark, but none of them went into my pocket.

The local papers reported monotonously from day to day that sanitary arrangements at the jail were to be completed almost immediately. Meanwhile, we suffered from the overpowering fumes of carbolic acid powder which was liberally strewn from one end of the compound to the other. This did little to alleviate our discomfort; it simply substituted one insupportable odor for another.

As if I had reached the nadir of human misery, my health began to mend almost from the moment I received the death sentence. Prison conditions had a contrary effect upon my fellows. One by one they succumbed to illness of one sort or another.

The district government surgeon, Messum, did what he could towards improving sanitation. He informed the inspector of jails that the sheds were too small and unhealthy for the number of occupants, that vermin had rapidly spread from the native quarters to those of the political prisoners, and that the lives of the older Reformers, as well as those who were ill, were endangered.

Dr. Messum made particular mention of Fred Gray, who was showing signs of acute melancholia and threatening to commit suicide. Poor Gray had been especially upset by the fact that the Boer government had just confirmed the sentence of banishment against the Reformers. In his Wednesday report, Messum recommended Gray's immediate release; Thursday was Ascension Day, a public holiday; on Friday the landrost was so busy signing visitors' permits that the doctor's letter received no attention until noon. Meanwhile, to use the words of the Johannesburg *Times,* "The enforced idleness, the terrible ennui, the heart-sinking, brain-snapping suspense in which they have to drag through the weary hours—all these form a punishment which the most remorseless arbiters of fate could not render more horror-inspiring."

Early Saturday morning, May 16th, Gray borrowed a razor and cut his throat. The universal horror aroused by this act was heightened by the fact that he left a widow and six children. The tragedy formed the only topic of conversation, even in Johannesburg, and the expression of grief there was almost as profound as within the prison itself.

When the time came for the removal of Gray's body, we formed a solemn procession and reverently carried his coffin as far as the gates. Ten thousand people attended his public funeral in Johannesburg. Several hundred conveyances followed the hearse to the grave in a spontaneous tribute to one who was regarded as a martyr. Conspicuously placed among the floral offerings was a wreath bearing a card, "In memoriam, F. Gray; from his friends in prison." Despite the fact that he was a suicide, he was given Christian burial. The clergyman who pronounced the final words at his grave said his epitaph should read, "Tortured to a cruel death by murderous suspense."

To offset the feeling of depression, we were cheered a few days later by an afternoon of humor and hopeful good omen. "The Star of the Stars and Stripes," as the Johannesburg *Times* called Mark Twain, was on a round-the-world lecture tour, and took advantage of an engagement in near-by Johannesburg to pay a social call on the American prisoners. I had great hopes for the effects of this afternoon on our spirits as I was familiar with Mark Twain's genial personality and witty conversation. While I was a student at Yale, I met him a number of times at Hartford, Connecticut, where I often went to spend week-ends with General Franklin, president of the Colt Arms Company.

In the glare of the South African sun which beat into the courtyard, Samuel Clemens, with his white hair and spotless linen suit, was a refreshing sight. I grasped his hand warmly in both of mine. "Mr. Clemens, I'm certainly glad to see you again. How did you ever find your way into this God-forsaken hole?"

"Getting into jail is easy," replied the humorist. "I thought the difficulties arose when it came to getting out."

I smiled appreciatively and introduced him to the rest of our company. He was particularly struck with the martial demeanor of Colonel Bettington, who had been one of the Committee's military commanders.

"This is a pretty dull sort of place, Colonel. Killing time, eh?"

"I suppose so," replied Bettington. "I'm a soldier and must kill something."

"You've got all the big bugs here, haven't you?"

"Yes, two hundred million were in my cell last night." The colonel rubbed his shoulders.

"What! Two hundred million big bugs?"

"Good Lord, no! Two hundred million pounds in good hard English money."

"Where do you keep it?"

The colonel pointed to Solly Joel, leaning against the wall. "There's some of it standing over there. Barnato Brothers, you know."

"And what's he doing in here? Hasn't he enough money to buy himself out?"

"So far he hasn't had any success, but we still have hopes."

After an hour or so of amusing conversation, Mr. Clemens prepared to depart, refusing our invitation to wait until we were ready to leave.

As he left the prison yard, a cub reporter accosted him. "Mr. Clemens, how did you find living conditions in the prison?"

"Why do you ask?"

"Some of the prisoners have complained to Kruger that the jail was no fit place for gentlemen. Although the president replied he was not aware that jails were intended for gentlemen, just the same we'd like to have your impressions."

"Has Mr. Hammond, or any of the other Americans, made any complaint?"

"No," admitted the youth; "the grievances were urged by their friends."

"Well," said Mark Twain, "I am not surprised that Mr. Hammond has made no complaint. I knew him as a young engineer out in Nevada where he used to spend a good deal of his time in mining camp hotels, and compared with those accommodations Hammond is now living in luxury."

The reporter carefully noted this down on his pad and Mark Twain went on to say that he was really greatly pleased with the jail; he had found some very charming gentlemen there, and he thought it was an ideal rest cure for these tired businessmen. He only regretted his stay was so short that he could not take advantage of the peaceful conditions in the jail to rest his own tired nerves. He said he could not imagine a place where one would be less troubled by the importunities of his creditors and the only feature he did not like about the jail was that there were too many lawyers among the prisoners, and somehow or other he never could hit it off with lawyers.

Next morning a very sharp criticism of the jail authorities appeared in this Boer paper, which was one of the Joubert papers hostile to Kruger. The article declared the jail was supposed to be a place for punishment and *not* a pleasant rest cure, and the paper called upon the government to take drastic measures of a punitive nature. The prison authorities responded by diminishing our rations, which had been none too liberal before.

None of the prisoners had seen this news item, and we could not account for the increased severity of our jailers' treatment of us; conditions had seemed intolerable before. Some friends on the outside, however, learned the reason and at once sent a deputation to Bloemfontein, several hundred miles south, to intercept Mark Twain, who was on his way to Cape Town to sail for England. As soon as he saw the paper containing his interview, and realized its unfortunate consequences, he hastened back to Pretoria to make clear to President Kruger that he had merely been trying to be humorous. In truth, he considered our quarters disgraceful and quite unfit for political prisoners. His explanation was apparently satisfactory; the severity of the discipline was once more relaxed.

Several years later I met Mark Twain in New York and was invited to a delightful luncheon. He told this story as a joke on himself and promised redress by giving me a banquet whenever I cared to name the day.

In the latter part of May, my wife was taken seriously ill, and the Boer government allowed me to go to her at Johannesburg. Du Plessis came with me as guard but after twenty-four hours of home life he became bored and returned to Pretoria, leaving me to my own devices.

As soon as my wife was out of danger I returned voluntarily to prison. It amused me to find a heavy guard lined up at the station and to be marched solemnly into the jail. One of my jailers considerately offered to relieve me of my small hand bag, but I determinedly maintained my grip on what was a precious load of contraband tobacco.

By this time the prison authorities knew that none of us would take advantage of Boer trustfulness, and other Reformers were also granted week-end privileges.

During one of our numerous conversations, Du Plessis said that Kruger was curious to know why the Reformers had pleaded guilty. I asked Du Plessis to tell the following story to the president with my compliments.

"A Texas horse thief had stolen an animal from the very judge before whom he was later brought for trial. The judge, as an interested party, wished to prevent any criticism of partiality, and turned over the case to a subordinate court officer, saying, 'Proceed with the case while I go for a rope.'

"Tell His Honor, the president," I said, "that the Reformers were just as likely as the horse thief to get a fair trial."

Du Plessis told me afterwards that Oom Paul shook with laughter at the joke. It was too apt to seem funny to us.

Negotiations for our release had begun almost immediately after our imprisonment. So long drawn-out and involved was Kruger's policy towards the Reformers that it became known as "magnanimity by inches." For some time the leaders were definitely excluded from any arrangement that might be made. The other prisoners were asked to send in individual petitions in which they admitted the justice of the sentences imposed upon them, expressed regret for what they had done, and promised to behave in the future. Almost to a man they refused.

The result was a compromise. On the one hand, the authors of the petitions had to take into consideration the extremist Boer opinion that penitence was a condition precedent to release; on the other, many prisoners were reluctant to admit any guilt.

A way out was found in a formal application to the Executive Council to have the sentences reviewed. Each application had to contain an explanation of the circumstances under which the prisoner had joined the Reform Movement, and set forth any extenuating factors he could urge in his own behalf.

The suicide of Gray probably hastened a decision. On May 20th, ten of the prisoners were released, twenty-four had their sentences commuted to three months, eighteen to five months, and four to one year. A. Wools-Sampson and W. D. Karri-Davies refused to submit any petitions; consequently, their cases were not considered.

By this time there had been a strong revulsion of feeling in South Africa in favor of the prisoners. Part of the solicitude on our behalf was undoubtedly due to the Boers' belated realization of the economic benefits the Uitlanders had bestowed upon them. The country was facing financial ruin. Railroads were going bankrupt, options on Boer properties were not being taken up, the rinderpest was now within their borders, a plague of locusts had destroyed crops, and many of the mine owners had threatened to close down.

The little seed I had planted in Sir Gordon Sprigg's mind now began to bear fruit. In every single one of the South African towns, in some of which only Dutch was spoken, and including such a stronghold of conservatism as the Orange Free State, a concerted movement got under way to effect our release. J. Bryant Lindley, an American who had lived in Cape Town for many years, directed this movement. It was generally felt that there had been gross discrimination towards prisoners who had pleaded guilty to the same offense, and that some were being held by the Boer government as political pawns.

The gathering pressure of public opinion eventually had its effect. On May 30th, with the exception of the leaders and the two impenitents I have just named, all the prisoners were released on the payment of $10,000 and, in lieu of banishment, a promise to keep out of Transvaal politics for three years.

So far as the four leaders were concerned, the government would make no public statement except that it was busy. But privately it was intimated that, if we were prepared to pay for our liberty, the matter could probably be arranged. Our attorneys sent a letter to the Executive Council suggesting some monetary arrangement, and offering $40,000 as ransom for each of us.

At once there arose loud Boer professions of reluctance to accept what they termed blood money. But they were a thoroughly practical people not unacquainted with high finance and assessed a value of $250,000 on each of the leaders. I protested that this asking price was too high for me, although my fellow prisoners could have paid the sum without feeling its loss.

Meanwhile, some of the Reform Committee, now once more free, had swallowed their pride and gone to Kruger to petition for our pardon. This was the famous "dog interview." Kruger maundered on about dogs, and how the little dogs had been punished but the big dog (Rhodes) had escaped, and how dogs crawled to lick their masters' boots after being punished.

He would make no definite promises.

There was one thing far more effective than this attitude of humility, and that was the rising tide of sentiment throughout South Africa: from the Cape Parliament, from the inhabitants of Natal, from the Orange Free State, and even from the Afrikander Bond, which Kruger could not afford to antagonize.

Overwhelmed by the unanimity of protest, Kruger hastened his policy of "magnanimity by inches," and little by little his price came down to $125,000. This payment was to be accompanied by an expression of appreciation of his generosity. We replied that we would rot in prison before we would both pay him and thank him for accepting our money. We would either pay or thank; we refused to do both. This created a temporary impasse which lengthened our period of detention by several days.

At this point, a delegation of one hundred and fifty mayors of South African towns arrived at Pretoria to petition in person for our release. Kruger could delay no longer. On June 11th—five months after our arrest—we leaders were set free without having to express our gratitude. My fine of $125,000 was paid by Cecil Rhodes as an advance on the profits due me according to the understanding arrived at in my first interview with him at Groote Schuur.

We had to choose between banishment and nonparticipation in Transvaal politics for three years. Colonel Frank Rhodes chose the banishment and was escorted over the Natal frontier, whereupon he promptly joined his brother Cecil who was engaged in fighting the Matabele. Phillips, Farrar, and I, together with a handful of Reformers still remaining in Pretoria, boarded a special train, provided not by the Boer government but by the citizens of Johannesburg.

Johannesburg, which had offered to pay the ransom, celebrated our release wholeheartedly. Several thousand people met the train as it pulled into the station. The crowd lifted the Reform leaders to their shoulders and carried them to a victoria, which was then drawn triumphantly through the town. The next evening we were guests of honor at a banquet presided over by Barney Barnato.

Karri-Davies and Wools-Sampson remained in jail. When I returned to South Africa in 1897, I went to see them. I told them they were giving great concern to those who had formerly been in prison with them, and that many of their friends thought they should accept Kruger's offer of release. Particularly if Boer and Briton should come to blows, their presence as hostages in Pretoria Gaol might prove an embarrassment to their own government.

They were already an embarrassment to Kruger, who was becoming increasingly anxious to be rid of them. After having served thirteen months, the Boer government expelled them as a compliment to Queen Victoria on her Diamond Jubilee.

Before the Raid had taken place, I had already decided to move my headquarters to London, where I could continue to act as consulting engineer for Rhodes's mining interests. The important technical problems had been solved; I had the utmost confidence in the ability of my staff to carry out all operating details. Had it not been for the Raid, I should have gone sooner. I now wound up my affairs in Johannesburg as quickly as possible.

While still in prison I had reserved passage for myself and my family on the *Drummond Castle* from Cape Town but the delay in coming to terms caused us to miss the sailing. Kruger's dilatoriness in opening the jail doors had undoubtedly saved our lives. The *Drummond Castle* went down off Ushant, only two of her passengers and crew being rescued.

By a curious coincident there were Hammonds on board. My son Harris, then at school in England, saw this name on the list of those missing. But the same day he received word from his guardian in London that we were not on the boat.

Many times in my life I have been touched by the attitude of the men working under me. Certainly elaborate and formal expressions of esteem cannot always be taken at face value; but with so many years intervening, and with the loyalty of my associates still warm in my memory, I should like for various sentimental reasons to quote a letter which meant much to me.

THE CONSOLIDATED GOLD FIELDS OF SOUTH AFRICA, LIMITED.

Johannesburg, June 20, 1896
South African Republic.

John Hays Hammond, Esq.
Johannesburg.
Dear Sir:

It is with feelings of great sorrow, that we, the members of your staff are about to part from you.

Our respect for you as a man, our admiration for you as an Engineer, and our affection for you as a friend, is most strong.

An ambitious man is inclined to allow nothing to stand in his way in the attainment of his ends. You, on the contrary, have always been anxious to further the interests of those who have been associated with you, and have guarded their interests more zealously than your own. You have never allowed an opportunity to pass, where there was a chance to advance some one whom you felt deserved it. The kindness and consideration you have shewn, has endeared you to us in the strongest degree. You have drawn us to you, not by your great success, but by a genuine and lasting feeling of affection.

It is scarcely necessary for us to speak of the great work you have done on these Fields, or of what the Rand owes to you. That is too well known. We simply speak to you personally, that you may understand our feelings for you, and our sorrow that you are to leave Johannesburg.

That health and happiness may attend you and
yours is our most earnest wish.

> V. C. CLEMENT
> S. B. CONNOR
> EDWARD MELVILLE
> POPE YEATMAN
> W. LEONALD HOLMS
> H. C. SIMPSON
> F. M. WATSON
> E. H. GARTHWAITE
> W. WYHERGH
> E. H. BOOTH
> S. J. TRUSCOTT
> E. KEMPER-VOSE
> R. M. CATLIN

A dozen or more Reformers traveled to Cape Town on a special
train as guests of the Cape Colony government. We were cheered
as we pulled out of Johannesburg, and cheered again at Bloemfontein, in the heart of the Boer country.

From the newspapers I had learned that a Select Committee of
the Cape of Good Hope House of Assembly proposed to determine,
if possible, the exact connection between Rhodes and the Raid.
When I reached the Cape Colony border I was not surprised, therefore, to receive a summons to appear before this committee on
June 23rd.

It was well known that the Select Committee was being run by
an anti-Rhodes faction, actuated by political animus. The chairman was W. P. Schreiner, a brother of Olive Schreiner and formerly
a member of Rhodes's cabinet.

I made up my mind in no way to add to Rhodes's difficulties by
incriminating him or exposing him to further criticism. Furthermore, Rhodes had his hands full with the uprising of the Matabele
in Rhodesia and was unable to defend himself in person.

On the other hand, a refusal to testify might involve me in considerable red tape and compel me to remain in Cape Town for some
weeks. The situation was particularly embarrassing to me since my

wife was shortly to be confined, and I was anxious to have her in England. But after we had discussed the subpoena she told me she would rather have her baby in Cape Town than have me go against my conscience.

I arrived just in time to present myself at the place and hour specified. Following a preliminary verbal skirmish, Mr. Schreiner asked me certain questions which tended to incriminate Rhodes.

I declined to discuss Rhodes's connection with the Reform Movement. The committee reiterated its questions, but I still would not reply. Helpless in the face of my refusal, they asked me to withdraw for a few moments while they discussed the policy they should adopt. They intimated that they could hold me as a material witness if I continued recalcitrant.

In about half an hour I was again summoned before the committee, and was asked on what grounds I refused to give this testimony. I replied out of the depths of my ignorance of international law: "I'm not a British subject. I've already paid the Boer government for my share in the rebellion. As an American citizen traveling from one friendly republic to another, I'm not obliged to give evidence against my will, and any attempt on your part to extort it is entirely *ultra vires.*"

I was pleased to note the perturbation of the committee and realized that I was actually within my rights in taking this stand.

I was asked once more to retire. When I reappeared, they said they would have to take legal advice and would notify me whether or not I should be detained in Cape Town. Thereafter, they confined their questions to other matters.

This gave me an opportunity to place on record the Reform Committee's relations with Dr. Jameson and to demonstrate that his precipitate action had been largely responsible for the failure of the Reform Movement.

Somewhat to my surprise, Mr. Schreiner and other members of the committee invited me to lunch with them next day. They complimented me on the loyalty I had shown to a friend, and particularly on the legal correctness of the stand I had taken. I admitted to them then that, even as I was laying down the precepts of international law, I had been uneasily wondering whether Grotius and

Puffendorff would have approved my incursion into their special field.

That very afternoon, two weeks after my release from Pretoria Gaol, my family and I set sail from Cape Town.

My wife was as much pleased as I to get away from South Africa. "Revolutions are expensive games to play," she said.

We landed at Plymouth, July 11, 1896, and immediately took a house at Bickley, near London. In August my third son, Richard, was born. For the next four years London was my business headquarters and my home.

CHAPTER TWENTY-ONE

The Aftermath of Revolt

LONDON HEADQUARTERS—DR. JAMESON'S TRIAL AND
CONVICTION—RICHARD HARDING DAVIS CABLES
INSIDE STORY—I VISIT JAMESON—DR. JIM BECOMES
SIR STARR—MY WIFE'S DIARY IS PUBLISHED—
RHODES IN LONDON—HE TAKES FULL RESPONSIBIL-
ITY FOR RAID—KRUGER AND I DISCUSS UITLANDER
GRIEVANCES—KRUGER'S OPINION OF THE KAISER—
I MEET DR. LEYDS AGAIN—BOER WAR AND AFTER—
JOSEPH CHOATE'S ADVICE—I URGE MAGNANIMOUS
PEACE TERMS—"BOTHA WAS ALWAYS RIGHT"

*A*fter months of African sturm
und drang, life in London
was calm and peaceful. My headquarters during the first year
were the Consolidated Gold Fields offices, at 8 Old Jewry; later I
established myself in Threadneedle Street. My time was divided
between work for the Rhodes interests; trips once or twice a year
back to South Africa to inspect the mines of the Consolidated Gold
Fields and other companies which I represented as consulting engineer; and in building up a new clientele in London. At Rhodes's
special request I had renewed my engagement with the Consolidated Gold Fields.

Almost as soon as I returned to London in July, 1896, I realized
a feeling on the part of the British public that the Reformers had
been responsible for the failure of the Raid. We had been selected

as scapegoats and were being ridiculed in journalistic lampoons and music hall skits. The opprobrium was undeserved and I could not understand why Jameson had so long kept silent. We Reformers had not been able to speak in our own defense while we were still in South Africa, for fear we would do Jameson an injury pending the preliminary hearings of the High Court of England against him and his principal officers. These hearings had dragged on for months, during which time the Reformers suffered in silence. We felt aggrieved at Jameson for allowing charges of cowardice to be alleged against us. Of course, we did not expect Jameson to incriminate himself, but he must have known that the sole responsibility for the failure was his own.

The first charge brought against Jameson and fifteen of his officers was in the Bow Street Police Court:

> That they with certain other persons in the month of December, 1895, in South Africa, within Her Majesty's Dominions and without license of Her Majesty, did unlawfully prepare and fit out a military expedition to proceed against the dominions of a certain friendly state—to wit, the South African Republic, contrary to the provisions of the Foreign Enlistment Act, 1870.

On June 15th, after three and a half months of preliminary proceedings, Jameson and five of the fifteen officers were picked out for trial. The indictment contained twelve separate counts.

The trial began July 20, 1896.

Ian Colvin in *The Life of Jameson*, says:

> The jury were asked to find upon a series of questions—as to whether or not the defendants were engaged in a military expedition from Mafeking and Pitsani Potlugo against the South African Republic, and whether Pitsani Potlugo was under the dominion and sovereignty of the Queen.
>
> The motive for asking the jury for this sort of verdict is suggested by the illustration used by the Chief Justice:
>
>> 'Of course you remember the shipwrecked crew who, finding themselves on the ocean without

any means of obtaining food, sacrificed the life of one of the persons of the boat.'

Clearly, the Bench feared that the sympathies of an English jury would go against State policy.

The jury retired at 4:20 in the afternoon, and debated their verdict for an hour and five minutes.

When they returned it was with an answer in the affirmative to all the questions on the paper.

'That amounts, gentlemen,' said the Chief Justice, 'to a verdict of guilty. Do you now find against all the defendants a verdict of guilty?'

'My Lord,' the foreman replied, 'the jury have thought fit in answering these questions to append a rider: "The jury consider that the state of affairs in Johannesburg presented great provocation." My Lord, we have answered your questions categorically.'

'Then I direct you that, in accordance with those answers, you ought to find a verdict of guilty against the defendants.'

Here Sir Edward Clarke rose to his feet, 'My Lord,' he said, 'I wish . . .'

'I cannot allow any intervention,' said the Chief Justice.

'My Lord, I am calling attention . . .'

But the Chief Justice was determined to have his way: 'I cannot allow it, Sir Edward Clarke,' he said. 'At this moment I cannot allow it.' And then to the jury: 'Gentlemen, I direct you that in point of law that amounts to a verdict of guilty, and it is your duty to see if you cannot come to an agreement.'

'My Lord,' said the foreman, 'there is one objection to that. We answered your questions categorically. We cannot agree upon a verdict.'

'That,' said the Lord Chief Justice, 'is a most unhappy state of things. If there is one juryman objecting to a verdict he ought to reconsider the matter. These questions, answered as they are, amount to a verdict of guilty and to nothing else. They are capable of no other construction, and therefore I direct you—and I direct my observations particularly to the gentlemen to whom you refer as disagreeing with the rest on the verdict—that you ought all to find, in accordance with these findings, a verdict of guilty.'

The jury hesitated for a time and consulted among themselves, and at last the foreman yielded the point:

'My Lord,' he said, 'we are unanimous in returning a verdict of guilty.'

Against this skilful and masterful piece of shepherding Sir Edward Clarke proposed to appeal: he wanted to ask for a new trial, but Jameson and his officers refused to allow him: they preferred to take judgment.

Jameson and Sir John Willoughby were sentenced to imprisonment for fifteen months at hard labor. Major Robert White was given a sentence of seven months, and Colonel Grey, Colonel Henry White, and Major Coventry, each five months at hard labor.

Jameson was taken first to Wormwood Scrubs, dressed in prison garb and treated like a common criminal, but shortly afterwards was moved to Holloway Prison and became a "first-class misdemeanant." Jameson was in bad health, suffering from gallstones. In November, 1896, he was operated on and shortly afterwards released from further punishment. He moved to his chambers in Down Street.

On the very day of Jameson's sentence, July 27th, Richard Harding Davis, whose influence on the press at that time was great and whose attitude was therefore important, remarked to my Yale classmate, Colonel George Creighton Webb, that he "would rather be in Jameson's shoes than in those of John Hays Hammond." He went on to express his contempt for me and the other leaders of the Reform Movement, and called us cowards because we failed to keep our promise to go to Jameson's aid.

Webb spoke up in my defense. "That shows you don't know the inside facts about the Raid. If you're interested in getting both sides of the story, I'll arrange to bring you and Hammond together, and then I'm sure you'll change your views."

Webb arranged a dinner at the Savoy. Without informing me of Davis's preconceived ideas, he induced me to recount my adventures. I related the more familiar details and in addition I described the many attempts on the part of Boer Secret Service agents to extort confessions from us in order to involve Rhodes and in that way escape punishment ourselves. But I asserted with pride that not one had turned state's evidence and betrayed a fellow prisoner or implicated any other person.

Early in the conversation Davis's incredulity showed that he was in the other camp. By the end of dinner he was half convinced that his first impression of the Reformers had been wrong. But I wanted him to verify my statements and offered to put him in touch with Captain Harry Holden, Jameson's intimate and trusted friend. From him he could get many particulars confirming my version. Davis interviewed Holden and was fully convinced. Since he was first and foremost a newspaperman, he composed a feature story and cabled it to the American newspapers. He did the Reformers a great service. Davis and I struck up a personal friendship which remained unbroken throughout his life.

After Jameson's release from Holloway Prison, and while he was convalescing at Down Street, Rhodes returned to London. At the urgent request of Rhodes, Maurice Gifford, and other friends of Jameson, I reluctantly accepted his invitation to come to see him. Gifford brought the message and said that Jameson wanted to talk over old times with me and had promised not to mention the Raid.

I had always been fond of Jameson and was really sorry that he was so ill, but I still resented his implication that the Reformers were cowards. Gifford tried to reassure me, saying that Jameson had never included me in his contempt. I insisted that we had all worked together and should be judged together.

"You mustn't be too hard on poor old Jameson. He's been through a lot and he's ill."

"I guess you're right, Maurice, we'll let bygones be bygones."

In spite of our determination, the Raid inevitably came up in our conversation. Apropos of Jameson's coming to our assistance I resorted to an allegory to avoid unpleasantness.

"Once there were two neighbors. One had built himself a house of which he was inordinately fond. In this house he had a laboratory in which he carried on chemical experiments. The other had made a fire engine of his own invention.

"The chemist one day hailed his neighbor, saying, 'My good friend, tonight I shall try a delicate experiment, which, if it fails, will burn up my house and family. Will you stand by with your crew in my back yard, and come to the rescue if you are needed?'

"The neighbor was pleased at the prospect of trying out his fire engine and gladly agreed. The chemist returned to his test tubes. Presently there was a commotion outside; he threw open the window and called out, 'See here, you fellows, don't turn on the hose until I call.'

"But the firemen were carried away by the idea of an actual test of the engine. The water suddenly burst forth, the excited neighbor directed the stream on the chemist's windows, and it crashed through the glass. This so startled the chemist that he upset the lamp, and the whole elaborate structure went up in flames."

Jameson smiled grimly and the subject was dropped.

Jameson's health improved, and during the next few months we resumed our old friendly relations, but I did not see him again in London after he gave his testimony before the Select Committee appointed by Parliament to inquire into the circumstances of the Raid, the incursion by armed force into the South African Republic. His testimony was given in the summer, and then Jameson returned to Rhodesia to resume his position as administrator. On my last trip to Rhodesia shortly before the outbreak of the Boer War, I spent a night with Jameson at his camp on the veldt, where there were a group at dinner including Lady Sarah Wilson. We did not meet again until the coronation of King George V in 1911.

Jameson served in the Boer War, and was present at the siege of Ladysmith. After the war he took an active part in the political life of Cape Colony and was prime minister of that colony from 1904 to 1907. He received a baronetcy in 1911—Sir Starr Jameson. He became president of the British South Africa Company (Chartered) and held this position until his death, November 26, 1917.

In February, 1897, while I was on one of my business trips to South Africa, my wife's diary, *A Woman's Part in a Revolution,* was published in London. This small volume was described by James Bryce as "one of the brightest, freshest, and most graphically vivid and direct of all the accounts that have appeared of one of the most curious and interesting episodes in modern history." Her account of the Raid did much to allay prejudice against the Reformers.

While the Second Matabele War was still in progress, Rhodes had received a summons to appear before a Select Committee of Parliament. The committee was appointed "To inquire into the origin and circumstances of the incursion into the South African Republic by an armed force and into the administration by the British South Africa Company, and to report thereon, and further to report what alterations are desirable in the Government of the territories under the control of the Company."

When Rhodes received the summons he answered: "The investigation can wait. I am busy fighting the Matabele."

After the Matabele were suppressed, Rhodes started for London— to face the "unctuous rectitude" of his countrymen, as he expressed it—via Durban and Cape Town. In each place he was given a great ovation. In January, 1897, he arrived in London where he was welcomed with a demonstration also, from all except some of the stockholders of the Chartered Company who considered he had jeopardized their interests to carry out what they pleased to call his own selfish political policy.

On the day of his arrival I went to see him at Burlington House, his headquarters whenever he was in London. His sitting room was already filled with friends. When I appeared in the doorway, Rhodes rushed to greet me, and grasped me by the hand. It was our first meeting since the Raid.

"Hammond, my dear fellow, you don't know how glad I am to see you."

He then drew me aside into the bedroom where we could talk privately. He seemed eager to explain his apparent indifference to the fate of the Reformers. This had been one of the focal points of criticism of him.

I replied to his first words: "You don't need to explain. I fully understand your position. You had your hands full with the Matabele. The Reformers never doubted your sympathy for them."

Kruger's animosity to Rhodes had made it useless for him to intervene for the Reformers.

Later I was told by those who had been with Rhodes in Rhodesia that, when the news of our death sentence reached him, he exclaimed, "Good God! Surely Kruger wouldn't dare to do a thing like that." For the rest of the night he paced up and down his tent, chafing at his utter powerlessness to help us out of our dilemma.

The anguish of mind which had afflicted him since the Raid was shown by his remarks to my wife when he saw her for the first time since they had parted in South Africa. The Baroness Burdett-Coutts, one of the dominant figures in the later Victorian era, gave a dinner and reception in honor of Rhodes. From his position beside the baroness in the receiving line, he caught sight of my wife and left his place to welcome her.

"I am so glad to see you again, Mrs. Hammond. Many things have happened since you and I last met. I remember that you asked me then whether I had ever spent a sleepless night, and I said, 'No!' But since then I have spent many sleepless nights. Often in my adversity I have recalled the pleasant visits we had at Groote Schuur. I suspect that you then looked upon me as being afflicted with the 'big head.' I must have seemed to you so cocksure and self-satisfied. Is that not true?"

My wife's reply was tactful, but did not confute his conjecture.

He answered her unspoken criticism. "Mrs. Hammond, I have had a serious setback; but I trust that eventually I shall profit by this. My perceptions are now awakened to many things which formerly I did not recognize or realize."

The proceedings were impressive enough to have frightened any ordinary man. A committee of the House of Commons were just "plain folks" to Rhodes. At the trial he, the accused, dominated the scene. While the examination was in progress he called for beer and a sandwich and between mouthfuls answered the questions put to him.

The morning of the second day of the Select Committee's investigation I was to have breakfast with Rhodes at Burlington House.

I caught an early train from Chislehurst, where we had moved. Two gentlemen in the compartment with me were discussing the testimony Rhodes had given the previous day. They were obviously friendly to him, although they regarded many of his answers as evasive and feared an unfavorable impression had been created by his attitude.

I repeated the gist of the conversation to Rhodes over the breakfast table. After a moment's reflection, he replied:

"Perhaps that is true. So much has happened since that many of the details have slipped my mind."

"Don't you think it would be a good idea to tell that to the committee?" I asked. "The public is evidently getting the impression that you're trying to conceal something."

He immediately summoned his attorney, Hawksley, and got in touch with Alfred Beit and George Wyndham, asking them to come to the hotel. After discussing the matter, we agreed that every effort must be made to counteract that impression.

When the hearings were resumed later that morning, Rhodes frankly stated that he did not remember the dates or wording of certain messages, but he said he was willing to assume full responsibility for all telegrams and letters sent in his name by myself, Jameson, or any of the others who had figured prominently in the Raid. He added, he would go even further and would take upon his shoulders full responsibility for all that happened. This courageous attitude brought forth praise from all England, even from his political enemies.

Punch, which had not always been favorably inclined towards Rhodes, printed a cartoon representing the "great man" as a giant tied to the ground by his Lilliputian investigators. One of these was Labouchère, the editor of *Truth,* who had charged Rhodes with profiting on the stock market through the Jameson Raid. This made Rhodes so furious that "Labby" was forced to withdraw the accusation, admitting it had been based upon vague and totally unfounded rumor.

Although Rhodes was acquitted of having ordered Jameson to invade the Transvaal, the conclusion of the committee was that the Raid should be condemned without qualification, because by it "pub-

lic confidence was shaken, race feeling embittered, and serious difficulties were created with neighboring states."

When the hearing was over, Rhodes still had to deal with his stockholders. Their resentment was not lessened by the bill which
Kruger had rendered: £677,938 for material damages; and a cool
million for intellectual and moral injuries.

Unless the Raid had left the Republic morally bankrupt, the latter
item would seem rather steep.

Both claims were promptly rejected by the Chartered Company.
Perhaps the shareholders considered that Kruger had already
profited enough from the Reform Movement; the Reform prisoners
had, after all, paid him almost a million dollars in ransom money.

Ultimately many of these stockholders revised their unfavorable
opinion of their leader. In 1899, I went with Rhodes to the last
meeting of the Chartered Company in London at which he was
destined to preside. The hall of the Cannon Street Hotel was filled
to capacity and the crowd overflowed into the corridors. In front
of the building a throng had gathered to catch a glimpse of the man
who was the first since Wellington so completely to capture the
imagination of the British world. The uproar became deafening
and the calls for Rhodes insistent. He put his arm around my
shoulders and drew me to the balcony overlooking the vociferous
assemblage. This ovation marked the final stage of Rhodes's return
to the Olympian heights.

During the year following the collapse of the Reform Movement,
the progressive Boer element had forced the appointment of a government commission to investigate the Uitlander grievances. A
thorough and impartial examination was made and a report of seven
hundred pages drawn up. The whole constitutes a damning indictment of the government, as the following extracts from the report of the commission testify:

> Your Commission are pleased to state that at present
> there exist all the indications of an honest administra-
> tion, and the State, as well as the Mining Industry, must
> be congratulated upon the fact that most of the mines
> are controlled and directed by financial and practical
> men who devote their time, energy, and knowledge to

the mining industry, and who have not only introduced the most up-to-date machinery and mining appliances, but also the greatest perfection of method and process known to science. But for these a good many of the mines now producing gold would not have reached that stage. . . . When the fact is taken into consideration that up till now the mining industry must be held as the financial basis, support and mainstay of the State . . .

Your Commission entirely disapprove of concessions, through which the industrial prosperity of the country is hampered. Such might have been expedient in the past, but the country has now arrived at a state of development that will only admit of free competition according to republican principles. This applies more especially to the gold industry, which has to face its own economical problems without being further burdened with concessions that are irksome and injurious to the industry and will always remain a source of irritation and dissatisfaction.

As to the sale of liquor:

It has been proved to your Commission that the Liquor Law is not carried out properly, and that the mining industry has real grievances in connection therewith, owing to the illicit sale of strong drink to the natives at the mines, and they wish especially and strongly to insist that the stipulations of Article 16 of the law shall be strictly enforced. The evidence given on this point proves that a miserable state of affairs exists, and a much stronger application of the law is required.

Regarding explosives:

Before entering on this subject, we wish to put on record our disappointment with the evidence tendered on behalf of the South African Explosives Company, Ltd. We expected, and we think not unreasonably, that they would be able to give reliable information for our guidance respecting the cost of importation, as well as of local manufacture, of the principal explosives used for mining purposes; but, though persistently questioned on these points, a few facts were elicited and we regret to say that they entirely failed to satisfy us in this important respect. . . .

The Mining Industry has thus to bear a burden which does not enrich the State or bring any benefit in return, and this fact must always prove a source of irritation and annoyance to those who, while willing to contribute to just taxation for the general good, cannot acquiesce in an impost of the nature complained of.

The nature of this report was a surprise to President Kruger and his entourage, who denounced Mr. Schalk Burger and others who had signed the report as being traitors to their country, i.e., the Transvaal.

In spite of my connection with the Reform Movement, I retained the friendship of many of the Boers, particularly among the younger men, and when I was in the Transvaal in 1899 they asked me again to take up the cudgels in defense of Johannesburg community and the Uitlanders generally.

I did not care to undertake such a mission to Kruger, but there seemed no way out of the difficulty. I accepted with the stipulation that I be furnished with an interpreter who could be depended upon to render my conversation verbatim. Because of Oom Paul's well-known tendency to sudden wrath, I feared that his sycophants might be led to temper my remarks in translation.

There never was any trace of personal animus in my dealings with Kruger, although I naturally deplored his intolerance, fanaticism, and obstinacy. In fact, he seemed to have some regard for me, which I suspected was mainly due to his admiration for my wife. On many occasions he referred to her as a "grand woman" whom he held in the highest esteem because she had remained to face danger and to help her husband.

When I arrived at Kruger's home in Pretoria, the president greeted me with the question, "How is my sister?" I must have shown my bewilderment, because he continued, "I mean Mrs. Hays Hammond; she is my sister because we both believe in God." I thanked him and assured him that she was in good health.

I then said that I had just come from London and had called specially to tell him about the feeling of the people of England regarding his treatment of the Uitlanders. I said I was convinced that there would be serious trouble unless he adopted a conciliatory attitude at the meeting he was to have within a few days with Sir Alfred Milner, the high commissioner. Kruger replied that so long as Queen Victoria lived there could be no war. I insisted he was wrong; although Queen Victoria was opposed to war, and wanted to end her days in peace, eventually the pressure of sentiment throughout her dominions would force her to protect the rights of British subjects in South Africa.

Kruger remained undisturbed. "That's all right, I'll come to an agreement with Milner."

A few days after the meeting of Kruger and Milner at Bloemfontein, I spent an evening with the high commissioner at Cape Town. In the course of our political discussion, he told me what had occurred at the interview.

Because of Kruger's reputation for craftiness, Sir Alfred Milner had been uncertain of his ability to cope with him. Kruger first made offers which Milner promptly turned down; they were not adequate to secure redress of the grievances of the Uitlanders. Kruger repeatedly said that, if he made further concessions, he would not dare face the Volksraad. He employed his histrionic talent so effectively as to bring tears to his own eyes; the only reaction in the mind of the Englishman was disgust.

Despairing of reaching any satisfactory compromise, Milner told Kruger it was futile to prolong the discussion and rose to go. Kruger now perceived that his disingenuous tactics had failed; he drew from his pocket a proposal of terms from the Boer government which were far more liberal than any previously discussed. Milner was incensed by this duplicity, stated that even these additional concessions were unsatisfactory, and abruptly terminated the conference.

After the Bloemfontein meeting there was unmistakable evidence that the Transvaal and the Orange Free State were preparing for war.

422 The Autobiography of John Hays Hammond

On October 9, 1899, these two republics sent their ultimatum to England and two days later the Boer War began. The Boers fired the first shot and Kruger directed war operations until the British came within striking distance of Pretoria. He then departed unobtrusively to seek aid in Europe. He never returned. Tante Sanne, too old and ill to face the uncertain future, was left to the kindly understanding of the British. She died a few months later. For the few remaining years of his life, Oom Paul lived in comfort on the large fortune he had amassed during his years of power. In 1904 he died in exile, near Vevey on the shores of Lake Geneva.

I have always believed that the "little Englander" attitude of the Liberal party towards the Boers, largely inspired by political considerations at home, was responsible for Kruger's obstinacy in refusing to settle the Uitlander grievances. There is no doubt that Kruger was tenaciously holding to a policy of noncompromise in the expectation that the Liberal party would eventually return to power.

General Smuts, while attorney general of the Transvaal, in February, 1899, told Fitzpatrick that the Boers would stick it out until there was a change of government in England. "The Liberals will come into power, and this time we shall get all we want."

The diplomatic entente between Kruger and Germany naturally grew more intimate after the Raid, though it had already begun in the early nineties with the inauguration of Germany's policy of colonial expansion. It had been rendered more secure by the Kaiser's bestowal of the Order of the Red Eagle upon the president of the Transvaal Republic.

Kruger, in his fear of Rhodes's imperial schemes, had turned to Germany, whose rapidly growing influence had not yet become a serious menace. By playing one power against the other, he hoped to maintain Boer autonomy. He and his people were imbued with a sense of numerical inferiority which made them bluff. In the end, this proved their undoing.

Some months before the Jameson Raid, Kruger had spoken at a banquet given by the Pretoria Germans in honor of the Kaiser's birthday. In the homely figures of speech which he habitually used, he compared the Transvaal to a little child who had to wear small clothing. "When a child's clothes are made, they must not be made to fit a man; but as the child grows up, it requires bigger clothes— the old ones will burst. . . . We are growing up, and although we are young, we feel that if one nation tries to kick us, the other will try to stop it. . . . I feel certain when the time comes for the Republic to wear still larger clothes you will have done much to bring it about. . . . I wish also to give Germany all the support a little child can give to a grown-up man. The time is coming for our friendship to be more firmly established then ever."

Kruger had previously allowed Dr. Leyds to go to Germany to secure the promise of the Kaiser's aid in the event of an Uitlander uprising at Johannesburg. When the Raid took place Kruger's expectation of support from the Kaiser was more than justified by the famous Kaiser-to-Kruger telegram:

I HEARTILY CONGRATULATE YOU ON THE FACT THAT YOU AND YOUR PEOPLE WITHOUT APPEALING TO THE AID OF FRIENDLY POWERS HAVE SUCCEEDED BY YOUR UNAIDED EF- FORTS IN RESTORING PEACE AND PRESERVING THE INDE- PENDENCE OF YOUR REPUBLIC AGAINST THE ARMED BANDS WHICH BROKE INTO YOUR COUNTRY.

Queen Victoria's indignation at the Kaiser's action was so out- spoken as to amount to a reprimand. The Kaiser's own advisers pointed out how near his telegram had brought Germany to the brink of war; he thereupon tried to explain away his hasty and ill- advised act.

Kruger, whose bravery has never been questioned, is reputed on good authority to have said: "I have no more use for the Kaiser. I have a contempt for any man who is afraid of his grandmother."

In March, 1899, Rhodes visited Berlin and there had an interest- ing interview with the Kaiser. The conversation touched upon the Kruger telegram.

"What's your feeling about it?" asked the Kaiser.

"So far as your interests are concerned, I think it was a great mis- take, Your Majesty. But you unwittingly did me a service."

Rhodes went on to say that at the time of the Raid he was looked upon as a bad boy who needed punishment. His own people were quite ready to perform this task, but their wrath was diverted towards Germany by the prospect of the latter's interference and he had got off.

Arthur Balfour said to Fitzpatrick: "The Kaiser is an extraordinary fellow—one does not know if he is mad, has some deep-laid plan, or is just puffed up with vanity. You will hardly credit it, but only a few days ago he wrote privately to his grandmother, the Queen, enclosing a complete plan of campaign which he had ordered his general staff to prepare for the use of the British army against the Boers."

This was practically the plan adopted independently by Lord Roberts in the Boer War.

On my last trip from South Africa to London I took passage on the *Dunvegan*. I was on deck talking with Sir James Sivewright when I saw Dr. Leyds come aboard. I still had a vivid recollection of how he had blocked all our attempts to bring about a rapprochement between Boer and Uitlander. Moreover, there was no doubt that the major part of the blame for our prison treatment rested on his shoulders.

Sir James accosted him with the remark, "Here, Dr. Leyds, I fancy you and Mr. Hammond have met before."

"I think," I replied, "that I had the honor on a previous occasion."

"Yes," responded the doctor with a cool smile, "I recall we have met before."

Thereafter, Dr. Leyds and I saw nothing of each other until the steamer stopped at Madeira to take on coal. Our staterooms were on the same side of the ship and directly exposed to the dirt and noise of coaling operations.

The captain said to me: "I was afraid you'd be kept awake in your stateroom. Since I have to be on the bridge all night, I've made arrangements to shift you to my cabin. Would you object very much to sharing it with Dr. Leyds?"

"Certainly not," I said.

When I entered the room Dr. Leyds was already there. We bowed

PRESIDENT KRUGER WITH BARNEY BARNATO'S LIONS

A CONTEMPORARY CARTOON

RUDYARD KIPLING

coldly. We undressed in silence. I was preparing to take the cot and leave the bed to him when the steward entered.

"The bed has been prepared for you, Mr. Hammond," he announced.

His tone was decisive. Realizing that on a British ship feeling against the Boer secretary of state was intense, even among the stewards, and that the question of which should have the bed might involve national prestige, it seemed advisable not to protest.

I pulled the covers up to my chin and, just before snapping out the light, I wished Leyds a formal "Good night."

The response was even more frigid. The darkness concealed my involuntary smile at the irony of having my implacable enemy for a roommate. I still marvel at my moderation in not throwing him overboard, for my contempt and hatred for Dr. Leyds had not in the least diminished since Pretoria days.

During the Boer war, I made many addresses in America on behalf of Great Britain to enlighten the American people as to the circumstances that had led to hostilities. The consensus of opinion in the United States was undoubtedly anti-British. Boer propaganda had been extraordinarily effective. Acting on the maxim, "One tale is good before the other is told," the Boers had been shrewd enough to get in the first word.

In 1902 while in London I was asked to make an address at a banquet given me by Lord Albert Grey. I knew that among the guests would be many of the leading colonial statesmen then in London attending a conference on imperial relations and that I should be expected to express an opinion on South African affairs.

A few days before this occasion I had dinner with Joseph H. Choate, Hay's successor at the Court of St. James's.

"I have to make a speech two nights from now and I dread it," I remarked. "If only I had your gift of expression, I'd know what to say and how to say it."

Choate replied: "Why, you're the very man for the job. You have all the background. I've often heard you say how much you admired the Boers who did the fighting. In your opinion, it was men like Kruger and Leyds who caused all the mischief, wasn't it?"

I agreed.

"Well, then, it seems to me there's a logical analogy between the end of our Civil War and present conditions in South Africa. Why wouldn't it be a wise move to point this out to the peacemaking diplomats? Tell them how magnanimously Grant treated Lee at Appomattox, but how everything was ruined by the harsh treatment meted out to the South by our reconstruction politicians. These men gathered here in London are responsible for the future of Great Britain in South Africa. Much will depend upon the spirit in which they approach the negotiations."

I used Choate's suggestion as the keynote of my address. I began by deploring the fact that American sympathy lay with the Boers; that this seemed particularly unjust, since we now had the opportunity to reciprocate the sympathetic attitude of Great Britain during our war with Spain. I told them not to take too seriously the professions of friendship made by the Newport element; this was no real index of American thought.

As I was testing out the temper of my audience, I was encouraged by the "Hear, hear," uttered by Lord Beresford, which evoked further approval from other distinguished guests.

In conclusion, I pointed out that Boer and Englishman together had to work out the political and economic destiny of South Africa. I urged a peace settlement that would grant to the Boers at once what they would ultimately and inevitably attain by their superior political strength. *Bis dat qui cito dat.* My sentiments were vigorously applauded. Mr. Choate later added his congratulations, and said that my speech had contributed in some measure towards the granting of generous terms to the conquered.

It has always been a source of satisfaction to me that the Peace of Vereeniging proved my contention that, in the end, magnanimity is the wiser and more statesmanlike policy.

If the Reform Movement had been successful, I believe a *modus vivendi* between Boer and Uitlander would have been established. If, through diplomatic intervention, the full rights of the Uitlander could have been secured, enlightened self-interest would thereafter have made it to the advantage of all South African states to compose their differences for the common welfare and the Boer War would have been postponed, if not averted.

There are perhaps no ifs in history, but it is interesting to speculate on what might have happened if the Boer War had not broken out in 1899. In the intervening years Germany had built strategic roads in German Southwest Africa as a military threat to the whole British position from Cape Town to the headwaters of the Nile.

Germany's African ambitions were undoubtedly grandiose. She planned to build up an enormous legion of black soldiers as an inexhaustible reserve of cannon fodder. With her roads, with her disciplined host of native levies, with the aid of the well-armed, skillful, and courageous Boer Army, in 1914 Germany would have struck a blow in South Africa which might well have overwhelmed all possible opposition on the part of the British South Africans and the pro-British Dutch, and would have helped to give her that world-victory she so nearly secured by the suddenness of her attack upon Belgium and France. Her treasury would have been replenished with the gold of South Africa; naval bases at Durban and Cape Town would have placed her submarines within easy striking distance of every sea route south of the equator; the resources of the South American continent would no longer have been at the disposal of the Allies; the participation of India and Australia in the war would have been seriously hampered.

Immediately following the outbreak of the World War, certain irreconcilable Boers made a compact with the governor of German Southwest Africa to announce the independence of South Africa and to declare war against England. Germany promised to send help from Southwest Africa, and, in the event of a German victory in Europe, to recognize the South African claim to full independence. Furthermore, Germany was to have Walfish Bay, and the new South African Republic was to be allowed to compensate itself with Portuguese-owned Delagoa Bay.

Botha obtained possession of this treaty and tried to dissuade the rebels from joining forces with the Germans in 1914. Failing in this, he headed a volunteer commando of Boers in what is regarded as a remarkable campaign, captured the rebel leaders, and put an end to the movement for revolt in the Transvaal.

Even before the Raid, Botha and I had been good friends. At the Imperial Conference in England in 1907, Botha and Jameson struck up a friendship. Many of the British extremists never forgave the doctor for dealing with Botha.

"Are you aware," argued one of them, "that Botha was one of those men who wanted to shoot you at Pretoria after the Raid?"

Jameson smiled. "Ah," he said, "Botha was always right."

It was largely owing to the co-operation of Jameson and Botha that the Union of South Africa was formed in 1910, with Botha as its first prime minister. Moreover, many of the Reform Committee prisoners became identified with South African politics after the Boer War, and held office under the Union government. Prominent among these was Sir Percy Fitzpatrick, who defeated Botha himself in a friendly but strenuous contest for a seat in Parliament.

In 1911, General Botha was in London as the special ambassador from South Africa to the coronation of King George V; I was special ambassador from the United States.

Botha greeted me with, "It's been some years since we met, Your Excellency."

"The last time we were together, General," I replied, "I didn't meet you; I saw you in the courtroom when I was sentenced to death. I'd like to thank you now for being one of the first to start the petition for commutation."

"Isn't it extraordinary," he exclaimed, "that you and I should meet again under the present circumstances!"

"Not any more so than that you and Dr. Jim should have held high office under the same government. By the way, are you and the doctor still friends?"

"Indeed, yes," he answered, "I had the pleasure of recommending him, as well as several other old friends of yours on the Reform Committee, for the Honors List. I think he is the salt of the earth and as soon as this affair is over, I'm going with the doctor on a fishing trip to Scotland."

The following day I had luncheon with Jameson, and asked him his opinion of Botha. Jameson, at that time leader of the political opposition to Botha's government, answered, "He's as good a friend as I have."

That evening I dined with King George and was able to furnish him with some sidelights on South Africa, that seemed to interest him. I repeated the conversations that I had had with Botha and Jameson, and expressed the belief that, so long as men of their quality held the political control of South Africa, Great Britain might be confident of a loyal colony.

CHAPTER TWENTY-TWO

London Days, 1896-1899

LONDON SOCIAL LIFE—ANTIQUITIES—THE OLD TILE
CLUB—POLITICS AND BUSINESS IN LONDON AND
WASHINGTON—BARONESS BURDETT-COUTTS AND
PRINCESS LOUISE—RICHARD HARDING DAVIS AND
E. ASHMEAD-BARTLETT FIGHT THE GRECO-TURKISH
WAR—RUDYARD KIPLING AT GROOTE SCHUUR—I
CROSS THE TRANSVAAL BORDER PEACEABLY—DOUBT-
FUL MINING PROPOSITIONS—JOHN HAY—BAD
NAUHEIM—KING LEOPOLD II, OF BELGIUM—SOUTH
AFRICA AGAIN—I RETURN TO AMERICA—DEATH OF RHODES

*T*he years during which I made London my business headquarters were among the most enjoyable of my life and gave my wife and me an opportunity to know something of the color and the grace of English life at a fascinating period in its history. It was just before the machine age, and the twentieth century irrevocably changed its social aspects and made anachronisms of traditions that in their time were both sound and delightful. After the informal, relatively isolated, and occasionally rough life in Africa these few years came as a very acceptable contrast.

The family was united again for the first time in some years. Immediately upon our arrival, we took a house at Bickley in Kent, where Dick was born. Harris had been at school in Malvern for several years and we resumed our role as his parents, a responsibility which Lady Elizabeth Cust had kindly undertaken in our absence. Now Jack was also put in school, at Eastbourne.

I had settled down in my office in Threadneedle Street, with Kelsey, who had been with me in South Africa, as my secretary. Even now I was never in England for a very extended period, still having to do the traveling which an engineer's career exacts. My first commitments were, of course, to Rhodes and his concerns. Nevertheless, I found time to investigate and consult for other persons and companies. I traveled widely, sometimes on business, sometimes for pleasure. I made occasional short trips to Italy, France, and Germany, and to Switzerland where I was interested in building a tramway system. I made several trips to Africa and an extended journey through Russia, at the invitation of Count Witte, to study its natural resources. In 1899 I made my last voyage to South Africa. This chapter, therefore, is titled with a latitude to say nothing of longitude.

Many mornings, when I was in England, I would go up from Bickley, or from Chislehurst where we later lived, to my office in the City. I soon discovered that I must either change my American habits of business hours or find a great deal of unoccupied time on my hands, after arriving in London for the day's work. The English indubitably get their work done, but to the American, accustomed to arriving early at his office, it is a mystery how they do it. They come to work, not so long before lunch, spend a generous hour at lunch, and just as they are getting into the stream of the afternoon's business, they stop for tea.

Although I may have found this disconcerting, it afforded me time to pursue one of my favorite pastimes, that of indulging myself as an amateur antiquarian and also to reflect that Americans have much to learn from this method of organization, for many of these seeming gentlemen of leisure are among the most efficient businessmen in the world.

I have seen many different countries during my life and have always been interested in things of historical significance and particularly those bearing on the artistic and material development of civilization. In old London now called "The City," the remnants of the old Roman walls, some of them running to lengths of a hundred feet or more, first absorbed me. I would often go to the British Museum and search into books for information on various engrossing ruins I had seen and at one point my mental picture of the early Roman city was so vivid that I felt competent to undertake its reconstruction.

I followed the fortunes of both Ben Jonson and Dr. Samuel Johnson through alleys, bystreets, and taverns; in fact, it was at the "Old Cock" tavern in the Strand, the "Mitre" in Chancery Lane which Dr. Johnson entered by way of the "Cat and Fiddle" alley, that the doctor often held forth with Boswell. But it was at the "Turk's Head Inn" in Gerrard Street, Soho, that members of the Literary Club founded by Johnson—Goldsmith, Boswell, Burke, Sir Joshua Reynolds, and Garrick—more often met. These coffeehouses were most attractive landmarks on one's ramblings.

Visiting places described by the inimitable diarist, Samuel Pepys, was an unfailing delight. Pepys, who lived in what is now the City, describes the Great Plague of 1665 and the fire which came the following year, lasted three days, and swept away almost the whole of old-time London. But the fire was a blessing in disguise as it effectually destroyed the germs of the plague and led to the building of better streets and better houses. It is an injustice to regard Pepys as a philanderer and a socialite—to use the objectionable modern term—for he was an energetic man of affairs and rendered conspicuous service in the upbuilding of the British Navy when he occupied the responsible position in the Admiralty.

In what is now the crowded section of London, around the Hotel Cecil, there were many secluded spots, "Where one would live in the world but not of it, or, of the world but not in it." I have found recreation in those spots.

I have enjoyed an occasional visit to the country churchyard at Stoke Poges, where Gray's *Elegy* was written and where he is buried. This is one of my favorite poems, and it gave me infinite delight to have my children voluntarily memorize it at an early age.

As a lover of Chaucer, at times I would trace the course of his travels as far as possible along the old Canterbury Road. I could well appreciate the charm of the Canterbury Road in lovely spring days and understand what charm meant when he said, "Than longen folk to goon on pilgrimages." Perhaps the fact that

A Coke [cook] they hadde with hem for the nones,
To boille the chiknes with the mary-bones

may have added to the zest with which the old pilgrims undertook their journey.

In its historical interest ancient London appealed to me more strongly than did any other European city with the possible exception of ancient Rome.

My curiosity and interest in these literary traditions were insatiable; if mines had no longer offered a livelihood, I believe I could have done rather well for my family and myself as a tourist guide.

In the evenings and over week-ends my wife and I entertained many friends we had known in both America and South Africa and people we now met in London. Richard Harding Davis was with us frequently, and a charming companion we found him. In the evenings at Bickley we would sit and talk for hours. It was here that he not only developed the idea for his novel *Soldiers of Fortune,* but wrote part of it. My literary friends tell me that it is difficult for the subject to recognize himself in fiction. This may be true, but I doubt if any of my friends would have seen in the six-foot, well-turned-out Clay—relatively a mirror of fashion—any resemblance to me. At any rate, I accepted the compliment and Davis and I continued our friendship until his death. Soon after my return to New York he invited me to the first night of the play, dramatizing this book. I enjoyed the evening very much.

It was with Davis that I first took up bicycling. In my student days at Freiberg, this sport was beginning to have a vogue, but as I gazed at the strange-looking objects with a huge front wheel and a small wheel strung ignominiously on behind, I preferred to walk. At this time in England, however, bicycles more nearly resembled those now in use.

Our garden at Bickley was a labyrinth of paths cutting in and out of many kinds of bushes and vines. To add zest to our self-instruction, we two beginners, with some misgivings, laid out a sort of bicycle steeplechase around the garden, which seemed to us as hazardous as a Mexican mountain trail. A large rosebush stood at the most difficult turn. I add, without modesty, that Davis more frequently than I found himself enmeshed in the thorny Charybdis. Poultney Bigelow, *sui generis,* was also a bicycling companion of mine in those days.

As we became more intimately a part of London life and our circle of friends widened, we soon realized how varied and continually fascinating was the make-up of Victorian society. It was a happy mixture of people who were active in many different capacities at the time or who had been in the past. We came to meet a number of businessmen, actors, various members of the nobility, writers, politicians, artists, and their wives. Among the friends I made in those days was T. P. ("Tay Pay") O'Connor. Tay Pay and I naturally did not hit it off on South African politics and I never succeeded in convincing him of the justice of the British cause in the South African War. I saw much of him during my last visit to London in 1929, shortly before his death, and he was "of the same opinion still." Tay Pay's bias was undoubtedly due to his Hibernian ancestry.

My friendship for W. T. Stead was founded on our mutual admiration for Cecil Rhodes who had already fortunately converted Stead to his South African policy. Stead was attached to Rhodes because of the latter's unquestioned sincerity in his efforts to promote world peace. At the time I met him Stead was editor of the *Pall Mall Gazette* and the *Review of Reviews.* He had written *If Christ Came to Chicago!* and *The Americanisation of the World.* He was a great spiritualist and his book, *Letters from Julia*—communications from the spiritual world, became famous. I never met him on any occult ground. The last time I saw him was during the coronation celebration in 1911. I was looking forward to a visit from him when he sailed from England in April, 1912, on the ill-fated *Titanic.*

Among the first of my old New York friends with whom I renewed acquaintance in London were John Singer Sargent and Edwin A. Abbey. In the artistic life of London we found some of our most stimulating friends. In fact, later when I came to know John Hay, as ambassador to England, it was with this group of intimates that we spent some of our pleasantest evenings.

My New York days had not been without such associations. When

I established my office in New York in the early eighties I met Sargent and Abbey at the old Tile Club. This club no longer exists, but it had an atmosphere so unique and charming that I should like to recall it here. In a way the Tile Club had some of the delightful features of Samuel Johnson's Literary Club, but was entirely lacking in the old-world atmosphere, obviously somewhat difficult to achieve in the basement of 48 West 10th Street, New York City, where it met monthly.

Since it was an association of artists, my calling as an engineer disqualified me. But I knew all the members intimately, among them William Merritt Chase, A. B. Frost, "Bill" Laffan, who was Charles Dana's right-hand man on the New York *Sun;* Frank Millet, F. Hopkinson Smith, Augustus Saint-Gaudens, Elihu Vedder, and Stanford White. Frederick Dielman is now the sole survivor.

The members took turns at cooking some special dish. Bill Laffan was the best cook in the crowd, but because of his laziness the members rarely enjoyed his virtuosity in this line. Frank Millet used to superintend Black Daniel, the old club steward, in the preparation of Turkish kibaab. Black Daniel was a typical servant of the old slavery days, and when he found that my great-grandmother was a Ringgold from Maryland, he, with great pride, would say, "Yassuh, I'se one ob de Maryland Ringgolds."

I was once, and only once, asked to try my hand at cooking. I had been talking of the native dishes I had learned about while in Mexico, although I failed to mention that I had never attempted to convert the recipes into actualities. I accepted the challenge, rolled up my sleeves, and from memory tried to produce tamales, chile con carne, or some other tempting Mexican dish. I'm afraid I did not stick to the recipe in the amount of condiments and highly flavored ingredients, for I was more liberal than the Mexicans themselves in the lavish use of spices and peppers. I was prepared to receive a chorus of compliments for my culinary art and it seemed incredible that the comments were, if anything, hotter than the dish I had prepared for them.

Through my Tile Club friends I came to know many others of their circle. Stanford White introduced me to Edwin Booth, who was then living at the Players' Club, in Gramercy Park. At that time

Booth was broken down in health and a recluse. Although some thought him difficult to get on with, I always found him pleasant. He asked me to come and see him often. He was interested in hearing stories about Mexico and the mining towns of our own West, in many of which he had played as a young man. He enjoyed reminiscing and was eager for news about the people he had once known and the changes that had taken place. He liked to hear about the actors I had seen as a boy when they played stock in San Francisco at the old California Theatre. We'd talk at length about such men as John T. Raymond, Lawrence Barrett, and John McCullough.

In London it was chiefly through Alfred Parsons that I kept in touch with the artistic and literary world. We had many mutual friends in the Tile Club, and he had once visited my family in San Francisco on his way home from a trip to the Orient. Parsons was a bachelor, a painter, and a most fascinating host. As an avocation from his painting, he became greatly interested in landscape gardening and laid out some of the most beautiful private gardens in England. On the walls of homes in both England and America one can still find lithographic reproductions of his *In a Copse, November.* It was a picture which caught the popular fancy, and consequently today's critics shrug and label it "Victorian."

At Alfred Parsons' "Open House" one met the wittiest and some of the most worth-while people of all sets in London, particularly the painters. It was here that most frequently I saw Abbey, Sargent, William Black, the novelist, and a host of others. In putting young and struggling artists in touch with those who had already made a name for themselves, Parsons performed a fine service.

Years later, when my wife and I went to live in Washington and found ourselves a part of the political and diplomatic life of our own country, I was immediately struck by its contrast to this same type of life in London. Not only was there in London a mingling with the world of artistic and business affairs, such as is rarely the case in America, but members of various English political parties could meet at the same table or in the same drawing room and brilliantly and without restraint or rancor discuss the most heated questions of the day. Even today this is not true in Washington. Perhaps this is due to the fact that many of our congressmen are little men, desperately worried over the outcome of the next election, harassed by lobbies and by their constituents, and more worried over their own survival than over good government, while in England statecraft is a life career and even if a man goes out with one election, he may either find an office or come back in the next. In America a man is likely to be out of office for years.

In London, Parliament is near the City, which corresponds to our Wall Street, and business and high finance are integrally connected with government. It is considered only reasonable that lawmakers should take various problems to the men who have firsthand information and the judgment derived from long experience. Indeed, many members of Parliament are actively engaged in business affairs in the City.

In Washington, politicians so far as possible avoid close contact with men of standing in business for fear of suspicion or investigation. The cry of "Wall Street" has been the death knell of many sound acts of legislation.

Another factor which added to the diplomatic or social life in London was the Englishwoman's ability to act brilliantly and intelligently as hostess at the most complex gatherings. Long before she gained the right to vote, she had an informed and accurate knowledge of "my country's politics." She is adroit at leading conversation and keenly aware of the moment when it is wise to retire from the center of the stage. Women have played an important role in the background of English politics, but they have done it with subtlety rather than publicity.

Of an evening in London one would find oneself in the midst of a thoroughly cosmopolitan assemblage. Under the same roof one might meet Viscount Grey, the statesman, Lecky, the historian, Kipling, the writer, and Lady Elizabeth Cust's son, Sir Lionel, head of the National Portrait Gallery, the Duke of Argyll, and Sir Edward Elgar, the composer and conductor. Among the charming women were Lady Vincent, called the most beautiful woman in London, and Madame Antonio de Navarro, formerly the lovely Mary Anderson of the stage. Add to these the usual sprinkling of foreign diplomats and noted explorers, the dash of leaders of great business enterprises, and the ever-present number of beautiful and distinguished women, and the scope of interest in the inspired conversation would be unlimited. Yet one must remember that this was before the time when the business office spread into the drawing room.

I have mentioned only a few of the friends we made. My wife had a genius for bringing together our friends, and I delighted in it. Her great interest in music naturally led her to include many musicians in this circle, and one of the closest was Elgar. Years later I made a speech at a dinner given for him in New York.

Elgar was a man of the world and informed on many subjects other than music, which was lucky for me. While I might enjoy the sonorous notes of his *Pomp and Circumstance,* I doubt whether my appreciation would include one of his symphonies. To be perfectly honest, I have difficulty in telling one note from another, although in my boyhood days I occasionally led the band in the drum corps of my company at the school military exhibitions.

I have sat through many painful hours of opera and concert in one good cause or another, chiefly to please my wife. She was a fine musician and was studying music in Dresden when I first met her. While I was courting her, I went up from Freiberg and took her to dozens of operas and concerts. I finally developed some small appreciation of Wagnerian opera, but I must confess that this came through following the schematic structure, which appealed to me as a great feat of mechanical thinking. It has always seemed to me that Wagner would have made an excellent engineer.

Our son Dick inherited a strong musical talent, obviously from his mother. Before he was three years old he showed a decided interest in it, and would try to climb onto the piano stool to reach the keys. One of his prized toys was a little primitive phonograph. He could pick out *She Was a High-Born Lady, Follow the Man from Cook's,* or *My Lodger Is a Nice Young Man,* simply by his familiarity with the slots and dashes on the paper disks. This aptitude was developed and Dick studied music for many years in Paris. His compositions have been played or sung by Ganz, Sokolsky-Freid, Braslau, Torpadie, Graveure, and others.

One of the most noted hostesses of all Victorian London was the Baroness Burdett-Coutts. She was born in 1814 and was an elderly

woman when my wife and I first met her, distinguished and grace-
ful in appearance and alert and clever in mind. The daughter of
Sir Francis Burdett, she added the name of Coutts on inheriting the
large fortune of her grandfather, Thomas Coutts, the banker. She
was close to Queen Victoria by whom she was created a baroness
in 1871.

King Edward VII spoke of her as "After my mother, the most
remarkable woman in the Kingdom."

Baroness Burdett-Coutts gave much of her time to the organizing
and carrying on of various charities. Her friendship with Charles
Dickens arose from their common interest in the poor of London.
In 1881 she married William Ashmead-Bartlett, who took her name.
Ashmead-Bartlett was born in America of English parents.

Her house at No. 1 Stratton Street, Piccadilly, was filled with rare
paintings, porcelains, ivories, old silver, Shakespeare folios and other
first editions. I frequently dropped in after business hours to have
tea with the baroness. She did not interfere with politics, but she
was much interested in Africa and we often discussed the problems
of the blacks under the English and the Boers. At these afternoon
gatherings one would invariably meet most of the nationally and
internationally known people of the time.

Holly Lodge, her suburban home, was one of the most beautiful
in London. On a hillside some hundred feet above London, it was
surrounded by magnificent gardens, and on a clear day one could
look down on the town. It was an ideal place for out-of-door entertaining. In the spring Season, she and her husband gave delightful
garden parties. It was at one of these that I had one of my more
serious encounters with royalty. The Duchess of Albany was being
pushed around the grounds in a rolling chair. There was also present
an Indian maharaja. The baroness asked me to present him to the
duchess. I asked to be reminded of his name and was told that the
reason the baroness wanted me to make the presentation was because
she couldn't remember it. No wonder. He had about forty titles.

I started, feeling a little like Alice in Wonderland, and was making fair, if somewhat halting progress in mentioning his many titles
when the young maharaja stepped forward and in the best Oxonian
English said, "Kindly allow me, sir"—and finished the job himself.

Both the duchess and the baroness seemed content and I, needless to say, was relieved.

The baroness had known the Duke of Wellington in her girlhood. It is said that she refused his offer of marriage. It was her custom, each year, to observe the anniversary of the Battle of Waterloo by giving a dinner. As the years went by these dinners became nearly as important as other more official memorials.

While my wife and I were at Bad Nauheim in 1905 we received an invitation to spend this anniversary with her. We were honored but somewhat surprised to find ourselves the only guests. But she was ninety-two now and growing weaker. She felt close to us for many reasons, among them the fact that she was our daughter Natalie's godmother. Her mind was as clear and active as ever. She wore the cabochon emerald that Wellington had given her, and talked of him and his services to England and repeated stories he had told her of his campaigns and battles. It was the last time we saw her. She died a few months later.

Mr. Burdett-Coutts' brother, E. Ashmead-Bartlett, M.P., was an extreme pro-Turk. He had been an observer in the Greco-Turkish War of 1897; Richard Harding Davis had been a war correspondent with the Greeks. After the return of both these friends of mine to London, I invited them to lunch to meet each other. I thought it would prove interesting and I promised myself some light on the unofficial and inside history of the war. We were hardly seated when Ashmead-Bartlett said something about the cowardice of the Greeks. This was challenged by Davis, who flared up in defense of them and then attacked the Turks. The argument became so heated that the two almost came to blows. This would have been a serious fight as both were powerful men, and it required all my tact to quiet them. The purpose of the lunch was defeated and the subject had to be dropped. War had very nearly broken out again over the glassware and china.

Another of England's most gracious ladies is Princess Louise, the fourth daughter of Queen Victoria. The princess has always been especially kind to Americans. She understood our unfamiliarity with court life. Her receptions were simple and her warmth of personality unaffected. She was most kind to both my wife and my

To John Hays Hammond
with the cordial regards of John Hay

JOHN HAY (1838-1905)

In Memoriam,
December 30, 1906,

ANGELA,
BARONESS BURDETT-COUTTS.

BARONESS BURDETT-COUTTS (1814-1906)

sister when they were presented at Queen Victoria's court. Her husband was the Marquis of Lorne, afterwards Duke of Argyll, whom we always enjoyed seeing. His charming simplicity is illustrated by his remark to my sister, when he heard we were looking for a house and were considering various locations: "Perhaps you'd better not think of the section around Buckingham Palace. *My wife's family* find it too relaxing." Among my literary treasures are the complete works of Walter Scott, which had been a gift to the duke from his mother, and which he gave to me shortly before his death in 1914.

I saw a great deal of Sir Edgar Vincent, later Lord D'Abernon. He was tall and handsome and wore a beard—strangely enough, becoming. Among all the English diplomats, he was one of the most versatile. He was an outstanding banker, financial adviser to the Egyptian government, and governor of the Imperial Ottoman Bank, and from 1920 to 1926 ambassador to Germany. He wrote many books, and one of the best arguments in the cause of peaceful international relations is the three-volume diary account of his activities in post-war Germany, *An Ambassador of Peace.*

The last time I saw him was when I visited England in 1929. He was just preparing to head one of those famous English goodwill tours. This one was to South America and, of course, to promote English business and commerce. He invited me to go with him to which I demurred saying that it would be impossible to get passage at such a late date. He assured me that he would arrange for the passage himself and that all diplomatic courtesies would be extended me. I hesitated again and asked him how he dared suggest that I, an American, go along, for I might be tempted to stir up some business for my own countrymen and myself.

"I'll take my chances on that," he replied. I persisted in my refusal, for I saw no reason why I should be a part of a junket to drum up trade for the British, though this was not my sole objection.

Following a good lead, however, I did make a trip to the east coast of South America a short time after.

During the winter of 1897-98 I made another trip to South Africa, and on the same boat with me were Rudyard Kipling (Rudyard was named after a place where his father and mother first met), his wife, and his father, Lockwood Kipling, the artist. They proved excellent traveling companions and we have maintained our friendly contact ever since. Rudyard manifested his " 'satiable curtiosity" by prowling endlessly from engine room to bridge getting information which, as he said, he filed away in his memory for future use.

When we arrived at Cape Town, I went, as always, to spend a few days with Rhodes at Groote Schuur and report on the mining properties in which he was still interested and of which I was still consulting engineer. Rhodes had finished with his Parliamentary Inquiry and had returned to Cape Town, once more to enter politics, and to work for his "North."

Rhodes asked me if there were any interesting passengers on the steamer and I mentioned the Kiplings. Then I asked his permission to bring them to lunch; from that meeting sprang a genuine and deep regard between these great imperialists which terminated only at Rhodes's death. Rhodes had built a guest house on his place at Groote Schuur, and Rudyard was asked to make it his winter home, which he did for several years.

My assistants, Yeatman and Webb, had met me at Cape Town to report on operations on the Rand. We made the return trip to Johannesburg together, and I invited Lockwood Kipling to accompany us.

At the Transvaal border we had to change trains and go through the customs. Precautions against smuggling had greatly increased in stringency since the old days when I had played Ali Baba with the oil drums. Yeatman and Webb seemed apprehensive. They asked me several times whether I had a pistol with me, saying that the Boers were sure to make a thorough search for arms. They believed that I, particularly, would be suspected should my identity become known. Their anxiety, though to me amusing, became tiresome.

To quiet them I bet them I would not suffer the indignity of personal search.

At the border Yeatman and Webb went ahead of me into the wire enclosure where the baggage was being examined. After they had submitted to a search of their persons for concealed weapons, the inspector turned towards me.

"Let me see your commanding officer, please!" I demanded in a firm voice.

He pointed to a man standing in the doorway. I walked over and introduced myself.

"Oh, yes, Mr. Hammond, I seem to have heard of you before. What can I do for you?"

"Do you think it necessary to search me?" I asked. "I don't deny that I have done some gunrunning over these borders in my time, but I like to do my smuggling on a large scale. I'd have no use for firearms now. I assure you my intentions at the moment are entirely peaceable."

The official smiled pleasantly, and said: "I'll see you're passed through without examination. Is there anyone else in your party?"

"Yes," I replied, "I've a friend with me." I discreetly avoided mentioning the name of Kipling as it was anathema to the Boers at that time because of the extremely imperialistic character of Rudyard's verse. Moreover, I didn't care to disturb the confidence just shown in me. The official beckoned to a porter and told him to reserve a compartment for us and to see that our luggage was put on the Transvaal train.

It was a warm day, and the official asked me whether I would join him in a glass of beer. I gladly accepted. He thereupon unlocked the door which led from the wired enclosure to the bar. While waiting for the train, we sipped our beers, smoked, and chatted.

As I leaned with my back against the bar, I could see out of the corner of my eye Yeatman and Webb staring wistfully, their anxiety this time centering on themselves rather than on me but I took no notice of them.

Finally the Boer inspector remarked: "Mr. Hammond, there are two gentlemen out there. I think they're trying to attract your attention. Do you know them?"

I glanced casually in their direction. Their gestures became more agitated. I turned back to my beer and said, "I can't place them for the moment."

But their pathetic appearance gradually worked upon my sympathies and I relented.

I turned and called, "Come on, fellows, there's just time for a quick one before the train leaves."

When I was back in England in 1898, I was dining one night at the Burlington Hotel in London with Rhodes and two or three other friends. Rhodes received a cablegram from Kitchener, saying, "We have whipped the Mahdi. Your brother Frank well. I will win my bet." I asked Rhodes what the bet was and he said that he had made a bet with Kitchener that he would extend the railroad from Cape Town farther north than Kitchener would extend it south from Cairo, within the next five years.

The Cape-to-Cairo railroad was most dear to Rhodes and was an old point of contention between Rhodes and me. I pointed out to him again that the cost of maintaining the Cape-to-Cairo road would be greater than the economic returns would ever warrant, and that he ought to take into consideration the fact that all freight for western Europe and England would have to be transferred from railroad to ships at considerable expense and there would be no saving of time. Also, very little time would be saved by passengers who chose the land route. Rhodes, however, was so committed to the completion of this project that after a few arguments which became somewhat heated the subject was dropped.

Later, in lunching with Baron Reuter, of the Reuter News Agency, I remarked that at last the English had another great general. He said, "Of course you refer to Kitchener."

"Yes," I replied; whereupon he said, "You are entirely mistaken in your estimate of Kitchener."

Reuter then went on to say that the Battle of Omdurman was not one that would reflect great credit on Kitchener's generalship, since as a matter of fact he narrowly escaped defeat owing to lack of precaution in his advance. The Mahdists, it seems, had led him into an ambuscade and if it had not been for the remarkable bravery of a force of a few hundred soldiers under General Kelly, one of Kitchener's officers, in relaying, charging, and dispersing the enemy, thus affording Kitchener time to reorganize his column, the British would have suffered a serious defeat.

Neither did Kitchener's career in the Boer War, a few years later, add luster to his laurels as a military commander. It was fortunate for the British cause that Lord Roberts was in command early in the war; he superseded General Buller, who had got the British Army involved in many difficult situations. Kitchener was, however, a great executive, and I think he must have had many of the qualities of General McClellan in our Civil War; a great organizer but not a great fighter. We all recall Lincoln's impatience at the inaction of General McClellan; the President good-humoredly sent word to McClellan that if he did not have any use for his army he wished the general would lend it to him.

In the great World War, Kitchener failed to rise to his opportunities, not realizing the supreme need of sufficient munitions to carry on a war of that character. Only the perception and energy of Lloyd George retrieved that blunder.

All over the world, when I set up an office, people came to me with mining propositions. Sometimes they were sound, sometimes worth investigating, at other times tragic or comic. The most tragic, I think, was the case of Whitaker Wright who came to me after I had established headquarters in London.

"Mr. Hammond," he said, "I have some gold properties in Australia. I'd like you to look them over and come in with us as consulting engineer. We've a fine board of directors as you'll see by this list."

I took the paper and noted suspiciously the inclusion of many titled directors. Since I was familiar with Wright's questionable mining reputation, I suspected that these noble lords were being prepared for fleecing.

Wright held out the inducement of a yacht for my accommodation if I would go in with him; even so, I refused.

Only a few months later Wright's financial structure toppled. He had tried to freeze out his partners by bearing the market and buying in at the bottom, but he overstepped the bounds of legality.

At his trial, he might have embarrassed those well-known gentlemen who, in return for substantial directors' fees and through misplaced confidence in Wright, had lent their respectable names to his enterprise.

There was consternation in London. But Wright refused to give any evidence involving others. He had even destroyed all records which might have inculpated some of them. Perhaps fearing that his own high resolve might weaken, he took some cyanide of potassium from his pocket as he left the dock and, before the guards could prevent him, he had swallowed a fatal dose.

Since it was during these years in London that I first met John Hay, whom I consider one of the finest Americans I have ever known, I should like to digress long enough to tell something of our relationship.

Trifles often help to turn acquaintance into friendship. Soon after I met him I heard one day that he was ill. Stopping at a florist shop, I selected some flowers, and wrote a card, "From John Hay's Hammond." This pleased the fancy of the genial diplomat, and after that we saw a good deal of each other.

Although I had not known Hay before, I had, of course, heard about him from boyhood. I was ten years old when Lincoln was shot; John Hay had been his most confidential secretary. The imagination developed in his early career as writer and journalist, tempered by his legal training and matured by intimate association with Lincoln, together with the terrific events at the Capital during the war and the President's assassination, gave his mind a balance and a varied brilliance that cannot be forgotten by anyone who heard him talk or has read his letters. Hay was the ideal diplomat. As ambassador to England and later as secretary of state in this crucial time of financial crisis and our war with Spain, he more than any other American cemented our bonds with England. The English admired and liked him no less than did his fellow countrymen.

It was just at this time, during the Spanish-American War, that he and I became so intimate. Through the co-operation of Rhodes, I acted in a sort of liaison capacity between Hay and certain important personages in the British government. Hay was very anxious to meet Rhodes in an informal way, so when Rhodes next came to London, I arranged a luncheon for Ambassador and Mrs. Hay, Mr. and Mrs. Rudyard Kipling, Rhodes, James M. Barrie, my wife, and myself. We had a delightful time and enjoyed a spirited talk for two or three hours. Rhodes then told Hay the whole story of South Africa as only he could tell it, and Hay was won over to Rhodes and his aspirations. When Hay returned to the United States in 1898 and became secretary of state under McKinley, he was able to impress upon the President the true situation in South Africa.

When the Spanish-American War first broke out, I was in London and was greatly pleased to see how English public sentiment in general favored us. All the other nations of Europe sympathized with Spain. As evidence of the British sympathy to the American cause, they often referred to it as the Yanko-Spanko War.

During this time, I happened to sit next to General Lord Wolseley at a dinner and I asked him how he thought the conflict would end. Wolseley said: "You know I am in sympathy with the United States, as I served in your Civil War as a British observer, and I have a very high regard for the American soldier, but I am much afraid that your country will be rushed into the war by politicians, and your country is not prepared. It takes a lot of preparation to transport troops, even for a short distance. England with her great navy and merchant marine would find it difficult to move troops to any part of the world in a short time, and I am afraid that the United States might be set back, but, of course, ultimately you will win, and I hope you do." Subsequent events proved the justness of this criticism.

After enjoying Hay's companionship while he was in England, I did not see him again until we met at Bad Nauheim in 1905. I had had pneumonia in America, after visiting the Utah Copper Company. The weather was very cold and I had to walk through the snow for two or three miles down a canyon to the railroad. Moreover, there wasn't a drop of liquor at the Utah copper mine, as the superintendent would not allow it about the place. I've always believed that if I had had some whisky I might have escaped pneumonia, but then I might not have seen John Hay again.

My wife really inveigled me into going to Bad Nauheim. While I was recuperating, she tried to get me to make the trip there, but I refused. Then she pretended that she had heart trouble; she thought she ought to go to Bad Nauheim and take treatments. I was naturally greatly concerned, so we went. The result was that I got the treatments, and her heart trouble quickly disappeared.

John Hay was completing his treatments at Bad Nauheim under

Dr. Groedel. During this time the American ambassador to Germany was Charlemagne Tower, who later became a good friend of mine. He came to Bad Nauheim with an invitation from Kaiser Wilhelm for John Hay and myself to visit him in Berlin. We would have enjoyed such a visit exceedingly and were disappointed that we could not accept the invitation, but our physicians strongly urged us not to leave until after the completion of the cure. We asked the ambassador to express our regrets to the Kaiser, with the hope that we might be able to visit him at another time. Unfortunately this occasion never presented itself, as the "reisender" Kaiser was away on one of his frequent trips by the time we were ready to leave the baths.

Mrs. Hay went to Paris for a few days and left her husband under the care of my wife and me. We used to meet with other friends daily at five o'clock to listen to the band and drink tea, chocolate, or beer. Hay called our meeting the "Catch Your Eye Club"; whenever we saw an American any of us knew, we would catch his eye and invite him to come over to our table. For obvious reasons it occurred to me that it was more fitting to call ourselves the "klätscherei" or gossiping club.

Hay was a delightful companion during those days at Bad Nauheim. We talked naturally of many of the presidents including Lincoln. Hay told me: "I sat up with Lincoln the night the election returns for his second term were coming in. He was far from confident; in fact, he was exceedingly nervous. I have been with several presidents on similar occasions and not one of them showed any confidence in being re-elected."

During one of our conversations he told me that King Leopold of Belgium was importunate in seeking a meeting with him. Hay said: "I know what the old codger has in mind; he wants to explain away the atrocities in the Congo, and I am not going to see him." The king arrived the next day, so Hay left word at the desk of the hotel that his doctors had ordered him to see no one and he was not to be disturbed. Then he and I went off for a long walk. About five o'clock, he said: "Let's go back now. I guess the old rascal has come and gone by this time." When we reached the hotel there was King Leopold in an armchair in front of the elevator, waiting for Hay.

There was nothing left for Hay to do but make an apology and talk with the king.

That evening Hay told me that the king had not wanted to talk about the Congo at all; instead, he talked about the Manchurian Railway. Hay added, "He is really a very likable fellow."

Royalty does not move without being noticed. Robert Williams told me long afterwards that he feared King Leopold's visit while I was there meant that I would secure from him the Katanga concessions, and this fear impelled Williams to hasten to a conclusion his own negotiations for that property.

There was a curious thing about Hay. With all his intellectual power and the fair degree of his earlier success as poet, biographer, and essayist, it is said that after he went to England he was always sorry he had published any books in lighter vein. Perhaps he feared the accusation of being literary would interfere with his importance as a statesman.

Hay's greatest obsession was his contempt for the United States Senate, which had turned down the Hay-Pauncefote Treaty, though it was finally signed in November, 1901.

Hay was a man of quick wit, as is illustrated by the following anecdote. He, William M. Evarts, at that time secretary of state and likewise famous for his wit, and the British lord chancellor, who was paying a visit to America, went sightseeing to Mount Vernon. The British chancellor turned to Secretary Evarts and said: "That is a pretty tall story about Washington throwing a dollar across the Potomac. It is a very wide river."

"Oh," replied Evarts, "a dollar went farther in those days."

Then Hay capped the climax by quickly saying, "George Washington did something better than that; he hurled a sovereign across the Atlantic."

Our visit together at Bad Nauheim was destined to be our last. John Hay was anxious to return home, but Dr. Groedel advised him not to go back to America and start any business until he had finished his nach kur. Unfortunately Hay disregarded this advice and returned home. He spent a few weeks in Washington in the heat of the summer and then went to his home in New Hampshire. He died there, the day I arrived in the United States.

In 1898, while in London I had received a new business offer. My arrangement with Rhodes allowed me to accept other work in South Africa, of course, provided it involved no injury to his interests. Therefore, no professional ethics were concerned when Leopold Hirsch, head of the great stock brokerage house of L. Hirsch and Company of London, informed me that his client J. B. Robinson, later Sir Joseph, wished me to take charge of his gold-mining properties, the Randfontein Estates.

I had heard a great deal about Robinson's unpopularity among the mining operators of the Rand; he was especially jealous of Rhodes, his avowed enemy. His astuteness in negotiating land purchases from the reluctant Boers are still far-famed in the Transvaal.

In 1886 he was almost penniless. Hearing of the discovery of gold on the Rand, he had persuaded Alfred Beit to back him to the extent of one hundred thousand dollars in the purchase of farms in the Witwatersrand district. Since the partnership did not thrive, it was decided to divide the property. Robinson's share, the Langlaagte, produced nearly five million dollars in five years but he was disgruntled because that of Beit proved much richer.

Robinson carried on a long private feud with Rhodes, paying extravagant prices for diamond fields wherever and whenever he thought it possible to injure the De Beers Company. He boasted that, since he was now worth sixty million dollars, he could afford it. Because Rhodes and Kruger were inimical, he affected to be an adherent of the latter. Afterwards he broke with Oom Paul because, as he said: "Kruger is so corrupt he can be bribed by anyone. I've done it myself."

Because of his eccentricities, Robinson had few friends on the Rand, and was likened to a "rogue elephant." For that reason I told Hirsch quite frankly that I would not consider seriously any offer made by Robinson, since I believed I could not get along with a man of such arbitrary disposition.

When Hirsch reported this to Robinson, his only reply was, "Well, at least bring Mr. Hammond to have tea with me some day at Dudley House."

Some weeks later I accepted this invitation.

It was interesting to observe a man who utterly lacked aesthetic appreciation living in one of London's most famous and beautiful houses. He was proud of it because it was expensive. He was incapable of realizing that the value of such an architectural treasure could not be estimated in pounds, shillings, and pence.

He asked me bluntly why I objected to becoming associated with him. With equal candor, I answered that, according to report, no self-respecting man could remain long in his employ.

"Can you be more explicit?" he asked.

"For one thing," I replied, "I've been told by your engineers that you interfered constantly with their work."

"True, Mr. Hammond, I've employed many men in whom I have afterwards lost confidence. But if I paid you as much as I expect you to ask, I wouldn't dream of trying to run things myself. Furthermore, I'd agree to give you absolute control of all mining matters."

"I'll have to think this over for a few days, Mr. Robinson," I answered as I took my leave.

I sent a cable at once to Harry H. Webb in Johannesburg in whose estimates of ore values I had great confidence. I asked him to let me know whether it would be possible to make the Randfontein Estates property a financial success if there were sufficient working capital and if it were under my absolute control.

On the strength of Webb's favorable assurances I accepted the position with Robinson, and selected Pope Yeatman to become general manager.

A few months later I went to South Africa and made a personal examination of the properties. Without any hesitation our recommendations were accepted, and we had the satisfaction of seeing our policy carried out.

When Rhodes and other friends heard that I had become consultant for Robinson, they told me I could not get along with him for three months. Actually, I remained his consulting engineer for two years—that is, until my return to America. Other mining men who knew Robinson were amazed when I told them I had found him one of the most liberal men with whom I had ever done business. He gave me his unqualified support and, after I had resigned, did the same for Yeatman, whom he retained as general manager.

Towards the end of 1899 I came to the conclusion that it would be desirable to transfer my headquarters to New York. My reasons were due partly to business conditions and partly to sentiment.

I sought out Rhodes at Burlington House to tell him of my decision. Rhodes expressed regret, and asked whether I could not be persuaded to reconsider and instead go back to South Africa as general manager of all his interests there.

I hesitated for a moment, and then shook my head. "I'm sorry but I can't do it. I appreciate your offer, and I know how important the position is, but it's not in my line. It's a job for an administrator. Right now all that mining on the Rand amounts to is cutting salaries and reducing operating costs. You know the kind of work I like— solving new technical problems or pioneering in new districts. There's plenty of territory in the United States and Mexico still left to explore."

Rhodes nodded in agreement. "But wouldn't you be interested in politics? I feel confident I'm going to have a new lease of political life, and I'd hoped to have you work with me."

"I'm certain your career has hardly begun yet," I answered him, "and I should regard it as a high honor to be associated with you, but South African politics don't seem to be in my line. I confess I've had enough politics."

I then gave my final reason. I told him that, in spite of my fondness for England, I did not wish my children to become expatriates. Harris was almost ready for college. If I were to remain longer in England, the natural thing would be for him to continue with his friends to Oxford. I recalled my own happy years at Yale, and liked to picture my sons receiving their education in a similar environment. It seemed to me that I could recapture some of my early enthusiasms through their experiences. I looked forward to seeing them take their places in the small college world.

Rhodes understood and sympathized with my feeling, and so we parted. This was my last talk with him; in a few months he was besieged by the Boers in Kimberley.

While dining with me in New York on March 26, 1902, Lord

Albert Grey received a cablegram from Dr. Jameson saying that Rhodes would not survive the night. This came as a great shock to us, though we had known that his days were numbered.

Not merely did I wish my children to be educated in the United States, but I desired to renew my business connections here. At the beginning of the Spanish-American War the price of American securities had dropped considerably, though I had not the slightest doubt that with the ultimate victory of America they would rise again.

Because I had been out of touch with American investments for so long a time I asked the advice of Otto Kahn, who was then in London. Accepting his suggestions, I sold out a large part of my South African mining securities, and invested the proceeds in American enterprises. Once again, I threw in my fortunes with those of my own country.

CHAPTER TWENTY-THREE

Russia, 1898, 1910, 1912

AN OFFICIAL INVITATION TO RUSSIA—WITTE THE
STATESMAN—DODGING THE NIHILISTS—EXAMINING
THE URAL MOUNTAINS—OUT FOR THE WORLD'S
PLATINUM SUPPLY—AN OASIS IN SIBERIA—THE
INDUSTRIAL DEVELOPMENT OF RUSSIA—WITTE
NEGOTIATES PEACE WITH JAPAN—A SECOND
JOURNEY TO RUSSIA—I GIVE THE CZAR GOOD
ADVICE—BARON ROTHSCHILD AND THE JEWISH
PROBLEM—THE UNITED STATES ABROGATES HER
COMMERCIAL TREATY WITH RUSSIA—THE U. S. S. R.

*W*hile I was in London, a fresh opportunity presented itself to enlarge my mining experience. In the winter of 1897-98 the financial firm of L. Hirsch and Company was working with Serge Julievitch Witte, the Russian minister of finance, to stimulate the investment of English capital in Russia. Leopold Hirsch had several interviews with Gregory Wilenkin, the Russian government's financial agent in London, and with Dr. Rafalovitch, who acted in a similar capacity in Paris.

As a result of these conversations, Witte invited me to come to St. Petersburg with Hirsch and make a survey of Russia's industrial potentialities, particularly the mining resources.

Our party consisted of Hirsch, his friend, Captain Money, a retired English army officer who managed the details of the trip, and myself. Almost immediately upon our arrival at the Hotel Europa, a droshky was ready to take us to the Ministry of Finance.

I looked forward to meeting Witte, the man who almost single-handed was attempting to change the course of his country's history. At once he reminded me of Cecil Rhodes. Both were over six feet tall and proportionately broad, and would dominate any assemblage by size as well as personality.

Witte had fine clear eyes, set far apart. His face, though intellectually distinguished, bore an expression of sadness. No other Russian I have ever met had his drive, his energy, his ability to cut through red tape. Yet, blended with this practical activity was a certain Oriental imperturbability that contrasted sharply with Rhodes's nervous energy and responsiveness. It is not likely that the possibility of failure had ever occurred to Rhodes before the Jameson Raid; from Witte one gathered that he was prone to envisage the eventuality of disaster.

At that time Witte was regarded as the magician who was about to metamorphose the somnolent Muscovite with his cannikin of vodka into the busy happy workman with a full dinner pail—a plan that had the merit of never having been tried in Russia. In the eyes of the world, Russia was a land of vast and incalculable natural resources awaiting only the fructifying touch of foreign capital.

Witte was one of the most highly qualified of the great statesmen of his day as an empire builder, although perhaps in the economic rather than the political sense. Rhodes was interested in the industrial development of a country chiefly as a means of expanding the British Empire territorially; that is, his aspirations were pre-eminently political, while Witte's paramount interest was for the economic expansion of his country. In his ambition to bring Russia to a high state of industrial development, Witte was willing to sacrifice such frontier territory as was not essential to the country's political integrity. He fully comprehended the political weakness of an overextended empire.

Like Rhodes, the Russian statesman was deeply sensible of having a mission to perform. Either would have been a great factor in the history of any nation and would have exerted commanding influence. Both were exceptionally self-reliant and resourceful; both were dictatorial. Rhodes was the more willing to compromise, but even Witte was at times compelled to make concessions in order to maintain position and influence.

Witte had a far more difficult problem. At court he had to face a camarilla opposed to any economic or political change that would militate against its control of Russian affairs. Also, he had to compel a hidebound bureaucracy and an ignorant populace to subscribe to his plan. On the contrary, Rhodes could appeal with confidence to the enlightened self-interest of the Englishman.

Witte was the ablest and most farseeing man who has guided Russia. He was born in the Caucasus in 1849. His father was a minor state official of Dutch descent; his mother belonged to the Russian nobility. He attended school at Tiflis and then went to Odessa for further education.

In the ordinary course of events he would have become a member of the local bureaucracy. Instead, he went into the employ of the Odessa Railway Company. In a few years he had become general manager of the Southwestern Railway Company, and there he won his technical reputation handling troops and supplies during the Russo-Turkish War.

Business opportunities in Russia at that time were decidedly limited. Advancement through merit was possible up to a certain point; thereafter favoritism played a dominant role. Witte's opportunity came when he was commanded to run the imperial train over his road on a schedule he considered too fast for the Little Father's safety. He absolutely refused to obey orders, and this obstinacy brought him to the Czar's attention.

The Czar recognized that, although honesty and ability are essential for business success, the real test of a man's value to his employer is the manner in which he conducts himself in an emergency; there are times when judgment must override rules, regulations, even the orders of a superior.

There were in the ranks of the Russian nobility few men capable of handling efficiently the portfolio of national finance. Witte was offered this position, but declined. After much persuasion, he agreed to accept the specially created post of director of railways, and in 1892 became minister of ways and communications. Finally, when

Vishnegradsky fell ill, Witte took over the duties of minister of finance, and in 1893, in his forty-fourth year, received the formal appointment.

I was familiar with Witte's aims and generally in sympathy with them. He was convinced that Russia must be tributary to industrial countries so long as it remained exclusively agricultural, and there could be no extensive development of Russian resources without capital. This must be sought abroad. He had to persuade foreign money that Russia was a safe place for investment. In spite of every type of opposition and intrigue, he succeeded in initiating his program.

One of his major victories was to put Russia on the gold standard. First he stopped the speculation in Russian rubles on the Berlin Bourse, and then contracted the paper currency. This financial achievement had been carried through the year before my visit.

The foundation of Witte's economic theory was "educational protection," which resembled the ancient and honorable plank in our Republican party's platform. Witte put high duties on raw materials and manufactured products which could be produced in Russia, although he knew that this policy would result in higher prices to the Russian consumer and that any measure touching the consumer's pocketbook would be unpopular. He deliberately accepted this unpopularity.

The tariff provoked German hostility. Witte welcomed these reprisals because they gave him an excuse to throw off German industrial domination. At our first interview he frankly stated that this was his object in seeking the aid of English capital.

"Isn't the real reason, M. Witte," I asked, "that you have sucked the Gallic orange dry?" France had supplied Russia with large funds.

Witte's face remained impassive. I continued, "Have you also considered seeking American capital?"

He looked at me for a moment, and then said: "Mr. Hammond, the United States is not an international money power. You are occupied with building up your own country. You have not yet reached the stage where you can afford to export capital."

There was so much truth in the statement that I could not counter his observation with any conviction.

From Witte's office we went to his home for luncheon. With great show of politeness, Hirsch and Money insisted that I be the one to accompany the minister in his small droshky. I climbed in and seated myself beside the great man. My involuntary smile and glance of understanding betrayed my thoughts to my English companions, who showed signs of embarrassment. Witte did not trouble to hide his own amusement at their discomfiture. They had apparently taken to heart the recent publicity given by the European press to nihilistic attempts on the lives of Russian officials. Their droshky remained discreetly distant from ours.

Mme. Witte presided over the luncheon table. She was a charming and highly intelligent woman who, I felt, understood Witte's plans and was a constructive influence in their accomplishment. The conversation ran chiefly in political channels, and both M. and Mme. Witte expressed opinions which, in certain diplomatic circles, might have been regarded as unnecessarily frank.

Witte showed particular interest in Rhodes and what he had been trying to do in Africa. The conversation turned naturally to the English attitude towards Russia. Since I lived in England, but was not English, I felt free to express my opinions.

"M. Witte, you have asked me several questions about Rhodes, and I have tried to tell you my estimate of him. It seems to me that if Rhodes were autocrat of England and another like him held the same position in Russia, these two would be able to settle the differences between their respective countries. The English autocrat would concede Russia's necessity for a Window on the Mediterranean, provided Russia would cease agitation on England's Indian frontier. Both men would recognize that, for the peace and welfare of the world, the two countries should harmonize their foreign policies."

"Of course you know, Mr. Hammond, that I, as minister of finance, have little influence on the foreign policy of my country, but you may rest assured that I know how essential it is for Russia to be friendly with England."

When we were ready to start back to the office, Hirsch—his fears calmed by the fact that we had arrived for luncheon intact—expressed a desire to ride with Witte.

"No," demurred Witte. "You'll pardon me if I seem to consider my own safety. Mr. Hammond will prove a more efficacious body-guard, because he is an American. I am sure the Nihilists would show him more consideration than they would an Englishman, in spite of the fact that England is well known to be the asylum of 'persecuted Nihilists.'"

Any apprehension I may have had was now allayed, and I relaxed sufficiently to take an interest in the strange city life through which I was passing. Each time I attempted to look about me, I found my view obstructed by the corporeal majesty of the driver. Witte explained to me that the private coachmen were selected from the fattest of their class. The importance and standing of the master was gauged by the weight of his coachman.

This was an interesting sociological sidelight, but I was more comforted by the thought that our driver might serve as a shield from an assassin's bullet. And it occurred to me that armor plate would be an acceptable means of enlarging a coachman and pro-tecting his master.

In order that I might have an accurate picture of the occurrence of minerals in Russia, I had sent ahead several engineers under S. J. Truscott, one of my most competent assistants in South Africa and author of the recognized standard work on Rand mining. He is at present professor of mining at the Imperial College of Science and Technology in London. A preliminary report was awaiting me at St. Petersburg. On the basis of this report I laid out my route to include the most likely prospects. We had permission to examine the Crown properties and authority to open them up if they proved worth while.

Witte had warned me to be on guard against German interfer-ence. He had also advised me under no circumstances to attempt to bribe a Russian official. Although the graft scandal was greatly magnified, it seems that little of the money paid to the middlemen for their influence in high places ever accomplished its object.

My party of inspection included Hirsch, Money, and a German interpreter. Everything was done to facilitate our preparations. The minister of transportation, Prince Khilkov, who had learned practical railroading as a locomotive engineer on one of our western lines, placed his private car at our disposal. One room was given up to an enormous map over which we all pored endlessly. The five-foot gauge used on all Russian railroads produced a smoothness of motion that was very agreeable. The tedium of the long trip was relieved by frequent stops at stations where all the passengers were served glasses of hot tea. I have never been able to accustom myself to fondness for their boiled bitter beverage, but I succumbed without a struggle to the attraction of this liquid as served from the Russian samovar. We lived well: smoked salmon, caviar, bortsch, veal, and cheese appeared often on the menu.

Our first detailed examination was to be made in the Ural Mountains at Ekaterinburg, where shallow prospecting shafts had been sunk on the gold veins in anticipation of my arrival. None of these properties was worth exploitation, however, and the prospects so far developed were not available for purchase. It was near these shafts that the Russian royal family was murdered; their bodies were cremated and the ashes of the bones, with buttons and other indestructible objects from the wearing apparel, were thrown into the shafts, where they were later found.

The platinum deposits were more tempting as a business proposition. Ninety per cent of the world's supply at that time came from the Urals. Since it had to be sent abroad for refining, English firms had secured the monopoly of the manufactured product and could establish its market price. Platinum was then selling at about $5.00 per troy ounce, and Russia was producing about two hundred thousand ounces a year. In 1912 the price in New York had risen to $45.00 per ounce, and at the depth of the depression, in 1932, was still $36.45. Colombia and Canada are now important producers, and in 1932 California produced two thousand ounces as a by-product from working the auriferous gravels.

Hirsch was planning to secure a monopoly of the platinum deposits, and to make an agreement with the Russian government whereby the ore might be reduced and refined in Russia. As a preliminary step we secured options on all the important properties except that of Count Schouvalov, of the Russian diplomatic family. On our return to St. Petersburg, we approached Count Schouvalov on the subject. He expressed willingness to join in the proposed amalgamation, and invited us to luncheon for the purpose, we assumed, of discussing details. After luncheon the count explained that he did not handle his financial affairs himself, but would turn us over to his business agent.

Our plans eventually came to nothing because we put too much dependence upon the honesty of the Schouvalov representatives. While Hirsch and I were absent in England awaiting final decision on this property, Belgian financiers secured it. Our ambitious scheme for cornering the world's platinum market had to be abandoned.

After a few days spent in investigating the mineral potentialities of the Urals, we resumed our trip by way of the Trans-Siberian Railroad. From its terminus at Marinsk, in South Central Siberia, we started south with native guides and two troikas on a trip of several hundred miles to the headwaters of the Yenesei River in the Altai Mountains. Sometimes by muddy roads, sometimes by rocky trails, we made our way through the rolling, sparsely wooded hills of this rarely visited portion of Russia.

While we were still in St. Petersburg, Witte had secured for us a government order enabling us to commandeer conveyances and horses wherever and whenever we should need them. This document proved particularly efficacious when we arrived one night, long after dark, at a small village. Everybody was drunk, including the mayor. We needed a change of horses immediately as we were in haste to catch the weekly train from Marinsk. We seized the mayor, stuck his head under a pump, righted him again, and shoved the order under his nose. Sobered by the sight of the imperial seal, he promptly produced fresh horses.

Traveling in a troika over the almost impassable Siberian roads is comparable in discomfort only to a journey in a dead-ax wagon over the rough trails of western America. Hirsch moaned disconsolately at each jolt. Hitherto his greatest physical exertion had consisted of cantering along the bridle paths of Hyde Park or reeling in salmon or stalking deer on his estate in Scotland.

On the northern slope of the Altai Mountains we found a hospitable host and comfortable quarters at the Ivanisky estate, the only one of any importance within a wide radius. In fact, it was two hundred and fifty miles from the nearest railway and a thousand from any important town.

Ivanisky was over eighty. Forty-odd years before he had been sent as a political exile to Siberia. There he was joined by his wife. Under the laws regulating exiles, those who agreed to discontinue political activities were allowed considerable latitude after a time and could take up their residence in Siberian localities remote from police supervision. Ivanisky was now at liberty to return to Russia, but he told me he preferred to spend his remaining years in Siberia. His relatives and nearly all his friends were dead, and he had succeeded in creating a civilized form of living in the wilderness.

In his youth Ivanisky had acquired some knowledge of mining, and had found employment in a small gold mine owned by a fellow exile. At the latter's death he had inherited several hundred acres of gold-bearing gravels, or placers. The working methods were crude, but produced from fifty to a hundred thousand dollars a year, depending upon the amount of work done upon the mine, which in turn varied with the income he required. I examined the property and made him an offer. Without hesitation he turned it down. He admitted the sum was fair but he considered it far safer to keep his gold in a bank of gravel than to deposit it in any bank of Siberia.

Ivanisky found diversion in his lonely life in raising trotting horses. The Altai country was not at all adapted to this purpose, there not being a level acre within many miles of his stables. Nevertheless, he had laid out a half-mile undulating track and had even sent his head trainer to California to study scientific breeding methods.

This genial old gentleman delighted in dispensing hospitality, and provided pleasant entertainment. The sole amusement for him and his wife during the long winter nights was to listen to the raucous music ground out by a primitive phonograph. Its repertory was almost entirely made up of negro minstrel songs and the so-called humorous dialogues of the day. The old couple did not understand a word of English.

Since they were eager to know exactly why they were amused, I translated the jokes and songs into Russian through our German interpreter. Whatever faint elements of humor might once have existed must somehow have evaporated in my rendition, and I fear that unwittingly I did these simple old people a disservice. They never laughed so heartily after that.

Using Ivanisky's estate as a base of supplies, we outfitted for a trip into the mountains. Our route lay through a country devoid even of trails and, though it was May, great patches of last winter's snow still lay on the northern slopes. Fortunately, our sure-footed Cossack ponies were able to avoid the treacherous places encrusted with thin ice. Before advancing over questionable ground, they would snuff off the covering of soft snow and delicately paw at the suspected spot. Thanks to their amazing sagacity, we met with no mishap except an occasional tumble into a snowbank.

One night a mounted messenger from Marinsk arrived at our camp with a telegram. When we had left St. Petersburg, the Spanish-American War was in progress and the American ambassador, Ethan Allen Hitchcock, had promised to keep me informed as to the result of the naval engagement which then seemed imminent.

The whole evening was devoted to deciphering this message. It had been written in French, the language of diplomacy, and so transmitted to Moscow, translated into Russian there, and then forwarded to Marinsk. When it finally reached us, our interpreter translated it from Russian into German, and I made an English version for Hirsch and Money.

The text had been so mutilated in transmission that all we could make out was that there had been a battle between Cervera's fleet and our own. It was impossible to be sure which side had won, although the Americans seemed to have been victorious. Naturally, I preferred this interpretation. In spite of many telegrams of inquiry, we never did know exactly what had happened at Santiago until we reached Moscow.

We were almost as much out of touch with the world as were some Americans I once heard about who raised foxes on an island off the coast of Alaska. Trips were made from the island twice a year to deliver the skins and to get provisions for the colony. At these times they would pick up a file of papers dating back to their previous trip, and would conscientiously read them in the proper order from the earliest issue to the latest. During the Spanish War, they were so interested in events that they reversed the process and read from last to first.

On our way back to Marinsk, we broke our journey for a day at Ivanisky's home. The entertainment began early and was continuous. We were not accustomed to champagne toasts and "no heeltaps" in the morning. Bumper followed bumper all the afternoon and evening, alternating with caviar and hors d'oeuvres. At midnight we sought our beds, tired but happy.

To our consternation, breakfast consisted chiefly of champagne. But we managed to present a steady front and converse fluently until it was time to start.

As we stepped into our troika, Ivanisky bade us farewell: "God speed you, but pardon the lack of true Russian hospitality of which I am guilty. You are the first guests who have ever left my house sober."

With pardonable pride, we thanked him and settled down for a few moments' quiet before we reached the river which cut across the road. There on the brink of the river stood young Ivanisky to bid us farewell. He had taken a short cut and driven furiously to arrive ahead of us. He proudly pointed to his own troika where we saw a case of champagne.

At this point we broke down and abjectly pleaded incapacity. Pointing to the rain-swollen torrent, we explained that, even perfectly sober, we would find it difficult to keep the dugout from capsizing. As we climbed into the troika on the farther side, we caught a glimpse of Ivanisky junior. In each hand he held an upturned bottle from which the precious contents were flowing to the ground. Then, according to Russian custom, he dashed the empty bottles on the rocks.

On our return to St. Petersburg, we saw Witte again. I told him that the natural resources of Russia offered most attractive opportunities for the investment of British capital. The physical geography of many parts of Russia and Siberia strikingly resembled our own West, and for that reason I was inclined to be especially enthu-

siastic over the prospects. It was apparent that the problems in
Russia were similar to those encountered in the United States.

The construction of railroads was going steadily forward under
Witte's constant pressure. But many other problems had not yet
been seriously considered. Improved methods of agriculture were
vitally needed, and with them the erection of grain elevators at
strategic points. Furthermore, refrigerator cars were required to
move perishable products over the vast distances.

I told Witte that I was greatly impressed with his plans for an
intensive industrial development of Russia and Siberia. I then
pointed out certain factors which would prevent foreign capital
from seeking Russian outlets. In the first place, the laws of Russia
were not favorable to such investment. Certain legal clauses made
confiscation possible without what citizens of other countries would
term "due process of law." Witte acknowledged this objection and
expressed his willingness to modify the legislation regarding tenure
of property by aliens.

The second obstacle was the control exercised by the Russian
bureaucracy over all phases of Russian economic life. Its blighting
hand reached to every smallest detail of administration. If English
capital were to be interested, much red tape would have to be
eliminated.

Most important of all to capital was the alarming state of the
political situation. Sir Nicholas O'Connor, the British ambassador,
Mr. Ethan Allen Hitchcock, the American ambassador, and I had
a joint interview with Witte. The seizure of Kiaochow by the Germans had been followed by the Russian appropriation of Port
Arthur and Dalny in Manchuria. Furthermore, in 1896 Russia had
secured permission from China to construct the Chinese Eastern
Railroad. While I was in Russia, the Trans-Siberian was extending
a spur to Port Arthur.

These preparations for the economic and political exploitation
of China were being viewed with the profoundest suspicion by
England. She could not help believing that the Bear was on one
of his ever-recurrent prowls and would be unlikely to content himself with such honeypots as had already fallen to him.

Witte admitted that little could be done about English capital until the political horizon cleared.

My first Russian trip brought no concrete results, but it did bring me in touch with the Russian Empire.

I next saw Witte at Portsmouth in the summer of 1905. My observations in Russia in 1898 had convinced me that American commercial interests in the Orient would be best served by a Russian victory in the Russo-Japanese War.

I made an address before the American Academy of Political and Social Science at Philadelphia in which I firmly stated my views. This came to Witte's attention, and he was prepared to regard me as a genuine friend to Russia at a time when Russian friends in the United States were few: from Roosevelt down, the American populace was inclined to sympathize with the Japanese. Witte seemed honestly pleased to find one American who was prepared to give him sympathetic hearing.

He talked with me frankly about the problems he had to face. He had come to the United States as peacemaker against his will. The war had not been of his making. He regarded it as the work of a court cabal. As an economist he recognized only too well the disaster war would inevitably bring to Russia. It represented the downfall of his hopes for a regenerated nation. The Russian treasury had been depleted, foreign loans could be obtained only on ruinous terms, and the army and navy had been decisively defeated.

In confirmation I recalled that in 1898 Witte had expressed opposition to the Russification of the Far Eastern territory. He had been unquestionably an advocate of world peace: he realized that the enormous cost of their national defense put the European nations under a severe handicap in trade competition with America.

Witte conducted himself with remarkable sagacity although he was no diplomat by training. He recognized American hostility and set out to counteract it. A hater of publicity, he allowed himself to be photographed as much as the American press desired and in this way did much to overcome the prevailing pro-Japanese sentiment. His old friend, Dr. E. J. Dillon, long a British newspaper correspondent in Russia, gave him valuable assistance in winning over the American press. When the Japanese insisted on secrecy at the peace sessions, he declared for the admission of newspaper correspondents. The representative of autocracy, he conducted himself with democratic simplicity. Although fully cognizant of Jewish antagonism, he paid a visit to the ghetto in New York City. At no period of his life did he show himself more favorably than during the negotiations.

He had come to the peace conference shackled by the instruction that he was to surrender not one inch of Russian soil or pay one kopeck of indemnity. Many people regarded his attitude as one of sheer bluff. But he really believed Russia "had only just begun to exert her full strength and to attain co-ordinated effort in her military plans." He pointed out that Japanese credit was practically exhausted, and that she could not extend her military operations much farther westward because of the increasing distance from her base of supplies. Furthermore, Russia was at the moment negotiating with French bankers for a loan with which to prolong the war.

Although Russia did cede half of the Island of Saghalien, this was due entirely to the Czar's personal intervention. Witte was generally regarded as having scored a great diplomatic victory at Portsmouth because Russia was not burdened by the imposition of a war indemnity. His reputation as a statesman was greatly enhanced by this victory, although the tardy expression of appreciation of his imperial master caused him deep chagrin; he was not even given his title of Count Witte until some time later.

During the years since I had seen Witte, we had fought and won our war with Spain. The United States had projected itself on the European vision, not only as an economic but as a political world power. I jestingly reminded Witte of the statement he had made to me in 1898 about our financial provincialism.

"You are right," he replied, "in asserting that the United States is now a star of the first magnitude in the financial heavens, but it will be long before she becomes an international banker."

He could not foresee that a decade after this discussion America would have lent almost as much money to the countries of Europe as the total sum of England's foreign investments.

In 1910, Gregory Wilenkin, the same financial agent of the Russian government with whom I had previously dealt in London, came to the United States. He tendered me an invitation on behalf of M. Kokovtzov, successor to Witte as minister of finance, to visit Russia again. The object this time was the development of Russian industries by the use of American and English capital expended under American auspices.

Remembering that the outcome of my former trip had been abortive, I wanted assurance of Russian sincerity. Wilenkin told me I had been chosen because of my previous survey, and also because the government believed that my recommendation would convince hesitant investors of the soundness and profitability of Russian opportunities.

Taking my wife and Jack with me, I started for Russia late in November. The news of my departure had been cabled ahead to Berlin where I planned to stop a few days. When I arrived I found reporters from German newspapers prepared to interview me. I did not wish news of my true object to get about, and supplied no more information than was necessary to allay suspicion. My few days in Berlin were mainly occupied in securing political and economic information from Ambassador David Jayne Hill as to the relations between Germany and Russia.

Heretofore, about two-thirds of the trade of Russia had been in the hands of the Germans, who were making every effort to keep it there by preventing the extension of commerce between Russia and other nations. I learned that a large part of United States exports to Russia were going through German channels and were being credited to that country. Germany, of course, enjoyed the advantage of proximity to Russia and most favored nation clauses under the Treaty of Bjorke, made by Witte in 1905. Through political pressure applied by Germany on Russia, at that time in the throes of the Russo-Japanese War, the treaty was tantamount to establishing a German economic protectorate over a large section of Russia, and had become a heavy burden on her industry.

I felt that, since Russia had within her boundaries most of the raw materials required for her basic industries, her natural policy should be to establish a protective tariff adequate to build up her home manufactures. The greater earning capacity thus created would result in higher standards of living, and with her immense population she would provide a great home market for her own industrial products.

It is my confident opinion that under the right kind of government and increased industrial development Russia would have been able to create in the not remote future a national wealth greater than that of any other nation in Europe with the single exception of Great Britain.

While we were in Berlin, Herr Emil Rathenau, head of the Allgemeine Elektricitäts Gesellschaft, an immense corporation comparable to the General Electric Company, and father of Walther Rathenau, called at our hotel and asked for John Hays Hammond. When he was shown into our suite, I found that he did not wish to see me. He wanted to consult my son Jack, whose developments in radio had already gained him a position of repute in the scientific world.

Later we dined at the Rathenau home and found the whole family deeply interested in current world problems. Herr Rathenau in particular had a great admiration for the Kaiser, to whom he gave much credit for the industrial expansion of Germany because of the close contact he maintained with the leading industrialists.

M. Wilenkin, who had accompanied us from London, arranged that we should be shown every courtesy at the Russian frontier. Our baggage was passed without examination and a private car was attached to the St. Petersburg train. I was cordially received in the capital by the various ministers of the Czar, including not only Kokovtzov, but Prime Minister Stolypin, his minister of foreign affairs Sazonov, as well as the ministers of commerce and agriculture, Timaschev and Krivoschein.

W. W. Rockhill was then American ambassador to Russia, but owing to strained relations over Manchurian railways he had not yet been able to present his credentials to the Czar. I was careful not to involve him in any way in my affairs. Because of my known personal relations with Taft at that time it would have been unfortunate had my visit borne any official tinge.

To get the imperial imprimatur on my agreement with the government officials, an audience was arranged for me with the Czar at his palace of Tsarskoe Tselo, some fifteen miles from St. Petersburg. Although the audience was scheduled for four in the afternoon, the Foreign Office sent me careful instructions to present myself in evening dress. Nothing was said as to the type of waistcoat prescribed. In order to be on the safe side, I wore a white one and carried the ordinary black evening model in my pocket, prepared to make a lighting change if necessary.

Somewhat amused at my own trepidation over meeting the Autocrat of all the Russias alone, I took the train and was set down at the station. It was already dark but I managed to make out a gorgeously arrayed Cossack standing at the door of a royal equipage. It was the only vehicle at the station. I peered in all directions, but could see no other passenger for whom it might be intended.

Since I was unable to speak Russian, I could make no inquiry. Without further formality, I stepped into the carriage, the Cossack shut the door, and off we drove. After a short ride we stopped at a small building which I was certain could not be the palace. Nevertheless, the Cossack opened the door of the carriage. It was apparent that I was expected to alight. I was taken to a small reception room where it was so warm that I removed my overcoat and sat down.

After a few minutes I was summarily hurried back into the same carriage and driven furiously down the same hill I had just ascended. I lowered the window and poked my head out. In spite of vigorous protests delivered in English, German, and French, that I did not want to go back to the railroad station, the driver remained impassive. I had given up trying to make him understand when the carriage turned suddenly into a side road, and delivered me at the imperial palace.

This time I had to wait only a few moments before the Czar, attired in Cossack uniform, appeared. He advanced quickly, shook hands cordially, and offered me a chair. Then pleasantly, in perfect English, he expressed the hope that I was enjoying my stay in Russia.

I knew that imperial audiences were customarily short, and thought I could not afford to take up half this valuable time in verbal exchange of courtesies. Therefore, I disregarded the diplomatic usage which prescribed that the Czar should lead the conversation.

"Your Majesty," I began, "I feel honored by your confidence in me, and I assume you wish me to speak frankly, and not take up your time with pleasantries."

"Yes, Mr. Hammond," he replied, "I want you to be perfectly frank."

"I can reassure Your Majesty that, were I so indiscreet as to betray any confidence you might place in me, you could remedy this by nominating me for the Ananias Club, formed a few years ago by President Theodore Roosevelt."

"I've heard about that club," the Czar admitted with a smile.

"Well," I went on, "if Russia is to go on a constitutional basis, Your Majesty will find an Ananias Club an exceedingly useful institution."

The Czar then expressed curiosity as to why the United States had been so sympathetic with Japan during the Russo-Japanese War. I told him a certain degree of American sympathy inevitably had gone to Japan as the smaller nation. Also, there had been an impression that the war had been fomented by concession seekers belonging to the court camarilla. Mustering all my courage, I suggested that the Russian government might have forfeited some American sympathy because of the frequent Jewish pogroms.

The Czar did not seem angered. "I can understand the American point of view in the latter case. But there are six million Jews in Russia—more than half the number in the entire world."

"Couldn't the administrative regulations which restrict Jews to certain congested localities be modified?" I asked. "Wouldn't a policy of dispersion eliminate the sore spots?"

His Majesty told me with a smile that the idea had already occurred to him.

I then introduced the subject of the advantages Russia could obtain by the use of American capital for its industrial development. "We are best fitted," I urged him, "to understand your problems because they are so nearly identical with those of our own West."

This was the same argument I had used years before with Witte.

"Also," I continued, "you will find it profitable to employ Anglo-American rather than German capital. The Germans aim to stifle the growth of a Russian bourgeoisie and, if they succeed, it will retard Russia's financial and commercial independence."

Emboldened by the Czar's acquiescence in my views, and absorbed in my mission, I continued to give him good fatherly advice as to how the interests of Russia, politically and economically, could best be served.

At the conclusion of our conference, the Czar assured me of his approval of the plans I had outlined and, wishing me success, bade me a cordial au revoir.

Immediately following my audience, Sazonov called to see the Czar, who told him that he had just had an interesting and informative interview with a man who spoke to him as "man to man and not as subject to sovereign."

The following day Baron Rosen, for many years the popular Russian ambassador in Washington, called at my hotel and left the following note:

> Hotel de l'Europe
> St. Petersburg
>
> January 15, 1911
>
> I have just seen M. Sazonov who told me that you had had a prolonged audience with the Emperor and that His Majesty was very greatly pleased with you.
>
> ROSEN

Ambassador Rockhill was also gratified with what I had accomplished and predicted that my visit would prove a great advantage to America's commercial relations with Russia, adding that I had also done much to promote the entente cordiale of the two nations.

An interesting dinner was given for us by M. Kokovtzov, at which M. and Mme. Stolypin, M. and Mme. Sazonov, and other prominent members of the Russian government were present.

Stolypin was always regarded as a leader of Russian reactionary officialdom. Several attempts had already been made on his life. In fact, he had a badly mutilated hand as the result of a bomb thrown a few years before.

Stolypin expressed a great desire to see America, but when my wife asked him to give us the pleasure of reciprocating his hospitality, he shook his head and said, "You little realize the danger my presence would bring to your peaceful household."

A few months later he fell a victim to the bullet of an assassin at the Royal Opera.

The result of my visit was most promising. I had the assurance of the highest Russian officials that, so far as consistent with Russia's treaty obligations with other nations, preference would be given to American and English capital in the various enterprises we were to undertake.

Entirely at my own expense I sent two American experts, A. P. Davis, chief of the United States Reclamation Service, and W. W. Mackie, who had worked for me in mapping out the reclamation of the Yaqui Valley, to make an investigation of the agricultural recources of the southeastern part of the Russian Empire and particularly to report on the feasibility of irrigating the Hungry Desert of Turkestan.

The reports of Davis and Mackie were presented by me to the Russian government and formed the basis of developments recently undertaken by the Soviet government, employing Davis as advisory engineer.

The investigation of the Stewart brothers who had erected the grain elevators along the Great Lakes confirmed the opinion I had formed in 1898, that Russia would benefit by having a similar system. At that time I had ridden through field after field of crops unharvested because of lack of storage and transportation facilities. There was still a crying need for refrigerator cars, and this was provided in the concession from the government.

In a tentative way, better equipment for loading and unloading cargoes in Russian ports was also discussed with the departmental heads.

It was my ambition to achieve in Russia the crowning work of my career as one of those "unprincipled American exploiters" who are arraigned so often at the bar of public opinion for their ruthless exploitations of the defenseless foreigner.

When I left Russia I was convinced I had the most important packet of commercial opportunities ever presented for the prospective benefit of two nations. I had succeeded not only in opening up a great field for the profitable investment of American capital and the expansion of her commerce, but also in breaking the economic shackles which held agricultural Russia subject to industrial Europe.

In Berlin, where I remained a few days to look into the much-vaunted efficiency of German industries, the object of my visit to Russia was freely discussed by the press and considerable apprehension, I learned, was created in German official circles.

From Berlin I went to London, where I found a keen desire among financiers to participate in the Russian enterprises.

Lord Rothschild was particularly interested to know not merely what I had accomplished, but whether my plans would have any effect upon the unhappy status of the Jew in Russia.

"I know from your pleasant business and social relations with Barnato, Hirsch, and the Guggenheims that you must sympathize with our efforts to alleviate the misery of our persecuted brethren."

"The Jewish question in Russia, as the Czar himself admitted, is undoubtedly 'difficult'," I replied. "The Jews have been subjected to every conceivable form of ignominy and, as all humanitarians will agree, have been cruelly maltreated. The issue has developed into a vicious circle of crimination and recrimination between the government and the Jewish population. The authorities justify themselves by claiming that, if Jews would abstain from participation in revolutionary politics, they would be treated more liberally; the Jews retort that, if they were treated more liberally, there would be no occasion for them to seek redress through political activities."

Rothschild pondered over my comments and then said: "Suppose for a moment that the Jewish bankers in London should participate in financing these projects of yours. Would Russian anti-Semitism extend to Jewish bankers in London?"

"Yes," I replied honestly, "there is universal resentment against the Jewish bankers of Europe, and also of America, because they lent money to Japan during the Russo-Japanese War. This has been used as a rallying cry by the liberal party of the Kadets."

A few days later I sailed for America. When I reached New York I was greatly surprised to learn that the government was seriously considering the abrogation of our commercial treaty with

Russia, in retaliation for the refusal of that government to grant America's request for passports into Russia for American Jews.

I studiously avoided any action that might be represented by President Taft's political enemies as an endeavor to influence legislation on this subject. As a matter of fact, the passport question was never at any time discussed between the President and myself. Moreover, I fully realized that any attempt to frustrate the movement would be futile. But I did warn my Jewish friends that the desired passports never could be secured by threats of hostile legislation against Russia.

The United States did abrogate the commercial treaty. The resultant ill feeling utterly destroyed any hope of carrying out my plan of obtaining American capital for Russia.

Although my mission failed, the theory on which I was proceeding was correct. There are in Russia extensive deposits of iron, coal, lead, copper, gold, platinum, and other valuable minerals, and petroleum in addition to its vast agricultural and timber potentialities.

Under the right kind of government Russia would be found an attractive field for foreign investors. As I told Witte in 1898, the vast opportunities grip the imagination of Americans, because the problems presented in the industrial development of Russia would not be new to the American captain of industry.

Furthermore, in the new era Americans would enjoy a significant advantage over the peoples of other countries, because there can never be political jealousy between Russia and the United States. Russia has always held America in high esteem and admiration, and the Russian people feel a sincere friendship for Americans.

Russian labor may be lacking in technical skill, but it is the opinion of Americans who have conducted mining and other industrial operations in that country that a most efficient class of artisans could be developed from the great Russian proletariat.

While it is true that the Russian peasant is illiterate and densely ignorant, he possesses exceptional resourcefulness. Contrary to the popular impression, he has a peaceful and kindly disposition, but his limited knowledge of the world makes him an easy prey to any political and economic doctrines foisted on him by unprincipled agitators.

In 1898 the fundamental laws of Russia described the power of the Emperor as "autocratic and unlimited," but after the opening of the first Duma, following the revolution of 1905-06, the word "unlimited" disappeared, although the name and principle of "autocracy" was jealously preserved. The *Almanach de Gotha* described Russia as "a constitutional monarchy under an autocratic Czar." It was still a question whether the emphasis should be placed on "constitutional" or on "autocratic." The definition itself connoted the transition period through which the empire was passing.

But in 1910, so far as was observable on the political face of Russia, the revolutionary spirit had become modified, and the nation seemed destined to attain a more liberal form of government through political evolution rather than bloody revolution. Russia seemed on the eve of great industrial expansion and prosperity.

Yet within the brief period of seven years a world cataclysm brought forth a Bolshevik Samson who pulled down the temple of the mighty Russian Empire, a temple that was erected on the quicksands of political oppression instead of upon the solid foundation of the "consent of the governed."

To judge the potentiality of Russia as an important industrial nation by the progress she has made since the establishment of the Soviet government would be a mistake. Russia has not as yet had a fair opportunity to demonstrate her capacity in industry. In spite of the efforts of the Soviet government to develop industrial classes, progress has been disappointing even to the rulers themselves. Internal political conditions have made it impossible to attain the industrial development that would have been achieved under such a government as our own, free from political oppression and dictation in matters of industry.

The political theory of government at present obtaining in Soviet Russia is absolutely opposed to the fundamental economic principles of national development adopted by other nations.

Collectivism removes the stimulus and incentive for individual effort, without which achievement is doomed to failure.

The war against the Russian bourgeoisie is a mistaken policy inasmuch as that class is recognized throughout the world as the backbone of industry and commerce.

The political situation in Russia is well known. The will of an insignificant minority is imposed by force of arms upon a helpless majority of Russians. Our government has recently recognized the Union of Soviet Socialist Republics. Protagonists for recognition hold that every nation has a right to determine its form of government, and for this reason Russia was entitled to recognition. This, of course, is true so far as the activities of that form of government do not seriously affect other governments. However, the avowed Communist program of Russia is

> The dictatorship of the proletariat is nothing else than power based upon force and limited by nothing— by no kind of law and by absolutely no rule.
>
> LENIN, *Complete Works,* Vol. xviii, Page 361.

> "The American Communist Party must be improved and Bolshevized. For that end we must work in order to forge real revolutionary cadres and a real revolutionary leadership of the proletariat, capable of leading the many millions of the American working class toward the revolutionary class struggles."
>
> STALIN, in address, May 6, 1929.

> "The conquest of power by the proletariat is the violent abolition of the power of the bourgeoisie, the destruction of the machinery of the capitalist state.
>
> "We proclaim openly that our design can only be realized by the violent overthrow of the entire traditional social order."
>
> (The above policies were formally adopted and promulgated as the Communist program by the Sixth Congress of the Kommintern of the Communists' Internationale, which was held in 1925 in Moscow.)

This program is obviously a challenge to other nations to defend their peculiar forms of government. It is for this reason that I have consistently been opposed to the recognition of Soviet Russia. That Russia has not repaid the United States for loans made to the Kerensky government does not seem to me an insuperable objection to recognition. Other nations are in default in respect of loans we have made to them. The confiscation of American property in Russia comes under a different category and we should insist that our citizens be compensated.

I do not believe that there is danger of the overthrow of our government by the Communists. America is not fertile soil for revolutionary activities, but there can be little doubt that their insidious attempts to accomplish this are a serious menace to industrial peace. It would seem that Russia herself is pursuing a fatuous policy in antagonizing the rest of the world in her attempt to overthrow the government of other nations with whom her policy should rather be a spirit of co-operation.

We have incontrovertible evidence of further activity in many of our universities, and worst of all is the plan to Sovietize the youth of the country through the Young Communists League which is financed by older Communists.

Had there been unanimity among the foreign governments in refusing diplomatic recognition, I believe the Soviet regime would have long since ceased to function. Lack of uniform purpose has been due to the subordination of a great moral issue to the desire of developing commerce with Russia, and even this desire has failed of realization.

CHAPTER TWENTY-FOUR

The Turn of the Century

I BRING MY FAMILY BACK TO AMERICA—
HORSECARS TO TRAMWAYS—THE PURCHASE OF THE
CAMP BIRD MINE—EDISON TAKES JACK THROUGH
HIS LABORATORY—AUTOMOBILING IN THE 1900'S—
WASHINGTON SOCIAL TRADITION—THE STRIKE AT
TONOPAH—HOW STRATTON SOLD HIS MINE—THE I. W. W. IN
CRIPPLE CREEK — GOLD DREDGING ON THE YUBA RIVER

In December, 1899, after an absence of seven years, my family and I returned to New York. For the second time my name appeared on an office door in the Mills Building.

The business of a consulting engineer is made up of constantly shifting activities which call him without warning from one end of the earth to the other. My first summons was to Mexico to examine the El Oro and Esperanza gold mines. This experience will be described in the next chapter.

I had also secured a concession to install the first hydroelectric plant in Mexico to furnish power for irrigation. D. O. Mills, Charles A. Coffin, and others furnished capital and we built what is now known as the Guanajuato Power and Development Company, supplying current to the mines and irrigating systems in that district.

The extension of transmission lines over the mountainous country was an expensive undertaking. As might have been expected, there was a good deal of pilfering by the Indians, particularly of the large insulators on which the high tension lines were strung on the poles. Finally, the foreman offered twenty-five cents reward for each insulator returned. When I first went to Mexico in the early eighties I had bought my own chickens over and over again from my servants; and once more I had to spend hundreds of dollars for the company buying back insulators from the Indians. This trade was not always an advantage to them, however. After the line was put in operation, we occasionally found a dead Indian at the foot of a pole—in trying to make a little extra money on insulators he had been electrocuted.

With the backing of Wernher, Beit and Company, Henry A. Butters and I were now planning to electrify and extend the Mexico City horsecar system which we had lately purchased. I had already had some experience with tramways, for in 1895 Butters and I together had laid out the Cape Town tramway system. After the completion of this system, he and I started a similar type of project in Geneva, Switzerland. There we encountered the same obstructionist tactics from the politicians that we met later in Mexico. We were constantly threatened with a rival franchise until, in exasperation, we said, "When you clean out your bad politicians, we'll build you a tramline." But the interference continued and, after laying out the road and solving the engineering problems, we left the matter to a group of French investors who seemed better fitted to deal with petty officialdom.

Although my family could not accompany me on my professional trips, it was sometimes possible to have them near me. This was the case at Glenwood Springs in the Rocky Mountains, where I went for my health in the summer of 1900.

My wife and I were much interested in what we heard of the archaeological discoveries of the Mesa Verde region south of us. We outfitted at the Wetherill ranch in southern Colorado and set off exploring, taking Jacky with us. The country we had to traverse was almost without trails, and water was scarce. But despite its discomforts, the outdoor life proved of great benefit to me. Our enjoyment was enhanced by poking about among the cliff dwellings which had been preserved intact by the dry air of the desert. We found them practically as they were when abandoned by the Indians several hundred years ago.

COUNT WITTE (1849-1915)

TRAVELING IN A TROIKA

The winters of 1900 and 1901 were spent at Del Monte, California. One of our chief pleasures was to get up at five in the morning and ride with the cowboys in the roundups.

Del Monte brought to my mind many interesting and pleasant associations. In 1879, I accompanied my father and Governor Leland Stanford, president of the Southern Pacific Railway, Mr. Charles Crocker, vice-president, on a trip to Monterey just after the completion of the railroad to that terminus. They were looking for a site for the proposed new hotel and station. On the train going back to San Francisco, Governor Stanford asked my father to suggest a name for the hotel. Father said he thought Del Monte an appropriate name, but Governor Stanford seemed to think it inappropriate as there were no mountains in the neighborhood. Then my father explained that there was a fine grove of oak and other trees and that in Spanish "Del Monte" also means "of the grove." This name was finally adopted.

My brother Dick was employed to survey the grounds and construct roads through the property, which involved many thousands of acres. It was he who built the famous Seventeen Mile Drive on the Monterey peninsula.

Dick had a very constructive mind and together with Page Brown, San Francisco architect, laid out the beautiful section now known as Burlingame, not far from that city.

While we were at Del Monte, President McKinley and John Hay dined with us. My wife, full of enthusiasm over the archaeological interests of the Mesa Verde, concerning which she had delivered a lecture before the American Association for the Advancement of Science in Denver, persuaded the President that the region should be made into a national park.

During these early years of the twentieth century we took a house at Lakewood, New Jersey. We were so well pleased with it in itself and with its accessibility from New York that we made it our winter home for several years. There our daughter Natalie was born.

Thomas A. Edison, who lived at East Orange, was then working on a new process to extract gold from South African ore. He had encountered difficulties and asked me to come to see him in the hope that I could shed light on his problems. I was soon able to demonstrate that the obstacles were insuperable in the economic use of his process.

Jack—who was about twelve at that time—was with me, and we eagerly accepted Edison's invitation to go through his laboratories. He showed us the models of his first phonograph and complained that well-known musicians scorned to sing for his machine; with a quiet smile he added that he did not blame them. That was in 1901. He prophesied, however, that we should all live to see the time when the best of them would be glad to do so.

He gave Jack some original sketches of the first phonograph model, and it may have been the contact with Edison that stimulated my son's interest in the study of electricity.

Ten years later Edison wrote me: "I see that your son has adopted inventing as a trade. If he has a commercial instinct, he will succeed; if not, the poorhouse will be his ultimate destination."

On several occasions Edison said to me: "Every time I see you, you are wasting your time in civic matters, politics, or public affairs. Why don't you stay with your profession and be at the head of it?" He did not entirely follow his own counsel, for later he adventured into discussions of educational and social problems.

One of my first engagements in the United States was the examination of the Camp Bird mine, owned by Thomas F. Walsh, and located in Ouray County, Colorado. This examination was made jointly with Hennen Jennings, who was for many years with Wernher, Beit and Company on the Rand and rendered distinguished service in the development of the mining industry. In his South African work he was associated with Henry C. Perkins, another successful American mining engineer. At this time Jennings was living in London.

A favorable report had already been made on the Camp Bird property by T. A. Rickard and F. W. Bradley, who, in spite of experience and reputation, seem to have lacked the proper qualifications for evaluating mines. Rickard was at the time consulting engineer of the Venture Corporation of London. This organization had been formed to promote mines, particularly on the western hemisphere. Frederick W. Baker was the chairman and moving spirit.

On Rickard and Bradley's recommendation a short-time option on the property had been secured by our clients, the Venture Corporation of London and their associates. The estimate of net ore in sight made by Rickard and Bradley was about six million dollars. Our clients had deposited this amount, the purchase price, in a New York bank to be paid if Jennings and I approved.

Although we found some rich ore bodies, we estimated the net value to be less than three million dollars; there was nothing to warrant the investment of six millions. Our London clients accepted our recommendation to turn down the proposition.

The next year a recurrent attack of malaria necessitated another summer at Glenwood Springs. Walsh came to see me there and again brought up the question of the sale of the Camp Bird.

"I heard you recommended your clients not to buy my mine, Mr. Hammond."

"Yes, I did. I thought your figure was much too high."

"I'd like to talk with you about it again. You see, it isn't entirely a question of money with me. I've already made several millions out of the mine, but I don't want to be tied up any longer. I've been in these mountains for many years. My children are growing up. I want them to have an education and some social life, and I'd like to play around in politics myself. There's nobody I can trust to manage the mine properly. My manager, John Benson, can't stand the high altitude any longer, and I don't want to train a new man."

"Well, Mr. Walsh," I replied, "I'll arrange for another examination and make you a new offer based on what I find."

On this understanding I sent for A. Chester Beatty. On my first examination I had noticed the skill and efficiency with which this young graduate from the Columbia School of Mines was doing his work. He was then employed by his brother-in-law, T. A. Rickard.

"How much are you making, Beatty?" I had asked.

"Twelve hundred a year."

"That's not much, is it?"

"It does for me. I still have beer tastes though I hope to get to champagne some day."

"How'd you like to come to me for twice that amount?"

"I'd come for nothing," he caught me up eagerly.

"Well, I haven't any place for you now, but you're on my payroll from this minute, and when I find something for you, I'll let you know."

One of the first tasks I assigned him was that of sampling the Camp Bird after my conversation with Walsh.

When Beatty had finished his work, I joined him and checked up on the results. Our report was most thorough in details and positive in conclusions. This second examination confirmed the values previously found by Jennings and myself.

I then discussed the purchase price with Walsh on the basis of two and a half million dollars' worth of net ore in sight. "You've already had a valuation from Rickard and Bradley which is much higher than mine. You and Benson are practical miners with a lot of experience. Why don't you employ other engineers to ascertain the correctness of my report?"

"I'm perfectly satisfied to accept your estimate of the value of the ore reserves."

Three million dollars cash was agreed upon. I advised Walsh to take part of this in stock, and offered a certain additional payment if and when ore should be extracted beyond the purchase price of the mine.

I then cabled to the Venture Corporation that I was on my way to London to make a personal report. The time of the option being short, I had to leave the necessary legal work to be done in this country. Samuel Untermyer represented the Venture Corporation; Charles S. Thomas, formerly governor of Colorado and subsequently United States senator, represented Walsh.

The cash payment was made to Walsh according to agreement. But when the contract drawn up by Untermyer and Thomas reached London, there was some ambiguity as to the additional percentage payment due on future ore developed. The London attorney of the underwriting syndicate was greatly disturbed; he pointed out that, according to the phraseology of the contract, we were at the mercy of Walsh. He could legally have claimed a large sum of money. I told them that the lawyers were wrong in certain important mining technicalities and that I was sure Walsh would not take advantage of the lawyers' ignorance, but would accept the verbal understanding he and I had made.

I hurried back to Colorado and met Walsh and Governor Thomas, to whom I explained the anxiety of my London clients.

Walsh said: "I haven't read the contract. I left it entirely to Governor Thomas."

"Well, Walsh," I replied, "you and I are both mining men and you know very well I'd never have agreed to a contract like this."

I pointed out the error. His immediate response was, "You're quite right, Hammond; that wasn't our agreement at all."

He turned to Governor Thomas. "Charlie, change that to Hammond's understanding. He is right as to our agreement."

Walsh had the right to send expert accountants to check up mine output and engineers to report on underground developments. When he was asked by the Camp Bird Company why he did not avail himself of the privilege, he replied that so long as I was their consulting engineer he needed no one to protect his interests.

Walsh, honest himself, gave others credit for possession of the same quality.

The Camp Bird turned out to be profitable for all concerned, but the rich ore that added so much profit to the company was later developed under my personal direction in a section of the property not opened up at the time Hennen Jennings and I made our examination.

Walsh aspired to social position and attained it. He made friends in high places, among them Leopold, King of the Belgians. He died a wealthy man.

When the Walshes became my neighbors on the North Shore of Massachusetts, which had become our summer home, our children saw much of each other. My son Jack and Vinson Walsh acquired automobiles of the same make, in which they used to race each other. In order to keep them within bounds, their parents formed an automobile club, and invited them to join. They felt highly honored at this attention from their elders and accepted with alacrity. As soon as the fathers had paid the boys' dues, these same fathers hastily passed a by-law imposing fines and removal of license on any member who was reported for speeding.

There was one occasion on which I myself fell a victim to the same speed mania. Jack and I were coming home one night from dinner with the Walshes when a car tried to pass us. Jack imperceptibly opened the throttle. I sympathized mildly when he shouted above the noise, "It's Vinson!"

As the other car slipped past, we heard a defiant challenge.

Jack's feeling of outrage was transmitted to me. I said nothing as the speedometer needle began to creep up. We skidded around corners, madly raced on the straightaway, and my elation equaled his as we triumphantly passed the other car. Jack honked derisively.

That night there was no reprimand of Jack, and no one reported to the Automobile Club that one of the committee members had been speeding.

The last time I saw Vinson was at Newport an hour or so before he drove his car off a bridge, killing himself and seriously injuring his sister.

Jack was not the only one to give me a wild ride. Henry Clay Frick taught me that automobiling could hold new terrors. His home was at Pride's Crossing, about nine miles from Gloucester. One day Frick telephoned me that E. H. Harriman was visiting him, and asked whether I would like to take a spin with them around Cape Ann.

"I'd like to show you my new French car."

"I'll be delighted," I replied.

"All right, we'll be there in fifteen minutes."

"Better make it twenty," I replied as I hung up the receiver.

He was at the door in fifteen minutes. We started on the twenty miles of narrow, winding, unpaved Cape Ann roads. The chauffeur took the curves on two wheels and whenever we came to a village seemed to prefer the sidewalks to the streets. Hens squawked, horses reared, New England ladies scuttled into doorways. So loud was the rattle and bang of our vehicle that we were spared most of the vituperation which followed in our wake. Once we slowed down long enough to catch some salty comments which for a moment made me think I was in Billingsgate rather than in the main street of Gloucester.

We slithered to a stop at my front door.

Harriman and I had no breath left with which to swear, but Frick was not at all discomposed. He said, "Harriman, how do you like the wonderful scenery of Cape Ann?"

Harriman's trains never could travel fast enough to suit him, but now he gasped: "To tell the truth, Frick, your French chauffeur went so fast I didn't see much of it. Another time I think I'd better ask Hammond to take me in his car. I'd really like to see the scenery!"

"Sorry I won't be able to go with you," responded Frick, who, even on the golf course, had a mania for speed. "When I go riding, I have to go fast enough to dodge bullets." This remark referred to his experience at the time of the Homestead strike, when he was shot by Alexander Berkman.

Shortly after our return from South Africa my wife and I were invited to be the guests of honor at a dinner given by Mrs. John R. McLean, whom I had known as a young girl. She was Emily, the daughter of General and Mrs. Edward F. Beale. Her parents and my parents had been intimate friends in our early California days. Mrs. McLean was known as one of the leading hostesses of Washington. Upon starting for the dining room, we were somewhat surprised to have our hostess express the hope that we would not be offended at not being given the seats of honor—she had to follow the established rule of precedence. We were not offended, of course, but I was interested in this phase of Washington etiquette, which was then new to me.

It was on this occasion that I met Admiral Dewey, recently returned from his victory at Manila Bay. He told me how humiliated he felt at the criticism leveled at him by the American public for having given to his new wife (the sister-in-law of Mrs. McLean) the house which had been presented to him by the people of the country in recognition of his exploit. He said that it was the only gift he could have made to his wife. At this time Dewey was being groomed as a Democratic candidate for the presidency. He told me that the "boss" Democratic politician said to him, "Keep quiet and don't say nothing."

In 1903 I resumed my position as consulting engineer of the Union Pacific and Southern Pacific railroads, united under Harriman's control. My chief function was to examine mining districts and to determine whether it would be profitable to connect them by spurs to the main line. If it seemed to me that the ore bodies were sufficiently extensive I advised favorably.

I fell into the habit of lunching frequently with Harriman at his office. I considered him the greatest of our railroad builders, greater than Jim Hill or Paul Morton, or Ripley of the Santa Fe, all of whom I knew intimately. His great fault was his impatience at what seemed to him the slowness of others in grasping his ideas. His pronounced unwillingness to delegate responsibility was brought home vividly by an experience I had with him.

At that time I owned the Mount Whitney Power Company, which was supplying power for irrigating the newly developed citrus fruit belt near Visalia, California. I pointed out the profits Harriman could make by running an electrified branch line into the San Joaquin Valley for which we would furnish the power. Harriman told me to go ahead and secure land for the right of way without letting it be known that the Southern Pacific was the purchaser. Meanwhile he went abroad for his health.

I secured the necessary options and then went to Judge Lovett, president of the road. Julius Kruttschnitt, vice-president and general manager, was also present.

I said, "I need twenty-five thousand dollars to exercise the options." Lovett replied, "I'm sorry, Mr. Hammond, but I can't give it to you."

"But both you and Kruttschnitt were present when Harriman told me to go ahead. Don't you remember?"

"That's true," Lovett agreed, "but neither Kruttschnitt nor I have authority to make the payment."

"Well, then," I suggested, "why don't you cable Harriman and get it?"

"Harriman doesn't want to be bothered with business, and we'd rather not."

This struck me as a childish and inefficient way of doing business. I knew that the Santa Fe would jump at the chance to get into the citrus belt, and I couldn't let Harriman down. I left the Southern Pacific office determined to advance the money out of my own pocket.

HYDRAULIC MINING

THE BUNKER HILL AND SULLIVAN MINE

A present-day view showing concentrators, powerhouse, shops, change house and electric power lines at the mouth of Kellogg Tunnel

THE BUNKER HILL AND SULLIVAN MINE

*A print from an old picture taken at the time of its development,
showing the original concentrator and circuit work*

When Harriman returned from Europe, I told him of the difficulty I had encountered, and how I had had to use my own money to pay for his right of way.

"Here's Kruttschnitt," I said. "There isn't a better railroad man in the country, and yet you won't give him the power to handle a small matter like this. Why, I've seen you send for him to come all the way from Chicago to New York for a fifteen-minute interview. On top of that you sometimes keep him waiting for days. And he's your highest salaried man! But you'll let me come in and take up an hour over some trivial detail. It would save you time, money, and worry if you'd delegate a little more authority."

Harriman merely smiled. The next time he went to Europe, however, his subordinates were granted more leeway, and on his return he admitted that the wheels of the locomotives had gone around just as well during his absence.

One of the projects I suggested to Harriman was a sixty-five-mile spur track from Sodaville to Tonopah, Nevada. Up to this time the ore had been hauled over the desert by mule team.

My first connection with Tonopah had come from W. C. Whitney, with whom I became well acquainted after my return from London. He asked me to become consulting engineer for the Tonopah mine in which he had a large interest. I accepted this position.

Tonopah was one of the richest strikes made in Nevada in recent years. In twenty years $125,000,000 was taken out—nearly half of which came from the original mine—with a profit in dividends of $32,000,000. In the year of grace 1902, this camp was almost as "bad" as Bodie or Tombstone had been twenty-five years before. It was the last wild town of the West, though Goldfield, discovered a few years later, is entitled to honorable mention in this respect.

The discovery of the Tonopah district was the result of pure chance. As in the case of every famous strike, there were innumerable tales as to who was the discoverer and how the find had taken place. Prospectors necessarily lead lonely lives and must entertain themselves. They take to yarning much as sailors do, and eventually convince themselves of the truth of their own stories.

One day as I emerged from the shaft of the Tonopah, I found James L. Butler discoursing learnedly to a party of enthralled eastern tourists on the geological phenomenon which had led him to the discovery of the mine. When he caught sight of me he stopped abruptly. While he was still Lazy Jim Butler, rancher and prospector, he had told me quite a different tale.

I went on my way smiling. Butler had gone back on his burros in a most unsportsmanlike manner. The burro certainly has "a nose for a mine" even though he may not have horse sense; he is a worthy precursor of the modern geophysicist, as in the case of Kellogg's burro of Coeur d'Alene fame.

According to Butler's early version, in the spring of 1900 he and his wife set out from Belmont, Nevada, for a near-by district called the Southern Klondike. They camped one evening in a desolate spot at the foot of a hill. The next morning, finding that the pack burros had strayed, Butler set out uphill to find them. In order to speed them on their way back, he picked up a rock and was about to hurl it in their direction when he noticed it was mineralized quartz.

Mrs. Butler also claimed to be the finder. She said that while she was sitting on a rock pile waiting for her husband to find the burros, she saw a piece of loose rock that glinted with yellow specks. Gallantry impels me to accept her version.

Like the good prospectors they were, the Butlers gathered up some specimens and carried them the remaining ten miles to Southern Klondike. There Butler submitted them to the camp assayer, who refused to test them without the customary fee. This the Butlers could not produce, but they were undiscouraged by the rebuff. They picked up more fragments on their way back to Belmont, and took them to the young district attorney, Tasker L. Oddie. Butler offered Oddie a quarter interest in the mine if he could get an assay made.

Oddie took the samples to Walter C. Gayheart, an assayer, and in lieu of the usual fee of ten dollars, offered him half of his own share for making the assay. Gayheart agreed to this proposal and made a test in his spare time. The ore was found to run several hundred dollars per ton in gold and silver.

Every foot of ground anywhere near the richest outcrop of Mizpah Hill was immediately staked and restaked. Not having enough money to develop the claims, the original locators leased them on a percentage basis. Four million dollars were taken from surface digging the first year. Butler then sold his holdings to Philadelphia capital represented by O. A. Turner, C. R. Miller, and other eastern investors.

In 1901 the Tonopah-Belmont Company was formed with John W. Brock, president; Tasker Oddie, general manager; Key Pittman, attorney. As I have said, I was employed by this company as consulting engineer and spent considerable time in developing the property and erecting a mill for treatment of the ores.

It is interesting to note that fortunes made out of this mine enabled three men to devote their energies to politics. Pittman became leader of the silver faction in the Senate, Oddie was a senator and also governor of Nevada, and Miller was elected governor of Delaware.

While I was consulting engineer for Tonopah, I was asked to make an examination of a mine at Cripple Creek, Colorado, known as Stratton's Independence. This was at the time the greatest gold producer in that famous district.

Its original owner, William S. Stratton, had started out as a carpenter, but he was ambitious and in his spare time took lessons in assaying. Then he attempted prospecting on his own, and discovered the Independence mine.

The Venture Corporation had been trying to find outlets for its surplus money, and Stratton was now approached and asked how much he would take for his mine. It had not previously occurred to him to sell but he realized from the eagerness of their representatives that the highly favorable report submitted by T. A. Rickard had made the Venture Corporation exceedingly anxious to buy.

Stratton was invited to come to London at the company's expense to meet the board of directors. He proved no more tractable in England than in the States. As a last resort, it was decided to give him a banquet. At the appearance of the first course, they offered him five million dollars for his mine. He promptly turned it down.

As the dinner proceeded, the price rose to five and a half millions. Stratton showed some sign of interest, but was still unwilling. When the figure reached six millions, his eyes opened wider and he began to pinch himself. But his head had started wagging in the negative and he could not seem to stop it.

Except for the price, the contract was ready for his signature. At six and a half millions the pen was placed in his hand. But he said he liked his mine; he couldn't bear to part with it.

In desperation seven and a half million was written in and his fingers were firmly closed around the pen. Still unable to believe his eyes or his ears, he affixed his signature.

When I met him some time afterwards, I asked, "What would you have done if I'd offered you a check for five million dollars for the property before you had been approached by the Venture Corporation?"

"I'd have jumped at it!"

The Venture Corporation offered a large block of stock to some of my clients in London. I was at Glenwood Springs at the time. They cabled me to examine the property and advise them as to the purchase of the stock on the basis of ten million dollars for the property.

The manager of the Independence was ill when I arrived at the mine, and the foreman accompanied me on my tour. Although the foreman had known me by reputation and realized I was not easily to be deceived, he suggested that we begin our examination on the upper levels from which the pay ore was being taken. I suspect that he hoped I would devote most of my time to examining that part of the mine. I simply remarked that as the future of the property depended upon the value of the ore found in the deepest workings, I had better start my inspection at the bottom of the shaft.

When we reached the lower levels the character of the development work showed me at once that the grade and amount of ore had fallen off. The foreman admitted that the recent developments in depth had not been encouraging. In order to confirm my conclusion, I sent engineers to sample the mine. Their report convinced me that the estimates made by Rickard and his associate engineers had been altogether too favorable.

When my cabled report was made public in London, there was a crash in the market quotation of the stock. In spite of my unpopularity among those who were gambling in the shares of the company, the Venture Corporation employed me to replace Rickard as consulting engineer for the Stratton Independence mine. Under my management the shaft was sunk deeper by several hundred feet, but crosscuts and other exploratory work proved conclusively that the rich ore bodies had petered out.

While I was still engaged in this work there was a labor strike in the Cripple Creek region. Our employees admitted they were not dissatisfied with the conditions of their own employment, but claimed they had been compelled to join the strike under the overwhelming pressure of the I. W. W. organization, which had already closed the neighboring mines. The district was under martial law, so we supposed we would be safe in operating the mine with those men who had defied the strike order.

We took all possible precautions to protect our miners. One night after an inspection of the underground operations I ascended the shaft and returned to the manager's house where I was staying at the time. I had just gone to bed when word came of a bad accident at the mine.

Dressing as we ran, the manager and I hurried back to the shaft house I had just left. It was a shambles. Dismembered bodies were tangled with wrecked machinery. In an attempt at sabotage, some I. W. W. member had greased the brakes of the hoisting engine. As the cage, filled with men, rose to the surface, the brakes refused to grip and the cage shot up into the gallows frame. The engineer, helpless in the face of this horror, ran screaming from the spot.

I was overcome by this brutal deed.

When I heard a few days later that the I. W. W. were sending a delegation to the Camp Bird mine, I saw to it that I got there first.

Immediately I called a meeting of miners, mill hands, foremen, and clerks. "Have you any complaints against the company?"

"No!"

"Do you like your manager?"

They said he was all right. He had risen from the ranks, worked with them, and shared their risks. In fact, they thought him the best manager they had ever worked under.

"Do you get along with your cook?"

There was nothing to complain of about the food.

Having run through the list of possible grievances, I pointed out that I had always dealt frankly and fairly with them. I told them

I was gratified with the work and that, though I had great confidence in the manager, I was always ready to discuss any important questions with the men.   I reminded them that we had tried to make their winter hours in that isolated spot as pleasant as possible.   There was a comfortable clubroom equipped with gramophone, magazines, and other means of recreation.

My words were received with approbation.   Then I came to the point.   "Tomorrow there is a gang of I. W. W. coming up here from Cripple Creek to get you to strike.   Do you want to meet them here and let me be present while the matter of grievances is discussed?"

One man shouted, "We haven't any kick coming!"

Another rose and said, "Just leave it to us, Mr. Hammond; we'll take care of 'em!"

Instead of allowing the I. W. W. deputation to reach the mine, the miners sent a committee of their own down the narrow mountain road to a strategic point about a mile and a half from the mill.   There they met the invaders.

With menacing gestures, the leader of the Camp Bird contingent shouted: "You damn butchers, what are you doing here?   Go on back where you came from.   You're going over the cliff quick if you don't get the hell out of here!"

Miners of the old type were honest, courageous, and took great pride in their work.   I could invariably rely upon their loyalty in an emergency.   I never had a walkout in any mine under my management.

One reason for the popularity of my mines, I realized, was the fact that I paid top wages. I did not do this in order to draw men away from the other mines, but because they deserved it.   Furthermore, at a time when mining was much more hazardous than it is now, and when mine owners did not always employ doctors, I saw to it that medical attention was available at each of the mines in my charge. I also worked to secure the compulsory adoption of safety devices.

Soon after my return from London, I had become interested in dredging alluvial gravels at Oroville, California. Because of my extensive examinations of the section around the Yuba River at the time I was employed as expert on the United States Geological Survey, and subsequently as consulting engineer of the Mining Bureau of California, I believed that the Yuba and its tributaries presented an exceptionally attractive field for similar operations.

I suggested the idea to Jeff Doolittle, whom I had known some years before when he was in charge of hydraulic operations in Placer County. In spite of the fact that he was an expert on auriferous gravels, he inclined to the opinion that the difficulties were too great. The river bed was covered with many feet of debris, swept down from hydraulic operations in tributary streams. "I myself have washed down millions of yards," he remarked.

Prior to this time, forty feet was the greatest dredging depth attained. If we wanted to operate successfully, we had to build a dredge of much greater depth capacity.

Finally, I persuaded Doolittle that the project was feasible and agreed to secure the necessary capital. Because of my enforced absence in London, I had E. A. Wiltsee obtain an option on a thousand acres in the heart of what subsequently developed into the most profitable dredging area in the world.

Also, I made an arrangement with Fred W. Bradley for drilling tests. In addition to depositing funds for that purpose, I left him my power of attorney to handle the option—an act I was later to regret. Bradley's first report to me was favorable.

I had known Bradley for a long time and had considered him thoroughly honest. In 1890 I had been looking for someone to assist Clement, and Bradley had been recommended to me. During a blizzard I had traveled on snowshoes to a mine in the Sierra Nevadas which Bradley was then operating. I remained with him two days. I was impressed with his ability as a manager and engaged him as assistant for the Bunker Hill and Sullivan.

When Clement went to South Africa with me, Bradley was made manager of the property and proved himself a good executive. In recognition of his services I had given him an option for a year at a very low price on a large block of the B. H. & S. stock. Clement also gave him an option for a block of the same stock.

About three years later Bradley came to London to see me on other mining matters and told me he would like to exercise his option on the B. H. & S. stock. I told him that his option had long since expired; nevertheless, I would let him have the stock at the same price, though Clement refused to let Bradley have any stock.

Some months after securing the Yuba option, I was much surprised when R. D. Evans, a Massachusetts investor interested in mining ventures, called at my New York office to ask whether I would be interested in a gold-dredging proposition.

"That depends," I answered. "Where is it?"

"California."

"What part?"

"Yuba River."

I smiled. "Old man, you're a little late. I already have an option which controls dredging on the best part of that river."

He smiled in turn. "You mean you had an option until last week. Now I have it. I bought your option from Bradley, who wasn't going to renew it."

It was through W. P. Hammon, who was engaged in dredging operations not far from the Yuba, and Colonel Forbes that Evans had secured the property.

I was astonished. "I can't understand why Bradley should have changed his views as the last reports from him were favorable. I'd advise you to go slowly. Maybe he's found poor values, or too much clay. You'd better see him again and make sure the property is worth developing."

I suggested to Evans that he have further tests made by Charles Hoffman, a specialist in auriferous gravels who had been in Siberia with the Lena Company. These confirmed Bradley's first estimates of rich possibilities. Evans then formed a syndicate in which he offered me a fifteen per cent interest, which I purchased.

When I later examined the titles to the claims Evans had secured on taking up our original options, I found that Bradley himself had taken up options on some adjoining claims and had sold these to Evans at a profit. While I still had the property under option I had told my friend Cyrus H. McCormick that if the tests being made by Bradley came up to my expectations I would give him and other of my Bunker Hill and Sullivan associates the opportunity to invest in the enterprise. I had sent him Bradley's preliminary reports indicating that his first tests were exceedingly favorable. Later, Mc-

Cormick wrote to Bradley asking how it was that I had confidence in the property in spite of his adverse report. Bradley replied that Evans and I had nothing to lose by our investment: if it proved worthless, we could dispose of our interest to my English clients. As a loyal friend, McCormick showed me this correspondence and I immediately wrote Bradley expressing my utter contempt for him, and warned him to keep at a safe distance from me. This he carefully did.

Then I started suit against him for restitution of the money he had received for his options. The San Francisco fire destroyed the essential records just before the case was to be called. Also Doolittle, one of my most important witnesses, died suddenly about this time. I was compelled to drop the suit.

There was more than one reason for my indignation against Bradley. He had been basely ungrateful for professional favors I had done him. More than that, in order to cover his own unethical transactions, he attributed dishonorable motives not only to me, but to R. D. Evans, a high-principled man who had acted solely on Bradley's recommendation in the purchase of the property. Bradley persisted in expressing to my friends his belief that the property was of no value, even after dredging operations had shown a large profit and the phenomenal value of the property was proved.

The success of the Yuba operations has many times over justified the confidence I had in the soundness of the idea, and all credit is due W. P. Hammon for his skillful handling of the technical and business problems.

Much of my enthusiasm for the career of a mining engineer has been caused by the evidence of what technical knowledge and skill have accomplished. An old-time miner, with a five-dollar outfit of pick, shovel, and sluice box, could not have visualized the development of great dredges for use on alluvial gravels. Had he been asked whether it was worth while to wash twenty-five hundred pounds of gravel to recover thirteen cents, his comments would have been unprintable.

The first two dredges on the Yuba, costing $190,000 each, started operating in August, 1904. Eighteen dredges have since been constructed on the property at a cost of $4,723,000, paid out of earnings. These dredges have extracted 481,000,000 cubic yards, or more than was taken from the Panama Canal. Each dredge can operate profitably on gravel which returns no more than seven cents a cubic yard, although the average yield is over twelve cents. The Yuba Company's latest electrically operated dredge, with bucket capacity of seventeen cubic feet, costing nearly a million dollars, will dredge to a depth of 140 feet instead of the 65 feet reached by our earlier dredges. From 1904 to 1933, with a capital of $750,000, the company took out $37,500,000 in net profits.

All this statistical information is not a prospectus for the company; its shares have never been placed on the market and are still largely held by the original investors.

Subsidiary companies of the Yuba are operating in a smaller way in other parts of California and Montana, as well as carrying on dredging operations for tin in Portugal.

I have also been interested in the extension of dredging operations in Colombia, South America, on properties for which I obtained and transferred the option to the Oroville Dredging Company.

Recently the Oroville company secured from my old firm, the Consolidated Gold Fields of South Africa, an interest in gold gravels in New Guinea. The property is about a hundred miles from the coast and exceeding difficult of access, owing to dense jungles and high mountains. The estimated cost of a road, built through the lowest pass in the mountain range, four thousand feet above sea level, was in excess of $1,000,000. This road would have had to be cut through trackless, fever-ridden jungles peopled by head-hunters and cannibals. Moreover, because of torrential tropical rains and subsequent washouts, the upkeep of the road would have been prohibitive.

The only hope of success in the enterprise lay in the possibility of having the proposed dredges flown in parts over the mountains and assembled at the inland base of operations. This plan was finally agreed upon and three specially designed airplanes were put into service. The twelve thousand tons of material, to construct the three dredges now in operation, were flown in without accident and in a relatively short time. These planes are capable of making three round trips a day, whereas, had a road been possible, the round trip would have taken a tractor a week. The cost of transportation is still materially less than the cost of the road originally considered. The large profits derived from the three dredges now operating have warranted the importation of a fourth, which is currently under construction.

CHAPTER TWENTY-FIVE

The Guggenheim Exploration Company, 1903-1907

THE RISE OF THE GUGGENHEIMS—I MAKE A FIVE-
YEAR CONTRACT—ALVARADO PROVIDES FOR PAYMENT OF THE
UNITED STATES NATIONAL DEBT—MEETING WITH
DIAZ—TAKING A FLYER ON THE ESPERANZA—THE
HIGH-PRICED ENGINEER VERSUS THE "PRACTICAL
MINER"—ERROR IN THE NIPISSING—FINANCING
THE UTAH COPPER COMPANY—THROUGH THE
AIR IN AN ORE BUCKET—RIDER HAGGARD'S
HOBO—THE INTEGRITY OF THE GUGGENHEIMS

*T*he history of the rise of the house of Guggenheim to wealth and fame is comparable in many respects to that of Rothschild. Meyer Guggenheim of Switzerland had seven sons who were united by paternal guidance and fraternal loyalty. This cohesive quality which distinguished the Guggenheims would have been possible only in a Jewish family. Even among the wives there was no friction. Each woman who married a Guggenheim became a Guggenheim herself and worked for the solidarity of the group rather than for the advancement of her particular family unit.

All were possessed of the fine old German sentimentality and kindliness. My wife and I were constantly made aware of this. For example, they would never consent to my setting out on a trip to mining property unless I was in the best of health.

So long as Meyer Guggenheim lived, he was the patriarch of the clan. Although I met him on only a few occasions, I always had a great admiration for him. After having previously made what was then regarded as a comfortable fortune in spices, he came to Philadelphia in 1848 and set himself up as an importer of embroideries.

In 1879 he put twenty-five thousand dollars into two silver mines at Leadville, Colorado. Benjamin Guggenheim was sent to Colorado to take charge of his father's mining interests. He became dissatisfied with the terms under which the custom smelter was treating his ores, which, though refractory, had a high silver content. He persuaded his father to buy fifty-one per cent interest in a near-by smelter. Meyer Guggenheim insisted that all seven sons be given equal shares in this new business he was launching for them. Out of this small beginning grew the great American Smelting and Refining Company.

Daniel, the second son, was recognized as having the greatest executive ability. For this reason his brothers acknowledged him as head of the clan and accorded him unswerving loyalty. When any decision had to be made, the others would come for judgment to "Mr. Dan," as he was called in the organization. They knew that everything he did was directed towards the advancement of the family rather than for his own aggrandizement.

Isaac, the eldest son, devoted his time to the financial aspects of the business. Simon, later senator from Colorado, was interested chiefly in the technical details of treating ores. In the early years Benjamin and William controlled the smelting operations. Murry was the salesman of the company. He would buy the unrefined ore and find markets for the refined product. Solomon was interested in all phases of administration. He was the outside man, what would now be known as the contact man.

It was natural for the brothers to extend their activities to the mining of ore so as to assure a steady supply for their smelters, which in a comparatively few years were scattered throughout the West and Mexico. The Guggenheim Exploration Company was formed expressly to locate mining properties. The Guggenheims were primarily interested in smelting and not in mining; the latter was always incidental

One of the important stockholders in the Guggenheim Exploration Company was William C. Whitney, who was not only a great

power in the financial world, but had attained political eminence as
secretary of the navy under Cleveland. Because of his winning personality, I had come to find his companionship most agreeable.
He had often talked to me about the Guggenheims and had even
suggested the possibility of my becoming connected with them.
With this in mind, in 1903, he arranged a luncheon at the Midday
Club for me to meet Daniel Guggenheim.

He introduced me pleasantly by saying: "This is the man I've
been urging you to get for our Exploration Company. He's worth
any salary he may ask."

We spent the lunch hour discussing the question of my joining the
Guggenheims, and at a later meeting tentatively agreed on a salary
and a five-year contract. Before signing this, I consulted Whitney
and offered a substitute plan to him.

I told Whitney that personally I would rather work with him
than with a company. Between us we could raise all the capital
needed. I knew the western country and was sure we would be
offered the cream of the new discoveries. Whitney agreed that this
was worth considering.

Then I made the following proposition: Whitney was to pay all
the expenses of my mining staff and back me in any venture I might
recommend. At the end of two years we would figure the value of
the properties I had acquired. Whitney would then agree to pay
me out of future earnings what he considered the value of my contribution. I had great confidence in him and knew that any figure
he mentioned would be fair.

The idea appealed to Whitney. He asked if I would be willing to
take his son Harry in with me. The young man was just getting
started in his business career, and this would be fine practical experience for him. Naturally, I was glad to do so.

This was as far as the scheme went, because the Guggenheims
objected. They said to Whitney, "No, you have a large interest in
our company and it's better to have Hammond working for the
organization as a whole than for you alone."

Accordingly, I made a five-year engagement whereby I became
consulting engineer and general manager for the Guggenheim Exploration Company. This contract not only covered my salary, but

gave me a percentage interest in propositions taken on my recommendation. In principle it was the same as my contract with Rhodes.

My first duty was to scrutinize the company's holdings, get rid of poor properties, and install new managers wherever the present ones seemed incompetent. I was also to take charge of the various mining operations and at the same time I was to be on the lookout for new and promising ventures.

I was expected to attend daily board meetings. These were impromptu affairs which occurred almost without warning, no one could tell where. Messengers could be seen scurrying from floor to floor rounding up the executives with last-minute bulletins of where the meeting was to be held. Before long these meetings became a bone of contention between the Guggenheims and me.

The firm had invested in an unprofitable mine in Mexico, the Zaragoza. The manager kept sending monotonous and long-winded dissertations on its minor past performances and its infinitesimal future expectations. He usually guessed wrong the first half of the month, and apologized for his mistake the second half.

One day at the board meeting Murry handed me a particularly long and inept report from the Zaragoza and, as usual, asked my opinion.

I lost my patience completely. "Good Lord!" I shouted, "don't you realize that your entire investment in the Zaragoza would only pay my salary for about a month? I'd be saving money if I bought it myself and shut it down, yet you are taking up half of my working time in these endless discussions. These post-mortems are just a waste of my valuable time and yours! I can't get anything important done if you insist on talking trivialities!"

"Well!" Murry exclaimed, as I departed. "J. H. H. certainly has a temper!"

The result of my outburst was that the daily meeting was changed to a monthly one, and I attended only if I could fit it into my schedule.

But the day came when I, of my own accord, asked for a full meeting of the board of directors of the Guggenheim Exploration Company. I was ready to recommend the purchase of the Central Lead Mine of Missouri. I had learned its history from Arthur Thatcher,

504 The Autobiography of John Hays Hammond

a well-known St. Louis mining engineer, who had been its manager before it was closed down some years previously. I secured a working option on behalf of the Guggenheims and my assistants had made drill tests to ascertain the value of the ore deposits. When these proved favorable, I made a careful inspection of the property myself.

With my head crammed with statistics and my arms laden with maps, I made a personal appearance before the directors. The maps were enthusiastically spread out on the long table and I began a lengthy, detailed, and earnest explanation. The directors wandered idly around the room evincing no interest, not even glancing at my maps.

Finally Isaac Guggenheim turned and asked, "How much money is involved in this transaction?"

I replied, "The property itself and a plant to work it will cost about a million dollars."

In a good-humored but pointed manner, Murry said: "Well, J. H. H., why are you spending so much time on such an insignificant matter. If you recommend its purchase we should buy it without further delay and not waste any precious moments of your 'valuable time'!"

My own words used against me. I laughed along with the rest and took them off to Delmonico's for lunch.

While looking over prospects in Mexico for the Guggenheims, I heard of a likely gold and silver mine at Parral, Chihuahua. The reputation of Pedro Alvarado, the owner of the Palmilla mine, had spread far beyond his own district. His peon father had been ignorant of the potentialities of his mine, but shortly after Alvarado inherited it, the Palmilla developed into a bonanza.

I have observed in the case of the nouveaux riches the desire to turn their wealth immediately into some tangible evidence of their improved economic and social status. Alvarado spent his first million in building a Mexican palace in the small village near his mine and equipping it with Parisian furnishings. One bathroom would have made his house unique in the village and certainly would have served his needs. In his desire to impress the world at large, he had twelve bathrooms installed. The possession of a piano was a sure sign of opulence, so he ordered not one but fifteen.

In the midst of his new-found riches and magnificent surroundings Alvarado retained his simplicity and kindheartedness. He established Sunday as gift day and invited the poor of the town to receive the silver pesos he himself doled out from a large basket. He was also a man of great civic pride, and made a promise to pave the streets of Parral in silver, a promise he was never able to fulfill.

Alvarado's generosity took more impressive form in a patriotic letter to President Diaz in which he offered to pay the national debt. When the affluent Don Pedro's suggestion went unnoticed by the Mexican government, he changed his allegiance and made a will providing for the payment of the national debt of the United States. After he had been swindled, as he thought, by the exorbitant charges of the American plumbers who were installing the twelve bathrooms, he cut the United States out of his will.

Within a few years he had accumulated and spent several million dollars. In his ingenuousness, he expected his wealth to last forever. He dug deeper and deeper into his mine until he struck underground springs. His pumps were inefficient and the lowest workings were soon flooded. Alvarado had never heard of King Canute's failure. He had a silver angel made and dropped this figure down the shaft of the mine in the pious belief that it would cause the waters to recede.

At that time general conditions in Mexico were unbelievably primitive with practically no hotels available. In my work I could not afford to be at the mercy of chance accommodations and found a private car indispensable. I had named it "Kya Yami," which in Zulu means One of My Homes, and it was indeed one of my homes for I spent many days and nights on the car in different parts of Mexico and in our western mining districts. The car served also as a traveling office so that members of my staff could join me on my trips and discuss business matters. Fortunately, as consulting engineer of the Harriman system I had free passes for "car and party" over the railroads of this country, Canada and Mexico, and the cost of transportation was not prohibitive as it is today.

Before I met Alvarado, he had seen the car standing on a siding and a friend of mine showed him through. He inspected it thoroughly.

As he emerged he asked, "Whose car is this?"

"It belongs to Mr. Hammond, the consulting engineer of the Guggenheim Exploration Company."

Alvarado at once replied: "I'd like to have a consulting engineer. Is Mr. Hammond a good one?"

"He's supposed to be," answered my friend. "He gets a pretty good salary."

Alvarado came to a quick decision. "I believe I will employ him."

"I don't think you can. He's already under contract to the Guggenheims."

"Well, then," countered Alvarado, "why shouldn't I buy their mines?"

"I don't think you have money enough," replied my friend.

"That doesn't worry me. I can take care of that—but if I get Mr. Hammond as my consulting engineer, I suppose the car will go with the transaction. Of course," he added astutely, "he'll have to make some allowance for its being secondhand."

But Alvarado and I never came to terms on this proposal—nor, for that matter, on the sale of the mine. Although I found him not unwilling to part with his property, his valuation was out of all proportion. Certainly Palmilla would not have been worth recommending to the Guggenheims. Eventually he sold it to an American company which has operated it intermittently, but without profit.

Today Alvarado is practically destitute, living alone in his crumbling palace and existing upon the meager sums received occasionally from those old friends who remember his former generosity.

When I went to Mexico in 1900 to examine the El Oro and Esperanza properties, John Hay, then secretary of state, gave me a letter to President Diaz, calculated to make him regard me as an important as well as trustworthy figure in the business world. Upon my arrival in Mexico City I lost no time in presenting it.

I was ushered without delay into the presence of the president, who, in spite of his seventy years, was still erect and soldierly in his bearing. Most noticeable were the white hair, white mustache, and white bushy eyebrows, the snowy lines of which contrasted with the swarthy complexion. His Mixtec Indian blood proclaimed itself in the high cheekbones and large dark eyes, half covered by drooping lids so that they gave no inkling of the purpose behind them. Like Rhodes and Witte, he had a massive frame, a fit instrument for the dominant will directing its movements.

In the memory of most people Porfirio Diaz was a cruel dictator. They have forgotten that as a young man he was in a large measure responsible for the overthrow of the French in their occupation of Mexico. Moreover, in a sense he was the first Mexican patriot in that he recognized a national individualism as opposed to the heterogeneous racial characteristics and borrowed cultures.

The idea of Mexico's coming of age became strongly fixed in Diaz's mind when he was a youth. He was a man of decided culture and learning. He went to college and later studied law at Oaxaca. Shortly afterwards—in 1847— he joined a guerilla band and fought to defend his country against the American invasion of 1848, then later to defeat Santa Anna whom he rightly considered a fool and a traitor.

From then on Diaz was definitely a military man—a rebel and a skillful revolutionary leader. In his almost fanatic belief in the destiny of the people of Mexico and his conviction that they were being grossly mismanaged by their executives, he plotted revolts against Juarez and Lerdo de Tejada.

Finally, in 1877, he entered Mexico City victorious and with the acclaim of the people he had so ably defended.

The methods Diaz used might be criticized according to the ethics of our reputedly more enlightened democracy, but his justification was that he had employed them in behalf of his country. It was Mexico's good fortune to have as her leader during these important years a man for whom the means justified the end, but for whom that end was Mexico's welfare.

Diaz understood English much better than he could speak it. With such Spanish as I had at my command we were able to understand each other perfectly. The first question the old dictator asked me was, "What can I do for you?"

"Not a thing in the world," I assured him.

He looked his surprise. "This is an unusual, if not a unique, experience for me. Should you ever change your mind, Mr. Hammond, I shall be glad to be of service."

Then he added slyly: "I hope you will not attempt any revolution here. I'm afraid you would not get off so easily as you did in South Africa."

I laughed. "No, it would never occur to me to start a revolution where none was needed. Though you yourself, Mr. President, must admit that revolutions are sometimes necessary."

Diaz made no comment, but his mustache twitched with amusement. The conversation then shifted to a discussion of the development of Mexican resources. He warned me of one obstacle I would almost certainly encounter. I would be approached by lower officials who would ask for money, saying it was necessary to square the higher politicos.

"In reality," said Diaz, "very little of the money paid in bribes goes beyond the pockets of the petty grafters. If you have trouble of this sort, come to me and I'll settle it."

Occasionally I heard from my staff in Mexico that they were having difficulties with the local authorities. I thought up a scheme. Whenever a crisis seemed imminent, I would see to it that announcements of my departure for Mexico City appeared in the local Mexican newspapers, intimating that I was going to pay a visit to Diaz. This was usually enough to bring the greedy politicos to reason before I had reached the capital.

From my first meeting with Diaz a pleasant relationship developed. Whenever I happened to be at Mexico City, Diaz sent his military aide to bring me to the palace for a little chat about my work and things in general. I was one of the earliest representatives of foreign capital in Mexico, and the president was eager to consult about many phases of industrial development in his country. He was encouraging American businessmen to invest in mining and oil concessions in order to open up the country to the industrial revolution.

His theory was that, if Mexico was to be freed from ignorance and poverty, he must make use of the enterprise and money of more progressive nations. He knew capital would not enter in sufficient amounts unless he could reduce danger and risk to a minimum by maintaining before the world a stable government. This government would have to be strong enough to protect the lives and property of the foreigners who were to be the instruments to his great purpose. Under existing conditions in Mexico, despotic rule was the only kind possible.

Diaz's attitude towards capital as the weapon he was forging to free Mexico was well illustrated by what happened one day when I called on him in company with José Casasus, Mexican ambassador to the United States.

We were kept waiting for over an hour at the National Palace while the president was conferring with his secretary of foreign affairs. Diaz seemed surprised when he saw us, and displayed irritation for not having been notified of my presence. He said that, so far as the ambassador was concerned, he was a Mexican, for whom mañana would do as well as today. As for the secretary of foreign affairs, he also could wait. But I, as one of his "collaborators in the development of Mexico," deserved instant admittance day or night, for "Mexico herself" waited on me.

Besides being a shrewd diplomat, the old dictator did not lack a sense of humor. I remember once being summoned to his summer palace at Chapultepec, one of the most beautiful places in the world. Outlined against the snowy background of the towering volcanic peaks, Popocatepetl and the White Woman, Iztaccihuatl, and located upon a conspicuous hill in a grove of ancient cypress trees, it afforded a splendid view over the Valley of Mexico.

As I looked down over the precipice I wondered how the American troops in their march on Mexico City had managed to scramble up its steep slope. I remembered that my father had been one of the leaders in the storming of Chapultepec.

Diaz and I were strolling about the grounds when a light rain, hardly more than a mist, began to fall. With a glance at my shiny top hat, Diaz remarked, "I'm afraid your hat will be ruined."

He thereupon sent an attendant to bring me more fitting headgear. I confessed that I had bought the top hat about an hour before expressly for this occasion, explaining that toppers were not de rigueur at the mines.

The attendant returned with one of Diaz's own sombreros. I made the exchange and the hat sank down over my cranium. It made an excellent umbrella, although I had to use both hands to keep it off my ears.

The thought that the skies had intervened to render futile my carefully arranged formality of appearance struck the old man as funny. He never forgot it. Whenever I appeared, arrayed in all the glory of my beaver, Diaz would glance at it gravely and utter a pious ejaculation of gratitude that he had once been able to save it from destruction. Indeed, I kept it at my hotel in Mexico City for presidential audiences. For all I know, it may still be there, or it may even have graced the head of one of the post-Diaz presidents.

During one of our conversations, Diaz asked me whether I had ever been at his birthplace in Oaxaca. I told him the story of how, in 1885, I had recaptured the baggage and ore which had been stolen from me by bandits.

He smiled knowingly. "So you were the young engineer. I heard about your exploit at the time. Mr. Hammond, you lost the opportunity of your life. If you had killed any of those bandits, I should have given you a gold medal for each one, because it would have saved me a great deal of expense. I had to send a party of rurales to clean up Oaxaca. Today you will find it as safe as New York City."

"That isn't saying much, Mr. President," I replied. "But I know what you intend to imply."

I have already mentioned that I had gone to Mexico in 1900 to look over the El Oro and Esperanza properties, located ninety miles northwest of Mexico City. J. B. Haggin, of Haggin, Tevis, and Hearst, had sold the El Oro to an English organization, which called itself the El Oro Mining Company. Before I left London I had been employed by them as consulting engineer, a position which I held for about a year.

As for the adjoining Esperanza mine, in 1899 I had secured an option on it for a group of English investors, including the Venture Corporation of London, On my suggestion, F. W. Bradley, then manager of the Bunker Hill and Sullivan, had been engaged to make an examination of the property. Bradley recommended the purchase at the agreed price of six million dollars. On the strength of his report, we organized a company in London with the necessary capital.

Before proceeding further, I pointed out to my colleagues that, since Bradley had long been one of my own assistants, it would be well to have a report from an engineer representing the prospective purchasers. Accordingly, Ross E. Browne, whom I knew to be one of the best of our American mining engineers, was sent to make another examination.

The expectation was, of course, that his report would confirm that of Bradley; we were only making assurance doubly sure. To our consternation, Browne's estimate fell far below Bradley's. His statistical analysis was so convincing that we decided not to float the company. My own examination made the following year confirmed Browne's report. The lower levels were in poor ore; the mine was en borrasco, as they called it.

I still believed that further development would open up fine mineral deposits. E. A. Wiltsee remained there to secure an option on the property. He advised Sonnenberg, the owner, to come to see me in New York. Sonnenberg accepted this advice and offered me the mine for three million dollars, exactly half Bradley's original evaluation. This was the blunder which made me first lose confidence in Bradley.

I sent Beatty and several assistants to sample and map the property thoroughly. Their favorable report, coupled with the reduced price, persuaded me to start for Mexico to conclude the purchase.

Before I could reach Mexico City, however, Sonnenberg died, and I was obliged to conduct my business with his executors. It turned out fortunately for me that this particular matter had been left solely in the hands of an honest lawyer, Luis Mendez.

There had been bad blood between the owners of the El Oro and Esperanza mines. Immediately upon the death of Sonnenberg an agent of the El Oro Company endeavored to get an option on the Esperanza property. To that end, he offered to deposit twenty-five thousand dollars for an option of thirty days, during which the company's experts could examine the mine. I reminded Mendez that Sonnenberg had promised me the option: that I had been put to considerable trouble and expense in having the property examined, and was now ready to purchase; moreover, that Sonnenberg himself had several times told me that, because of the existing feud, he would under no circumstances sell the property to the El Oro Mining Company of London. Mendez readily admitted that the estate was under moral obligation to sell me the property, and finally agreed to give me the thirty-day option without my putting up any money.

I myself felt a moral obligation to offer a fifty-one per cent interest to the Venture Corporation because they had been associated with me at the time we had formerly considered the purchase. The remaining forty-nine per cent I intended for the Guggenheim Exploration Company.

It was a Friday afternoon when I arrived at New York. The first payment on the three million dollars had to be made the following Wednesday at Mexico City. I went at once to see Daniel Guggenheim, but he displayed no interest whatever in my proposition.

I did not press the matter, but started for Whitney's cottage at Sheepshead Bay. At this critical juncture I went to him because I knew him to be a man of courage. With that ability to grasp a situation quickly which distinguished his entire career, he agreed to assist me in the undertaking. We tried to reach Guggenheim by telephone Saturday morning, but were unable to get trace of his whereabouts. Finally, it was agreed that Whitney and I should take over the property ourselves.

When I located Mr. Dan on Monday and told him what we had done, he expressed surprise. I then said: "Whitney and I are going ahead to float this company. I know that the Venture Corporation will take up fifty-one per cent. Do you want the other forty-nine? If not, we'll buy it ourselves."

He bought this section of the flotation on behalf of the Guggenheim Exploration Company, and it was not offered to the public.

The Venture's fifty-one per cent was being dealt in on the London market. When bonanza ore was discovered in a newly developed part of the property, there was a boom in Esperanza shares. I told Mr. Dan that the high price of the stock was not justified, since the bonanza ore would soon be exhausted, and the mine had no future except as a relatively slow and steady producer. Our profits were not to be derived from stock manipulation, but from the operation of the mine. As soon as earnings fell off, there would inevitably be a slump in the shares. This would reflect discredit both on the Guggenheim Exploration Company, which owned the property, and on me, who was managing it.

Guggenheim immediately agreed with me. We cabled the London brokers who were engaged in booming the Esperanza shares to the effect that, if the shares advanced higher, the Guggenheim Exploration Company would dump its holdings and break the market.

This brokerage firm, which had been a client of mine in South African days, indignantly cabled that in the future its members would not touch any flotation in which the Guggenheim Exploration Company was interested. I replied by letter that they would be given no opportunity to repeat such an unwarranted manipulation of stock, and when they realized that the conservative policy of the Guggenheim Exploration Company was for the protection of the investor and not for the profit of the speculator they would be glad to participate in that company's flotations. They came to repent of their hasty action, and many times in the future were desirous of dealing in our securities.

The mining investor is constantly obliged to take risks, even when prospects seem most favorable. In purchasing the Esperanza we were risking a half million dollars, since there was not more than two and a half million dollars' worth of net ore in sight. Moreover, most of the deeper developments seemed unfavorable.

But I knew from my previous examinations that the El Oro, on one side of the Esperanza, possessed a long shoot of pay ore; on the other extension, the recent discovery of rich ore bodies at the Dos Estrellas convinced me that the geological formation justified our risk. As consulting engineer, I ordered certain exploratory work done, and was fortunate in discovering large bodies of unusually high-grade ore in a new section of the mine. Those who had invested in the Esperanza then enjoyed a series of handsome dividends, amounting in a few years to twelve million dollars.

At a banquet, not long after opening up the new development at the Esperanza, I was seated next to my old friend, J. B. Haggin. He was evidently in an unpleasant frame of mind. In discussing mining conditions, he remarked sourly, "Well, Jack, you have a lot to answer for in mining."

"Yes, Mr. Haggin," I said, "what's your particular grievance?"

"You've ruined the mining industry with the high salaries and engineering fees you pay," he replied. "Though I'm not reproaching you for the very large salary you're now reputed to receive," he added.

"That's a matter of opinion," I said. "It's true that I've paid fairly high salaries and fees, but I get expert engineers who are really worth their salt. Mr. Haggin, when it comes to purchasing a property you still stick to the 'practical miner,' though you've made all your money through the technical knowledge and ability of trained engineers developing and operating those properties. And you haven't even paid them adequately. Your practical miner with a 'nose for a mine' is all very well, but I'm not sure that I, personally, feel complimented."

Haggin humorously mentioned having seen a cartoon from a recent issue of a London paper in which I was represented with a greatly magnified nose. According to the caption, Barney Barnato said to his brother in 1892, "They have a miner over there in America who can smell a gold mine a thousand miles away. Let's send for this man Hammond."

"I've always contended a sense of smell is not enough," I remarked. "Shall I go on?"

"Go ahead."

"Well, you brought the subject up, and I want to prove I'm right. You were the first capitalist to invest any considerable amount of money in the El Oro district. I admit you secured the El Oro mine through the recommendation of your practical men, but unfortunately, through their bad advice you afterwards sold it to some of my English clients. Following their suggestion, again, you refused to purchase the Esperanza when it was offered to you. On my recommendation the Guggenheims and the Venture Corporation bought it.

"In this very same district I secured for myself, Charles D. Lane, and Ernest A. Wiltsee an extension of the El Oro in depth. Although this ground had been condemned as valueless by the manager of the old El Oro Company, I purchased it on the recommendation of my experts and, after some development work, I sold it to the new El Oro Company at a handsome profit. Now don't you think it was good business for me to employ a more expensive but a more competent type of mining engineer?" Mr. Haggin was somewhat chagrined but had to admit the force of my argument.

I still maintain that my theory is sound and I repeat what I have said already, that I believe the specialist is worthy of his hire. Of course, even experts sometimes make mistakes. Pride goeth before a fall. Because I could not help being somewhat proud of my previous successes, it was a great shock to find that my first favorable report on the Nipissing silver mine of Canada was not justified by subsequent examinations made under my direction. This report had created a sensation on the market, because the Guggenheims had invested a large sum in the purchase of the Nipissing Company stock on the strength of my recommendation.

My optimism had been based upon estimates by engineers in whose integrity and ability I had implicit confidence. Unfortunately, they had overestimated the value of the ore; it was the first time they made an error of that kind. I accepted, and still do accept, full responsibility for my optimistic report. Shortly afterwards, as the result of a careful personal examination, I informed the Guggenheim Exploration Company that my previous estimate of values had not been justified.

I was much criticized at the time. The Guggenheims, although they admitted they had been disappointed in this particular investment, stood loyally by me. They publicly stated that their confidence in my judgment had not been shaken by this error. It was rumored that I was to resign my position with the company in consequence of the Nipissing episode. This was corrected by the following statement in various newspapers, including the New York *Herald*, December 8, 1906:

> There is no foundation for the report that John Hays Hammond, mining expert for the Guggenheims, is to resign his office as a result of the Nipissing episode. Official denial of the report to this effect was made yesterday.
>
> This statement may be taken as representing the

views of the Guggenheims in regard to the recent Nipissing developments.

There is no mining company or set of mining engineers infallible. If a mistake was made in our first views of the Nipissing property we were at liberty to rectify our attitude later. Mr. Hammond has examined the properties for the Guggenheim interests which later came under their control and have resulted in enormous profits—enough to triple the losses sustained in the Nipissing deal.

My mistake in the Nipissing had been due to placing too high a value on the stock of the company. After the Guggenheims retired, the mine still continued to produce silver and to pay dividends. Since my report, eighty-two million ounces have been mined, and $29,940,000 have been paid in dividends.

One of the outstanding acquisitions of the Guggenheim Exploration Company was the Utah Copper Company. In 1899, Victor Clement, representing Joseph R. De Lamar, purchased a one-quarter interest in Colonel Wall's Mountain of Copper, at Bingham, Utah. Up to this time there had been no development on the property.

Clement made a careful examination, running drifts and crosscuts, and engaged R. C. Gemmel, the state engineer, to do the sampling and D. C. Jackling to run the mill tests. Under a comparatively barren cap, the mountain was found to be a mass of porphyry which assayed slightly less than two per cent in copper. The ore in sight was vast in amount but of such low grade as to make unprofitable the ordinary method of mining by means of tunnels and shafts.

Clement advised the use of steam shovels to terrace down the mountain and run it through a mill. Jackling, who subsequently carried out the development independently, adopted this plan. The deterrent to this procedure was the reluctance of capital to expend an estimated three million dollars in development before one ingot of copper could be produced. The property, therefore, remained idle. Clement became involved in a dispute with De Lamar and resigned his position. In 1901 he began to devote himself to his Mexican mines.

The following year De Lamar still had his one-quarter interest in the property and Colonel Wall held a three-quarter interest. Wall was anxious to have the mine developed. He was disappointed in what he considered De Lamar's lack of co-operation, and offered a favorable option on his own interests. Clement was still convinced of the value of the deposits and had kept up his friendly relations with Wall. He now suggested that, if I could secure De Lamar's quarter holdings and interest capital in London or New York, we could take up the property ourselves. We agreed to put a hundred thousand dollars each into the venture for further prospecting work.

De Lamar was willing to part with his interest at about its cost. He told me frankly that he had no faith in the enterprise.

In January, 1903, Clement had to go to Mexico again, and we agreed that on his return we would close the negotiations. But Clement died in the hospital at Saltillo in April. I happened to be in Mexico at the same time and so was able to assist in the last sad rites for that fine engineer and my loyal friend.

When I reached New York again, I heard that Daniel C. Jackling had succeeded in closing a deal with Wall by which the MacNeill-Penrose group had acquired control of Utah Copper. The capital for extensive development was not forthcoming, however.

In 1905, John C. Montgomery, Colorado mine promoter, came to see me with the proposal that I, as the Guggenheims' consulting engineer, should interest them in financing the Utah Copper Company. I told Montgomery I was familiar with the history of the property and would recommend it. I put the proposition before Mr. Dan with a view to securing his support at our next board meeting.

There was needed, I said, someone with imagination enough to see beyond the great initial outlay and to grasp the eventual success of large-scale operation. My own faith in the enterprise was evident, since I had been willing to go into it with Clement. This demonstration of confidence, coupled with my arguments and figures, convinced Mr. Dan.

I then sent Seeley W. Mudd and Beatty to make a new examination and a thorough drill test of the property. Their report, in October, 1905, was favorable and the Guggenheim Exploration Company then underwrote a bond issue of three million dollars and bought a large block of the stock.

I became consulting engineer and later managing director of Utah Copper. Jackling was put in charge of operations. The adjacent property was acquired and consolidated for more efficient operation, and the striking success of Utah Copper under Jackling's able management is a matter of contemporary copper history.

In August, 1907, the big concentrator at Garfield went into operation. Since that time 225,000,000 cubic yards of ore and waste have been moved, or almost exactly the total yardage displaced in building the Panama Canal. At least four times this amount will have been dug before Utah Copper is exhausted as a mine.

The gross income from the sale of copper, gold, and silver has been $596,000,000. Total disbursements, including dividends, construction of plants, taxes, etc., have been $300,000,000, and the company has paid in dividends alone $185,000,000. The number of men on the Utah Copper Company payroll is about 3500, with 500 others whose livelihood comes directly from the company's operations. These men represent a high class of labor, all skilled workmen and well paid. With their families and the families of those men indirectly required for the life of a community, there is in the Bingham district a population of twenty-five thousand or more supported directly or indirectly by operations of the Utah Copper Company.

The success of working the large low-grade copper deposits by the Utah Copper Company gave rise to discoveries of deposits of this kind in other parts of the United States and in Chile, and the development of what is known as the Porphyry Copper Industry. The magnitude of operations in this industry is shown by A. B. Parsons in his book, *Porphyry Coppers*. "From 1905 (the beginning of operations of the Utah Copper Company) to 1931 inclusive, the output was $2,871,300,000 of which $50,000,000 was derived from gold and silver contents. Of this large sum $800,000,000 has been allocated to dividends and bond interest; $391,000,000 to taxes, local and federal; transportation, refining and selling copper; $840,000,-000 to supplies, fuel, equipment, machinery, and power at mines, mills, and smelters $840,000,000, for payrolls at mines, mills and smelters."

As Mr. Parsons states: "In a mining community payrolls make towns. The townspeople include a great many doctors, lawyers, school teachers, preachers, bankers, merchants, butchers, garage men, restaurant and laundry proprietors, insurance agents, hotel keepers, movie-house owners, and the employees of all these necessary members of a normal community. Even bootleggers and politicians are not unknown in some of the towns. And all these indirectly derive their livelihood from the mining or ore-treating operations. Farmers, dairymen, and poultry raisers find excellent markets for their produce in the mining town. For every man employed either directly in producing copper or in serving the man who digs or smelts, there is on the average a family of four."

In 1906, I sent my assistant, Pope Yeatman, to Alaska to examine the Kennecott Copper Corporation's property. The Guggenheims secured an interest in it on his favorable report. Later on, Yeatman and his assistants, Edward Berry and E. T. Stannard, the latter subsequently president of Kennecott, had charge of the development for the Guggenheims of the Braden Copper Company and the Chuquicamata property, both in Chile. An expenditure of many millions of dollars was necessary in the development of these properties for large-scale operation, and the attainment of the low working cost will ensure their importance as factors in the world copper production. The Incas smelted copper ores from the Chuquicamata mine in the fifteenth and sixteenth centuries.

Pope Yeatman succeeded me as managing director and consulting engineer of the Guggenheim Exploration Company. He resigned the office in 1916, after a period of nine years.

One of the properties on which I had to report for the Guggenheims was the Silver Lake mine in Colorado. I had already visited the mine in 1901 for English clients, at which time I had found that the owner was an old Freiberg classmate, Ed Stoiber, who was lacking in aggressiveness.

Stoiber's wife possessed all the traits which were missing in his kindly disposition. She was determined that Ed was not to be imposed on by anyone but herself, and relegated him to the background when there was business to be done.

On my arrival I was introduced to Mrs. Stoiber by Ed. After some preliminary conversation about Freiberg days, the talk turned to business. Mrs. Stoiber, apparently fearing that I might get the better of her husband, projected herself into the conference.

I began by saying: "Now let's see what condition the mine is in. First, how large are the profits, and what are your prospects?"

The replies were evasive and vague, and my dissatisfaction must have been obvious. Before long Mrs. Stoiber asked to speak to Ed privately, and they withdrew from the room.

In a few minutes Ed returned. "Well, Jack," he said, "I don't think this is the kind of mine your English firm would like. If I were you I wouldn't recommend it." After a moment's hesitation, he added, "I hate to advise you to do this, because I know you'll lose your fee."

"That's all right, Ed. Don't worry about that. You're an old friend—that's enough for me. I won't even bother to examine the mine."

Without further ado I returned to Glenwood Springs and dismissed the Silver Lake property from my mind.

I was much amused when, some little time after I joined the Guggenheim Exploration Company, the directors asked me to make an examination of this same mine. They had purchased it a few years before, probably led astray by the exaggerated value of the property in the opinion of Mrs. Stoiber. Having already spent a million dollars in developing it and erecting a plant, the Guggenheims thought the mine ought to begin showing some profit.

It was decided that I should make the trip with three of the brothers, Daniel, Solomon, and Simon. While plans were being made, I told the Guggenheims that I was afraid the journey would be unprofitable, and I then related the story of my first visit there.

Young Harry Payne Whitney accompanied us and did much to enliven the excursion. The train took us as far up the valley as the company's office. The mine itself lay at an elevation of thirteen thousand feet, about three miles away as the crow flies.

The ore was brought down in iron buckets traveling along aerial cable lines. Their use by employees of the company was prohibited since they were regarded as unsafe for passenger traffic. Unfortu-

THE GUGGENHEIMS

WARDNER, IDAHO

nately, the night preceding our planned inspection of the mine there was a heavy storm, and in the morning the horse trail was buried so deep in snow that it would be impassable for days to come. It was essential that I, at least, see the mine, and time pressed. I decided to go up in one of the empty ore buckets, although it was only under the strongest protest that the manager finally gave me permission to do this.

Whitney wanted very much to accompany me. He used all his persuasive wiles, first on the manager and then on me, and was greatly disappointed when I flatly refused to take him. I told him I was not going for the fun of it: it was a business necessity in which he could be of no service.

Wrapped in a heavy fur coat against the cold, I cramped myself down in a bucket. The manager telephoned that I was on my way. After swaying for a half-hour over the snow-clad rocks and gorges far below, I reached the mine and was dug out of my uncomfortable conveyance. I had barely straightened up when I saw Whitney's head poking out of another bucket approaching the landing stage.

I was angry, because I felt responsible for him, but was unable to restrain a smile at his comical appearance. I demanded, "Where did you come from, you nuisance?"

He grinned back at me, promised not to get in the way, and followed me to the office.

There we were met by a delegation of outraged miners who complained in strong language about the cook. Now, to complain of the food is the most fundamental and treasured right of a miner. I inquired whether there was any fault to be found with the supplies furnished by the company. The spokesman replied that the grub was good enough in itself, but the fault lay with the cook, who was giving them the same thing day after day. "We'll be damned if we'll stand it any longer!"

I then called the cook, and asked him whether he thought the company was furnishing suitable provisions. He admitted it was.

"Now, cook," I said, "you came here with a good recommendation, and I wonder if you're living up to it. How many ways do you know of cooking potatoes?"

"About six."

I appealed to his vanity. "And how about bread, eggs, corned beef, pudding?"

To prove his culinary art, he began to enumerate the different dishes he could make.

"All right," I said, "the men will appoint a grub committee, and each week one of them will make out a menu and submit it to you. Then you'll cook up what they want from your supplies. If you give them an occasional surprise, they'll be your friends for life."

I saw he had half a mind to leave, but I looked significantly at the snow-covered mountains. His eyes followed mine; apparently he decided he was better off where he was. I heard later from the manager that peace was reigning at the cookhouse—at least, for the time being.

Whitney watched proceedings with amusement. He followed me into the mine and all day scrambled nimbly up and down ladders and over piles of rock. His athletic prowess stood him in good stead. In the evening we went back to the mill in two buckets as we had come.

I have never seen anyone make friends more quickly with miners, prospectors, and other old-timers than Harry Whitney. He had a personal magnetism and a disarming friendliness that made him popular in the West as well as in the East. "You could beat even Teddy if you would go into politics," I used to tell him.

Harry also had his father's good judgment and generosity. In many later years of business dealings with him, there was never an enterprise in which we were associated wherein Whitney did not only urge my receiving the profits due by definite agreement, but also an additional sum to which he thought I was entitled. I, of course, declined these generous offers.

When the Guggenheims, Harry, and I arrived at Salt Lake City, my secretary told me that a man had been waiting several hours to see me. A personable-looking fellow was shown in.

He said, "Mr. Hammond, I don't suppose you recognize me."

When it was evident that I did not, he added, "I'm the 'hobo.'"

My mind flashed back to the time two years before when Rider Haggard had been a guest in my car going from California to New York. As the train wound its way over the Sierra Nevadas, I had been relating some of the famous holdups that had occurred on this same road. The scenes I had depicted were still vividly present to his mind when, late at night, he went to his compartment.

Before long James, my negro cook, came rushing into my room and in great agitation asked what was wrong with my guest. He explained that, noticing Haggard's light still burning, he had gone in to switch it off. With pistol in hand Haggard had leaped from his berth and threatened to shoot.

The next day I told Haggard that it was permissible to defend himself against bandits, but he would have to be careful with James; in addition to being the best cook I had ever had, James was also the best shot.

At breakfast Haggard regretfully remarked that he had never encountered a hobo in the flesh.

My son Harris, who usually accompanied me on these western journeys, spoke up. "There's a hobo been riding the brake beams of our car all night. I found him this morning and gave him something to eat. He's back there now."

At the next stop, Harris produced him. The hobo was grimy with dirt and cinders, ragged, and nearly frozen from the cold ride through the snowsheds and alkali desert. I introduced him to Haggard.

The hobo's face lighted up as he said, "You don't mean the famous Rider Haggard?"

"Yes," I said, "the very same man."

"Mr. Haggard," he said, "I've read all your books—some of them several times," and he rattled off their names.

I called James and told him to get our new guest washed up and give him a coat, since he was to have dinner with us.

We spent an entertaining evening listening to his tales of hobo life. Finally I asked the man whether he wasn't tired of being a tramp and whether he would take a job if I were to give him one. He accepted eagerly.

When we reached Ogden, I sent him off with a railroad ticket and a letter to the manager of a mine near Salt Lake City.

In parting, I added: "Here's a chance for you. I hope you'll stick to the job."

Now, some two years later, here was this same hobo transformed into a respectable and steady workman. He reminded me of my parting words as I had despatched him to a more profitable life, and said, "I did stay with the job, and now I have a chance to get a better position in the smelter you're building here."

I told him I would talk with the manager about him and would also write to Rider Haggard. I knew he would be pleased. The manager reported later that the man had turned out well and deserved his promotion.

On this same trip I was walking up and down the station platform with Sol Guggenheim, while waiting for a change of engines. We were discussing the notorious lawsuit then being tried at Butte, between H. H. Rogers, of Anaconda, and Heinze, the mining magnate. The bribery, corruption, and blackmail in this long and expensive litigation were causing more scandal than has been raised in any other mining case.

J. P. Morgan had said to me, "It reflects on every business in Wall Street, and it ought to be stopped."

I had been asked to serve as umpire between the parties to the suit but before I could act I joined the Guggenheims.

Sol said: "I can't understand why Rogers keeps up such a dirty mess. He may get a few million out of it, but he'll only give it right away to charity. Wouldn't you think he'd have more sense than to sacrifice his good name for that? I think it's a damn shame!"

"I agree with you, Sol," I replied, "and I'm glad to hear you've such a high ideal of business ethics. In the future I'll never have to worry about any rumors of sharp practice connected with your enterprises."

At the end of 1907, when I tendered my resignation to the Guggenheim Exploration Company on account of ill health, I was asked to renew my contract, and the Guggenheim brothers expressed regret at my leaving.

In the four years I had been with them I had formed a friendship with all the family. Although Dan and Isaac are dead, this friendship still continues with the surviving brothers.

I look back on my association with them as one of the most satisfactory periods in my mining career. This was partly due, of course, to the generous amount of my salary but chiefly to their estimable personal qualities. They backed me loyally. I found them scrupulously honest in their business methods, men of courage and broad vision, although outside of their knowledge of the smelting industry they had little personal experience in mining matters. They took an interest in their church, their charities, and social service.

I consider myself qualified to express high admiration for their business integrity, their sense of civic duty, and their solicitude for the welfare of their staff.

CHAPTER TWENTY-SIX

Prospecting in Politics

I had been in active service as a mining engineer for more than a quarter of a century. I had built up a corps of younger men on whom I could rely for efficient field work. It was not only unnecessary for me to follow activities in the field but considerations of health now made it unwise. I found I had leisure to do other things.

Up to this time I had not engaged in American politics, although in a life as active as mine one necessarily deals with statecraft and learns to know the weapons and the rules of the political game. I never cared for it. I have never fancied myself as a handshaker, a godfather to the nation's children, or a demagogue.

In America one must be "all things to all men" to run successfully for public office. Although it is the duty of honest and intelligent men to take part in the executive affairs of the nation, one reason why many industrialists and businessmen hesitate to do so is because political activity lays them open to suspicion and puts a noose around the neck of their business freedom. Also they have been accustomed to direct dealing and find themselves waterlogged by the need for compromise and the entangling routine of "parish pump politics," as Rhodes expressed it.

It is true that positions and offices were at various times offered me—some of which I would have accepted—but, unfortunately, these offers came when other conditions made acceptance impossible. As a result of combinations of circumstances, I found myself in the political arena without portfolio.

The reason—and the only reason—for my entry into politics in the early nineteen hundreds was my warm personal friendship with William Howard Taft. I liked to be with him. I admired him. His intelligence, integrity, and fine balance were qualities requisite in a leader at that particular time. He welcomed my advice and I felt that I might be of some use to him.

Out of all my family I am the only one to break away from the tradition that a Southerner must be a Democrat. My relatives thought me a misguided turncoat; I consider it independence. While still a student at Yale, I had agreed with the Republican stand on the tariff issue and my attitude had persisted and developed. But in becoming a Republican I had not renounced my allegiance to many of the time-honored principles of the Democratic party. I felt that Cleveland's election came at a time when the Republican party had been so long in power that a change was needed. Cleveland was the type of president best fitted to the occasion, and was highly esteemed by men of all parties for his level-headedness, his soundness of purpose, and his courage.

I have been personally acquainted with all the presidents from Grant on—with the exception of Chester A. Arthur—and had opportunities for close observation of their activities. Hayes, Cleveland, and some of the later presidents I knew more intimately.

The first time I saw President Cleveland was in 1886 when the appointment of my brother Richard as surveyor general of California was under discussion. Cleveland realized that Richard had strong support from California, but feared that some objection might be made to his youth: he was only twenty-seven. The position was one of great responsibility because of the predatory efforts of powerful private interests to get hold of valuable timber lands in California.

My brother's competence and record for inflexible honesty finally prevailed, and the President appointed him. After that he was locally called "general," much to the amusement of my father who really was a major.

Golden Gate Park in San Francisco owes much to my brother Dick. He was president of the Park Commissioners for several years and was especially interested in building the children's playground. In my boyhood days I used to camp and hunt among the sand dunes on which the park is built. My cousin, William Hammond Hall, a young civil engineer, imported shrubs from abroad and transformed these sand dunes into a beautiful park.

After that first meeting, I did not see Cleveland again until the summer of 1908, when I was living at Lakewood. He was desperately ill and had been moved from his home at Princeton to the Lakewood Hotel in the hope that the change would be beneficial. When they were ready to return to their home, Mrs. Cleveland was extremely anxious to get her husband away without his having to run the gauntlet of photographers who prowled around the grounds at night and lurked by day behind their black cloths on the hotel veranda.

I succeeded in throwing them off the scent by appearing with Mrs. Cleveland and the baggage in front of the hotel. She allowed herself to be photographed while the ex-President was taken out a rear door and installed in my son Jack's automobile. When we were sure Jack had a sufficient start, Mrs. Cleveland and I stepped into our waiting car and departed, leaving behind us a row of dumfounded newspapermen.

A few days later Cleveland died. I served as one of his pallbearers.

I was out of the country during most of the years of McKinley's presidency, and my occasional contacts with him were purely social. He was always kindly and good-natured, but behind this front-porch manner I divined a greater degree of stamina than many people gave him credit for. Shortly before his assassination McKinley had paid off his political debts and had begun to assert his authority.

Roosevelt, his successor in office, was a spectacular figure the world over. While I was in England, I followed with interest his vivid career in the Spanish-American War and as a forceful governor of New York State. He was a man marked by physical and moral courage, and by an inexhaustible drive. The self-made man is popular in America. Roosevelt, with a background of illustrious ancestors and ample means, substituted vigor and personal magnetism for humble origin as his method of capturing the admiration of the masses. Moreover, it was apparent that he was politically astute and would forge ahead in politics.

After my return to America I saw President Roosevelt on many occasions.. It was at the White House during his administration that my friendship for Taft, then secretary of war, was intensified and that I saw much of the famous trio, the other member of which was Elihu Root, secretary of state.

On one occasion these men, and Mrs. Roosevelt, were present at a luncheon at the White House to which I was unexpectedly summoned by wire from New York at the time of the I.W.W. trouble in Colorado.

At the table, in his impetuous manner, Roosevelt boomed jocularly, "Well, Mr. Hammond, I hear you think I'm losing my political courage!"

I was embarrassed by so blunt a statement, but understood his reference. A few days earlier I had dined with Paul Morton, secretary of the navy, and had expressed the opinion that Roosevelt should have complied with the governor of Colorado's requisition to send troops to suppress the lawless activities at Cripple Creek. I had further stated that in my opinion the refusal had been based solely on political considerations.

Morton must have repeated this conversation to the President; I was fairly caught. I frankly admitted that my sentiments had been correctly reported and that I still held them.

Roosevelt seemed amused that I should acknowledge having accused him of political cowardice. "Why," he said, "most of my friends on The Hill blame me for showing too much boldness. They say I've meddled in too many things—Panama, for example."

"Mr. President," I said, "I'd like to discuss this Colorado situation with you after lunch, explain my criticism, and hear your side of the story."

When Mrs. Roosevelt retired, the President reintroduced the subject. "You criticized me for not having sent troops to Cripple Creek at Governor Peabody's request. Peabody must have known that before federal troops could legally be sent to Colorado, the resources of the state itself had to be exhausted. He had no business asking me for help until the state militia was no longer able to handle the situation. There are plenty of people who'd like to catch me doing something for which they could impeach me. Your friend Taft will bear me out."

Turning to Taft and Root, he said, "I wish you both would send Mr. Hammond all our correspondence with the governor. He can then see for himself."

I said quickly, "There's no need of that, Mr. President. I will take your word for it."

A few days later I had to go to Colorado, and, while I was there, made a point of seeing the governor. I asked why he had issued an appeal with which he knew the President could not legally comply.

He finally agreed that Roosevelt's stand had been correct and admitted that he had hoped to avoid antagonizing either capital or labor by shifting the responsibility to the federal government.

I had been a staunch supporter of Governor Peabody, but now I freely expressed my opinion of his double-dealing and said I would make it my business to do all I could to prevent the re-election towards which he was so cautiously pussyfooting. My friends prominent in Republican politics were disgusted with Peabody's action and contributed their influence to his defeat.

During these years I was seeing Taft constantly, and our families became close friends. I often went to Washington to see him; he and Mrs. Taft came to Lakewood and New York to visit us. The renewal in 1902 of our acquaintance of Yale days, with its informal—indeed, almost accidental—quality, I count as one of the happiest events of my life. Taft later described it in an article in the *National Geographic Magazine:*

After I returned from the Philippines temporarily in 1902, I stayed with Mr. Root in Washington while I was being subject to the grilling of a congressional committee, which cross-examined me for 30 days in the spring of that year. During that examination I ran over to New York and went to the University Club for luncheon.

While I was there a waiter brought a card from a gentleman who was also taking luncheon, which was followed by the owner of the card, and he proved to be my old college friend, John Hays Hammond. He had been out of college 26 years, and I had been out of college 24, and we had not met since we graduated.

He had been to South Africa and helped to develop its wonderful mineral wealth, had been convicted of treason against Oom Paul and the Boer Republic, had been sentenced to death, and had only escaped by the intervention of England and the United States. He left college a mining engineer, to be engaged in peaceful occupations in the West. I had left as a lawyer, to pursue the humdrum professional life as a member of the bar in the Middle West, and had just then come back from the Orient, as the chief executive of 8,000,000 people, the oldest Christian community in the Orient.

There was a metamorphosis in the case of both of us that seemed to be striking, and when I told Mr. Root about it he said, "And they say there is no romance in this American life."

With all these comparable experiences and the opportunities for discussion which they offered, we naturally reverted to our college days. Taft had not changed greatly in character—he was the same genial Bill Taft—although his physical bulk had increased. One got the impression of a large rather than a fat man. At college he had been a powerful boy, with a decided aptitude for undergraduate politics and academic study. He was in my brother Bill's class, two years behind me. Bill was very fond of him; in fact, he broke the habits and beliefs of a lifetime to vote for Taft in 1908. Through Bill I met Taft and saw a good deal of him at New Haven, although he was two years younger. In fact, at that University Club luncheon we recalled that it was I who had initiated him into the mysteries of poker. He was not a particularly promising pupil. Some months later, however, I was badly beaten by him. When I recovered from my surprise I realized that brother Bill, a recognized authority in the game, had been coaching Taft on the quiet. I promptly went to Bill for some coaching myself. The defeat lurked in the back of my mind for years, but the opportunity to retaliate at the poker table never came.

In 1904 when Taft returned from the Philippines, where he had been governor general, to become secretary of war under Roosevelt, we first began discussing politics and the activities in which he was engaged. He was having dinner with me one day in New York. Afterwards, we strolled down Fifth Avenue; that was the quietest place in which to discuss a subject without interruption. James G. Blaine once said that a stroll on Fifth Avenue afforded him the best means of a private conversation.

Taft asked my opinion of the Panama Canal; whether the army should take over the work or whether private interests should be allowed to complete it.

I said that I believed the army engineers would probably not do as good a technical job as civilian engineers, but that there would be less opportunity for graft and less scandal if the canal were put under military supervision. Taft said that was his opinion also. Efficiency would have to give way to integrity. The remarkable ability shown by Goethals and other army officers in the digging of the canal proved my misgivings unjustified.

While Secretary and Mrs. Taft were visiting at our home in Lakewood at the time my wife and I were celebrating our silver wedding in 1906, President Roosevelt called Taft by long-distance telephone and offered him, for the second time, the post of associate justice of the United States Supreme Court. Taft was inclined to accept.

Mrs. Taft and I urged him to refuse, assuring him that many of his friends felt as we did. Had he been offered the chief justiceship, we would have raised no objection. That would, indeed, have been the achievement of his life ambition.

I based my opposition on the ground that he was the logical candidate for president in 1908. If he now accepted a life tenure on the bench, he would be shutting the door on any further political advancement. Moreover, he could be virtually certain of an appointment to the Supreme Court if a vacancy occurred during any ensuing Republican administration.

Up to this time Taft had held numerous important political offices and in every case had acquitted himself admirably: assistant district attorney and then judge in Cincinnati, solicitor general of the United States, judge of the Federal District Court, chairman of the Philippine Commission and later governor general, and at present secretary of war. Even his work in the Philippines had been thrust upon him. This proved to be practically the reorganization of a whole nation by one man. He displayed courage, diplomacy, and executive brilliance in the work, but he really did not like politics. His natural inclination was always towards the law.

Towards the end of 1907 it became apparent that Taft was to be the Republican choice for president. He was the only man above the status of a favorite son, and Roosevelt was letting out the tucks in his own mantle to make it fit Taft's shoulders.

I had recently resigned my position with the Guggenheims and now actually ventured into the field of politics in behalf of Taft. I was to spend the winter in California and my wide acquaintance there might be of value in supporting his candidacy for the presidential nomination, which was already gaining momentum in Republican circles. This proved to be true. I made many trips throughout the state and in other sections of the West and in most cases found it easy to enlist support. Oddly enough one of my most ardent lieutenants in this cause was Jack Burke, who had been my violent business enemy in the Bunker Hill litigation. Burke insisted enthusiastically that I campaign in my own behalf as running mate with Taft, a suggestion which Taft had already made to me.

On my return to New York in the spring of 1908, I called on E. H. Harriman and in the course of our conversation told him that I was now taking a hand in politics.

"Hammond," he said, displaying the American businessman's attitude, "I'm surprised at you wasting your time in politics. Your valuable abilities as an engineer shouldn't be discarded for intrigue and demagogy."

I smiled and asked him what kind of man he did want to see taking care of the affairs of the country and told him he ought to know that I wasn't likely to play cheap politics. Then I said jokingly that Wall Street didn't have enough money to "buy" me and under no consideration would I go out appealing to the mobs, and assured him seriously that I had no political ambitions for myself.

Apparently this made some impression on him. A few years later, in Washington, he asked me to come and see him and Chauncey Depew. They proposed that I run for the Senate.

I asked from what state.

"Why, New York: you live and do business there; or California, where you were born; or Idaho, where you've developed so many mines."

I thanked them both and declined, reminding Harriman that I had not changed my mind about seeking office for myself.

Harriman was definite in his approaches and opinions. He either liked a man or he didn't. For instance, there was no love lost between him and Roosevelt. When Charles D. Walcott, secretary of the Smithsonian Institution in Washington, was collecting money for Roosevelt's African expedition, he asked me to get Harriman to contribute. "Give money? No," said Harriman. "While he was president I would have gladly paid all his expenses to get rid of him, but not a cent now."

Harriman added that what particularly disgusted him was Roosevelt's posing as the discoverer of the Ten Commandments. He said, undoubtedly the big businessmen of the country at certain times in the past had been ruthless in their methods and not as scrupulous as they should have been. But at that time they had all been engaged in a free-for-all fight with devil-take-the-hindmost and did not realize how objectionable their methods were. He concluded by saying, "We will all be more conscientious in the future." If they had been, the history of 1929 to 1935 might have been a very different story.

The fact that I enjoyed a flutter in the direction of the vice-presidency should not really count against my statement that I was not seeking personal advancement. I should have liked being on the ticket with my friend Taft. My name was being mentioned in this connection in the newspapers, as were those of several others. The vice-presidency was quite open; no one seemed to have any lead.

I discussed the matter with Taft. He named two men who were seeking the nomination for vice-president, neither of whom he favored, and said he hoped I would make every effort to defeat their candidacy. He expressed the opinion that with them out of the way the situation at the convention might take such form as to allow him to give me his support, and he assured me that he would be delighted to have me as his running mate. It must be remembered that this was before the convention, when Taft's own nomination was by no means certain and it would have been sheer folly for him to commit himself. Also, I was given to understand by friends that Roosevelt had no objection to me, but Roosevelt would have all he could do in keeping the convention from a Roosevelt stampede, and in securing the succession for Taft.

I went to the Chicago convention but not as a delegate. My plan was to use my influence wherever it would be most useful to Taft.

Shortly after our arrival my friend, Arthur Sewall, brought Congressman James S. Sherman to see me. Unfortunately, I was away at the time and did not hear of Sherman's offer to be my convention manager until too late.

After many telegrams came in to party headquarters urging me to try for the vice-presidential nomination, and after John C. Montgomery, a western mining man and an old friend, had offered to be my campaign manager, I said "Barkis is willin'."

We opened an office in a hotel room and my son Harris, just out of college, came on to help. I am afraid we were just hopeful amateurs at the game. Harris tells the story of one of our negro constituents who came in one day and said to him: "Well, Mistah Hammond, yo' fathah sho' ain't takin' dis campaign ver' seriously."

"How's that?" Harris demanded.

"Well, sah, I ain't seen much of his money bein' spent aroun' heah."

Harris tells another story. One morning two negroes called to see me. They were referred to Harris, who had not forgotten the "glad hand" spirit of college days. One of the men took Harris aside and told him that the other was by far the most influential colored politician in Indiana and Illinois. Harris said he would be glad to meet him. The most influential colored politician was introduced to Harris as "my old and esteemed friend whom I have known for forty years or more. Mr. Hammond, let me introduce you to Mr. Jackson," whereupon "Mr. Jackson" indignantly drew himself up to his full height and said to his esteemed friend of forty years, "Didn't I just tell you not more than five minutes ago that my name's Johnson?"

Harris suddenly recalled that he had an engagement elsewhere.

When it was certain that Taft, the Midwesterner, was to get the nomination instead of Hughes, the Easterner, Hughes's adherents became bitter and claimed that steam-roller methods had been used in flattening out their candidate. My friends advised me that the nomination of Congressman "Sunny Jim" Sherman, the very man who had offered to be my manager, would add to the strength of the national ticket; in this way compensating the New York delegation for the rejection of Hughes. I withdrew and turned over to Sherman such potential support as I had.

Taft and Sherman were nominated. A few weeks later the Democrats at Denver once more chose William Jennings Bryan as their standard bearer, and the campaign opened.

The Republican National Committee set up headquarters at Chicago, as well as New York, in recognition of the growing importance of the West in Republican party politics. Taft resigned his Cabinet post and went to Cincinnati; he remained there until September when he took the stump for four weeks in the eastern, midwestern, and border states.

An example of Taft's fearlessness and direct honesty in meeting issues is shown by the address made in Chicago, September 23rd. The audience was composed largely of members of the organized labor groups. Taft chose to talk to them about his unpopular decisions in labor cases when he had been United States circuit judge.

> "I am not here to apologize for anything which I did when I was on the bench. I am here only in view of the fact that I have been attacked on this ground, to take up those decisions, to ask your attention to them, to explain here in my humble judgment why it was necessary to reach the conclusions and take the action

which I did, and then, if you gentlemen of organized labor think that this is a reason why I should *not* be selected President of the United States, you will not hear a bit of complaint from me. That is your privilege. You are electors and you have the right to judge of a man by his official action, whether it be on the bench or in any other capacity."

Taft took up several cases, analyzed them, and explained the necessity for his decisions. It was bold, franker than political speeches usually are, and met the issue squarely. It was typical of him.

Mark Sullivan says that Roosevelt advised Taft—and it must have been apropos of this speech, "Don't talk on delicate subjects—stop citing court decisions." Roosevelt was perhaps more astute, Taft was certainly more forthright.

Roosevelt's political wisdom and open support were generously given to Taft. But some of Taft's friends thought Roosevelt's public utterances were at times too patronizing. He seemed to be creating in the public mind the impression that Taft was not capable of standing on his own feet. When Governor Haskell, of Oklahoma, brought up the question of government guarantee of banks, Roosevelt took issue as though he himself were the candidate.

At the urgent request of some Taft supporters, I undertook the delicate mission of intimating to Roosevelt that in his effort to help Taft he was keeping himself too much in the limelight. I had no fear of being thrown out as I had always found him willing to listen, however violently he might disagree with me.

I told Roosevelt that I was perhaps in a better position than he to hear political gossip and that there was a lot of talk about Taft's lack of independence, and about his being forced to rely on the President for everything he did. I said that I thought it was partly because Taft had insisted on consulting him on the acceptance speech, against the advice of certain supporters who were not friendly to Roosevelt. This had made a bad impression in political circles. Taft openly declared that he felt he should confer with Roosevelt, not only out of a sense of loyalty but because he had high regard for Roosevelt's political acumen.

Roosevelt eyed me quizzically for a moment and then remarked: "I guess you're right. In the future I'll put on the soft pedal."

I tell the incident to show that Roosevelt was not always as arbitrary as represented. On other occasions I found him equally willing to discuss controversial subjects.

Shortly after Taft's nomination Roosevelt asked me to take up the reorganization of the National League of Republican Clubs. He wrote me, and also sent John A. Stewart, long identified with Republican politics, to explain how I could help the campaign by undertaking this work. The existing organization was inactive, and the clearing away of a few obstacles would rejuvenate it and I could be made president.

Frank H. Hitchcock, formerly first assistant postmaster general under Roosevelt, was at this time chairman of the Republican National Committee and Taft's campaign manager. We had to exercise considerable tact to avoid giving the impression that we were encroaching upon his province. He seemed jealous of any interference and apprehensive of not receiving due credit for success in the election.

At no time was he sincere in his support of the league; he undermined it whenever he had the opportunity. He was particularly anxious that no funds for its support should be diverted from his organization. Instead, he invited me to Republican headquarters and then was tactless enough to ask me for money. In view of the unfriendly attitude he had always betrayed, this was certainly surprising.

He complained: "When my friends induced me to accept this job, they said they'd give me ample funds. They're not doing it."

"Well," I retorted, as I turned on my heel, "I wasn't one of those friends. I wouldn't let you squander a penny of mine under any condition."

This open expression of my sentiments did not improve his feeling towards me. He had other worries, however. Whenever a difficult campaign problem presented itself at New York, he would take the Twentieth Century train for Chicago to seek advice from western headquarters. He would at once be confronted with two major problems in Chicago, and would skip back to New York on the next train. He spent most of his time railroading himself out of political realities.

The function of the Republican National Committee was to carry on party propaganda; that of the National League was to form local clubs of young and new voters in every county and city. Some thirty-eight units were organized, with a total membership of a million or more.

We could not draw on the National Committee for funds, nor did we need much money; our organizers were volunteers who gave their spare time to the work. Membership in the league involved the payment of no fees or dues, and the amounts that had to be spent for rent, literature, campaign buttons, and similar items were donated in small sums. My own party contribution was for the support of these clubs.

I appealed to the young men to interest themselves in political questions; I wanted them to be Republicans, of course, but more especially to be politically active. In my addresses I deplored the private citizen's lack of concern with local and national political questions.

It was my view then, as it is now, that good government in a democracy is possible only when responsible citizens envisage self-government as a personal and serious duty which cannot safely be delegated to professional politicians. I urged American youth to assume its civic duty and make its influence felt.

I thoroughly enjoyed the big parades of voters from our clubs which arranged for Taft's visits to the larger cities. The flickering torches, bands, excitement were an interesting and picturesque part. I liked to feel that thousands of young voters were aiding Taft's march into the White House.

After the election the Tafts went to Augusta, Georgia, to spend the winter, and invited my wife and me to accompany them. When not engaged in political discussions, the President-elect and I spent our time playing golf or attending barbecues.

We played a whole series of games which came out exactly even. On the day before Taft left for Panama, we had a final round to decide which was the better golfer. At the seventeenth hole we were still tied. On the eighteenth Taft teed off and topped his ball, which landed in a quagmire, leaving him what seemed a hopeless shot.

I turned to him and said triumphantly, "Well, old man, I guess I have you now."

With great deliberation I proceeded to drive, and made a beautiful long shot, which unfortunately hit a tree and bounced into a position fully as bad as that of Taft's ball. We both arrived on the green in the same number of shots, with my ball about six feet from the cup, and his fully thirty. There was a large gallery of fans. They seemed to inspire Taft but made me decidedly nervous. He took aim carefully and holed out by what seemed to me a miraculous putt. At this crucial moment, I flubbed and left him the victor by one stroke. He never failed to mention this victory snatched from defeat and plagued me unmercifully whenever he could contrive an opportunity.

Roosevelt often criticized Taft's enjoyment of golf. He thought it not a democratic enough game for a president, but Taft would laugh and go on playing. Just what form of exercise a man weighing over three hundred pounds should take was not suggested; possibly tennis or running, or pole vaulting.

Taft had selected golf on the recommendation of his physician. Roosevelt regarded this as a great political handicap and on several occasions warned Taft to that effect. Through Mark Sullivan, Roosevelt told him "that he should take his exercise in some form more familiar to the plebeian." "It is true," Roosevelt said, "I myself play tennis, but that game is a little more familiar. Besides, you never saw a photograph of me playing tennis. Photographs on horseback, yes, tennis, no, and golf is fatal."

For a time after his inauguration Taft took up horseback riding but he never really enjoyed it. In this connection one recalls the cablegram sent by Secretary Root when Taft was governor general of the Philippines. Taft had been seriously ill after a surgical operation and his friends in Washington were anxious about his health. When he recovered he cabled Root that he had just completed a long horseback trip into the interior of the country and felt fine. Root expressed pleasure at hearing this, but inquired as to the condition of the horse.

Taft's genial personality was as efficacious in winning him friends in the South as it had been everywhere else. On all public occasions he was greeted with sincere enthusiasm. He would rise slowly to his feet and, with his familiar chuckle, say: "I'm accepting your enthusiasm as a personal tribute and not as a sign of political approbation. Four years from now, of course, I know you'll go to the polls and vote against me."

His platform manner was peculiarly his own. He did not ingratiate an audience. He won them. To describe the "famous chuckle" to which everyone refers in remembering him, one should have the pen of a Dickens. I have never heard any other sound like it, nor expect to again. Taft's laughter was a form of physical enjoyment. It would start far ahead of the point of an anecdote, when he began to think of something that amused him and was making up his mind to tell it. It began unexpectedly and softly, grew in volume and repetition, and was used to punctuate his sentences. This chuckle started chuckles in his hearers. One of the most exciting memories of anyone who ever heard him make a speech was his ability to throw huge audiences into spasms of delighted laughter. This was neither a pose nor a trick. Taft was a great lover of laughter—and he liked to share his enjoyment.

Taft's popularity suggested to me that the Republican party in the South might be resuscitated by the formation of Taft Clubs. I hoped they could be entirely dissociated from the corrupt, carpetbagger organization which made the southern Republican politician a disgrace to his party. Hitchcock's hostility, however, quashed the idea.

If the Republican following were to be increased in the South, Taft's attitude on that ever-recurrent and troublesome problem of the negro politician had to be made clear. My southern heritage made me sympathetic with the Southerner's attitude toward the negro, politically and socially. I was afraid Taft might get into difficulties about this but was reassured when he told me that he would not think of giving a negro any important political position in the South, although if Massachusetts wanted a negro postmaster, it could have one. I said I felt sure Massachusetts would not be insistent as to that.

Taft spent much of his time in Augusta weighing carefully the make-up of his Cabinet. He talked with me freely about the various possibilities and asked whether I would accept a secretaryship. I told him I preferred to serve him in an unofficial capacity.

It has often been alleged that Taft promised Roosevelt he would retain certain members of the old Cabinet. It is quite possible that Taft in his jovial and expansive way may have remarked at one of the last meetings under Roosevelt, "I hope you fellows will come along to help in the new job the President has picked for me." But I am certain from what Taft told me that he gave no specific promise to appoint any particular individual to a certain post, and that he acted in good faith. It was in the matter of these appointments that the difficulties began which made Taft's administration so stormy a one from the personal angle. I know that when he was first considering appointments he did not intend to make George von Lengerke Meyer secretary of the navy; he had already offered me that portfolio and I had declined it, though he had Meyer in mind for a Cabinet position as a favor to Senator Lodge, to whom he felt politically indebted.

Senator Henry Cabot Lodge had a personal interest in the appointment of Meyer, to eliminate him as a possible candidate for Congress against his son-in-law, Augustus P. Gardner, who came from the same Congressional district in Massachusetts. Lodge came to Augusta to see the President-elect and asked outright, "Are you intending to put Meyer in the Cabinet?"

Taft replied: "Yes, Senator. Roosevelt has already suggested it, and I myself shall be glad to have him there." He did what he thought politically wise in the Meyer appointment, but even in this case he believed Roosevelt had made a suggestion rather than a request.

Taft certainly did not regard himself bound in the matter of James R. Garfield, secretary of the interior. In January, 1909, Taft wrote Garfield that he could not retain him.

Though he did not want Garfield in his Cabinet, he was anxious to choose a secretary of the interior who would continue the conservationist policy so dear to Roosevelt's heart. Richard A. Ballinger, as head of the General Land Office, had rendered excellent service and seemed the logical man for the job.

Taft asked me to go to New York and convey personally the offer of appointment. I invited Ballinger to breakfast and explained my mission. He said he appreciated the compliment but regretted he could not accept the post because of his limited personal means. He added that he had promised his wife to give up government work and return to his law practice in Seattle.

I reported this decision to Taft.

"Well," Taft said, "I'll get Henry to see what he can do."

Henry W. Taft, his brother, a member of the law firm of Cadwalader, Wickersham, and Taft, was apparently able to summon more cogent arguments in the line of civic duty, and Ballinger succumbed.

In place of Luke E. Wright, secretary of war, Taft appointed Jacob M. Dickinson, of Tennessee, an ex-Confederate soldier and a Democratic railroad attorney. He was a man of fine character and proved himself loyal to the President. When trouble began between Roosevelt and Taft, Dickinson told me he felt he was rendering Taft a disservice by remaining in his Cabinet, since, as a Democrat and a Southerner, he could contribute no political influence. I promised to report his attitude to Taft, although I was sure Dickinson's reasons would have little weight. Dickinson was not to be shaken from his decision, however; shortly afterwards he resigned, and was replaced by Henry L. Stimson, an intimate friend of Roosevelt.

For the appointment of Chief Justice White, of Louisiana, another southern Democrat and a Catholic, Taft was severely criticized by Republican organizations throughout the country. He had a particular interest in this office, since it was the one which, above all others, he would have chosen for himself, and regarded White as best qualified for the position. He courageously refused to consider anyone else.

The conscientious discharge of what he regarded as his duty is further evidenced by his appointment of two other Southerners as associate justices of the Supreme Court: Horace H. Lurton, of Tennessee, in 1910, and Joseph R. Lamar, of Georgia, in 1911.

Although Taft knew I wanted to remain a private citizen, two months after his inauguration he announced my appointment as minister to China. The first intimation I had of the matter was through the newspapers. Taft immediately sent for me to come to Washington.

When I arrived he greeted me enthusiastically with the words: "Well, what do you think of the idea, Jack? I knew you didn't want to be ambassador to any European country, as you saw no opportunity to render conspicuous constructive service, but you can't say that about China. We need a man there who can deal with the problem of developing her natural resources and industries. You've had that type of experience in Russia and elsewhere. In my opinion you're just the man to be minister to China."

I insisted that I couldn't do it. I told him that I appreciated the honor, that I'd rather have that post than any other in his gift, but that I'd been out of my own country many years and didn't think I should take my family away again, especially as I had children ready for college.

Reluctant to take "No" for an answer, Taft sent for Philander C. Knox, his secretary of state. Knox also urged me earnestly to accept and finally asked me whether I was declining the post because it was not an embassy: "If that's the reason, we can take care of that. We'll make it an embassy."

I explained that I felt the foreign policy was dictated by the State Department, and the envoy was merely the intermediary—a glorified messenger boy.

"Well," retorted Knox, "you've heard of such things as 'cutting the cable.'"

"Yes," I replied, "but I'm declining on personal and no other grounds."

It was embarrassing for me to have to decline after the appointment had been made public, and I also feared that it might embarrass the administration even more. Taft advised me to state my reasons frankly to the press, and to explain that the appointment had been made without my knowledge.

That same afternoon, the President, Knox, and I were playing golf at the Chevy Chase Club. In a pause in the battle I asked Knox:

"Why don't you go to China this summer after Congress adjourns and take me with you? We could study the country at first hand. You'd have the distinction of being the first secretary of state who'd ever been to the Orient."

Knox drove far down the fairway. With his eyes still following the trajectory of the ball, he remarked complacently, "Hammond, I'm just learning to play this game, and I'm not going to let anything so unimportant as China interfere."

Taft appointed Charles R. Crane of Chicago. Crane was criticized for having cast aspersions at Japan while on his way to his post. Influenced probably by Huntington Wilson, the undersecretary who at the time was doing most of the work of the department, Knox first recalled Crane and then telegraphed the news to Taft who was in San Francisco.

Taft was much concerned about this and told me that a reprimand would have been sufficient punishment, but added: "Knox is in the saddle and that's his department. If I interfere he'll say, 'If you don't let me run my department the way I want to, I'll get out.' "

In high dudgeon Crane betook himself and his wealth to the opposing political camp where, through judicious campaign expenditures, he did much damage to his former political associates. Finally, in 1920, he reached port when Woodrow Wilson appointed him again minister to China. He served there with distinction and later in other diplomatic missions.

In 1909, at Taft's solicitation, I moved my family to Washington. My wife and I had for many years entertained the hope that after I retired from business Washington might be our home.

Before, during, and after Taft's term of office, our relations were those of pure friendship. In our many hours together we talked of all manner of things, naturally of state and business matters among them. He came to ask my advice, considered it competent, and I sought advice from him on many occasions. It was give-and-take, although he sometimes thought I was too eager to be "up and doing," while I felt that his judicial mind weighed matters too long. I was always extremely careful to avoid giving the impression that I possessed inside information or that I had any special influence over the President. It is difficult to explain an association of this sort without giving rise to misunderstanding. I know that Taft appreciated my efforts not to presume on our friendship, and it is my wish to avoid the appearance of it even in these pages. Our confidences were those of friends. He was one of the best-loved friends I ever had.

My visits to the White House had their lighter moments. I was at the executive office one day when the chairman of an important New York antisaloon society was announced.

As I started to leave, Taft said, "Don't go, Jack—I may need help."

A stern-faced lady appeared in the doorway. "Mr. President," she began, "I've made this trip from New York especially to express the admiration of the members of my society for your noble action in turning down your glass when you were offered wine."

A twinkle appeared in the President's eye. "Madam, if I am to speak honestly, I must admit I'm not entitled to any credit. I'm strongly in favor of temperance, but I'm a teetotaler only because my physician advises it. I've no objection to drinking wine. As a matter of fact, many of my intimate friends drink it. For example, Mr. Hammond here."

The lady gave me a look of disapprobation, rose, swished her skirt as women did in those days—and because of the revival of fashions in dress with the years they are now doing it again, as I observe—to express disapproval, and remarked witheringly as she stalked from the room, "I'm greatly disappointed to hear this about you, Mr. President."

In the next issue of her society's paper the President was arraigned as a backslider from grace.

Taft's great bulk was made the subject of caricature and jest. It was fortunate for him that he was not oversensitive on this subject, and could joke about it himself. He once told me, with his hearty chuckle, the story of his visit, while governor general of the Philippines, to the court of Czar Nicholas. As he and Mrs. Taft alighted from their carriage at the imperial palace, there was a loud ripping sound; the seam of his trousers had burst. There was no time to return to the hotel for a change of clothes. Mrs. Taft rose to the emergency; she borrowed needle and thread from a lady-in-waiting and hurriedly sewed up the rent. Fearful that her hasty stitches might not hold during the audience, Taft moved crabwise before the Czar and on leaving backed out of the room.

In spite of his size, Taft had an unusual air of dignity. He was a jovial man—a fat man if you will—but above all a most distinguished one. His laugh, his beaming smile, his optimism, and his kindliness became famous the world over, and unlike large men generally, he was careful of his attire. Often his love of people and his delight at being with them made him seem easygoing. He was rarely on time for appointments, not because he meant to be late, but because he found himself interested in whatever he was doing at the moment and unable to break away.

Taft has been criticized for having changed his views on important matters, but in each case that came under my observation he was amply justified. I have known him to go back on a promise made to friends from whom he had every reason to expect truth, but only when he discovered they had misrepresented the facts. He disliked saying "No" because he was essentially a man of kindly impulses, desirous of doing his friends favors when these were consistent with the public interest. Politicians soon found it useless to recommend a measure because of political expediency alone or because it might be helpful to Taft's own political fortunes. The interest of the country was uppermost in all his decisions.

As I have said before, his intellectual interests were basically judicial. He admired the jurist rather than the statesman. We once passed the statue of Chief Justice Marshall on Capitol Hill together.

Noticing that Taft glanced at it, I asked curiously, "Wouldn't you rather have been John Marshall than president?"

"Of course," he replied. "I'd rather have been Marshall than any other American, except perhaps Washington—and I'm inclined to think that I'd even rather have been Marshall than Washington."

CHAPTER TWENTY-SEVEN

Debates and Battles

*T*his chapter and the following are in no way intended as an apologia for Taft's presidential career; they are merely an explanation of his attitude, expressed to me on the debated issues of those four years.

In the first place, Taft has not always received informed acknowledgment for the constructive legislation passed during his administration. He did not dramatize nor spectacularize it as many presidents would have done, but its value has been increasingly evident. Later administrations have received credit for such measures as the federal budget and a national banking system, which he had recommended long before. He did not use publicity to cut short his enemies, but quietly pursued what he believed to be the business of being president, placing accomplishment in office ahead of ambition for re-election, and paying little attention to the fact that his deeds were being currently obscured by the sound and fury of his political opponents.

It is undoubtedly true that politicians of long experience were able to upset legislation and commit sabotage because of the unorthodox and unselfish way in which Taft conducted himself, but I believe this to be a devastating commentary on the fundamental condition of American government and not on the character of President Taft.

Many people considered that Taft would have become a second John Marshall had he given up his whole career to the bench. Some of his friends, partly misled by his own preference for the law, thought his going into politics was a mistake. In fact, the popular estimate of Taft as president is more or less confused with a conviction that he would have accomplished greater things as a jurist.

In 1908 the country did not need a fighting leader such as Roosevelt; it needed a president who would carry out the general program laid down by Roosevelt and promised in the party platform.

Unlike some presidents, Taft took the party platform promises seriously and used them as a legislative program. Among other things, he strengthened the Interstate Commerce law so that appeals could be taken from the commission to the Court of Commerce. He instituted the parcel post and postal savings bank systems, secured the passage of the income tax amendment, encouraged many bureaus for government scientific research and supervision, and urged a bill providing that campaign funds and their uses be made public.

Had there been any issue requiring direct action, I am sure Taft would have risen to meet it. Obviously, he did not carry a chip on his shoulder nor did he welcome controversy.

Naturally the first question confronting any president is the vexing problem of official appointments. Taft was, with his usual balanced timing, slow to make up his mind. With four or five names under consideration for a particular job, he would spend many days and still have come to no decision as to which candidate to appoint. He was as precise and as thorough in weighing a man's qualifications for office as he would have been in the courtroom in deciding on a question of life and death. While this was admirable, it was often irritating.

I used to tell him that he was wasting too much time in dealing with patronage. I asked him why he did not select one of these men, and, if he seemed all right, appoint him. What difference did it make if his recommendations were based on the selfish motives of the man's backers?—he might be good in spite of them. I added: "You can find out as much as you need to know about him in twenty-four hours. If you make casual appointments fast enough, the press will be kept busy reporting them instead of filling the pages with criticism of your selections. While this is going on, you can be making up your mind about the really important appointments. That's the way Roosevelt did."

On one occasion only did I interfere in Taft's political family. Charles D. Norton, who was then secretary to the President, had been assuming unusual authority and pretending to have a greater degree of influence over the administration than he actually possessed. In the presence of newspaper correspondents, at his summer White House at Beverly, Massachusetts, Taft had several times jocosely referred to Norton as "underpresident" and his "alter ego."

Norton was a Chicago businessman, whose fine appearance and ingratiating manners invariably created a favorable first impression. In time, however, everybody except the President began to see that Norton's practice of setting one person against another was seriously damaging Taft's prestige.

Various people, both representatives of the press and members of the Cabinet, asked me whether I would not protest against Taft's being misrepresented by Norton.

"You are closer to Taft than we are," some of the Cabinet urged, "and your position is a disinterested one. The President won't let us say a word against Norton."

I replied that I was sorry but didn't see how this concerned me at all, that I couldn't understand how they had allowed themselves to get into such a humiliating position. I asked them why they didn't write individually to the President and tell him that they would be forced to resign if he insisted on keeping Norton.

On thinking this matter over, I decided that anything which concerned Taft so intimately was my problem also. For Taft's own sake, such a situation must not be allowed to continue.

Accordingly, I went to the White House and found the President in the executive office. "Mr. President," I began, "I'm sure you'll recall that on the way to your office in the State, War and Navy

Building one day shortly before your nomination I pointed to the White House and asked, 'Bill, do you see that building? You'll soon be living there.' You replied that I was pretty optimistic. I asked you then to make me a promise. With all our admiration for President Roosevelt, we agreed that he often acted impulsively without seeking advice from his friends or without making sure information was not being kept from him. I asked you to promise me that, when you were in the White House, I should always have the privilege of telling you anything that concerned your welfare, however disagreeable it might be. You shook hands on that, didn't you? Now I've come to tell you about Norton."

Taft listened to me attentively. Then he said, "Thank you, Jack."

We shook hands and I left. Within a few days Norton handed in his resignation. Charles D. Hilles succeeded him.

Hilles never was afraid to tell the President what he thought about anything. He said to Taft once, "I'm going to resign unless you get rid of Postmaster General Hitchcock or get him under control."

Fortunately there was no need for Hilles to resign as he and others of us finally did succeed in curbing Hitchcock's pernicious political activity.

Almost at the beginning of his administration Taft had to make a choice as to which of the two elements in the Republican party could be persuaded to join him in helping to carry out Roosevelt's policies. On the one hand were the old standpat Republicans, to whom party allegiance was paramount. They were regimented under such leaders as Senator Nelson W. Aldrich, chairman of the Finance Committee, and "Joe" Cannon, speaker of the House. These men knew exactly how to go about securing the results they wanted, although their methods might not have been approved by reform elements.

Taft has often been accused of not knowing how to handle politicians and of not having political flexibility. His plans were thoroughly thought out before he launched them and he was not inclined hurriedly to readjust a program because of changing circumstances. His critics point to his association with Cannon and Aldrich, who during the last two years of Roosevelt's administration had bitterly opposed him. They claim that these "unscrupulous politicians" led Taft around by the nose. This is emphatically not true.

Actually he used them instead of being used by them, although the public was not generally aware of this. When Roosevelt's insurgent partisans later attacked Taft on these grounds, his defense was that an antagonized Cannon or Aldrich would have wrecked the legislative record of his administration.

Taft had come into office personally endorsed by Roosevelt and his political household. He believed he had a right to call upon them for aid, but they promptly deserted him.

He turned then to the leaders of the Old Guard. As he explained to me, "They were my enemies when they were Roosevelt's, but since his friends have deserted me, I've had to accept the help they brought me." He had no great personal friendship for either of them nor did he always approve of their methods. But his aim was progressive legislation, and he realized that they were the only instruments to serve his ends.

Aldrich was an artist in steering legislation. He knew exactly how many Senate votes he could count upon. If an additional one was needed, he would hold out bait to Congressional ambitions. The promise of a desirable committee position or even such a trivial thing as the bestowal of a larger office in a better wing of a government building often proved irresistible.

Aldrich never spoke much in the Senate. It never disturbed him when Robert M. La Follette, of Wisconsin, the archrebel of the party, thundered for hours against the System (referring to Wall Street affiliation), the tariff, or predatory wealth. Aldrich, Brandegee, and their followers, confident of results, would meanwhile be pleasantly lunching in another room. When the time was ripe, Aldrich was certain that his cohorts would go into action and deliver the votes. This method of procedure gained him his reputation for political cynicism.

Far less in numbers but headed by the redoubtable La Follette, and including Dolliver, the veteran, experienced Cummins, and the oratorical Beveridge, the radical Republican movement was monthly gaining strength.

I used to divide these insurgents into four classes. First came the Simon-pure socialistic element, masquerading as Republicans. To these the Democrats were welcome.

THE TAFT FAMILY AND MYSELF

PORFIRIO DIAZ (1830-1915)

Second were the unintelligent intellectuals, the theorists without any practical knowledge of governmental affairs.

Third came the unctuous rectitudists, the reformers, and the fanatics concerning whom I thought no statement could be more apt than that often quoted by Arthur T. Hadley from one of the old philosophers, "Virtue is more dangerous than vice because the excesses of virtue are not subject to the restraints of conscience." In this latter class belonged what Roosevelt himself termed the "lunatic fringe." Its members had the same high ideals and the same casuistic belief that the end justified any means which had inspired the extreme abolitionists of the 1850s and 1860s and the prohibitionists of the 1920s.

The fourth insurgent class was the sane Progressive element. Many of these Progressives remained my friends, although I have always regarded their desertion of Taft as a betrayal of the party and responsible for Taft's failure to secure a second term.

In 1910 the Progressives still stood for control of the Republican party from within by public-spirited and patriotic members. This meant the reduction of power of the old-line machine politicians. It was increasingly apparent that there was danger of a split in the Republican ranks as the Progressives as well as the Democrats gained ground in 1910, although the insurgent Republicans at that time were not advocating extreme and impractical measures. These men, however, were to be the Bull Moosers of 1912.

The Republican party platform inherited from Roosevelt had specifically promised a downward revision in the tariff. Roosevelt carefully sidestepped this dangerous issue during his administration, leaving the Dingley Tariff, passed under McKinley in 1897, still in force.

The purpose behind introducing a new bill was twofold. In the first place, the Dingley Tariff had not produced enough revenue to run the government; in the second place, it was felt at the time that the tariff rate should provide for the protection of home industry by equalizing the difference between the lower cost of production abroad and that in the United States. It was believed that by inserting a maximum and minimum clause it would be possible, within limits, to adjust tariff rates, irrespective of production cost or discriminatory legislation in foreign countries.

Almost immediately after Taft's inauguration he called a special session of Congress to revise the tariff, and Sereno E. Payne, chairman of the Ways and Means Committee of the House, introduced a tariff bill. Taft realized as well as Speaker Cannon did that "no matter how great an improvement the new tariff may be, it almost always results in the party in power losing the election."

Hearings were held at which Andrew Carnegie and other industrialists testified that no higher tariff rates were necessary to equalize American and European costs of production. This applied to but a few industries. Both Senate and House bills were then sent to the Senate Finance Committee over which Aldrich presided. Without his approval no tariff measure had any hope of success. The Senate Committee promptly made certain articles on the free list once more dutiable, raised rates which had been reduced, and generally restored the reactionary features to the tariff bill. Aldrich approved these amendments, with reservations. Against the vociferous but futile objections of the insurgents, this machine-made bill was pushed through the House and the Senate.

Up to this time no vocal dissent had come from the country at large. Taft, according to his theory that the President should not steer bills through the legislature, waited until the act had gone to conference. He did not approve of many features of the bill, particularly the famous Schedule K on woolens. He believed, however, that the Payne-Aldrich bill was preferable to the Dingley bill, which had become an anomaly. The new measure at least established a Tariff Board to keep track of the relative costs of production and to recommend necessary changes in rates. Taft also approved of the free trade provision for the Philippines. In fact, he believed this bill might break the ground for the general downward trend in rates to which he had on many occasions committed himself. This was at the time when considerable objection was urged against a high tariff because of the high cost of living—sometimes humorously referred to as the cost of high living—a subject much agitated at the time.

Unfortunately for the administration, the self-seeking manner in which sectional and industrial interests had lobbied for rates had aroused the ire of the four able, honest, but radical midwestern Republican leaders.

Taft was perplexed as to what course to pursue. One Sunday in Beverly, a few days before signing the bill, he talked the whole matter over with me. He admitted his dissatisfaction with the bill as it stood.

He summed it up by saying: "I can veto this tariff bill as Cleveland did the one presented to him. Perhaps such an action would make me popular with the country, as it did Cleveland, but it would mean a hostile Congress for the rest of my term. Furthermore, if I should send a veto message, the confidence of the country, which is just recovering from the panic of two years ago, would probably get a setback. More important still, perhaps, is the deficit of $100,-000,000 which can best be made up by the revenue features in the new bill. The Tariff Board and the minimum and maximum features will allow us to make adjustments."

Believing the benefits of the bill outweighed its disadvantages, Taft signed it, but sent a message to Congress explaining his action and criticizing certain of its phases. Nevertheless, the public inveighed loudly against the bill; in its mind Taft had become *particeps criminis*.

The tide of insurgency in the Republican party was steadily mounting, particularly in the West. Some of us who were close to the President believed that if Taft had an opportunity to explain to the Westerners the eventual benefit to be derived from his policies, they would be less likely to block the progress of his legislative plans. To accomplish this it was proposed in 1909 that Taft take a trip through the West.

Taft's friends urged that a bill to give the President a traveling allowance should at once be put through Congress. Political enemies opposed this, basing their arguments partly on the waste of public money and partly on the waste of the Executive's time in what they regarded as a partisan junket. Some of the President's friends suggested that, if Congress would not make this appropriation, they would supply the necessary funds, and that courtesies would certainly be extended by the railroads as they had been in other administrations. But Taft resolutely refused to consider the trip unless Congress would pay every penny of the expenses.

To create support for this measure at Washington, without Taft's knowledge some of us arranged for a concerted demand from clubs, chambers of commerce, and newspapers in the West. Their enthusiasm was so effectual that criticism was stifled and the bill passed.

The President set out on his trip. Among the first stops was Winona, Minnesota, which became famous as the scene of Taft's classic but unintentional blunder on the tariff. His habit was to write his speeches just before delivery, and he rarely read them over. There was little time for composition on the train and, when he reached Winona, he carelessly asserted in his speech that the Payne-Aldrich bill was "the best tariff law the Republicans ever made, and therefore the best the country ever had." Unfortunately, he made this blanket endorsement without forcibly referring to his reservations made to Congress at the time he signed the bill.

Taft realized almost immediately that he had made a definite mistake. I am sure he meant only to say briefly what he had already said to me—that it was the best tariff bill that could be passed at the time.

This speech, coupled with Taft's signing of the tariff act, brought the insurgents in full cry against him.

A few days later, when I saw Major Archibald W. Butt, the President's military aide, who had served in the same capacity in the Roosevelt administration, he greeted me with the remark: "It's too bad you weren't with him. He bubbled all over and has done himself great harm."

Business engagements in California had prevented my accompanying the presidential party on the first part of the trip. Since I was to be in the West, Taft had asked me to see Gifford Pinchot in Los Angeles and try to induce him not to resign as chief forester. Pinchot had tendered his resignation as the result of his disapproval of Ballinger.

The conservation issue and the Pinchot-Ballinger fight gave another ground for attack on the administration by the insurgents. People whose memories reach back to Roosevelt have not forgotten the wave of discussion that swelled in those years over the phrase Conservation of Natural Resources.

The whole matter was exceedingly involved but the main facts were as follows:

Timber, coal, and oil were being rapidly used up; the alarming picture of a starving and shivering population at a time not far distant began to possess the imagination. That there was gross waste in the exploitation of natural resources was a fact, and that America should pause to take stock of the situation was necessary.

Theodore Roosevelt wisely saw the need and acted with decision and energy. Recognizing the professional interest that a mining man has in this subject, he appointed me in 1905 to serve on a committee to suggest revisions in mining law. One of our recommendations at that time was for the leasing, not the sale, of public lands for coal mining. On March 24, 1906, as president of the American Institute of Mining Engineers, I attended a joint meeting of the engineering societies where the subject for discussion was Conservation.

Later, in May, 1908, President Roosevelt called a congress of the governors of the various states and territories to meet at the White House to discuss the whole question of conservation. I represented the mining engineers; in my address I explained the "professional" view: avoid waste and concentrate on utilization.

In June, President Roosevelt appointed me a member of a federal commission, the formation of which had been recommended by the governors. That my own view was consonant with his may be seen by these words from his letter to me:

> Our object is to conserve the foundations of our prosperity. We intend to use these resources; but so use them as to conserve them. No effort should be made to limit the wise and proper development and application of these resources; every effort should be made to prevent destruction, to reduce waste, and to distribute the enjoyment of our natural wealth in such a way as to promote the greatest good of the greatest number for the longest time. . . . There is no break between the interests of State and Nation; these interests are essentially

one. Hearty cooperation between the state and the national agencies is essential to the permanent welfare of the people. You on behalf of the Federal Government will do your part to bring about cooperation.

Another White House meeting was called for January 19, 1909, and on January 18th I gave a dinner at my house to the governors attending the White House meeting. At this point in the history of conservation it should be noticed that the views of Roosevelt were moderate enough to gain the co-operation of the states.

Unfortunately, his secretary of the interior, James R. Garfield, and his chief forester, Gifford Pinchot, waxed overenthusiastic. They came very near taking the position that natural resources were a trust to be held solely for the benefit of future generations, and were not to be enjoyed in full measure by those now living. It was an exaggerated and a sentimental view, but it exactly suited the crusading and capricious spirit of my friend Pinchot.

On the order of Roosevelt many million acres of public land in the West were withdrawn from private development.

All the western states protested against what they considered eastern dictation. Sentiment grew so warm that, at a congress called at St. Paul in 1911, western voters and western governors insisted that their states should have control of the resources within their own borders. They were willing to conserve, but they wanted to conserve for their own citizens and in whatever manner seemed best to them.

Apart from this sectional quarrel, there was a sound objection on economic grounds to the closure of public lands. Individuals and corporations who already owned forests, mines, and water-power sites, it was alleged, were thus given an unfair advantage in protecting them from increasing competition, and so assuring them of larger profits.

My own viewpoint on conservation was neither prejudiced in regard to my personal holdings nor discolored by sentimental preconceptions. The engineer is interested in improving processes of recovering metals from mined ores, and in utilizing to a greater degree the energy stored up in coal and oil.

The mine owner complained of the Sherman Anti-Trust Law because it compelled competition. He was often forced to take out of his property only what could be recovered at low cost. This was called gutting the mine. Also, competition in mining led to overproduction. I was opposed to the drawing of leases that forced the lessee into speedy, incomplete, and uneconomical exploitation. In the development of oil fields I opposed the waste of natural gas. So far as concerned public welfare, the major political aspect of the conservation debate, I favored the intelligent utilization of natural resources when needed by the present or any other generation.

The conservationists were then greatly alarmed by the predictions of oil geologists that the fields would be depleted within a very few years. Since that time geological surveys have led to the discovery of other great oil-producing areas, whose subsequent exploitation has resulted in an embarrassment of riches. The present effort of the oil industry is to limit production, not through fear of the depletion of oil reserves in the near future, but because overproduction has forced oil companies to operate on too low a margin of profit.

As I have described in the preceding chapter, Taft appointed Richard A. Ballinger as secretary of the interior to succeed Garfield. Because Pinchot believed that Ballinger was not carrying out Roosevelt's original program, he considered this appointment as treachery to Roosevelt.

After Ballinger had been in office only a few months one of his subordinates, Louis R. Glavis, was egged on by Pinchot to accuse him of dishonesty in the disposition of Alaska coal lands. Taft asked Ballinger for an explanation, received it, and decided the accusation was groundless. The moment the accuser was dismissed from the service, Pinchot sent in his resignation as chief of the Forestry Bureau. Taft wrote Pinchot a friendly and conciliatory letter: he said that he had personally gone over all the evidence against Ballinger, and that as a lawyer he thought himself better qualified than Pinchot to determine the validity of the charges. His examination of the evidence had led him to exonerate Ballinger. In conclusion he asked Pinchot to withdraw his resignation.

Pinchot had been fishing at Catalina Island. At Taft's request I arranged to meet him at Los Angeles immediately upon his return and forestall any newspaper interviews he might be indiscreet enough to give out.

I asked Pinchot whether he had received Taft's letter. He replied, "It was one of the finest letters one friend could write to another." He appreciated Taft's friendliness, but persisted in his intention to resign. I then persuaded him to go with me to Salt Lake City, where I was to join the Taft party the following day. Pinchot and Taft discussed the matter, but failed to come to an agreement.

Shortly after this Pinchot renewed his public charges against Ballinger, and these led to a senatorial investigation. Though Ballinger was acquitted by the Republican majority in Congress, the Democratic minority were supported by the insurgents in the insistence on his guilt. Ballinger found his usefulness seriously impaired by these attacks and a few months later resigned and went back to the practice of law.

Ballinger's enemies whispered that he had made many thousands of dollars out of his public office, but that accusation I know to be false. Through some of my personal friends who were intimately acquainted with his financial standing, I subsequently learned that he was practically without funds when he left Washington.

I had no reason to feel friendly towards Ballinger. At that time I was interested in an important hydroelectric development in the West which brought me in contact with the Department of the Interior. In the belief that I ought not to be the recipient of favors from an administration in which the President was known to be my personal friend, I did not press my legal claim for permits from the department, and Ballinger on his part did not issue them.

After Ballinger had resigned I explained to him that his timidity and fear of criticism had kept him from doing his full duty towards me. My claims had been approved in principle by his predecessor Garfield and would undoubtedly have been granted had Garfield remained in office.

As for the accusation heard in some quarters that I was interested in the Alaska coal lands for the Guggenheims, that was utterly false. I was no longer connected with the Guggenheims. Furthermore, I had gone on record as urging the withdrawal of the Alaska coal lands from entry. Besides that, I had advocated the construction of railways and their control by the federal government to prevent any possibility of monopolies in the development of the resources of Alaska.

After I joined Taft at Salt Lake City, I accompanied him for the rest of his trip through Utah, Montana, Idaho, Washington, Oregon, California, Arizona, New Mexico, and Texas. Although he had been abroad a number of times, in Europe, the Orient, and the Philippines, Taft had a limited knowledge of the industrial development of the Far West.

In many ways it was a difficult trip, but Taft never lost his good-nature. One of the things not generally realized about Taft—again because of the popular feeling that so large and jovial a man is inclined to be lazy—is that he had an extraordinary ability to work long hours at a stretch in order to finish a task. His power of concentration and of excluding the nonessentials was almost unique. In this way he burned up an enormous amount of energy. One interesting sidelight on this was his need to compensate by taking unusual amounts of food and sleep. I have seen him eat inordinately without any self-consciousness. I have seen him often fall quietly asleep in the midst of a conversation with his friends, not because of lethargy or overeating but because of the fact that he had been concentrating for as much as fifty continuous hours on a given piece of work. On our trip he was often required to stay up until very late to speak from the rear platform of the train to groups assembled to see the President; or, he had to get up at an unconscionable hour in the morning. In these circumstances most people are in a go-to-hell mood; not Taft. He would come into my compartment, which was next to his, and say, "Jack, how are you feeling this morning?" He would then consume his breakfast and start cheerfully on the day's round of speeches and sightseeing.

Particularly on this trip it was an effort to keep Taft running to schedule. First the politicians would have him speak, and then the real estate men would drive us miles and miles over dusty roads through arid country, just to be able to say that the President had been there. Often after such a wild-goose chase I returned in a state of extreme annoyance, but Taft never said an irritable word; he had the greater capacity for swallowing dust.

At Butte, I was able to show Taft something of the copper mining industry. With his usual sense of humor, he expressed himself as doubtful whether the shaft of the Anaconda mine would be big enough to accommodate him, but I assured him that it was sixteen feet square and I thought we could manage to squeeze him through safely. We packed him into the cage. When we reached the bottom of the mine, I showed him how levels were run and timbered and how the drilling machines cut into the solid rock inch by inch.

Taft had never been in a mine before. He was genuinely interested in observing how mining operations were conducted. I did not try to take him over the thousand miles of underground workings, but I did regale him with what I considered astonishing, though accurate, statistics.

His comment at the end of the trip was that of most individuals: "I had no idea what it meant to get the copper out. I had a vague notion that it could be picked up from the ground. Why, it takes tons of rocks to get a few pounds of copper!"

As a matter of fact, the total metal production to January 1, 1934, of the Anaconda Copper Mining Company, including copper, zinc, lead, silver, and gold, had a value of $2,180,000,000, extracted from 150,000,000 tons of ore. To extract this ore, shafts, levels, raises, and stoping were made to an aggregate length of thirty-three hundred miles, or more than the distance across the continent.

A few years after Taft's visit, the agricultural interests for forty miles around Butte banded together to secure an injunction forcing the company to shut down. They complained that the arsenical and sulphuric fumes were killing all vegetation in that huge area. The company was unable to deny the justice of the accusation, but asked for time in which to make remedial experiments, stating that a complete shutdown would entail hardship for many people.

Remembering his visit to Butte and recognizing that thousands depended for their livelihood on this industry, Taft accepted the suggestion of Attorney General Wickersham and appointed a Fumes Commission to make investigations while the company continued operating. Dr. Louis D. Ricketts represented the Anaconda Mining Company, which eventually paid out hundreds of thousands of dollars in a sincere endeavor to solve the problem. Dr. J. A. Holmes represented the government. When these men asked me to act as chairman of the commission, I was glad to serve for the benefit of the industry.

We employed specialists to carry out the experiments. Among them was Dr. Frederick G. Cottrell, who added greatly to his reputation as a chemist by the success of his experiments, which minimized damage from fumes and became the basis for solving similar problems in other smelting centers.

The functions we performed for the Anaconda Company have since been taken over by the Bureau of Mines. There had been much talk of such a bureau, but nothing had been done about it. The attendant clamor over the conservation movement, however, helped to pass the measure through Congress. In discussing the formation of this bureau, Taft asked me whom I would recommend for the post of director. My first suggestion was the labor leader, John Mitchell, who said he could not accept because of his connection with the unions. I then recommended Dr. Holmes, and Taft appointed him.

The duties of the Bureau of Mines now include the treatment of difficult ores, the disposal of by-products, and the development of safety devices for coal mines.

Incidentally, although I did no selfish lobbying, I have not hesitated to use what influence I possessed in behalf of adequate financial appropriations for scientific bureaus, such as the Smithsonian Institution, the Geodetic Survey, the Geological Survey, and the Bureau of Standards.

In May, 1910, I suggested to the President a Department of Public Works, to control the operation of the Panama Canal, the reclamation of swamps and the irrigation of arid lands, the protection of power sites on public waterways, the administration of the Forestry Bureau, and similar projects. My idea was that this department should have charge of the active work of the government in connection with the natural resources of the country, direct all the government's construction and engineering undertakings, and carry out the conservation policy. Taft was interested, but not overenthusiastic. The plan was opposed by Secretary of the Interior Ballinger, and nothing ever came of it. I still believe this to be a legitimate division of executive control and I hope that something will be done about it. Such a department would be of great service in solving problems incidental to the present period of depression.

In Spokane the President made a great speech on conservation; in my opinion, a better exposition of the subject than any Roosevelt ever made. Taft kept strictly to the problem, showed plainly that he knew what he was talking about, and had not been led to his conclusions by a burst of temporary enthusiasm. The President gave all credit to Roosevelt for the initiation of the policy and put himself squarely on record in favor of conservation.

At Phoenix, Arizona, Taft was offered a drink of water from the nearby Hassayampo River. I tipped him off to the legend that he who drinks of the water of this river can never afterwards tell the truth. But he took the risk. There is in Los Angeles a club of several thousand members, known as the Hassayampo Club, which exploits the legend by using the river water for initiating its members. The club members' high standing for probity in the community, however, would seem to disprove the claim of the potency of the water.

At Albuquerque, New Mexico, there was a reception followed by the usual round of oratory. Among the first speakers on the program was Albert B. Fall, prominently introduced as the "senator from New Mexico" should it be granted statehood. The problem of the moment was the proposed statehood of Arizona and New Mexico. Fall began his speech by saying that everybody had heard about the promises presidents were inclined to make on the spot, but he advised the audience not to bank too heavily upon them. When the President returned to Washington he would probably feel differently about the matter.

The audience was hushed with dismay at this open insult. Taft would have been perfectly justified in taking Fall's action as an affront. Instead, he smilingly said he was reminded of the story of an officious young attorney who attempted to lay down the law to the judge. The exposition was so poor that, instead of helping, it endangered his client's case. When the lawyer finished, the judge said, "In spite of your argument, I decide the case in favor of your client." Then Taft went on to state that Fall's injudicious comments had not prejudiced him against the statehood bill; he was still in favor of it and, indeed, shortly afterwards signed the bill.

Before the presidential party arrived in Texas, it had been arranged that the President of Mexico should meet the President of the United States at El Paso. Diaz, then in his seventy-ninth year, made the long journey from Mexico City to the border. For the first time in history the chief magistrates of the two republics were brought face to face.

Unusual care had to be taken to prevent an attempt on the life of either president. Each man had his special secret service and military guard, and the police of El Paso and Juarez had been given special instructions, but further precautions were thought necessary. Major Burnham, my old friend of South African days, at my request had preceded the President's party and organized a number of experienced men who had been his associates in past years—scouts, cattlemen, and customs guards—to help protect the presidents. He had them sworn in as peace officers.

Along the line of march a census was taken of the residents and occupants of every building that faced the route. This area was divided into sections each of which was put under the command of armed deputies. The people in each section were ordered to close and lock all their doors one hour before the procession. Other deputies, stationed in the rear, were ordered to halt anyone trying to enter or leave. As the procession started and the two presidents rode between the crowded lines of people, a space was constantly cleared on both sides, front and rear, so that it would be difficult to make any attempt at assassination with either bombs or firearms.

The peace officers were instructed to keep their eyes constantly on the crowd rather than on the presidents. There was little danger to be apprehended from those who were smiling or chatting with other people. But, if any deputy caught sight of a drawn and set face, he would signal to the next officer, at the same time quietly edging over beside the suspect. While one deputy would engage the man in conversation, and slip his elbow over his arm, the other officer would quickly run his hands over him for weapons, guns, or packages. Many times the suspect never realized he had been one. Over one hundred weapons were gathered in this way, although none of them may have been intended for purposes of assassination. During the day there was but one fatality: a young Mexican boy drove his knife into the heart of another because his view of the Great Diaz was obstructed.

Major Burnham later told me the details of the elaborate care taken, and there is one curious incident which I shall relate. As Burnham was standing near the entrance of the hotel into which the presidents were about to enter, he saw a sinister-looking man writing in a notebook. He gave the secret signal to another deputy, and they closed in. The deputy slipped his arm through the arm of the suspect and at the same moment Burnham grasped his wrist. Quickly flipping over the busy scribbler's hand, Burnham discovered that the pencil sticking out between the first and second fingers was actually the muzzle of a pistol especially designed to be hidden in the palm of the hand.

Although the man with the gun declared he was a newspaper reporter, he was obliged to finish his story in jail.

The meeting of the two presidents had particular political significance. Trouble was already brewing below the Mexican border. If Taft had been killed on Mexican soil, it would have stirred up a tremendous feeling of bitterness in the United States. If Diaz had been killed on American soil, all of Mexico would have been inflamed. Even if the bullet had been fired by one of their own countrymen the people would have been suspicious and infuriated. There were many revolutionists who would gladly have made an attempt on the life of one or other of the presidents.

Taft and Diaz, with their escorts, met in the middle of the bridge over the Rio Grande. After exchanging courtesies, they drove together through the streets of El Paso. In the afternoon Taft returned the visit. Secretary Knox, Archie Butt, and I accompanied him to Juarez to call on the great dictator. When Taft was taking his leave, Diaz asked me to stay and have a chat with him; he assured Taft that I would be conducted back safely.

This was my last meeting with the Eagle of Mexico. His hair was now white, closely cropped, and as in his earlier days, brushed straight up on his well-shaped head. His eyes were still dark, unblinking yet not unkind, bright and full of spirit.

I told him how delighted I was to see him looking so well. He replied that his health was still good, but nothing could alter the fact that he was growing old and rapidly approaching the point where he would lose the grip on affairs that he had maintained so long. He was desperately worried about conditions in Mexico and felt unable to cope with them.

"Mr. Hammond, I should like so much to be able to resign and travel through your great country before I die. However, it seems impossible. I thought I had prepared for my retirement by selecting Ramon Corral as vice-president and my successor, but he is not popular with the people.

"My friends have begged me," he continued, "not to give up office at present. Since I am responsible for the investment of hundreds of millions of dollars of foreign capital in my country, I feel that I must remain at my post until I can secure a competent successor. My chief trouble today is from men whom I have established as governors and other high officials. I am afraid they are taking advantage of the fact that I am too old to get about and ascertain for myself just what they are doing."

After a pleasant hour of informal conversation, he sent me back to El Paso in his own carriage.

The same evening Diaz entertained President Taft's party with an elaborate banquet at Juarez, served on massive old silver plate brought from Mexico City.

After the banquet we returned to our train. Exhausted by the nervous strain of worrying over the safety of two presidents, Archie Butt and I settled into our seats. Like Diaz, Taft had gone through the ceremonies with complete unconcern. He now commented: "You and Archie seem to have been jumpy all day, Jack. What's the trouble? Perhaps a highball would steady you."

Before answering, we gulped down the offered highballs. With a sigh of relief, I then said: "Thank God we're out of Mexico and the day's over. We've been half crazy for fear somebody'd take a shot at you."

"Oh," Taft replied, "is that what's been bothering you? Why should you have worried about that? If anyone wanted to get me, he couldn't very well have missed such an easy target."

CHAPTER TWENTY-EIGHT

Diaz-Taft

WHAT DIAZ DID FOR MEXICO—THE DICTATOR'S
DOWNFALL—WILSON'S VIEW OF THE MEXICAN
PROBLEM—CANADIAN RECIPROCITY—THE PANAMA
CANAL TOLL BILL—BANKING REFORM—TRUST
BUSTING—THE RIFT BETWEEN TAFT AND ROOSE-
VELT—THE POLITIC THING TO DO—A CONVENTION
OR A RIOT?—BIRTH OF THE BULL MOOSE—THE
GRAND OLD PARTY GOES DOWN TO DEFEAT—
TAFT'S NOBLE CAREER AS CHIEF JUSTICE

*T*he Mexican situation was most troublesome to Taft. Almost against his will, he was forced to take cognizance of it. His heart was set on other matters. Canadian reciprocity; banking reforms; the just and wise program he had hoped to carry out to improve domestic affairs were his most immediate concerns. The accumulating danger of trouble on our southern border could not be ignored, however. Mexico was both unstable in character and uncertain in government as my own experience in that country had vividly demonstrated.

Diaz once said to me, "If I could only impress on my people the value of time—as you say in your country, 'time is money'—the development of Mexico would proceed with unparalleled strides."

His critics have said that Diaz mistook the tangible wealth of the country for its welfare, and that its prosperity was one-sided and confined to a small part of the population. Diaz himself recognized this, and was troubled by it, but the fault was not entirely his. Not much improvement in material conditions can be possible so long as the character of the people is what it is.

Industrialism came as a great shock to Mexico. The mestizos and the pure Indians are not conditioned for the exacting demands of modern civilization. They live slowly. The sort of work that Cecil Rhodes drove through in Africa is entirely outside their comprehension, and any dictator who drives them invariably alienates himself from his people. Probably more than any other people in the world they believe that what was good enough for their grandfathers is good enough for them. Even Calles, years later, in his fight to end peonage and to raise his people from actual starvation was able to accomplish little because of the tremendous inertia of chronic racial weaknesses.

Diaz's accomplishment, in spite of three centuries of misrule, was extraordinary, and in my opinion stands without parallel in modern times. Praise is due also to the genius of his finance minister, José Yves Limantour, who, laboring under great difficulties, put the currency on a sound basis and found funds to finance the great projects of the president.

Diaz by main force dragged his people from the darkness of oppression and drew them towards progress. Some idea of the magnitude of his achievements may be gained from the following facts:

Before his presidency there were scarcely any railroads or telegraph lines; one of his first acts was to build thousands of miles of railroads and a network of telegraph lines. There was neither order nor due process of law anywhere and bandits swarmed unrestrained over the countryside. He set up courts of justice and enforced their decrees with inflexible honesty. He formed the rurales, a military police force which cleared the country of highwaymen and public malefactors of every sort. He opened ports, instituted a postal system, built schools, encouraged manufactures, established banks, introduced modern agriculture and industrial methods, patronized the fine arts, supported the professions, and won world-wide confidence in the integrity and good faith of his government. Above all, he fostered trade and commerce by inviting foreign capital to invest in Mexico's great mineral, oil, and agrarian resources.

When he became president in 1877, the country was bankrupt. He left it solvent, with a large reserve, nor did he squeeze this surplus out of the peons as is often supposed. It came directly from the profits derived from foreign investors, and the peons, an incompetent class in the history of Mexico, have never been so well off as under his intelligent and farseeing dictatorship. He made Mexico respected among nations.

With all his accomplishments, however, Diaz overlooked the necessity for the organization and encouragement of liberal groups in politics. Always aware of the general ignorance and excitable temperament of his countrymen, ninety per cent of whom were illiterate, he had felt obliged to suppress all criticism of his government with an iron hand.

As time went on, and the dictator became wholly absorbed in his great schemes for the development of Mexico, his early attitude toward liberal thinkers crystallized into unconscious opposition. He was essentially a man of action; an executive, not a doctrinaire. Like his favorite hero, Bismarck, he had little time or inclination for political philosophy. As a consequence, he came to lean more and more upon the cientificos, or wealthy business men, and to lose contact with the mass of the people.

These cientificos were advocates of modern methods in industry and business. A controlling proportion of them did not, however, apply this scientific progressivism to the government itself. Their attitude towards their own country was in many cases almost entirely self-seeking. The members of this corrupt faction used their influence to bribe officials and to obtain concessions by other dishonest means. In time, they succeeded in completely undermining the morale of the domestic administration Diaz had so carefully built up. Government patronage became the chief source of their prosperity; by a widespread system of interlocking directorates these moneyed men, who should have been the first to lend their support to the government, soon came to exert a sinister influence which in the end brought about its downfall and their own as well.

Diaz eventually realized the harmful nature of this unprincipled element, but it was too late.

In 1911 revolution broke out. The various elements of political thought, which for years had been undergoing a process of fermentation, had united under Francisco I. Madero, a sincere idealist, who was resolved to shake off the grip of the capitalistic government.

The dictator, old, infirm, and entirely out of touch with public sentiment, could not this time suppress a movement which, while ill-advised, represented a genuine conviction on the part of many of the younger generation that Mexico was being mismanaged. Early in his administration he had seen to it that trusted subordinates had been made governors of the various states. These men had been pledged to carry out his policies and to keep him informed. They did neither of these things.

When the revolutionists broke out of Durango and Chihuahua in the north into the more populous south, Diaz vainly endeavored to conciliate them by passing the government on to a successor in orderly fashion. But the Maderistas would have none of this, and on May 11, 1911, he was obliged to lay down unconditionally the power he had held so long.

Though recognizing his defeat, Diaz retained his old courage. When he was being escorted out of the country, his car was held up temporarily on the way to Vera Cruz and a mob of his political enemies threatened his life. It was with the greatest difficulty that this man of eighty-one could be restrained by his friends. Single-handed he wanted to tackle the crowd who were hurling insults at him. No one not conscious of his own rectitude would have dared this.

True to his sterling integrity and honesty, Diaz left office without having laid by a competency for a rainy day. However corrupt his underlings may have been, he himself will always be free of the accusation of graft. He did not run off with the contents of the treasury, as has been the recognized habit of deposed Latin-American presidents. Secretary of State Lansing, who married the daughter of John W. Foster, former minister to Mexico, assured me that the State Department had made a careful examination of Mexican finances and was convinced that the treasury had not been looted; on the contrary, it contained a surplus when Diaz left.

For the four remaining years of Diaz's life, he was supported in Paris largely by the contributions of friends. He died in 1915 at the age of eighty-five. His last words were, "My poor Mexico."

The Mexican revolution of 1911 placed Taft in a difficult position. The lives of many Americans were likely to be endangered by civil war. Furthermore, American citizens had been killed by Mexican bullets fired from across the border, and consequently in the United States a clamor for intervention had already arisen. Taft stated that he did not feel called upon to intervene, but as a precaution ordered the mobilization of twenty thousand troops to guard the Texan border.

His recognition of Madero as constitutional president did not bring peace in Mexico. Madero was impractical and weak and could not control his military leaders. When they began fighting among themselves, Taft put an embargo on the shipment of arms and munitions to Mexico in an effort to deprive them of the means for shedding blood.

In March, 1911, a commercial and industrial congress of the South was celebrated at Atlanta. Taft and Woodrow Wilson, then governor of New Jersey, were there. Incidentally, and with prophetic vision unsuspected by himself, Taft in his speech referred pleasantly to Wilson as the next president.

I returned to Washington on the train with Governor Wilson. We spent the early part of the evening in the drawing room occupied by my wife and myself. I always found Wilson personally charming, and this evening proved no exception. After a pleasant chat he asked to see me alone, saying he wished to discuss with me the President's policy in Mexico, with which he did not agree. We adjourned to the club car.

"In what respect," I inquired, "do you disagree with the President?"

"I think he is making a great mistake in sending troops to the border. What concern is it of ours what Mexico does about her internal affairs?"

"But suppose the President has certain information which you have not? For instance, there may be serious trouble down there in which American lives will be endangered, as well as the lives of foreigners who, under the implication of the Monroe Doctrine, look to the United States for protection. Shouldn't the President be prepared for such a contingency?"

"Now that you've explained it," admitted Wilson, "I can see how the presence of troops might be necessary, but—"

"Then what would you have done in his place?" I asked.

"I would have moved troops in secret, not to the border, but to points within striking distance," replied Wilson.

"But how could that be done without the Mexicans' knowledge? Secrecy would defeat your purpose by giving Mexico ground for suspicion about our intentions. Taft has sent troops openly to protect Americans at the border."

Wilson must have been troubled by the Mexican problem during the night, because he awakened the other passengers with an unearthly Princeton yell. His discussion with a Yale man might have been partly responsible.

Next morning I breakfasted at the White House—Taft had returned by special train—and related my conversation with Wison.

Taft gave the well-known chuckle and said, "I wish he had the Mexican problem on his hands."

Two years later Wilson inherited it.

February 18, 1913, Victoriano Huerta overthrew the Madero government.

A few days before the inauguration of Wilson I gave a dinner to a number of foreign ambassadors in honor of Sir Cecil Spring-Rice at my home in Washington. There were present Bakhmetiev, Jusserand, Bernstorff, Cusani, and Dumba. They had an enjoyable time together, recalling their early friendships as young secretaries in the various embassies of Europe, and addressing each other familiarly as Springy, Baky, Bernie, and Cusi.

Toward the end of the evening the conversation turned to Mexico, and I was asked whether or not President Taft would recognize Huerta.

I replied that the President would leave the recognition of Huerta to "old man Wilson" as he called him.

"Though," I added, "the President has no doubt that Wilson will share his views and recognize Huerta."

Since that seemed the logical policy for our government, all these diplomats hastened to cable their governments. Thereupon Huerta was recognized by all the powers represented at this dinner.

But to the surprise of all Europe, the United States never recognized him. Wilson could not stand the "unspeakable Huerta" and pursued his fatal policy of "watchful waiting."

Before Taft went out of office he offered to give Wilson the benefit of his wide experience and to make suggestions as to how the Mexican situation might be handled. Wilson brusquely let Taft know that he did not care for advice and was prepared to handle the matter in his own way.

My own familiarity with Mexican conditions led me to consider that because of Wilson's failure to recognize Huerta, Taft's overscrupulousness in deferring to Wilson had proved a mistake. Huerta was at least president *de facto* and I think should have been given the support of recognition by our government. Moreover, he was at this time friendly to the United States and willing to negotiate for a settlement of our claims against Mexico.

In 1911, at the time of the coronation of George V, I was dining with the King when he received word of Diaz's expulsion from Mexico. At the end of our conversation he said, "Mark my words—Mexico's troubles are just beginning."

In 1924, I was lunching with His Majesty at the Ascot races when he received word of the murder of a British subject by Mexicans. He was visibly affected, and asked, "Mr. Hammond, do you recall my prophecy of twelve years ago about Mexico?"

"Of course," I replied.

"It's come true," he affirmed. "Even after all these years of banditry they haven't a government strong enough to protect the lives of British subjects."

In spite of the time and thought required by the Mexican situation, Taft made great efforts at this time to establish reciprocity with our neighbor to the north. In exchange for the abolition of duties on agricultural products, Canada was to give us free entry for our industrial products. The President was aware, more than most of our statesmen have been, that co-operation and friendship with Canada would be one of the strongest guaranties of our own safety and of the peace of the world.

Philander C. Knox had the idea that, if this treaty were to go through, the friendship between Canada and the United States would be cemented so firmly that a closer Anglo-American accord would naturally follow.

After a long battle against a hostile Congress, Taft succeeded in pushing through a bill to attain this end. In the course of this struggle I was on two occasions asked to serve as unofficial messenger to Premier Wilfrid Laurier and to Governor General Lord Grey, whom I had known intimately when he was an officer of the Chartered Company in the old South African days.

Laurier warned me that the Canadians were extremely sensitive, and asked me to caution Taft "against creating any impression that there is political significance in this treaty. My political opponents are trying to make that an issue."

There was also considerable antagonism on the part of our farmers of the border states. They feared that Canadian agricultural products would flood their normal home markets under reciprocity. This seems to me to have been sectional shortsightedness, because in a few years industries would have sprung up near the border to supply Canada with manufactured goods, and these new centers of population would have furnished nearer and better markets for the farmers. But the people of the agricultural regions could not look ahead.

After Taft had won a hard-earned victory in the American Congress, he was destined to meet defeat at Ottawa. Premier Laurier was in favor of the idea, but opposition rapidly piled up because of incautious newspaper remarks in the United States concerning annexation. The result was that when Canada refused to pass a reciprocity bill, this country considered its friendly gesture had been churlishly received.

As Taft's administration drew to a close in 1912 the question came up as to tolls to be charged for passage through the Panama Canal, which was shortly to be opened. Taft's view, as expressed to Congress, was that, since we owned the canal and since our money had built it, and since foreign governments subsidized their merchant vessels, it was right for us to remit enough on the tolls to our vessels to make up the difference. Also, he thought that coastwise shipping was entirely a domestic matter; as foreign shipping was not allowed to participate in this trade, the United States was merely regulating its own commerce.

Great Britain at once pointed to the clause in the Hay-Pauncefote Treaty which said the canal should be free and open to the vessels of commerce and of war of all nations on terms of entire equality "so that there shall be no discrimination against any such nation, or its citizens, or subjects, in respect to the conditions or charges of traffic or otherwise."

Taft stuck to his interpretation in spite of outbursts of indignation abroad.

A few months later I was talking with Lady Pauncefote, whose husband had negotiated with Hay the treaty which is known by their joint names.

"Of course," she said, "you agree with the stand President Taft has taken on the Canal Tolls question."

"I don't know anything about its legal equity," I answered. "I haven't studied the question particularly, and therefore I suppose I agree with the President."

"Well, he's wrong," she asserted.

"How do you know?"

"Because my husband came back after he had made the treaty and boasted he had outtraded Hay on this point."

Congress finally passed the tolls bill with the coastwise exemption clause, although such lawyers as Joseph H. Choate expressed disapproval. Wilson, who, it is said, had in his early career been touched with Anglophobia, stood in the 1912 election for the bill. Indeed, the Democratic platform itself advocated the exemption of tolls for American vessels. Afterwards Wilson gave in to vociferous English objections and had the clause repealed. This action, he said, "was in accord with justice."

Banking reform was another question constantly agitated during

THEODORE ROOSEVELT (1858-1919)

THE REPUBLICAN NATIONAL CONVENTION, 1912

Taft's four years. During this time the principles and framework of what eventually became Wilson's Federal Reserve Act had been carefully worked out, although the opposition of the insurgent elements was sufficiently strong to prevent its passage.

The actual movement for a unified banking system had begun with the great banking crash of 1907, when banks all over the country suspended payments and had to issue irredeemable currency to meet their obligations.

Senator Aldrich had been profoundly impressed with the idea that something should be done about the banking situation. He introduced and secured the passage of a bill to form a Federal Monetary Commission. At this time Aldrich was beginning to feel the need of accomplishing some great constructive work before leaving office. He was becoming sensitive at being called the head of the System and a reactionary. He bought books and pictures of Sir Robert Peel and Alexander Hamilton, whom he took as his financial mentors.

When the commission was formed, Aldrich took care that no other member should be chosen for his special knowledge of banking. They sailed for Europe to study the banking systems there. On arriving he scattered most of the members of the commission to look over banks wherever they wished. Then—with Henry P. Davison, of the J. P. Morgan firm, George Reynolds, a leading Chicago banker, and A. Piatt Andrew, Jr., assistant professor of economics at Harvard—he interviewed every important banker in London, Paris, and Berlin. He came home with the idea that the American trouble was due to lack of common organization and a common pool of resources. Ours was the only system subject to disastrous panics.

About a year and a half afterwards Davison took six influential bankers down to Jekyll Island off Georgia and there they worked morning, noon, and night for two weeks, whipping a banking bill into shape.

Just at this moment Taft was elected president. He first offered the Treasury post to George Reynolds, who had accepted to all intents and purposes when Taft went off on a trip to the Panama Canal. On his return he learned that when Reynolds informed his bank directors they promptly doubled his salary; consequently, he turned down the Cabinet position.

In the few days that remained before the inauguration, Taft was in a quandary about this appointment. I was in favor of Myron T. Herrick, of Cleveland. Taft finally offered the post to Franklin MacVeagh, who had a wholesale grocery business in Chicago and whose visionary ideas of reform had brought him a certain prominence. Taft wanted someone from the West, and he thought Mac-Veagh's innocuousness would probably have brought him but few enemies. He had formerly run for the Senate on the Democratic ticket and this was a Republican administration, but the slight anomaly was overlooked.

Taft was increasingly interested in banking reform, but as circumstances worked out his hands were tied. Aldrich naturally looked askance at the impractical MacVeagh, while MacVeagh regarded Aldrich as a sort of antichrist. The result was an impasse, made definite when a Democratic Congress was returned in the 1910 mid-term elections.

As soon as Wilson came in, he called a special session of Congress to put through the Federal Reserve Act, which in almost every way coincided with the Aldrich bill which failed of passage under Taft.

On October 26, 1911, proceedings were begun against the United States Steel Corporation, charging it with being a monopoly, particularly because of its purchase of the Tennessee Coal and Iron Company. This purchase had been made with Roosevelt's sanction during the panic of 1907. I believed with Roosevelt at the time that it was for the national interest that this amalgamation should be consummated.

Mark Sullivan says—in *Our Times*—this was the most important of all the suggested causes of the split between Taft and Roosevelt. The initiation of the suit implied that either Roosevelt had been deceived by the financiers or had been in league with them: "making me out either a fool or a knave," as Roosevelt expressed it. It was not until March, 1920, that the Supreme Court finally absolved the Steel Corporation, "a year after Roosevelt, long since purged of his bitterness toward Taft, had died."

Attorney General Wickersham made the statement, at a White

House luncheon in 1911, that he had started more antitrust suits during the three years Taft had been in office than Roosevelt had in his seven years.

I could not refrain from saying, "George, I don't see any reason for being proud of that record."

I realized that political expediency might require the policy, and understood his aspirations as attorney general to institute more anti-trust suits than his predecessor; but it has never been clear to me whether the overrigorous antitrust campaign was forced by the insurgents, or whether it was Attorney General Wickersham's own idea of his duty.

After forty years under the Sherman Anti-Trust Act, the country has now decided that corporations and combinations are by no means the unmitigated evils the reformers of 1890 thought them. Theodore Roosevelt used to distinguish between good and bad trusts. I agree with Franklin Delano Roosevelt, who wisely recognizes the necessity of "combinations in restraint of trade" to prevent the overproduction in agriculture and industry and the evils of cutthroat competition.

In the many party speeches I made between 1908 and 1920, I took the stand that the development of American business and commerce could be carried on most economically if large-scale operation were permitted. Overexpansion beyond the point of economic efficiency would be checked by the operation of economic laws, and much more wisely than by demagogues. Corporations should be judged, not by their magnitude but by their dominant purpose, and their methods, and the manner in which these affect the public welfare.

I suggested that federal incorporation or federal licensing would serve to control one of the chief evils of big business: overcapitalization. No one was more interested than I in destroying dishonest business, but I believed that the ballyhoo of the trust buster was not accomplishing much towards the welfare of industry. Nor, in the end, was the muckraking which came as an aftermath of Roosevelt's period of business reform of much assistance.

In my opinion the animus of Theodore Roosevelt against Taft was at the bottom personal. The rift in the fine friendship had been slowly widening, although I do not recall any one action on the part of Taft which Roosevelt could have construed as a specific personal affront. Until November, 1911, neither had made any public remarks against the other.

But zealots, such as Pinchot, and disappointed friends, such as Garfield, started in almost from the day of the inauguration to work against Taft. Pinchot rushed it abroad to meet Roosevelt when he came out of the wilds of Africa and poured into his ear his own version of the Ballinger episode and accused Taft of being hand in glove with Roosevelt's old enemies in the Senate and House, particularly Aldrich and Cannon.

Roosevelt could never understand Taft's way of doing things. Because Taft felt himself compelled to work with the System, Roosevelt thought he had abandoned the policies they had worked for together. Taft had not changed this program. He was deeply hurt by what he regarded as Roosevelt's unjustifiable coolness and, in his outspoken manner, allowed his friends to hear his comments. These, of course, were promptly reported to Roosevelt, and Roosevelt's were carried to Taft.

The cleavage was clearly marked in June, 1910, when Roosevelt called on Taft at Beverly. I had a faint hope that this meeting might bring the two men closer together, but the conversation never veered from the impersonal. When I saw Taft the following day, he told me of his deep disappointment at the outcome of the meeting. I expressed my regret but also my fear of difficult times ahead in politics.

From my own experience with Roosevelt, I realized how misunderstandings with him could arise in the most unaccountable manner. Shortly after his return from Africa, he made many speeches in New York State on behalf of the Republican party. The National League of Republican Clubs held a meeting at Carnegie Hall in New York City at which Roosevelt was to speak. When he arrived, he was hoarse from his other speeches and asked me in introducing him to express his regret at not being able to make himself heard.

I concluded my introduction with what I considered a pleasant tribute. "I wish to make an apology for the colonel. His voice is bad and you might find it difficult to hear him. But even the 'whisper' of Theodore Roosevelt can be heard around the world."

Roosevelt unfortunately mistook the sentiment I wished to convey. He left the platform without shaking hands with me. As soon as I learned that he was offended I hastened to explain.

He put his arm across my shoulders and said: "Your introduction was most complimentary. I misunderstood at the time what you meant."

My high regard for many of Theodore Roosevelt's admirable traits did not in any way mitigate my disapproval of what I have always considered his unfair treatment of Taft in connection with Taft's acts during his term of office.

A few years ago a well-known newspaper correspondent in Washington, a friend of both Roosevelt and Taft, told me of something that happened just before Roosevelt threw his hat in the ring for the 1912 presidential nomination. It admirably illustrates the difference between the two men. Roosevelt was making a trip through the West. A rousing reception was given him in Wyoming, and a long line of admirers passed to shake hands and greet him.

The reporter, who was standing by Roosevelt's side, whispered that a certain man approaching was a great admirer of the colonel, who undoubtedly remembered him.

The colonel whispered back, "No, I can't recall him."

"He's been at the White House, and lunched with you. His name's Watson."

"Oh yes, I know who he is now. How many children has he?"

"Five. No, he has six—another was born just a few days ago."

When Watson reached Roosevelt, both his hands were grasped and pumped heartily up and down. "My dear fellow, I'm so glad to see you again. I shall never forget the delightful hour we spent together in Washington. How are those five, oh no, I believe you have six children now?"

Watson, who was popular and politically influential in Wyoming, was from that moment an ardent Rooseveltian.

A few months after Roosevelt's tour, the same correspondent went to Seattle with Taft. He was again serving as unofficial introducer. He recognized an old Taft admirer approaching, and whispered, "Mr. President, there's a man approaching whom you certainly remember?"

"No, I don't. What's his name?"

The reporter murmured it in his ear.

Taft reiterated, "No, I don't seem to place him."

"Why, he's dined with you at the White House."

When the man's turn came, Taft took his hand in a friendly way and beamed upon him as he said, "They tell me I ought to remember you but, bless my soul, I cannot recall you at all!"

The former Taft admirer, who was a prominent politician in the state of Washington, went away and turned his strength against Taft.

On one subject Taft and I held decidedly opposite views and I was never able to convince him that I was right. This was the question of woman suffrage. I felt that, aside from expediency, women were entitled to the ballot and for years I had stood for equal rights. Even when the movement was still unpopular I often made speeches in its favor and told my audiences that the franchise for women was not a utopian ideal, and that, in spite of the popular contention to that effect, I did not believe woman would be giving up her prerogatives for her rights.

One afternoon, just before the convention of 1912, after lunching with Taft at the White House, I met a Washington newspaper correspondent who was a loyal friend to the President.

"Is there any truth," he asked, "in the rumor that the President is going to issue a statement that he will make no fight for renomination?"

"Why do you ask that?"

"Well," he said, "the newspaper boys believe it and they're about to give it semipublicity."

"On the contrary," I replied, "I can assure you that, while it is utterly distasteful to him to make that kind of a fight, he told me he was in it to a finish."

My statement was immediately made public. That evening I went to New York for a few days.

When I saw Taft, he said, "Jack, when did I tell you that I was in the fight to a finish?"

I explained to him that as a matter of fact he never had used just those words, but that, knowing him and knowing that he wasn't a quitter, I had merely anticipated his expression. If he had said anything, he would have said that.

He chuckled and said, "Perhaps you exceeded your authority, but it has worked out very well."

Taft then showed me a great pile of letters and telegrams he had received from his Republican friends and partisans, in which they congratulated him for his courageous stand and assured him that they promised undying loyalty since he was in the fight and would not give up.

A few days later, after New York State had elected a delegation favorable to Taft but not actually pledged to him, I was with him and a friend who said, "Mr. President, it must have been a great gratification to you, the way you secured the New York delegation and humiliated Roosevelt in his own state."

Taft replied, seriously: "You're wrong. While the victory is gratifying, it is also heart-rending, because the last thing in the world I wish to do is to humble Theodore Roosevelt. I owe him my nomination and election to the presidency. In spite of what has happened, he is very dear to me."

On November 16, 1911, Roosevelt came out in open warfare against Taft. It soon began to be evident that he would contest the nomination at Chicago the following June. Hughes, who had never been an avowed aspirant, dropped out of the race early. La Follette's attempt to float a Progressive movement, with himself as leader, had failed, for every Progressive preferred Roosevelt. La Follette was used merely as a stalking horse for the greater man and was unceremoniously discarded when he had served this purpose. Roosevelt was as necessary to the Progressive movement as Hamlet is to the play.

Even before the first session of the 1912 convention at Chicago, it was evident that one of the most dramatic events in our political history was about to take place. People were pouring into the city from north, south, east, and west. Hotels were jammed and on the streets were surging throngs. Roosevelt was unable to resist the call of the wild. When a voice from the cheering mob yelled, "How are you feeling this morning, Colonel?" he shouted back, "I'm feeling like a bull moose!"

A little later the stampede for Roosevelt began: it was called the Bull Moose movement.

I was at the Blackstone Hotel. It was so packed that sometimes it took me twenty minutes to make my way through the lobby. I was up very late, often all night, because the real work both before and during conventions is done behind the scenes in the hotel rooms.

According to my custom, I was not a delegate myself. I was, therefore, not subject to the duties of a delegate, such as being compelled to attend innumerable caucuses or be on hand for roll call. This left me master of my own time, and I could use my influence wherever it seemed to me most advantageous.

The convention itself was held in the big sprawling Auditorium on Michigan Avenue, the scene of most Republican conventions. The available seating capacity for spectators was far from sufficient to accommodate the thousands seeking entrance. It was attended by a great number of visitors who had obtained seats through influence with delegates and who followed the proceedings as intently as the delegates did. Some came to see the spectacle for itself; others, the nomination of the candidate; still others were interested in certain planks of the party platform to be adopted.

My wife and I sat in the box of my old friend, Fred Upham, near the stage. Upham was assistant treasurer of the Republican party, which position he had held for many years. Anywhere from thirty to forty people would be crowded in the box at one time. We hardly dared leave the scene of the excitement for fear we might miss something. Pages scurried in and out with food.

We could look down on the tumult. Balconies and boxes flaunted bunting, banners, and pictures of white hopes and dark horses. From galleries and floor came intermittent and inexplicable bursts of applause and song. The din was such that it was difficult at times to hear the speakers on the platform.

The great fight came over the choice of a permanent chairman. If Elihu Root were elected, it would assure Taft's nomination. One by one the contested Taft delegations were seated, and the regulars of the Grand Old Party assumed complete control. The galleries were filled with Roosevelt followers who kept up an incessant cry,

"We want Teddy! We want Teddy!" Senator Jonathan Bourne, of Oregon, had organized this claque.

One now sees in retrospect that the campaign was doomed to end in the defeat of the Republican party. As president of the League of Republican Clubs, I took an active part. Thinking back on the speeches I made, I seem to have spent much more energy in declaiming against Roosevelt than in attacking Wilson.

One reason for that may be found in the fact that Roosevelt was trumpeting challenges which we were forced to answer in kind. Not for him were the insubstantial platitudes of ordinary politics. Though he had fought to lead the whole party in June, as head of the Progressives he was forced to identify himself completely with their radical program. His attack on the political machine coincided with public indignation, and could not be rebutted, since we, too, were saying that the evils of bossism were indefensible. His advocacy of radical principles, particularly the shocking proposal for the recall of judicial decisions, gave us a better weapon, and we used it.

In a calmer moment I would not have complained of the ruthless domination that was characteristic of Roosevelt. Moral force is too rare in this world to be overnicely criticized when it does appear. And I am glad that I did not join with those who referred to paranoias, dementias, and other terrifying psychoses. In describing the "archdeceiver" I did rise once to a poetic quotation:

> "He is the one political Don Juan, who, like the
> lover in the play, 'speaks the kindest words and looks
> such things, vows with such passion, and swears with
> such a grace, that it is Heaven to be deluded by him!'"

I was no defeatist. I insisted in public that Taft would be elected, although I had private misgivings. I was sure the public would not choose Roosevelt but, even so, I had overestimated its intelligence. I said there was no danger that Roosevelt would hurt the party; but he did—he elected Wilson.

What might have happened had Taft been elected is idle speculation. But it seems to me a reasonable supposition that, if Roosevelt had stayed with the party in 1912, he himself would have been nominated and elected by the Republicans in 1916. He would have been an ideal president for the period and, when we finally entered the war, we would have been adequately prepared. There is no doubt that Roosevelt would have much preferred to be a war president for one term than a peace president in perpetuity.

I think Taft was genuinely glad he did not have to assume the burden of another four years in the White House. He had been much distressed by the campaign of personal vilification introduced by Roosevelt.

When Roosevelt and Taft ultimately buried the hatchet and became privately as well as publicly reconciled, Taft came to see me immediately, saying, "I know, Jack, you will be delighted to hear this."

It always gave Taft deep satisfaction to know that this painful quarrel ended before Roosevelt's untimely death.

I have a letter from Theodore Roosevelt dated January 2, 1919. It reached me just after I had read in the newspaper of his death and it must have been among the last he wrote. He wished my wife and me a Happy New Year.

Taft's pleasures were simple, golf and conversation being his chief diversions. He had little time for reading except when he was at Murray Bay in the summer, and then he read mostly biography. Once in a great while he would read a novel, but unlike many of our presidents he never read a detective story. One of his enthusiasms was Patricia Wentworth's historical romance, *The Devil's Wind.* He went rarely to the theater but had violent prejudices for and against the plays he saw.

One day when he was chief justice, Taft and I were walking across the Connecticut Avenue Bridge—now called Taft Bridge, in the renaming of which I was influential. He said, "Jack, do you know what I would like to do this afternoon?"

"Probably play golf," I answered.

"That is out of the question. I would like to see some good play that is free of all sex stuff, something like *Old English* or *Disraeli.* I saw George Arliss in both plays and liked them. I would enjoy something as good as those."

I wrote this to my friend Arliss and he replied that he was highly gratified and hoped that Taft and I would see the moving picture *Disraeli,* which he considered better than the stage play. Excellent as it is, I am not sure that I agree with him.

In some ways I think now that Taft was too straightforward and too high-minded to be a successful politician. These qualities, unless they are coupled with political sophistication, are often detrimental to individual advancement in public life. Taft was one of the truest sportsmen we have ever had in American politics. He took his defeat for re-election philosophically and smilingly, which did much to endear him to the American people.

But when President Harding appointed him chief justice of the Supreme Court in 1921, the country applauded this choice, and he himself rejoiced at the attainment of his life's ambition. His intellectual power and broad knowledge of national and world affairs admirably fitted him for this position. His Lincolnian geniality and charm, which had won admiration and friendship even from those who had been his political enemies, brought a mellower tone to the somewhat austere atmosphere of the bench.

He was without pose and without the craft of the demagogue, and was never guilty of self-stultification. In the few remaining years of his civic service, the debated issues of his presidency were forgotten and he became once more the well-loved Taft who was to possess a permanent place in the affections of the American people.

CHAPTER TWENTY-NINE

Pageantry Before War

TWO SPECIAL DIPLOMATIC MISSIONS—EUROPE
JUST BEFORE THE WORLD WAR—PRECORONATION
FUNCTIONS—SHAKESPEARE BALL—GEORGE V IS
CROWNED—I AM GREETED BY SOUTH AFRICAN
FRIENDS—ON THE ROYAL YACHT—PILGRIM SOCIETY
DINNER—PLANS FOR CELEBRATION OF PANAMA
CANAL — LONDON, BERLIN, ST. PETERSBURG, VIENNA, ROME —
EMPEROR FRANCIS JOSEPH—VICTOR EMMANUEL III
OF ITALY — PANAMA-PACIFIC INTERNATIONAL EXPOSITION

*I*n 1911 and 1912 I had the good fortune to travel over a great part of Europe on two special diplomatic missions. The exceptional advantages this afforded naturally could not be appreciated by me at the time. I visited the capitals of England, Germany, Russia, Austria, Hungary, Italy, France, and other countries. There I met and talked with many people who were vitally to affect the tragic history of the next decade, and I saw things of immediate and subsequent significance. Moreover, although it was entirely unpremeditated, I was able to amplify my background in world economic conditions and politics and to establish contacts which were invaluable to me later when I became engaged in aiding various efforts to establish machinery for international arbitration and for the maintenance of world peace.

Europe was still colorful with the pageantry of court life and, on the surface at least, was secure, even gay. Prosperity was unequaled. The average man was troubled by only the usual vexations of living. In the pubs in London, the beer gardens in Berlin, the famous restaurants of Vienna, and the Paris cafés there certainly was no sign of tension. Everywhere there was music, cheer, even complacency.

Yet in the midst of the coronation of George V—the most magnificent England has ever seen, in the official dinners and balls following, and later at the state functions and at the courts of various European capitals which received the members of the Panama-Pacific Commission one might have detected warning notes of political unrest; an unconsidered and truculent remark by the crown prince of Germany, undertones of hostility in Berlin, Count Witte, Russia's greatest statesman, ignored, discouraged, and removed from power by the sycophantic court at St. Petersburg; all this escaped us in the movement and drama of the current scene and seemed important only as we looked at it in retrospect from 1914.

In 1911, President Taft appointed me special ambassador to represent the United States at the coronation, to take place June 22nd. My staff was made up of Rear Admiral Charles E. Vreeland as naval aide; Major General A. W. Greely, the arctic explorer, military aide; and as secretary we had W. Earle Dodge.

My old friend, Mr. Burdett-Coutts, had sent word that he was definitely planning to turn over to us his house at No. 1 Stratton Street. The British government would, of course, have furnished an embassy for the occasion, but we accepted this offer because we realized that it was made not only in token of warm family friendship, but as a tribute to America.

The demand for lodgings of any kind in London was unprecedented. Houses were bringing thousands of pounds for a fortnight's rental. One advertisement read: "Room B—handsome well-furnished room with bastion window at corner of St. James's Street and Piccadilly, commanding complete view of the street as procession turns at the corner, and a triple window in Piccadilly, price 200 guineas first day." But our host refused to accept a penny for the use of his home.

I sailed on the *Cedric* early in June and arrived some days before the rest of my party. It was necessary to get my family settled and also to obtain a wardrobe appropriate for the various functions. The latter was no easy matter. We were met at the steamer and conducted to London by our friend, William Phillips, secretary of the American Embassy, whose unfailing kindness and efficiency contributed much to the success of the mission.

We installed ourselves at No. 1 Stratton Street—overlooking the beautiful gardens of Devonshire House—where in the past my wife and I had visited Baroness Burdett-Coutts so many times.

While we were in residence, our official standing was indicated by a sentry box occupied by one of the Royal Guard, with scarlet jacket, black trousers, a pipe-clayed belt, all topped off with a two-foot busby.

In the main hall was another sentry box, framing the figure of Hallett, the hall porter, who used to hop in and out so briskly that the children called him the tree toad.

The Burdett-Coutts home was filled with treasures, and the friends who visited us confessed that they were no longer eager to see the museums of London; they would seem dull by comparison. The presence of several healthy youngsters in the midst of all these rare and antique objects offered dangerous possibilities, exciting as they may have seemed to the children. My wife warned them to be careful in moving about and not to indulge in roughhousing.

Fortunately our host had unusual understanding of children and patience with them. He used to tell Dick the romantic histories of his treasures. One Phoenician carving was dated B.C.; he explained to the boy that that meant it had been fashioned before the birth of Christ. Dick was deeply impressed. That same evening he rushed excitedly out of his bathroom, waving a towel.

"Look," he shouted, pointing to the monogram, B-C. "It's on them all. The towels in this house were all made before Christ."

The old, shriveled custodian took us through the huge cellars, stretching out under the house for more than an acre. They contained innumerable varieties of fine wines and liquors, a large part of which had been laid down in the eighteenth century. We were to give a reception following the coronation. Mr. Burdett-Coutts said: "Here's some eighteen-sixty champagne. I think it would be nice to serve it at your reception."

I hesitated. "But we're having more than a thousand guests."

"Don't be concerned, sir," the little gnome broke in, "we have plenty."

A few days before the coronation I went to Folkestone to rest and await the time of my official reception.

All of the foreign delegations were supposed to gather at Calais, and then to cross the Channel together by special boats. Trains were to be provided to meet us at Dover and to take us to London.

On June 19th, I went to Dover and there met the three men appointed by the British government as my official aides. One of them was Lord Sandhurst. His was the only case, I believe, in which both father and son had been decorated with the Star of India. The others, Lieutenant Colonel B. R. James and Captain C. F. G. Sowerby, I had known in Washington when attachés at the British Embassy. Sowerby came to an untimely end when he accompanied Kitchener on his trip to Russia.

All three were close friends of mine. It was a constant source of entertainment to me to see the mixture of informality and official decorum. Now and then one of them would call me "Hammond," and then, smiling, immediately correct himself with: "I beg your pardon, Your Excellency."

When the special boat train reached London the coach with the American delegation stopped directly in front of the crimson carpet where the Duke of Connaught, the King's uncle, stood. He represented His Majesty on state occasions. The duke, who knew very well that I had been in England for the last ten days, first greeted me in the name of the British government and then, solemnly, but with a twinkle in his eye, asked me what kind of crossing I had had.

I replied, with equal solemnity, that I was a good sailor for whom the English Channel had no terrors.

Preceding the coronation a succession of receptions and state dinners were held. Already potentates, princes, lords, and representatives from almost every country in the world had arrived. The first event was a royal dinner at Buckingham Palace the evening of our arrival. This was "a family affair" of eighty-seven at which the heads of missions were guests. The other members of the various deputations were to gather at nine-thirty and form in line for the procession to the Picture Gallery where each head of a mission was to present the members of his staff to Their Majesties.

After the banquet the men assembled in the smoking room. His Majesty asked me to sit down beside him and we began talking about Mexico and Diaz.

He was so interested in the subject that he failed to notice that we had been left almost alone in the room. Since etiquette demanded that only the King could terminate a conversation, I was unable to suggest leaving, although I feared we were upsetting the routine. At last, a messenger came from Queen Mary to remind the King that she was waiting. He took a short cut to the Picture Gallery where the levee was to be held. I had to follow the prescribed route and join my deputation, but in spite of my best efforts I failed to arrive there in time to take the place in line assigned our delegation.

As I made my bow before the Queen, I apologized for the delay. Always gracious, Her Majesty smiled sympathetically, "I quite understand the circumstances, Mr. Hays Hammond."

The next evening was the occasion of the state dinner, after which the Duchess of Sutherland gave a ball at Stafford House.

A most picturesque, memorable, and indeed unique affair was the Shakespeare Ball given in Albert Hall. We attended as the guests of Mr. Burdett-Coutts. The transforming of this vast but unlovely interior into an artistic Tudor setting for the brilliant scene was of itself an achievement. The great of every branch of art, as well as all of society, took part in the ball. As usual in England, the costuming was rich and authentic. Various groups named from Shakespeare's plays gave old Elizabethan dances, and Ellen Terry in one of them shone out with her unsurpassed grace and spirit.

Many of those who had stands or rooms to rent, and also those who had purchased space from which to watch the coronation procession, took out rain policies. June weather in England is proverbially uncertain. Lloyd's rate was twenty per cent for a rainfall exceeding twenty-hundredths of an inch during the twenty-four-hour period.

The arrangements and control of the millions who witnessed the procession on June 22nd and the royal progress the next day were perfect. In fact, the whole coronation was managed with forethought for the last detail and with miraculous precision. Lord Kitchener may not have been the greatest of generals, but in this matter he showed phenomenal executive ability.

Early the night before the coronation people from all quarters of the United Kingdom were gathering outside Buckingham Palace. When dawn broke about three in the morning, twelve thousand police and sixty thousand soldiers from every dominion and colony, under the command of Lord Kitchener, took up their stand along the line of march. Anybody still asleep must have been awakened by the royal salute at three-forty-five when, following an ancient custom, the Queen came out on the balcony and looked down at the multitude.

The regalia—including the spurs and sword, the royal robe, the orb, the ring and the scepters, the historic crown of Edward the Confessor—were being carried from the Tower to Westminster Abbey and were guarded throughout the night by the Tower Guard whose duty it is to keep them always in sight. They wore uniforms dating from the time of Henry VIII.

Meanwhile workmen were putting the finishing touches to temporary columns and arches, and decorating them with gilt griffons, red lions, and white unicorns.

Even while this was being done light rain fell so that by morning the colored bunting was streaked. But the spirits of the people were undamped. At intervals there would be outbursts of *Rule, Britannia* and *God Save the King*. All was conducted in an orderly, reverent way. As late as five o'clock in the morning one could still move about easily between Buckingham Palace and the Abbey.

Lord Sandhurst, who was well versed in court etiquette and dress, came about eight o'clock to escort me to the palace. When he entered the study he was attired in a most gorgeous robe with a train fourteen feet long.

"I've never seen anything so magnificent!" I exclaimed. "Let's see you walk around. I want to watch how you manage that train."

He looked at me reproachfully. "God forbid, Your Excellency. Don't ask that of me. My wife has had me parading before the servants for hours. You know we don't wear these more than once in a lifetime."

Each official representative was assigned a seat in a carriage. I was to ride with the French admiral, Fauques de Jonquières, Prince Rupprecht of Bavaria, and Duke Albrecht of Württemberg. When I started to take my place, I found that the seat of honor on the right facing forward, assigned to me as representative of the United States, was already occupied by Prince Rupprecht.

I politely showed the prince my card designating my seat, and intimated that he should relinquish it. He paid no attention, but continued his conversation with the duke. Assuming, for the sake of politeness, that he did not understand English, I made the request in German, and somewhat more emphatically.

To the ill-concealed amusement of the French admiral, Prince Rupprecht then moved, though reluctantly. Obviously piqued, neither of the two Germans paid any attention to me or to Jonquières as our carriage proceeded at a walk. Two independent conversations were carried on during the three-mile course to Westminster Abbey.

This question of precedence may seem a small matter in the light of the democratic usage of the United States, but in those days its implications certainly went deep into the wellsprings of the old-world attitude towards us. Too often England and Continental Europe had patronized us in this respect. And bearing in mind Theodore Roosevelt's unpleasant experience when he attended the funeral ceremonies of King Edward VII as representative of the President of the United States, I determined there should be no repetition. On a visit to England just before the coronation, I had gone so far as to consult Princess Louise, who had later talked to the King and to the Earl of Chesterfield, the lord chamberlain at the time of the coronation. Chesterfield, formerly one of the directors of the Consolidated Gold Fields and a warm friend, not only of mine but of America, assured Princess Louise that we would be shown every consideration.

The survival of ceremonial that dates from the Middle Ages made this coronation the most brilliant spectacle the twentieth century had seen. Some may condemn this pomp and show as economic waste, but in my opinion pageantry satisfies a fundamental human need. Knee breeches do not necessarily change an American into a fawner on kings. The American official costume is, indeed, simple enough. It is so incongruous among velvets, brocades, and jewels that inconspicuousness, the purpose of its plainness, is sometimes lost and the wearer finds himself standing out like a square-rigger in a fleet of battle cruisers.

The morning after the coronation the Hammond family read in the London *Times*: "In the Procession of Royal representatives and guests were the German Crown Prince, conspicuous by his noble bearing, with the Crown Princess, with the Prince and Princess Higashi-Fushimi of Japan, whose Oriental robes contrasted with the plain evening dress worn by Mr. Hays Hammond." The *Times* did me an injustice. I wore the prescribed costume and was not embarrassed by the disturbing thought that American ambassadors were frequently mistaken for waiters owing to the absolute similarity of dress and despite whatever air of superiority they were able to convey.

The Duke of Norfolk, first peer of the realm, was acting as marshal for the complicated coronation ceremony, and the participants conducted themselves as though they were well-rehearsed actors. I, unfortunately, almost missed one of my cues. The secretary of our delegation was to be at the entrance to the Abbey with information regarding the seating arrangements; he was nowhere to be found. Luckily I caught sight of an old friend from the Foreign Office, who was an usher, and asked him where I was to be seated.

"You move right along with the procession until you get as near the throne as possible. Precautions have been taken that no one except His Majesty will occupy that seat."

The vibrant hush inside the huge church, which for centuries has been the burying place of England's kings and distinguished subjects, came as a sharp change from the tumult of the crowd outside, who were shouting continuously, "God save the King." As we went forward it seemed dark at first, in spite of thousands of lighted candles and faint rays of sunlight streaming down from high windows. As our eyes became accustomed to the dimness, we could see the great cross formation of the Abbey, and far down the long narrow nave, the sanctuary and the gold of the altar in the circle of bright lights burning at the rear of the church. In front of the altar stood King Edward's antique chair, and the Stone of Destiny on which so many English kings had been crowned.

We had entered the Abbey in the same order as we had proceeded through the streets: first the representatives of the powers, then the peers and peeresses, followed shortly by the immediate royal family.

As we took our places, pools of light filtered through stained-glass windows, the reflection of the brilliant colors and flashing jewels of the assemblage lay softly on the ancient gray stone walls.

The peers and peeresses sat tier above tier in the transepts and above and nearer the altar were the royal boxes. The tiers as well as the galleries ranging along the nave were draped with velvet hangings of blue and silver-gray. The prevailing colors seemed to be blue, gray, and white, with flashes of scarlet from uniforms and trains and the ceremonial garb of the prelates.

A large choir, drawn from the various churches of London, sang at intervals during the ceremony.

The Queen entered as the anthem began: "I was glad when they said unto me, We will go into the House of the Lord." As the Westminster choirboys chanted, "Vivat! Vivat! Rex Georgius," the King appeared in crimson and ermine, and proceeded slowly to the sanctuary. Their Majesties knelt in prayer, and the crowd became silent.

The Archbishop of Canterbury, standing in front of the altar, began the ritual. He administered the oath, and the King, after kissing the Bible, moved to the coronation chair and was anointed on the crown of his head, his breast, and the palms of both hands. Then came the investiture with sword, spurs, and ring. The imperial mantle was placed across his shoulders, and the orb put in his hand. As he held the royal scepter in his right hand and the rod of mercy in his left, St. Edward's crown was placed upon the King's head by the archbishop. The silver trumpets of the heralds jubilantly rang out, and the bells of Westminster, of London, of England, of the British dominions the world over, took up the antiphonal chorus.

George V ascended his throne. The Prince of Wales kissed him on both cheeks and on the hand. The senior duke, marquis, earl, viscount, and baron then did homage, each on behalf of his order.

After the shorter and simpler ritual of the crowning of the Queen, Their Majesties partook of Holy Communion. The great choir then sang the *Gloria in Excelsis* and the *Te Deum*.

Preceded by heralds, yeomen of the guard, standard bearers, court officials, state functionaries, Knights of the Garter, pages, and the Abbey clergy, the King now in purple velvet, the imperial crown on

his head, the orb in his left hand, the scepter in his right, left the
Abbey to the triumphant strains of the national anthem.

The ceremony was over. We filed out of the Abbey, in the order
of precedence established for the occasion.

I resumed my place in the carriage and the same aloof attitude was
maintained by the Germans during the rest of the procession. The
South African contingent, about a thousand strong, was occupying
temporary stands near the Ritz Hotel. I had known many of them
on the Rand, and all of them knew of my connection with the Jameson Raid. As our carriage passed they raised a loud cheer, in which
both Boers and Englishmen joined.

At this demonstration, I could not resist turning to Prince Rupprecht and remarking ironically that the ovation must be meant for
him. He did not miss the point. Neither he nor the South Africans
had forgotten the Kaiser's telegram to Kruger.

Two days later a great naval review was held off Spithead. Great
Britain's sea power, augmented by battleships of foreign nations,
formed a lane down which the King's yacht sailed, followed by
others carrying the coronation guests. Almost deafening gun salutes
accompanied the review.

I had been invited to join the King's private party on the *Alex-
andra,* where I particularly enjoyed meeting the younger members
of the royal family. At this solemn moment they were engaged in
teasing the Prince of Wales.

They were commenting on the intimate family details of the coronation. Young Prince Henry remarked: "David certainly looked a
sight. He was frightfully nervous. He kept fooling with his collar
and cuffs as though he thought everybody were looking at him."

No wonder David was frightfully nervous. As a lad of sixteen he
was seated in a large chair alone on the dais the cynosure of all eyes
until the arrival of the King and Queen.

This was too much for the elder brother. He started after Prince
Henry but slipped and sprawled on the deck, to the rollicking amusement of the other children. David braced himself and shouted at his
younger relatives. Then he regained his equilibrium and continued
the chase.

Simultaneously the crown prince of Germany, insensitive to the humor of this healthy domestic scene, joined the group. He was obviously in a bad temper. We were approaching our battleship, the U.S.S. *Delaware*.

The crown prince made some arrogant remarks about its new basket type of observation mast. He said it was too conspicuous, it would make an easy target.

I retorted that experts on naval affairs did not agree with him. Before the argument could grow too warm, the Kaiser's brother, Prince Henry, arrived. He was head of the German Navy and was able to suppress his fiery nephew by tactfully siding with me. Even so, the crown prince may have been right. Our navy has since abandoned that type of observation mast. The review proceeded without further international incidents. Even the royal children were well behaved!

A few days afterwards, at the garden party at Buckingham Palace, I met Dr. Hillier, a fellow prisoner at Pretoria. He was now respectable; in fact, a member of the House of Parliament. While we were reminiscing, the labor leader, John Burns, approached, and Hillier introduced me.

"Oh," said Burns, "I remember Mr. Hammond particularly well."

"Thank you. I feel complimented but surprised. It has been a long time since our last meeting."

"I never forget a man who has been in prison." Noticing that I did not understand the implications of this statement, he added: "Don't be embarrassed. I've been in jail myself once or twice."

As we three stood talking, Sir Abe Bailey, followed by Sir George Farrar, joined the group. Suddenly, without apparent reason, Burns burst into laughter, stretched out his arms, drew us together, and then whispered, "You see that fellow over there with all those jewels?"

I couldn't imagine what he was driving at.

He pointed to one of the Indian princes, decorated with several ropes of pearls, each pearl as big as a thumb, and with dazzling emeralds, sapphires, and rubies hung about him.

He then pointed in another direction. "See that chap over there? He's a maharaja. God knows how much jewelry those fellows are carrying around. Think of these fortunes in loot and five of us ex-jailbirds let loose in this crowd!"

For ten days we were feted and entertained. One of the most interesting events was the gala performance at His Majesty's Theatre. The King and Queen were in the royal box and the house was filled with coronation guests. Virtually all the theatrical talent of England was represented on the stage.

All the suites, special envoys, and deputations were scheduled to leave Waterloo Station officially on June 28th. Since I was to be the guest of honor of the Pilgrim Society that night, and of the American Society's banquet on July Fourth, something had to be done to veil my failure to depart. I approached the Duke of Connaught and asked him how, without infringing any rule of etiquette, I could avoid leaving the country.

He replied that it could be arranged, but that I should have to be conspicuously present in my frock coat and tall hat at the station where I could be seen by newspaper reporters and cameramen at the official leave-taking. I would then board the train, which would stop a few hundred yards down the track to let me out. All this seemed very elaborate but it was carried through and thus, at both my arrival and my departure, official decorum was maintained.

The Pilgrim Society's dinner for me was a delightful occasion. Warmest sentiments concerning Anglo-American friendship were expressed. Arthur Balfour made an excellent speech, in which he pointed out that the best evidence of the sincerity of this friendship was that Americans and English no longer took offense at the jokes perpetrated at their expense by their friends across the water. He was so enthusiastic about it that before the evening was over a Yankee newspaper correspondent said that Balfour must be planning to run for Congress.

I replied to Balfour's toast. Augustine Birrell, chief secretary to the lord lieutenant of Ireland, then gave a toast "to the American visitors" to which Chauncey Depew felt called upon to reply.

In spite of the fact that I was not officially present on British soil on the eve of the Fourth of July, my wife and I gave a reception at No. 1 Stratton Street. We had the pleasure of entertaining a great number of Americans as well as many of our English friends. At the stroke of twelve, a band stationed at the foot of the grand stairway, ushered in our national holiday with Sousa's *The Stars and Stripes Forever*.

The next afternoon Ambassador and Mrs. Whitelaw Reid gave the customary embassy reception at Dorchester House, and that night I attended the annual dinner of the American Society at the Savoy.

We spent several weeks in Scotland and then returned to America.

My second diplomatic mission during these years was in connection with the celebration of the completion of the Panama Canal. This was of far more than local interest, of greater importance than most trumped-up world expositions. The international significance of the completion of the canal was apparent, and it was believed that interest could best be aroused by sending emissaries to request the co-operation of European countries. In 1912, therefore, three years before the Panama-Pacific Exposition was scheduled to open, Charles G. Moore, its president, asked me to head a commission for this purpose. He pointed out that my previous business connections in Europe and my having been the President's representative at the coronation would be of value in securing a favorable reception.

I hesitated between my wish to serve California and my desire to take the stump for Taft's nomination, and I wrote to President Taft that I preferred to remain in America to support him in the preconvention activities.

The President replied that he hoped I would go to Europe because it was of the "utmost importance that the European countries be induced to take adequate part in the great memorial celebration . . . in the success of which I am taking more than a mere official interest."

This was true. As secretary of war, he had directed the construction of the canal and, naturally enough, had extended his interest to the celebration of its opening. I then accepted.

Because of this extraofficial interest, Taft issued a presidential proclamation, naming the members of the commission, and thereby giving us a quasi-diplomatic standing. Secretary of State Knox requested all embassies and legations in the countries we were to visit to assure us special governmental courtesies.

In addition to myself, the members of the commission were R. B. Hale, W. T. Sesnon, Rear Admiral S. A. Staunton, and Brigadier General Clarence R. Edwards. Naval and Military representatives

THE PROCESSION ON THE WAY TO THE CORONATION OF GEORGE V

THE PANAMA-PACIFIC EXPOSITION, 1915

accompanied us because of the federal character of our mission. My
son Harris and Charles F. Wilson, of the State Department, acted
as secretaries.

We sailed for England on the *Mauretania* on April 24, 1912, with
a great mass of propaganda literature. In London we made Cla-
ridge's our headquarters. Then began once more the round of dinners, banquets, lunches, speeches, and ceremonial visits we had
learned to know so well during the coronation; thenceforward these
filled every hour of the day and many hours of the night.

Everywhere we received most courteous official attention. We
met so many people at different functions that, while we were vitally
interested in the world and government affairs, there was little time
for anything but the most casual conversations.

We were greeted by the ruler of a country in person if he was in
residence; in his absence, by a representative of the government. In
hotels we were given the royal suite and walked under yards of
canopies and over miles of red carpets. Even station masters greeted
us in elaborate uniforms reserved for state occasions. Our official
status was in danger of overwhelming our intent.

In England, Ambassador Reid took us first to call on the secretary for foreign affairs, Sir Edward Grey, at No. 10 Downing Street,
and in the evening to Covent Garden.

The next day we called on various government ministers, including H. U. Wintour, head of the department on international exhibitions. In the evening, the ambassador gave a dinner for forty, among
whom were the Marquis of Crewe, secretary of state for India, Lewis
Harcourt, colonial secretary, Sydney Buxton, president of the Board
of Trade, Lord Sandhurst, at this time lord chamberlain, and Lord
Roberts. Lord Haldane, the secretary of state for war, came in after
dinner.

While we were in London, Sesnon called on Lord Desborough,
president of the London Chamber of Commerce, Admiral Staunton
on Winston Churchill, first lord of the admiralty, and General
Edwards on Lord Haldane.

The government gave us a luncheon on the terrace of the House
of Commons, with the Rt. Hon. Earl Beauchamp acting as host.

After lunch the speaker of the House of Commons deputed Mr.

Cadogan to escort the commission into the House, where we heard Mr. Balfour in debate on Home Rule. Afterwards "Honest John" Burns showed us through Parliament House and pointed out the room where Cromwell had signed the death warrant of Charles I, and other points of historical interest. He was the best cicerone we had on the trip. It will be remembered that Honest John was the only man to resign from the Cabinet on its vote, at the urging of Earl Grey, to declare war in August, 1914.

We were granted an audience with King George V, whose cordiality and interest set the tone for our reception on the Continent. Afterwards we were entertained at luncheon by the Earl of Granard, son-in-law of my old friend Ogden Mills.

In London, Mr. Burdett-Coutts gave a tea for the commission. It was pleasant to be back at No. 1 Stratton Street, and to have Hallett pop out of his sentry box just as usual and the handsome major-domo greet me in his dignified fashion.

Our five days' reception in London was extremely cordial, and from every side we heard expressions of keen interest and promises of co-operation. The newspapers were generous in their support and the prevalent atmosphere of goodwill made us feel that we had made a good start.

We went next to Berlin and were met by Messrs. Spencer and Ruddock, secretaries to the embassy, and taken to the Hotel Adlon.

Germany ordinarily encourages exhibitions and had a permanent committee to further and control the multitude of national affairs that are given every year. This committee was exceedingly interested in our proposals because it believed that the Panama Canal had a world significance as an outlet and a means of communication. From an engineering point of view alone the Germans considered it worthy of celebration.

Ambassador John G. Leishman entertained us at lunch at which were present Herr Solf, minister of colonies, and Herr Albert, undersecretary of the interior.

Nevertheless, the reception which was accorded our exposition plans was by no means so warm as we had expected. There seemed to be an undercurrent of hostility. This might have been caused by jealousy of England's cordial promises of co-operation. More probably it was a matter of commercial rivalry with American manufacturers, or resentment over the American tariff. But unmistakably the Germans were busy—too obviously so, preoccupied with plans which necessarily excluded all thought of expositions or even courtesy.

Admiral Staunton called on Admiral von Tirpitz and was received politely, but without great enthusiasm. When General Edwards said to the minister of war, General von Herrigen, that Lord Haldane had promised England would be suitably represented, the German remarked with decision, "And so shall we."

The Kaiser was absent in Corfu, but our personal relations with many influential Germans were friendly. At the reception given us by Bethmann-Hollweg there was a brilliant gathering and we enjoyed meeting old friends and making new ones. I remember talking with Prince Lichnowsky, who had just returned from his post as ambassador to Turkey and was to go to London, and urging him to promote that friendly understanding between England and Germany which I had always thought a sound idea. He expressed keen desire to effect this.

During our four days in Berlin, we saw thousands of soldiers goose-stepping through the streets. It was evident the Germans had their minds on other things than peaceful expositions. In spite of the official chill, one of our party remarked as the St. Petersburg train pulled out of the station: "It's a good thing we didn't stay in Germany any longer. They might have killed us with that elaborate kindness."

We had some feeling of uncertainty as to our reception in St. Petersburg. Before leaving London, I had been cabled by our Department of State that the efforts of Curtis Guild, ambassador to Russia, had failed to secure Russian support. Though the premier had consented to receive us, no other minister was willing to do so, and the trip to Russia might, in his opinion, wisely be abandoned.

Ambassador Guild joined us in Berlin and explained that, in view of the delicate situation in Russia caused by the abrogation the year before of our commercial treaty, the Russian press was hostile. Members of the commission, he advised, should not talk to newspaper reporters there. He himself planned to remain in Berlin until the mission had finished its alloted stay in Russia, so that his presence might not lend it political significance.

Prime Minister Kokovtzev invited us to his house, making clear that he was receiving us out of courtesy to us as American citizens and not in his official capacity. He then became more cordial and declared there was every reason why the relations between our two countries should be close and permanent; we really had no conflicting interests and more than ninety-nine per cent of our differences had been eliminated. But Kokovtzev at the moment did not see how Russia could participate in the exposition. On the other hand, if a satisfactory treaty could be speedily negotiated, Russia would be glad to exhibit.

The commission was received by Minister of Commerce Timaschev, whose ideas followed closely those of the prime minister, he, too, urging that a new commercial treaty be completed soon.

That same evening Charles Stetson Wilson, the chargé d'affaires, gave us an excellent dinner arranged on a scale of extravagant hospitality. There were many Russians present but only one member of the government, the prefect of police.

The official calls of General Edwards on General Soukhomlinov, minister of war, and of Admiral Staunton on Admiral Grigorovitch met with enthusiastic response and promises that the army and navy would be suitably represented in any international features arranged for the exposition if Russia participated.

Since the Czar was absent in the Crimea, we did not see him.

I returned to my hotel from an official visit to learn that my old friend, now Count Witte, had called in my absence. I hastened to his home and had tea with him. This was the last time I saw him. He was a disappointed, embittered man. The Revolution of 1905 had put an end to his ambitions for Russia's future. Although no liberal in our sense of the word, Witte had hoped to see the Russian Duma's influence replace that of the nobility. Instead, he had had to view a succession of ever more ineffectual Dumas succumb to the reactionary influence of Konstantin Petrovitch Pobedonostsev with his ideal of an absolute autocracy, supreme in church and state. Pobedonostsev was procurator of the Holy Synod and virtually the ecclesiastical dictator of Russia.

Witte, it has always seemed to me, was the only man who could have saved Russia from the consequences of her bloody revolution. He was the victim of a system against which he struggled in vain. The sinister and all-powerful influence of occultism, fostered by the Czarina herself, was thrown into the scale against him. His position in Russian politics became entirely anomalous. The court regarded him as too radical; the radicals, as too conservative. Although a great statesman, perhaps the greatest Russia has ever produced, in his own country he was unhonored and even abroad had not received the recognition he merited.

The minister of credit, M. Davidov, whom I had met in 1910, gave a banquet for forty guests. I had had some experience with Russian hospitality, but even to me this seemed a gastronomic marvel.

Set out on a long table was the necessary zakousky, an array of irresistible hors d'oeuvres, smoked fish, anchovies, cold meats, caviar heaped in shining gray, red, and black mounds. Punctuating the table like exclamation points, bottles of vodka made from grain, vodka made even from green leaves, alternated with champagne. General Edwards and I, who knew the ropes, were as abstemious as the temptation would allow. The rest of the delegation let themselves go and stood about fairly gorging themselves on the delicacies.

When all the American guests were thoroughly stuffed, one or two approached our host to compliment him on such a superb cold supper. At that moment the great doors behind us were folded back and dinner was announced.

M. Davidov achieved the acme of Russian hospitality—he provided for us the royal boxes at the opera.

Afterwards Davidov asked Harris, who was but little younger than he: "How'd you like to go on a bear hunt? I can get a special train to take us to the Urals. We can have a day's shooting, and then I can arrange for another special train to take you to Vienna."

Harris was reluctant to decline but, in spite of the lavish use of special trains, he was afraid he might not reach Vienna in time to rejoin the party.

We left St. Petersburg at midnight, May 13th, and reached Moscow the next morning.

Someone in the party told the story of two Russian peasants who got on a train together at a way station between these two cities.

One of them said to the other, "Where are you going?"

"Petersburg. Where are you?"

"Moscow."

"Isn't it wonderful that we are on the same train, between the two cities, and traveling together—and that you are going to Moscow and I to Petersburg. What miracles these modern scientists have performed for us."

We stopped off in Moscow only one day to visit the Kremlin, which was closed in anticipation of a visit from the Czar, perhaps a necessary police precaution in view of the activity of the anarchists. As a special courtesy, the prefect of police allowed us to visit the fortress of the Kremlin, its churches, and the treasure room. On my previous visit to Russia I had made many good friends, but they all seemed different now; there was suspicion, tension, and an atmosphere of national distrust. Their gaiety was hectic and their laughter was hollow. The old Russia was dying of her own physical and spiritual inertia.

As the train halted at the small station marking the Austrian frontier, we heard the sound of stringed instruments. On the platform was a five-piece tzigane orchestra, playing its gay gypsy music. Our courier informed us that many years before an Austrian, who had been long absent from his country and was returning home a wealthy man, heard gypsies playing at this very spot. He was overcome with emotion and provided that romany music should henceforth greet every entering train.

We reached Vienna at six in the morning and were met by Ambassador Richard C. Kerens and his entire staff. It was bad enough to arrive at such an impossible hour but to have to struggle into full evening dress when half awake was made bearable only by the comforts afforded by our special train. As we neared each new stopping place we could—if forced to—array ourselves in the proper clothes for any time of day and for any court requirement. It was some satisfaction to know that the welcoming committee was obliged to wear the same formal attire.

Kerens had been most energetic in his arrangements, and we were given a printed government program covering nearly every hour of our visit.

First we called on all members of the ministry and were received enthusiastically. After visiting the Natural History Museum, we attended a luncheon given by Dr. Faber, president of the Austrian committee. We were then taken for an automobile ride to Kobenzl, in the beautiful hills overlooking Vienna. In the evening we sat in the royal box at the Kaiserliche Königliche Burgtheater and from there went to a brilliant reception at the American Embassy.

The death of the king of Denmark, whose body had been found on the streets of Hamburg, necessitated the court's going into mourning. Consequently the invitations issued by Count and Countess Berchtold for a grand reception at the Ballplatz had to be recalled. Berchtold did, however, give us a small and unofficial dinner at his private palace. This gave us the opportunity of frankly discussing world politics. It is remembered by us as a most enjoyable occasion. Berchtold was one of the recognized brilliant statesmen of his time even if he did sign the ultimatum to Serbia in July, 1914.

A state luncheon was given us in the fine old Rathaus. The decorations of the big banqueting hall had been designed and carried out by Joseph Urban, who had been honored by the Emperor for his architectural and stage designs. Later he created magnificent effects of line and color for the Chicago Century of Progress Exposition, but unfortunately he died before he could hear the chorus of praise.

Our luncheon became quite festive. I had written a speech for the occasion and, with the help of our German courier, had translated it into German. I had attempted to keep it in a light vein and felt very well satisfied with my efforts when the audience showed itself highly amused and applauded inordinately.

But later my wife told me that Harris had written her, "Father certainly created an atmosphere of humor, but I am not sure whether the guests were amused at his stories, or were laughing at his German."

The Emperor Francis Joseph, in full uniform, gave us an audience at Schönbrunn. His soldierly bearing belied his eighty-two years.

His cordial manner immediately set the entire commission at ease.

His Majesty had dispensed with the presence of both our ambassador and an interpreter, although we never knew why. He was master of nine languages, but strangely enough, English was not among them. As I was the only one in the delegation who could speak German, I had to assume the burden of conversation. I apologized for not being familiar with the "hofdeutsch" used at court. I explained that my German was the student dialect learned at Freiberg thirty-five years before. The Emperor said pleasantly that he would be glad to hear the studenten-sprache, it would be a relaxation from court German. Thus encouraged I went ahead without regard to grammatical construction to tell him about the prospective exposition.

Dr. Dumba, Austrian ambassador to Washington, told me the Emperor had been pleased with our audience and as a memento of the occasion was sending his autographed photograph to the young man who used studenten-sprache. I was proud to receive this honor from the most formal court in Europe.

In Vienna I was interviewed by a clever newspaper correspondent who cross-examined me thoroughly on American tariffs, always a grievance in Europe. I had a difficult half-hour trying to clarify for his readers the Republican policy of high tariffs—perhaps an impossible undertaking.

Our Austrian visit was highly successful and enjoyable. We were shown full official courtesy and were promised hearty support for the exposition.

After four busy days in Vienna, we went to Budapest, where we were met by Dr. Ott, minister of commerce and representative of the city. The next day we were granted an audience by the Archduke Joseph. The Archduke Francis Ferdinand was also present. Two years later his murder at Sarajevo was to precipitate the World War.

After a round of official calls we were given a luncheon by Count Serenyi, the minister of agriculture. The same evening we were guests of the government at a brilliant dinner at the Orszagos Casino, where the minister of justice was the official host. The following day was filled with ceremonious meetings, and in the evening the city of Budapest was our host for a trip down the Danube to Margaret Island and a magnificent dinner presided over by Count Apponyi. The Hungarians justly pride themselves on their hospitality.

The Hungarian government then sent us by special train to Fiume, then Austria's port on the Adriatic. We spent the day at the torpedo works of Whitehead and Company, and watched with interest as torpedoes were discharged into the bay for our edification.

It was an overnight trip by steamer from Fiume to Venice. After a day's sightseeing there, we proceeded to Rome.

Italy was in the midst of the Tripolitan War with Turkey. General Edwards and Admiral Staunton were naturally following its progress with great interest. I had heard in court circles elsewhere that Victor Emmanuel III was exceptionally well versed in world affairs and one of the most brilliant European monarchs, but I was unprepared for his accurate up-to-the-minute information. Almost his first words were, "President Taft has lost Ohio."

This referred to the Ohio election of delegates for the Republican National Convention. He had studied the political map and already had made an accurate forecast of the effect on the election based on such incomplete returns. None of us had heard the news, and my pained expression surprised the king; after his recent meeting with Roosevelt, he had assumed that all patriotic Americans would be Rooseveltians.

The gloomy forecast that the Italian government would be too preoccupied with its war to bother with commercial questions was without foundation. The king made the remark that the rebuilding of San Francisco after the earthquake and fire was in itself a triumph sufficient to warrant the celebration, and asked to have explained many pertinent technical details concerning the operation of the Panama Canal. These questions might have been expected from an engineer but hardly from a ruling monarch.

At my last interview with him, in 1926, Victor Emmanuel showed much interest in my account of the world sources of gold supply. He then reviewed history and pointed out that after every great political and economic catastrophe, such as the World War, there appeared the practice of debasing the coinage, a dangerous practice indulged in by many governments since 1918.

After our audience the commission was lavishly entertained in Rome and met almost all the members of the ministry and other important personages. Premier Giolitti promised co-operation, and Cardinal Merry del Val, the papal secretary, asked that the commission indicate to him just what exhibits would be appreciated. The cardinal expressed regret that our departure for Paris that evening prevented an audience with the Pope.

From Rome the commission went to Paris where Ambassador Myron T. Herrick took us to call on the premier, Raymond Poincaré, and on President Fallières. We were promised full support on the part of France. The minister of war, Alexandre Millerand, was particularly interested in the canal, since, as he said, he had been minister of commerce during a part of the time the de Lesseps plan was in progress.

He seemed a little surprised that General Edwards asked for military participation, but said he would join if that were being done. Delcassé, minister of marine, promised Admiral Staunton that the French Navy would be represented.

Because of my anxiety to reach the Republican convention in time to support the candidacy of President Taft, I parted company with the commission at Paris; it completed its itinerary before returning to America.

In looking back over the trip, it seems to me that the show of interest we elicited was greater than had been expected. Unfortunately, the outbreak of war in 1914 made it impossible for many of the countries to carry out their participation on the scale they had proposed and hoped for.

On February 20, 1915, the Panama-Pacific International Exposition opened. The buildings were erected on made land by the shore of San Francisco Bay overlooking the Golden Gate. No more beautiful site could have been chosen; at night the fairgrounds were a splash of color, illuminating the sky, while the blue-black hills in the background twinkled with lights, and shining ferryboats scurried across the bay.

During the ten months of its duration over eighteen million people paid admission to the greatest international exposition ever held.

CHAPTER THIRTY

Peace and Preparedness

PEACE MOVEMENTS—TAFT'S INTEREST IN PEACE
SOCIETIES—I WORK FOR THE WORLD COURT—
WOMEN'S PART IN THE MOVEMENT—OUTBREAK OF
WORLD WAR—WOODROW WILSON'S ATTITUDE—HIS
RE-ELECTION—WE ENTER THE WAR—COLONEL HOUSE

*A*s I look back on the years
between 1910 and 1919,
years crowded with public and private business, it seems to me that
the problem of world peace occupied a great proportion of my time
and energies. My interest in search of a plan for the peaceable settlement of international disputes became complicated after August,
1914, with the urgent need for preparedness, and after April 2, 1917,
with the still more insistent problem of winning the war. But all
through this period the underlying and ultimate need seemed to me
to be the acceptance of the principle of justice in international relations. I do not propose to go deeply into the history of this movement, nor into the judicial and political arguments in support of it;
I want to give merely an indication of the attitude taken by a businessman and an engineer.

These chapters may seem somewhat lengthy to the general reader
but the issues discussed have profound importance in the present
international political situation. For instance, the activities of the
peace movements in this country eventuated in the creation of the
League of Nations—an ideal to which Woodrow Wilson dedicated
his political fortune and, in a large measure, his life.

The peace movement, under the influence of the Second Hague

Conference in 1907, had produced several propagandist societies, notably those supported and encouraged by Andrew Carnegie. A statesmanlike effort to translate ideals into political facts was made by Taft and Knox in general treaties with England and France, but the Senate refused to ratify them. Taft was greatly disappointed in this failure, but he never gave up his belief that some sort of court of justice could be set up to decide many of the war-breeding questions that arise between nations.

On February 6, 1910, Theodore Marburg, well-known publicist and subsequently United States minister to Belgium, gave a small dinner at his house in Baltimore. Among the guests was James Brown Scott, secretary of the Carnegie Endowment for International Peace, who had been technical delegate to the Second Hague Peace Conference. On this occasion we launched the American Society for the Judicial Settlement of International Disputes. The project was strongly supported by the administration, as is shown by the following quotations from letters read at the meeting.

President Taft:
> . . . If the proposed Court of Arbitral Justice at The Hague becomes an accomplished fact there will still remain the task of securing the adhesion of a number of Powers to the Court, and the very important task of so cultivating opinion in various countries as to incline Governments to resort to the Court when occasion calls for it. There is no other single way in which the cause of peace and disarmament can be so effectively promoted as by the firm establishment of a Permanent International Court of Justice . . . .

Secretary of State Knox:
> By the settlement of controversies susceptible of judicial determination before they have reached an acute stage the causes of war would be minimized and a first step taken toward the gradual decrease of armament . . .

Elihu Root:
> . . . I beg to say to your guests that I sympathize very

strongly with their object and believe that the proposed organization is adapted to render a great public service.

In another passage in his letter, Senator Root made a suggestion in the way of clarification of the society's objectives, which was acted upon:

> I assume that the new organization is to have a definite, specific object which may be indicated by emphasizing the word "judicial" in its title to indicate a distinction between that kind of settlement of international disputes and the ordinary arbitration as it has been understood in the past and is generally understood now.

Other letters expressed approval of the object of this meeting, notably one from Lyman Abbott and one from Woodrow Wilson, then president of Princeton University.

The officers for the new society were James Brown Scott, president; John Hays Hammond, vice-president; Theodore Marburg, secretary.

A statement detailing the purposes and policies of the society was prepared and given to the International News Service, which gave it wide circulation:

> The purpose underlying the formation of the American Society for the Judicial Settlement of International Disputes is promotion of the project to establish a judicial tribunal which will do for the civilized world what the ordinary courts of justice do for the individual and and to encourage recourse to it when established . . . The new society will enter upon no direct propaganda for peace, for arbitration, or for disarmament. Its aim is to advocate the most practical means hitherto devised of settling certain kinds of international disputes without resort to war and to leave to societies organized for that purpose the very useful work of bringing home to men the evils of war . . . Arbitration has been for some time, and will continue to be, of very great value, but it is merely the stepping stone to an institution far more

effective, i. e., the proposed International Court of Justice.

The task before the new society is to show the people of this and other lands . . .

1st. That the movement to reject war as a means of settling international controversies has already become a practical movement, made such by the achievements of arbitration and kindred institutions.

2nd. That the proposed Court of Arbitral Justice offers greater possibilities for the peaceful settlement of international controversies along permanent lines than any existing institutions . . .

The channels through which the new society proposes to work are principally two, viz: the issuing of brief statements of scientific accuracy by the leading men of various countries, and meetings of national scope.

It was now necessary to secure for our society the adherence of men whose names would carry weight with the public, and to enlist financial support. Theodore Marburg wrote to me on April 6th: "We are not deceiving ourselves as to the length or magnitude of our task; it will require many years of active propaganda by printed page and through public meetings before the leading nations of the world acquire the habit of using the proposed International Court of Justice instead of resorting to war."

Today, after a quarter of a century, there is still much to be done: the "magnitude of the task" was not overestimated.

On April 25th I wrote to Marburg:

I spoke to the President last night about becoming Honorary President of the American Society for the Judicial Settlement of International Disputes. He expressed his appreciation of the great importance of this work, and predicted success of the object which we are all making an effort to attain.

He also said that it would give him great pleasure to accept the post of Honorary President if he could do so with propriety, and that he would speak to Knox about it.

Secretary Knox approved and President Taft became honorary president. Woodrow Wilson was asked to become a member of the Advisory Council but declined.

It was thought desirable also to interest officials in Mexico and Canada. In June the secretary of state of Mexico, Señor Enrique Creel, accepted my invitation to become an honorary member We asked President Taft to invite President Diaz, Sir Wilfrid Laurier, and Earl Grey, governor general of Canada, for our coming annual meeting in December, but he could not see his way clear to issuing so official a request. We did not secure any of them, but Earl Grey sent me this telegram:

GREATLY REGRET IMPOSSIBLE ACCEPT YOUR MOST KIND
INVITATION DECEMBER FIFTEEN   SYMPATHIZE HEARTILY
WITH ALL YOUR HOPES AND WISH YOU THOROUGHLY
SUCCESSFUL GATHERING   GREY

The December meeting was addressed by President Taft, Jules Jusserand, the French ambassador, Joseph H. Choate, Charles Eliot, and others, and was considered a success. I was made president, and Simeon E. Baldwin, governor-elect of Connecticut, became vice-president.

In 1911 our society joined the American Peace Society in a national Peace Congress held at Baltimore in May. The situation in China was a disturbing one at the time, and in the course of my address I advocated the neutralization of China, and the guaranteeing of its integrity by the great powers. At that day none of us would have believed that within three years the Belgian neutrality treaty would become a mere "scrap of paper."

Whether or not this venture on shaky ground was wise I do not know. I remember asking Dr. Wu, the Chinese minister, Charles R. Flint, Paul Morton, E. H. Harriman, and a few others to a dinner, where our discussions were to be strictly confidential. In our conversation about affairs in China, Dr. Wu said that China was able to take care of herself and was at the time organizing a large army. I asked him whether it might not be better for China to continue her traditional peaceful policy, spend her hard-won revenues on internal development, and allow the powerful nations of the world to guarantee her sovereignty. To neutralize China would be advantageous to Europe, because, I pointed out as tactfully as possible, China might, if armed, become a threat to other nations.

"Quite true," said the minister, "that is good business, good diplomacy, and good politics; but could we trust you Western nations?" He went on to say that he was reminded of the fable *The Kite and Pigeons,* the moral of which is that "they who voluntarily place power in the hands of a tyrant or an enemy must not wonder if it be at last turned against themselves." He elaborated this by adding, *"Timeo Danaos et dona ferentes."*

When I was in London at the coronation of King George V, I attended the Pilgrims' Dinner and made an address on international amity. A. J. Balfour, I found, was enthusiastic in the cause of peace and made a telling speech on the value and practicability of a World Court.

Our society continued to hold public meetings and to issue quarterly pamphlets which were widely distributed. Annual conventions were held, I believe, up to the sixth one in 1916; the one planned for 1914 had been omitted at the request of our president, Charles W. Eliot. He characteristically wrote to the Executive Committee, "Events more effective than talk this year."

Another echo of the uncertainties of this first war year is found in Elihu Root's reply to Marburg's request that he become vice-president of the society for 1915 and, in regular course, president in 1916: "I shall be happy to act as vice-president for the year 1915. The question of the presidency for 1916, however, I think better be held in abeyance at present. That is a good ways off and I am not at all sure how I shall be situated at that time."

The society decided to concentrate its efforts on just one point— to gain support for the idea of an international court. There was no dissension in its ranks. It is true that some men, notably President Eliot, believed that force would be necessary to make effective the awards of such a Court, but the accepted official attitude was that the moral weight attaching to the Court's decisions would be sufficient to ensure their compliance; furthermore, that to advocate

THEODORE MARBURG

ANDREW CARNEGIE (1837-1919)

the sanction of armed force would raise such objections that our more modest aim would be nullified. We steered clear also of extreme pacifism, such as was being preached by more radical groups.

In place of the annual convention, a Peace Platform meeting was held at the Metropolitan Temple in New York on December 27, 1914, directed by John Wesley Hill and the International Peace Forum, of which I was vice-president. In my address I emphasized the similarity of the World Court to the United States Supreme Court. The analogy was not original with me, but it seemed a simple and familiar idea to impress upon the popular mind.

A day or two later, after talking with Marburg, I issued a call to a number of prominent men to meet me at lunch at the Midday Club on January 4, 1915. There I explained my idea of making an intensive campaign for the World Court through popular meetings and newspaper publicity. I did not consider that this activity would be regarded by anyone as in any sense unfriendly to the American Society for the Judicial Settlement of International Disputes, on the Executive Committee of which I continued to serve. (I did feel that that society's unwieldy title, suggesting a somewhat academic and "intellectual" tone, handicapped its effectiveness.) The outbreak of the World War had, it seemed to me, made it advisable to find a new approach to the problem. It furnished a concrete example of the failure of the old folk-ways of nations, and pointed the lesson that civilization must find its *modus vivendi* under Justice, impartial and recognized. Agreeing on the value of a new society under a new name, and of renewed and intensified effort, we proceeded to organize a World Court League and take it before the country.

I found enthusiastic support among my friends, many of whom were already working for the Court idea. Root declared for us, and Taft, whom I went to New Haven to see, agreed on the plan of a general campaign. In order that we might work in harmony with the Wilson administration, James Brown Scott interviewed Secretary Lansing and secured his approval. But we were unable to gain a public adherence from President Wilson. His reply of February 3rd said in part:

> I think it would be unwise for a member of the Administration to appear at a public meeting called for the advocacy of some particular measure of international organization, just at this juncture . . .

Marburg took the President's refusal quite to heart. In a letter written to me on February 8th, accompanying a draft of the President's letter, he wrote: "I enclose copy of a very disappointing letter from the President . . . You were right; I should have gone to see him in person."

Certain men we had hoped to have with us in a congress at Cleveland, planned for May, failed us. President Lowell, of Harvard, declined,

> . . . not through a lack of faith in the importance of an International Court of Justice . . . my objection to being on the general committee is that I got uncomfortably caught once in a peace movement, where I find that the names of the Trustees are being used for proposals which they have had no chance to consider, and which some of them, at least, do not approve; and I feel very shy about adding one's name to a movement in which one had not the time to take an active part. If I could be in Cleveland in May, it would be a very different thing.

Later, Lowell became actively identified with us in the League to Enforce Peace.

Joseph H. Choate's letter of refusal written April 8, 1915, is also interesting:

> I think there is no need to attempt to prove to the world that the people of the United States wholly approve of the project of an International Court of Justice, and I do not think the time has come to take any action that would be effective towards its prompt establishment, while the war is going on. The American public, in my opinion, does not need to be roused to a consciousness of the possibilities that lie in the creation

of such a court, and the discussion of it at such a congress in the midst of the war will receive no attention
from the nations who are engaged in the war, and who
will probably settle the terms of peace without assistance
from outsiders.

Of course, Mr. Choate knew as much as I did about the weight of
America's influence abroad, but my opinion was at variance with his.
I felt, and often said, that America's irreproachable neutrality, her
conspicuous advocacy of peace, her commanding position in finance,
industry, and commerce, her freedom from political alliances, her
cosmopolitan population had ordained her by Providence to take
the lead in the peace movement. Time proved that our influence
as one of the combatants was in some respects dominant at the
Peace Conference, but I believe that our advice would have been
listened to even if we had taken no part in the war, provided we had
created from a military point of view a strong position. It seemed
eminently reasonable and probable that a carefully thought-out plan
proposed by the United States and overwhelmingly supported by
its citizens would be welcomed by the nations of Europe when the
war was over.

Our minimum plan was for the creation of a World Court to deal
only with justiciable questions, and for the creation of an assembly,
or Council of Conciliation, to deal with nonjusticiable questions if
only to ensure delay and the publicity which a hearing would produce. This plan was so simple as to cause some men to say that it
was unnecessary to undertake a campaign to persuade Americans
that it was good.

Harold Howland, of the *Independent,* thought a postcard sent
through the mails, or the simple creed thrown on the screen before
motion picture audiences would be sufficient. Some thought the nations at war would have no time to listen, and they were to a degree
right. Archbishop Ireland replied to my letter, saying that he did
not have "much confidence in movements proposed at the present
time." Jacob Schiff thought that the "first thing is to bring to an
end the present conflict." Samuel Gompers, after consulting the
Executive Committee of the American Federation of Labor, replied,
"I am not in sympathy with some of the projects." Oscar Straus

approved but ended his letter with these words, "whether amid the awful clash and brutal noises of war men have ears to hear or not at the present time is a question which doubtless has had your consideration." Nevertheless, our World Court League grew rapidly by the accession of those who believed in the value and feasibility of our program. During the two years of its greatest activity, the officers were:

John Hays Hammond, *President*

Alton B. Parker

Bainbridge Colby

Charles Lathrop Pack *Vice-presidents*

D. D. Woodmansee

Henry Clews, *Treasurer*

Emerson McMillin, *Chairman of Executive Committee*

John Wesley Hill, *General Secretary*

Charles H. Burr, *Executive Secretary*

William W. Wilson, *Recording Secretary*

William Howard Taft, *Honorary President*

Charles W. Fairbanks

Oscar S. Straus

Lawrence Y. Sherman *Honorary vice-presidents*

Woodbridge N. Ferris

The limited object of the World Court League was defined thus:

> To advocate, and by agitation and appeal, to secure the support of all peoples in the establishment of a World Court for the settlement of all justiciable questions of dispute that may arise between Nations . . . a rational alternative to war.
>
> Until the efficiency of an INTERNATIONAL COURT has been recognized by the laws and practices of civilized Nations, the League likewise recognizes the right of every Nation to adopt adequate measures for National Defense.

The clause on preparedness expressed our sense of the danger to America of a spread of the European war, and our insistence that to plan for a reign of justice was not inconsistent with a vigorous defense program.

Our plan of operation was to hold public meetings throughout the country for the purpose of securing the adherence of clubs, chambers of commerce, state legislatures, and the masses. During February, March, and April we carried on a whirlwind campaign in the East and as far west as St. Louis. John Wesley Hill, as field agent, made the arrangements for meetings; and he, Henry Clews, Senator Lawrence Y. Sherman, of Illinois, and I addressed them. This initial campaign culminated in the First World Court Congress at Cleveland, May 12-14, 1915.

The congress was well organized and largely attended. Newton D. Baker, then mayor of Cleveland, greeted the assembly in an eloquent address. The subject of ex-President Taft's principal address was "The United States Supreme Court the Prototype of a World Court." Emerson McMillin and Theodore Marburg spoke on "The Composition of an International Court"; Henry Lane Wilson, on "Limitations of Jurisdiction." Judge Alton B. Parker, Warren G. Harding, Bainbridge Colby, and I, as president, on the practical value and feasibility of a World Court. These and other speeches were listened to with enthusiastic interest; the newspapers and later the magazines rendered excellent service in publicizing our proceedings; the officers and delegates were encouraged to carry on. The employment of sanctions to enforce decisions of the Court was rejected. My presidential address contained this expression of opinion:

> "As to the judgment of the court or the order of the Council of Conciliation, many of us believe that all nations would respond to the dictate of a World Court or a Council of Conciliation, irrespective of the exercise of any constraining influence other than that of the public opinion of the rest of the world.
>
> "This program, I believe, is practicable, whereas, it is very doubtful if we could obtain the agreement of the nations to the exercise of military force to compel obedience to the orders of the Court or Council in case of non-

compliance. This, however, would probably be a future enlargement of the power of the League.

"But this meeting has to do only with the creation of a World Court.

"A World Court would, in time, undoubtedly become representative of a world interest, subordinating the narrow interests of any particular nations to the welfare of humanity at large. The judges would become world judges, animated by the highest patriotism—the welfare of mankind—not a tribunal prepossessed with national bias.

"Many of us believe that the World Court can be established by the time of the termination of the present European War in connection with the discussion of the terms of peace. So, then, *in time of war let us prepare for peace, that in time of peace we shall not again have to prepare for war.*

"The belligerent nations at that time would, we believe, be willing to subordinate minor differences of opinion for the realization of this ideal, which they will regard as indispensable to their welfare. Since they all suffer from the evils of a great war, all neutral nations should make an insistent demand for the establishment of such a Court. Neutral nations have a common peril. In a World Court they would have a common safety."

Several interesting incidents occurred during the progress of the conference: A group of Polish patriots submitted a petition that we take up the question of Polish independence. A delegation of Zionists set forth reasons why Palestine should be made the seat of the Court. J. B. Livesay proposed a "Peace Society of the World."

On May 6th, Dr. Jeremiah W. Jenks and I had a conversation with Dr. Bernard Dernberg, the reputed unofficial spokesman of the Kaiser in this country. Dr. Dernberg knew of the event planned to terrorize the world on the following day—the torpedoing and sinking of the *Lusitania;* nevertheless, he calmly assured us that the Kaiser and the German people were in favor of a World Court!

In its meetings in 1916 the World Court League proposed to lay special emphasis on the study of the nature and the development of the United States Supreme Court, a study which should reveal useful analogies for an international court. A minor convention was held at Louisville, Kentucky, in April, and a special effort was made to secure favorable resolutions from state legislatures. The Second Annual Congress was held in New York on May 2-4, 1916. I wrote to Colonel House in April, explaining our program and assuring him that the war and preparedness issues would not be raised, and then asked that he get President Wilson to speak. Colonel House replied, "It is impossible for the President to make any commitments at present."

The World Court League now had the valuable assistance of an active and enthusiastic Women's Committee with the following officers: Miss Mabel T. Boardman, president; Mrs. Champ Clark, Mrs. Henry Clews, Mrs. Lindley M. Garrison, Mrs. John Hays Hammond, Mrs. Charles Evans Hughes, Mrs. Thomas J. Preston, Mrs. James Speyer, and Mrs. William Howard Taft, vice-presidents; Mrs. Alice Fisher Harcourt, secretary.

Our discussions were not so much on the desirability of the Court, for the public mind had really accepted that, but rather on its feasibility. As the *World Court Magazine* put it, the problem was no longer one of pure ethics; it was a problem of practical operation.

Taft discussed with great acumen the initial jurisdiction of a World Court, and the ways in which its jurisdictions could legally be extended so as to give it latitude for really effective ruling. General Leonard Wood spoke on the issue of preparedness: "Our country should be prepared to take its part with force when reason fails; there is nothing in the constitution of the Court which makes—or should make—its members pacifists." Senator Warren G. Harding said, "Yes, I believe in a World Court, I am very enthusiastic about it." My own emphasis was placed on the need for raising international questions out of the field of diplomacy and conciliation and arbitration into a field where not national but human welfare would be the first consideration: when a World Court became representative of genuine world interest, that is, of justice, nations would not be fearful of submitting disputes to its decision.

At the end of May our society joined with the League to Enforce Peace in their first assemblage. Our aims were to some extent the same, though it is significant that James Brown Scott, secretary of the Carnegie Endowment for International Peace, refused my invitation to speak at the assemblage on the ground that he could not lend, by his presence, support to the *Enforcement* aspect of the program. In taking this stand he was true to the principles of the Second Hague Conference and to the position of Andrew Carnegie.

Through the efforts of our Judicial Settlements Society, the Republican National Convention, in June, 1916, adopted a plank favoring a World Court, and the inclusion of it in Hughes's speech of acceptance. During the campaign I spent much of my time on political matters and eventually resigned the presidency of the World Court League.

The third peace movement in which I took an active part was Theodore Marburg's League of Peace, or League to Enforce Peace. As I served on the Executive Committee and then on the International Committee, from its beginning in 1915 up to 1919, I shall review briefly its history in so far as I personally know it.

Theodore Marburg gave a dinner at the Century Club in New York, on January 25, 1915, and there proposed a League of Peace. I could not be present but I was on hand at the second meeting, January 31st. The program included the World Court plan as its first step and then proceeded to put "teeth" into the Court, as I shall show later. Although I never could conscientiously advocate its more extreme measures, it contained so much that I agreed with that I gladly joined, served on its committees, and made speeches on those phases which I thoroughly believed in. I had the sincerest friendship for, and confidence in, Theodore Marburg, and the League was his greatest effort in the cause of peace. The two volumes of his *Development of the League of Nations Idea* give the full story, and form an important chapter in modern history.

The setbacks the League was destined to suffer were indicated in its early days. Theodore Roosevelt's reply to Marburg was, "But our prime duty is ourselves to be prepared." James Brown Scott said, "I do not see how we are justified to advance proposals—which we know would not, indeed could not, be accepted by our country." Marburg, Howland, and I were appointed to consult James Bryce, whose reply was that "a cautious and limited scheme has a better chance than such a large one as would satisfy you and Mr. Root and our British group." Howland, on the other hand, expressed the growing opinion that "The Hague Conventions are now in the scrapheap. They lacked the compelling force to make them effective under the conditions which existed, just before the outbreak of the Great War" and that a League of Peace will have to contain a "guarantee to be maintained when necessary by the use against offending nations of the united force of the nations of the League." *Quot homines tot sententiae.*

After several discussions and the examination of the criticisms, the Executive Committee agreed on a platform. Whereas the first proposal included the setting up of a League Police Force to compel obedience to the decisions of the Court, the committee decided to drop this provision as being too radical an invasion of national rights. It was hoped that the defenders of the two long-standing clauses of American foreign policy—"Monroe Doctrine" and "No Entangling Alliances"—would thus be placated. The name of the organization was decided on: The League to Enforce Peace. Preparation was made for the public inauguration of the League, and on June 17th a great meeting was held at Independence Hall in Philadelphia.

The platform was written by William Howard Taft, then the League's president.

> The principles and project of the League to Enforce Peace, as projected by the American Section of its promoters, are few and simple. Shortly stated, they look to the peaceable procedure for the hearing and decision of all international controversies, to be enforced by the joint power of the nations of the world. The force is to be applied in securing the due process under the agreements of the League. It does not extend to the enforcement of the judgment or recommendation of compromise which shall be the result of the hearing. The essence of the plan is the delay and deliberation involved in orderly procedure for the hearing and decision of the controversy. It is thought that most wars can be avoided by such a procedure, and the force is to be applied against the premature hostilities of any na-

tion which violates its plighted faith under the League by beginning war before the procedure of hearing and judgment has been completed.

On September 17th the Executive Committee passed the following resolution: "Efficient preparation for adequate national defense is in no way inconsistent with the purposes of the League, but on the contrary is essential thereto." Those who lived through the war years will remember how necessary it was at that time for our League to dissociate itself from the less conservative and more sentimental and visionary peace societies. As it was, our society was frequently misunderstood, and repeated pronouncements had to be made in the effort, not always successful, to assure the public that we were not "pacifist," "pro-German," or utopian. In the official announcement for the First Assemblage at Washington in May, 1916, A. Lawrence Lowell wrote:

> It is emphatically not a "stop-the-war" movement, neither is it an "anti-preparedness" organization, nor is it a "peace-at-any-price" endeavor. It represents an earnest effort by practical men, to secure joint action by the principal nations, after the close of the European war, looking towards the establishment of more permanent peace by the use of economic and military force.

Though I had failed in April in my effort to get President Wilson to attend the World Court Congress, the negative I received seemed to be due to the President's being overwhelmed with business and not to any unfriendliness. I knew, at any rate, that Colonel House was favorable, and we all felt that Wilson's speech at Des Moines on February 1st gave ground for thinking he was ready to espouse our cause openly:

> "I pray God that if this contest have no other result, it will at least have the result of creating an international tribunal and producing some sort of joint guarantee of peace on the part of the great nations of the world."

This statement I copied out and enclosed with a letter I wrote House on May 17, 1916:

There is to be a meeting of the League to Enforce Peace on May 26th and 27th at the New Willard Hotel, Washington. I am enclosing a tentative program for that meeting, also a descriptive pamphlet showing the object of the League.

At a meeting the other day a committee of the League discussed how best to present an invitation to President Wilson to speak on this occasion: and before sending an official invitation to the President they wished to ascertain whether or not it will be possible for him to accept it, knowing his urgent official engagements. I told them frankly that I did not know how far President Wilson would commit himself to the use of arms to compel signatory powers to the League to submit their controversies to a Court before commencing hostilities. I did say, however, that I believe that he could, consistent with his other declarations on the subject of a World Court, go so far as to advocate a policy of nonintercourse with a recalcitrant nation in such a contingency.

Mr. Theodore Marburg, one of the members of the Committee, gave me a quotation from a speech of President Wilson which I enclose.

Would you please let me know whether or not you can be of service to the League in this matter, and whether I should arrange to have an invitation extended to the President through you, or whether it would be better to send an invitation directly to the President. Your kindly offices will be appreciated by the members of the League and myself.

The World Court League, of which I am president and of which I spoke to you, has for its object the establishment of a World Court at the opportune moment. Our League relies for the enforcement of its decrees upon the pressure of the sentiment of the world, rather than the application of physical force. Both Leagues are agitating the establishment of a World Court.

Would you kindly let me hear from you by telephone

> or send me word where I may call to see you, should
> you wish to discuss the matter further.

This time we were successful. President Wilson attended the meeting of May 27th and stated that the United States was ready to take its place in "an universal association of the nations . . . to prevent any war begun either contrary to treaty covenants or without warning and full submission of the causes to the opinion of the world."

"I cannot tell you how pleased I am with your speech last night," Colonel House wrote the President the next day, "it will be a landmark in history."

By this time the League had been supported by resolutions passed in several state legislatures I had addressed on the subject, and it seemed opportune to secure a resolution from Congress. Marburg and Taft suggested to Wilson, therefore, that he have proposed in Congress an administration measure favoring the League. Wilson said that would not do, because of the opportunity it would offer for speeches against the measure on the floor. Taft agreed with Wilson, and Marburg reluctantly gave up the idea.

During the year 1916 our Committee on Foreign Organization proceeded to enlist the interest of the countries of Europe, those at war and the neutrals. Our literature was translated into several languages and sent to government officials and prominent persons. Marburg had been in France and England, from February to April, and had opened the question of the League with many influential people. Sir Edward Grey, shortly afterwards created Viscount Grey of Fallodon, was strong in his support, and his successor in office, Arthur J. Balfour, was hardly less interested. Correspondence was carried on with European chancelleries and we had conversations with foreign ambassadors at Washington. The result was encouraging. While the almost universal reply was to the effect that cabinets were too much engrossed in the immediate problems of the war to give proper attention to a plan for peace after the war, the League was accepted "in principle," and that was really all that could be expected.

As a crowning move in this international campaign we proposed to send Taft to Europe as our emissary. England was particularly anxious to have him come for the moral support of his presence. He was, of course, to talk with individuals only, and in the capacity of a private citizen; no attempt was to be made to promote inter-Allied conferences. Taft was persuaded to undertake the mission and went to President Wilson to ask his opinion. Wilson's answer was that he did not like it at all, and Taft replied, "Thank you, that ends it." The project was abandoned.

It began to be clear that unless Congress, and particularly the Senate, was in favor of the League the whole movement would be futile so far as American participation was concerned, and from 1916 on we determined to concentrate our efforts on the Senate and the House. Sir Edward Grey, on February 19th, expressed the fear that "the U. S. Senate will not adhere, which would make of the League merely a concert of the powers of Europe."

After we entered the war, like the other warring nations, we had to concentrate our efforts on winning it. The League should, however, as Glenn Frank said in an appeal to the members on April 24, 1917, meet its new obligations, which were to keep clear in the public mind that we were fighting for future security. The phrases of Wilson, "Make the world safe for democracy" and the "League of Honor," indicate the accord between us and the administration. The League had from its very foundation recognized the necessity of a policy of preparedness for defense, and throughout the two years of war supported the administration in its vigorous prosecution. On May 16-17, 1918, we held a memorable meeting in Philadelphia, the theme of which was, "Win the War for Permanent Peace."

That our work was of interest to the administration may be gathered from my letter to Taft, July 27, 1917:

> My dear Bill: The other night dining with Colonel House I had a chance to discuss with him the future of the League to Enforce Peace, and he expressed the wish that I should arrange a meeting some time in the near future, when mutually convenient, with you, President Lowell, myself and him, to discuss certain features of the plans. I believe that Colonel House can be and

would be of great assistance to us if we take the trouble
to enlist his co-operation . . .

Synchronized with all my work for peace, and arising out of it,
was the debate between the pacifists, in the invidious sense of the
term, and the advocates of preparedness, a controversy in which I
was necessarily active.

Before the outbreak of the World War, all of us who were identified with peace movements called ourselves pacifists. But with
the appearance of peace societies of the nonresistant order, it became necessary to distinguish between the peace-at-any-price groups,
among whom Henry Ford, Dr. David Starr Jordan, and Jane Addams
were prominent, and the groups that considered adequate national
defense consistent with the advocacy of peace.

As the war ran on into 1915, many Americans became concerned
over the state of our army and navy. A grudging Congress had
starved both, and the war waging in Europe had not roused either
Congress or Cabinet to action. The soothing reply to questions was
that the national defense was adequate—a reply that was contra-
dicted by both army and navy and, as later became obvious, by the
facts. The administration in its official insistence on neutrality
seemed bent on proving its neutrality by being unprepared. Not
even the sinking of the *Lusitania* on May 7, 1915, brought any
change in the official position.

At this juncture Henry A. Wise Wood came to see me, and after
our talk I took steps looking to the building up of the nation's defenses. What these steps consisted of, and the results that followed
upon them, were explained in a letter Wood wrote me four years
later, September 24, 1919:

> Professor William H. Hobbs, of Ann Arbor, Mich.,
> is bringing out a book entitled "Leonard Wood and the
> Preparedness Movement," which gives a history of both.
> I have supplied Hobbs with a great deal of data con-
> cerning the latter, among which is a reference to the
> exceedingly important part you played at a critical
> moment in 1915. Hobbs recounts this incident in the
> following words:

"A month after the *Lusitania* outrage the Conference Committee on National Preparedness was organized among the defense societies with Henry A. Wise Wood as chairman. The wisdom of this union of effort was at once to be proven, though the facts which we are here to present have not before been given to the public. The chairman of the Conference Committee was a friend of John Hays Hammond and both were during the summer the neighbors of Colonel House at his home near Cape Ann, Massachusetts. Since House was the unique confidential friend of the President, Wood made a strong appeal to Hammond to see if he could not through House get the President to move in the now desperate matter of our national defense. This Hammond did, but with no other result than a suggestion from House to get in touch with the Secretary of War. This failing to bring results, the appeal was renewed by Mr. Wood, though in a different way. In a personal letter he writes:

I hunted up Hammond and told him something really had to be done, saying that the sentiment for preparedness was rising so rapidly throughout the country that the inactivity of the administration would soon become a public scandal, and that the Democratic party would have only the President to thank if it should be utilized by its political opponents. I suggested that Hammond see House again and point out to him the *political* danger into which the President was running because of his refusal to take the steps necessary to prepare the Army and Navy for active service. Hammond said that he would act at once, and did. He saw House and told the latter that unless proper defensive measures were at once taken by the administration the President might expect the Republican party to make a political issue of Wilson's inactivity. Hammond told House that while the Republican party would not wish to make political capital out of such a matter, Mr. Wilson was so shaping affairs that the Republican party in order to fulfill its duty would be compelled to attack him for his dereliction. This, Hammond told me, greatly aroused Colonel House, who said that he would write at once to the President, at Cornish, and recommend that something be done. Immediately after Mr. Hammond's action came Mr. Wilson's half-hearted request for recommendations by the General Board of the Navy and the General Staff of the Army.

"These requests for reports on what was necessary for the National defense were sent from Cornish on July 21st and the reports of the two Boards were submitted to the President on July 30th. The reports of these expert Boards, containing, as they did, such vitally important information for the safety of the country, were not given to the public. In the public mind was the question, 'Was the President right when he assured the joint houses of Congress, and through them the nation, that they had been misinformed and that the national defense was already secure?' or did a desperate condition exist such as General Wood, Admiral Fiske, Congressman Gardner, and a number of former Secretaries of War had asserted? If these latter were right and the President wrong, it was obviously necessary to at once utilize every available agency to the end of supporting representatives in Congress when that body should meet and take up the consideration of the necessary appropriation bills."

Professor Hobbs will be glad to have you add any further matters that you have in mind, or to make such corrections in the above as you may deem necessary. My own view is that it was your action that turned the President from one course to the other and thus was a major influence in inaugurating our active military preparations.

This account agrees in substance with my recollection of the matter. I have only to add that Mr. Wood asked me to take the chairmanship of a defense committee, which I refused on the ground that to do so might handicap the cause since my son, John Hays Hammond, Jr., was at that time negotiating the sale to the government of his invention to control boats by radio.

Colonel House and I had been friends in our Hopkins Grammar School days in New Haven when he was a classmate of my brother Bill. Although Colonel House had been for many years a summer resident near Manchester (only a few miles from Gloucester), I had not seen him until after the inauguration of President Wilson when House dined with me at my summer home. At that meeting he told me that he was called "the John Hays Hammond of the Wilson administration." I said, "I hope you will have more influence with President Wilson than I had with President Taft; I failed to use such influence as perhaps I should have exerted."

As will become more and more apparent with the passage of years, Colonel House has been one of the greatest influences behind the scenes of American politics, and of world statecraft as well.

During the war Colonel House's cottage at Coolidge Point was a veritable "hub of the universe": every important diplomat who came from Europe was sent by President Wilson to consult with the colonel.

House has often been called "the man of mystery." There is nothing mysterious about him. He is a man without the usual pecuniary interests in life. The fact that no one can accuse him of private or selfish concern in his actions gives him great power and freedom of opinion. He has never liked publicity, which frees him from suspicion of greed for the limelight. He seldom appears in public. Today he sits in his home and receives, one after another, the great men of the world who use him as intermediary and spokesman because he is that most unusual phenomenon—a man without self-interest. He is actively behind the scenes in Franklin D. Roosevelt's administration, admittedly concentrating his keen analytical powers on international problems.

In the formation of the Wilson Cabinet, House was more influential than any other of Wilson's political advisers. In his *Intimate Papers,* House has understated the part he played in the Wilson administration. This I know, for it was my privilege to be his confidant in many instances just before and during the period of the World War.

When I first approached him on the subject, Colonel House assured me that he was in favor of preparedness and had given such support as he could to General Leonard Wood's citizen training camp at Plattsburg. At his suggestion I went to Washington and saw Secretary of War Garrison, who said that he had already taken steps to make the army more efficient for warfare. I talked with several other high officials, and also with Samuel Gompers, with whom I arranged a conference in a drawing room on the train between Washington and New York. At first he refused his cooperation, urging that preparedness was a militaristic aim that might be used later on to dragoon labor. Fortunately, before we reached New York, my arguments prevailed and Gompers became an important factor in the preparedness movement, as shown by his unswerving loyalty to the cause and by his splendid record during the war.

On my return to Gloucester I discussed the subject of preparedness with Secretary of the Navy Daniels, at a dinner at my home, August 25, 1915. Secretary Daniels at that time favored the idea of increased efficiency of the navy, though only a short time before he had made the public statement that the navy was already adequately prepared.

In the fall of that year I was a guest of Senator Frank Newlands, of Nevada, at a small lunch in San Francisco, attended by Senator Oscar W. Underwood, of Alabama, Senator Phelan, of California, and Norman E. Mack, Democratic National Committeeman for New York.

We discussed the national election to be held in 1916. I was the only Republican present, but we were all old friends and the discussion was perfectly frank.

I told Senator Underwood that I thought the Republicans would win, on the issue of the tariff. (At that time the Underwood Tariff was in effect.) Senator Newlands interrupted the argument by saying: "Jack, you are entirely on the wrong track. The tariff will cut no figure in the next national campaign. The people of the country are strongly opposed to our being dragged into the World War, and President Wilson will have a War Program in the campaign on the slogan that he will keep us out of war."

Although Mr. Wilson, on a speechmaking tour in January, 1916, uttered sentiments in favor of preparedness (at St. Louis, declaring for "incomparably the most adequate navy in the world"), he afterwards soft-pedaled, probably on political advice and carried on the campaign of 1916 as forecast by Senator Newlands. Private individuals and societies were left to agitate for preparedness. The Republicans used the issue as one point in criticism of the Democrats, and I remember that Vice-President Marshall, in his defense of Wilson in the *Forum* of July, 1916, could only weakly say that it ill befitted the secretaries of the Taft administration to criticize. As if nothing had happened between 1912 and 1916!

The League to Enforce Peace had a joint meeting with all the defense societies, and its speakers, myself included, took occasion to emphasize the need for preparedness. I made a point of it in my political speeches before various audiences: before the National Republican League in conference in Washington, December 13, 1915; before the Detroit Board of Commerce on December 27, 1915; and at the National Republican League Convention at Chicago, June 6, 1916. I reviewed the whole problem of preparedness, answering objections as well as I could, before the National Civic Federation at Washington on January 18, 1916. In January, 1917, Governor Whitman appointed me New York's delegate to the Congress of Constructive Patriotism held in Washington.

The "pacifists" were claiming that the defense movement was being fostered by the manufacturers of munitions, who were making vast profits out of the war and hoped to make still more. The point was an awkward one and gave rise to the proposal that private profit should be taken out of war. Colonel House had in mind this sort of solution when he wrote, apropos of measures that ought to be taken after the sinking without warning of the *Arabic* on August 19, 1915:

I would begin preparations for defense and for the war, just as vigorously as if war had been declared. I would put the entire matter of defense and the manufacture of munitions in the hands of a non-partisan commission composed mostly of business men—men like John Hays Hammond, Guy Tripp, and others of that sort.

Just before the election, on a New York-Washington train, I met the German ambassador, von Bernstorff, whom I knew very well. He asked me what I thought would be the result of the election. I replied by asking for his opinion, adding that I felt sure he favored the re-election of President Wilson. He wanted to know on what grounds. I said: "Because it is to the advantage of Germany that America does not join with the Allies, and Germany depends on Wilson to keep America out of the war. Furthermore, even if we are forced into the war on the side of the Allies, President Wilson's opposition to a preparedness program will ensure diminished efficiency in our support of the Allies." Naturally, von Bernstorff revealed nothing.

The failure to prepare during the years 1915 and 1916, up to the time of our joining the Allies (April, 1917), undoubtedly resulted in the loss of many precious months in equipping our nation to take part effectively in the early stages of our military campaign abroad. I think it is agreed that, had we been thoroughly prepared for war, it is quite likely that Germany would have refrained from some of the acts that caused us to declare war. In any event, it is certain that had we been properly equipped when we joined the Allies the war would have ended considerably sooner than it did and there would have been the saving of many lives and the costs of war. As General Wood said, "It is better to be ready for war and not have it, than to have war and not be ready for it." But alas! Woodrow Wilson yielded to political expediency.

CHAPTER THIRTY-ONE

From the World Court to the
League of Nations

*T*HE anniversary of Armistice
Day should stir us to great
exultation of spirit, because of the proud recollection that it was our
precept and example which had, by those early days of that never-to-
be-forgotten November, lifted the nations of the world to the lofty
level of vision and achievement upon which the great war for democracy and right was fought and won. Although the stimulating
memories of that happy time of triumph are forever marred and
embittered for us by the shameful fact that when victory was won—
chiefly by the indomitable spirit and ungrudging sacrifice of our
incomparable soldiers—we turned our backs on our associates, refused

637

to bear any responsible part in the administration of the peace, or the firm and permanent establishment of the results won by the war at so fearful a cost of life and treasure, and withdrew into a sullen and selfish isolation which is deeply ignoble because manifestly dishonorable.

With these words Woodrow Wilson began his last statement to the American people—his radio address on the eve of the fifth anniversary of the Armistice.

History offers few episodes more tragically bewildering than this, in which Woodrow Wilson points the finger of scorn and shame at the country he had led in a valiant war and had attempted to make responsible for an enduring peace.

When the end of the war was almost in sight, it seemed to me that the foundations of the League might be begun immediately. On October 29, 1918, I wrote ex-President Taft:

> President Wilson and Lord Bryce, it seems, are opposed to the creation of a League to Enforce Peace before the end of the war. It has always been my belief that such a League already established would be able to render great service in the settlement of many of the important details relative to the terms of peace, and it seems to me that the nucleus of such a League now exists in the Allied Nations. The Allies should create this League either independently of, or with the co-operation of the Neutral Nations, after which the present Enemy Nations should be invited to join the League. As the result of their experience in the present war the Allies should be able to devise an effective League. This League should assert jurisdiction over all Nations whether members of the League or not when the safety of the world is involved. Germany's Allies in this war would undoubtedly avail themselves of the opportunity of joining such a League, and however Germany might resent the League having been started without consulting her, she would eventually also find it to her interest to join it.

I sent a copy of the letter to Marburg, who replied under date of October 31st:

> Dear Jack: . . . I was also pleased to see your letter to Mr. Taft. You of course know that some few of us have been urging just this thing for a year past, having the hearty support of the French group in this movement. I fear that owing to President Wilson's attitude there is little hope of the project being realized, the more so because events connected with the war are moving so fast.
>
> But everything is working out just right. The great aim of the war, you no doubt agree, is the destruction of Prussianism, which can be accomplished effectively only by the German people themselves. President Wilson has risen wonderfully to the demands of the moment by emphasizing this side of it in his recent messages. It looks now as if we really would have revolution in Germany. If we get it everything else will be plain sailing. Without it we could not get an effective league and the future of the world would indeed be gloomy—the maddest kind of military preparation all around. . . .

Colonel House with remarkable discernment and vision advised President Wilson to go to Europe after the Armistice to size up the situation for himself and become acquainted with the leading European statesmen. He further urged him not to participate personally in the Versailles Conference but to return to the United States and from Washington direct the American representatives. This would undoubtedly have given Wilson far greater influence in the proceedings of the Conference.

House suggested that Taft and Root (or Taft and some prominent Republican senator) be on the American commission with three Democrats appointed by Wilson, one of whom should be a member of the Senate. Taft and Root would have added great strength, not only because of their wide experience in European affairs but because of the high esteem in which they were held by their country-men. Instead, Wilson appointed his secretary of state, Robert Lan-sing, Colonel House, Tasker H. Bliss, and Henry White, all of whom were regarded by the country as affiliated with the Democratic party, with perhaps the exception of Henry White who was at the most a lukewarm Republican and whom the Republican leaders regarded as a Democrat.

Since the President decided to act in person at the Peace Con-ference, these men had no standing other than as his personal assist-ants, to be ignored or dismissed at his will. Their names had not been submitted to the Senate for confirmation. The President in this fashion organized his Peace Mission only a few short weeks after the country had been chilled, even in the midst of victorious advance on the western front, by the dictum that "if you wish me to be your unembarrassed spokesman in affairs at home and abroad, I earnestly beg that you express yourselves unmistakably to that effect by re-turning a Democratic majority to both the Senate and the House of Representatives." This appeal was resented not only by the Repub-lican party which had rendered patriotic service to Wilson in the winning of the war, but by the country at large as evidenced in the return of a Republican majority in Congress.

Wilson sailed for Paris, December 4, 1918. With Colonel House in Europe, jealous and self-interested advisers began to influence the President that he should be on the ground himself in order to main-tain his ideas and—I say it with some hesitation, but believe it to be true—for his own exaltation.

Before sailing Wilson boasted that he was to match wits with the statesmen of Europe. He little realized that he was to sit in a game of poker with a "cold deck" provided by the conferees.

The League to Enforce Peace was now placed in an awkward position. In the first place, we were kept in the dark as to the course of negotiations for a League of Nations; in the second place, when news did come the clauses providing for drastic sanctions to be em-ployed against recalcitrant members of the League went further than our League to Enforce Peace had ever advocated. In both these dif-ficulties, however, the League to Enforce Peace supported the President blindly and loyally. When opposition began to appear, both Taft and Marburg stood staunchly and wholeheartedly by the Wilson program. Some of us could not do so.

On January 5, 1919, at the Maryland convention, the League to Enforce Peace passed a unanimous resolution in support of Wilson in his efforts to get a League of Nations established. A cablegram was sent from the convention to Wilson assuring him that the sentiment of the country was behind him and that the recalcitrant senators must eventually desist from their opposition to the League of Nations. I did not agree with these views and opposed sending the cablegram but without avail. I offered controversial material in my own speech in the following points: Do we need a League of Nations? If so, what power are we willing to delegate to such a League? What steps must be taken to create the League?

To the first question the answer was "Yes." To the second I showed a "reservationist" attitude: "If the authority delegated to the League in the enforcement of its decrees by armed intervention is considered too far-reaching, the authority might, I believe, be curtailed in some respects without seriously impairing the potency of the League."

In answering the third question I was more sharply critical:

> "Now what are the best steps to be taken for the creation of a League of Nations? The present is not the time for partisan politics, and I have, I am glad to say, not seen, as yet, any disposition on the part of statesmen of either party to make a League of Nations the football of politics. But, in the consideration of the supreme problem of world peace, it is the duty of those who have given the subject careful consideration to speak frankly and fearlessly, if such expression of views will be of ultimate assistance in the promotion of this all-important movement.
>
> "It does not seem that we are proceeding along the right lines—certainly not on the lines of least resistance—to attain the creation of a League of Nations. For obvious reasons, the nations of Europe, who have paid

such a great price to 'save democracy' and to whom the menace of war is more imminent, will be more ready to accept a subordination of their national sovereignty to consummate the project of a League of Nations than will the people of the United States. It is among the people of our own country that a campaign of education must be carried on.

"In all probability, at the Versailles Conference the European representatives will be empowered to conclude a treaty creating a League of Nations without reference to further sanction by their respective governments. In this respect, our delegates to the Peace Conference will be, unfortunately, seriously handicapped in their negotiations, inasmuch as any treaty they may make on behalf of our country would be merely tentative—subject to ratification by the United States Senate. The Senate may, perhaps, at times deserve criticism for ultraconservatism and for its reluctance to admit of any encroachment upon its prerogative as a party to our foreign treaties. I hold no brief, but as regards the present attitude of the Senate with reference to the proposed League of Nations, we surely cannot censure it in so far as it is noncommittal, nor for its refusal to give its endorsement *to plans of which the Senators themselves have not been apprised.*

"The proper procedure would be the development of some plan which would receive the endorsement of the Senate in advance of its submission to the other nations. A plan having this sanction could then be presented as the American Plan, the principles of which had already been accepted by the Senate, and which would have the approbation of the people of the United States.

"We should not be deterred by a false sense of delicacy in requesting from President Wilson and the American Peace Delegates an outline of their plan. If it meets our approval, we should take immediate steps to present our recommendations to the Senate, backed by whatever influence we may command, with the view to obtaining its endorsement and its co-operation.

"Inasmuch as the League to Enforce Peace has given to this subject more consideration than any other American organization, and has had, moreover, the advantage of the collaboration of the best minds of this country, its intervention in this matter could not reasonably be regarded as officious. This course would undoubtedly facilitate an understanding between the Senate and our Peace Delegates, thereby expediting definite and definitive action. Otherwise, the creation of the League of Nations would be subject to delay which would be from every point of view highly undesirable. . . ."

It is true that in giving carte blanche to the President in its resolution the convention discounted my objections, but I submit that my criticism touched on political realities as proved by the subsequent history of the League of Nations in the Senate and before the American people.

One of the very few in the audience to sympathize with my attitude was Major Fiorello H. La Guardia, who had just returned with a distinguished record in the World War.

On January 30th, I wrote to Theodore Marburg:

. . . I fear the President is not making the progress that we wish in connection with *his* League of Nations. Of course, it is most difficult to get the unadulterated truth from Paris through the press which is still virtually under censorship. It will be a great misfortune for the world unless some kind of a League is established to eliminate the causes of war. You see now the futility of soliciting the cooperation of Senators in a scheme of which the promoters themselves are so ignorant. Team-work is the only method by which anything could have been accomplished, and President Wilson is not strong on team-work. The day of dictation has passed in November last on the day of our Congressional Election . . .

On February 13th, Marburg wrote me:

I wrote you a post card from the station last night suggesting that, after all, you carry out the plan of having a few Senators at the dinner at your home tomorrow night.

I had with me last night only Senator McCumber and Mr. J. J. Rogers of the House, who, I understand, had a good chance of becoming Chairman of the Committee on Foreign Affairs for the House in the coming Congress. Francis B. Loomis also joined us. The little talk was exactly right, the Senator and Mr. Rogers participating freely and both accepting the program which you and I stand for, i. e., force limited to compelling inquiry, plus the various institutions we plan to set up. We were at it until quarter past eleven and canvassed the subject pretty well. . . .

With the work of the Peace Conference partly done, Wilson returned to America, arriving February 23rd. He then entertained the Senate Foreign Relations Committee at the White House, and discussed with them the draft of the League of Nations Covenant as it had been submitted to the Peace Conference on the eve of his leaving Paris. Although the document was not then submitted for the action of the Senate, more than one-third of the members of that body took the initiative in warning him of their opposition to the plan of the League of Nations as he had approved it. This was a sufficient number to prevent the ratification of the Treaty. To these Mr. Wilson gave public answer as he again took ship for Paris, March 14th. "When that Treaty comes back, gentlemen on this side will find the covenant not only in it, but so many threads of the treaty tied to the covenant that you cannot dissect the covenant from the treaty without destroying the whole vital structure."

The day Wilson sailed for Paris, a message came to me from the editor of the New York *World* asking that I telegraph him for publication in the *World* my views "as to desirability of League of

Nations," and any suggestions or criticisms I might care to make with respect to the "pending draft of the League's provisions." I give my reply in full for the light it throws on my drift into the "reservationist" camp:

My political affiliations are Republican, but I regard a League of Nations as a national and not a partisan matter. Politics must be entirely dissociated from the problem of World Peace. I am an earnest advocate of the creation of a League of Nations, properly constituted, believing that such a League of Nations would have prevented the recent great World War. The advocates of a League of Nations realize that no political organizations can do more than minimize the possibility of war. I do not believe that our Nation should endeavor to maintain an attitude of "splendid isolation" as to World politics. Our detached position, geographical and political, did not suffice to keep us out of the recent war. We are now a World Power and have world-wide interests. While we should aim to minimize "entangling alliances," we must, nevertheless, be ready to assume our international responsibilities if we are to insist upon our national rights.

A speedy settlement with Germany and her allies is of paramount importance, in view of the disturbed political and economic conditions of the world. To effect this speedy settlement, it is necessary that the Treaty of Peace with Germany and her allies should be separate from the Treaty creating a League of Nations.

I am opposed to the pending draft of the League of Nations. It is loosely phrased and generally ambiguous. Moreover, where the meaning is clear, it is in many respects highly objectionable.

For example, under article 10, the United States would be committed to "preserve, as against external aggression, the territorial integrity and existing political independence of all states members of the League." This means preserving the status quo of the whole World, which is an onerous obligation and the observance of which might in the future become highly undesirable. Our obligations should be confined to an agreement not to invade the territories of the members of the League. The League should, however, undertake to protect the territorial integrity of the newly constituted Nations under the mandatory system, with such power to readjust territorial boundaries as future experience might necessitate in the interest of justice and of peace.

A permanent court to try justiciable controversies should be definitely established in the Treaty creating the League of Nations. Otherwise, a separate Treaty will be necessary to establish such a tribunal. The members of the League should be compelled to submit all justiciable questions to this court.

While article 13 contains a provision that the contracting parties will carry out in good faith any award that may be rendered by a Court of Arbitration, article 15, which provides for the reference of disputes to the Executive Council or the Body of Delegates, contains no similar provision, except that the contracting parties agree not to go to war if the decision of the Executive Council or the Body of Delegates is unanimous.

Article 16 assumes vague obligations and requires both clarification and limitation.

As to mandatories, the United States should not only be willing to assume, but should insist upon being, the mandatory in the case of the need of a mandatory for the Western Hemisphere. Under the proposed constitution, the United States would not be compelled to assume any mandatory, but I believe if the constitution of the proposed League were satisfactory in other respects, the responsibility of a mandatory would not be an insuperable objection.

There should be in the constitution, a specific exclusion of the Monroe Doctrine in its broadest implication and the question of immigration and of tariffs and other domestic questions should be also excluded from the jurisdiction of the League.

As I interpret article 8 as to disarmament, the objection against it seems hypercritical, inasmuch as the extent of military equipment is a matter to be determined by the respective governments themselves in the first instance. It is true that thereafter the forces shall not be exceeded without the permission of the Executive Council. The enlightened self-interest of the respective members of the League would eventually dictate a common policy as to disarmament.

As the League is a matter of experiment, the contracting powers should have the privilege of withdrawing from the membership any time after a period of ten years.

It must be conceded by all that ententes and alliances, with their secret treaties, espionage, and nefarious diplomacy, have utterly failed. Let us try a League of Nations. The infamous Holy Alliance is no precedent to quote in opposing a League of Nations. The World will certainly not go back to competitive armaments in the future to maintain World peace, but the proposed draft must be made more clear, more specific, and amended in many particulars.

Marburg was not in agreement with my stand for reservations. After reading a copy of my telegram to the *World,* he wrote me (April 7th) avowing unqualified support of the Wilson program:

I quite share the view that the convention could be improved by certain amendments and we may of course look forward to such improvement as indicated by the Paris dispatches. I would have been willing, however, to accept the document just as it was, feeling the following to be a fundamental thing, namely, that practically the whole world, cooperating, is pretty sure to be governed by reason and to do justice. Personally, I should go so far as to say that I would be satisfied to have the United States go into a rough agreement to cooperate in this way through a central council without any written document whatever. I shall not, however, inflict you at this time with an argument on this line . . .

Woodrow Wilson did bring back in July the kind of treaty he said he would when he sailed in March, to submit to the Senate for the "advice and consent" of that body.

The Senate's opposition to the United States joining a League of Nations became more formidable as the subject was agitated. Many of us began to realize the impossibility of committing any future national administration to the plan of the League of Nations as approved by President Wilson, since whatever commitments the Wilson administration might make, even if approved by the Senate, would be liable to repudiation under certain contingencies by succeeding administrations.

To ensure a League of Nations compatible with our political institutions and the spirit of the nation, Senator Lodge, as chairman of the Foreign Relations Committee, had moved the approval of the Versailles Treaty, including the League Covenant, but with certain reservations as a *sine qua non* of the United States joining the League.

After weeks of acrimonious debate in the Senate, the President met with the Foreign Relations Committee on August 19th, and two weeks later set out to carry the fight to the country. It was soon reported that the senators who trailed him were gaining the larger and more responsive audiences; and it became apparent that "the irreconcilables," the "pygmy men," the "jaundice-eyed Bolsheviks of politics," as the President had variously called his opponents, were probing the deeper instincts and sensing the sounder traditions of American political life. Doubling back from the Pacific coast, on September 26th, near Wichita, Wilson's health snapped, and with drawn shades at which the nation gazed sympathetically his train carried him back to Washington.

On November 19th, the Lodge motion to ratify the Treaty with reservations was defeated by a vote of 55 to 39. On the previous day, President Wilson had addressed a letter to the Democratic leader, Senator Hitchcock, in part as follows:

> In my opinion, the resolution in that form does not provide for ratification, but rather for nullification. I sincerely hope that the friends and supporters of the treaty will vote against the Lodge resolution of ratification. I understand that the door will then probably be open for a genuine resolution of ratification.

"Thus urged," says Colonel House in the *Intimate Papers,* "the Democrats voted with the 'bitter enders,' defeating ratification. Had the Democrats disregarded the President's wishes, and voted for ratification, including the Lodge resolution, the treaty would have been ratified by a vote of 81 to 13."

A few days before Viscount Grey of Fallodon, then serving as special ambassador to the United States, sailed for England early in January, 1920, he lunched with me at my house in Washington. After lunch I took him and the other guests, Colonel George Harvey, Senator Brandegee, my son Harris, and Lord Glenconner (who died shortly thereafter and whose widow Viscount Grey subsequently married,) up to my study.

We discussed the approaching presidential election, and I voiced my fears that there would inevitably be an acrimonious discussion of the League of Nations question in which criticism of England's "six votes to our one" and other objections would be violently debated.

At that time I was in favor of entering the League of Nations with the Lodge reservations, and I think Colonel Harvey probably would have agreed with me, but Senator Brandegee was unalterably opposed to entrance in any way, shape, or form. I therefore asked Viscount Grey whether it was true (as Wilson had said) that modifications or reservations on our part would be totally unacceptable to our late allies. Colonel Harvey took up the question with alacrity and pressed Viscount Grey with great adroitness to issue a public statement on his return to England. This statement was to be to the effect that he (Grey) understood that the above impression prevailed in America, through statements of President Wilson, but that, on the contrary, such reservations as those proposed by Senator Lodge would be entirely acceptable to the Allies, and consonant with the Covenant of the League and the Treaty of Versailles.

Viscount Grey naturally declined to commit himself at this time, but later in the afternoon, when I was having tea with him at the British Embassy, he told me that upon reflection he felt sure he would be able to make such a statement as we requested, and that he could probably work out the details on shipboard.

Three days after his return to England, Viscount Grey was in Paris reporting to the prime minister and Lord Curzon, who were attending the first session of the League. On the 22nd, the King gave audience to Grey and the prime minister; and on the 31st, the London *Times* began a lengthy editorial with the significant sentence, "We publish a communication today which is probably unique in the history of diplomacy." "Lord Grey, who until recently was the British Ambassador to the United States, and who technically still occupies that position," continued the *Times,* "now feels it his duty to make public his views, and what he believes to be the views of the American people, upon the subject of his mission."

Viscount Grey ascribed the status of the Treaty in the Senate to two underlying causes: 1. A real conservative feeling for the traditional policy of the nation; 2. The provision of the Constitution under which the Executive and the Legislature have separate functions in treaty-making. "Let us first get rid of one possible misunderstanding," the statement says. "No charge of bad faith or repudiating signatures can be brought against the action of the United States. The Senate, by the American Constitution, is an independent body, an independent element in the treaty-making power. Its refusal to ratify a treaty cannot expose either itself or the country to the charge of bad faith or repudiation."

On February 6th, George Harvey wrote me, reviewing the discussion that had taken place at my home and giving further details about how Grey's historic statement came to be made:

... Grey certainly did go through in fine shape, didn't
he? When you come to think of it he carried through

the programme outlined to the very letter, even to the
time when the presentation of his views would prove
most effective. It is really quite gratifying to recall that,
after having thrashed out every detail of the reservations, and somewhat to his surprise, I suspect, finding
that there was nothing but the friendliest of feelings toward England on the part of those of us here who were
fighting the League, as we believe justifiably, he turned
to me and said, "But what can I do? My hands seem
to be tied." And I replied that the greatest service he
could render his country and our country and the entire
world would be by announcing shortly after his return
home that his Government fully appreciated the natural
apprehension felt by our people in making so radical
a departure from their age-long traditions and that with
this knowledge his Government stood ready to accept
the Lodge reservations. "Would you not," you remember he asked in return, "cooperate in according our self-
governing Dominions the recognition which they
thought they had earned?" You will recall how pleased
he seemed when I replied that, in my judgment our
people were quite as friendly disposed toward the Dominions as they were towards the Mother Country itself
and it was simply a question of framing a provision in
such a way as to give them all they were entitled to,
while maintaining for our own country moral and numerical equality with the Empire as a whole. This did
not strike him as an insuperable obstacle and since it
seemed to be the only one, he should concentrate his
efforts on his way home in striving to find a solution
which might be satisfactory and even welcome on all
sides, even going so far as to add that personally he
would be glad to have us have as many or even more
votes than Britain if that would tend to cement our
friendship because he did not believe we would ever
disagree on anything of consequence.

There was much more of course, especially with reference to the remark of King Edward to Von Meyer, printed recently in *Scribner's,* of which apparently he had not heard, as constituting in my judgment the true and wisest policy respecting the future relations of England and America. If, however, it should seem desirable to work out something more definite, the only association of nations into which the United States could possibly enter would be one based upon law and not upon force . . . in a word, along the Hague lines, insuring application of justice after full hearings by an impartial tribunal through resolute enforcement (by whatever means required) of all decrees rendered.

You will remember how he came as near clapping his hands as one could expect and responded enthusiastically, "Why, that is what I want. That is what we all want!" And then he frankly agreed that an aspiration to that end would be the Chief justification of America entering into an engagement in the hope that out of it, through the working together hand in hand of England and America would evolve the true solution of peace without tyranny.

Well, in any case, Grey certainly far more than fulfilled expectations and it begins to look as if the settlement of the whole business dates from your luncheon. It was a good party anyhow and one well worth remembering . . .

"The settlement of the whole business" did not turn out as Harvey expected. But Viscount Grey's statement had the immediate effect of undermining Wilson's dictum that the Treaty must be ratified, as it was commonly expressed, "without the dotting of an 'i', or the crossing of a 't'." Grey's insight, common sense, and understanding were pleasing to conservatives in America, but Wilson, wrathful, made sharp reply. It was felt on all sides that the Lodge motion could be passed any time within a few hours, if the President would give the lead. "Mr. Wilson is the man," a leading editorial read, "who threatens to block the way. He can do so only by degrading his presumably democratic office into a personal autocracy."

The Senate, under the suspension of its rules, voted to reconsider the Lodge resolution. Mr. Wilson remained obdurate, however, and on March 19th the Senate voted to send the Treaty back to the President without its approval. Wilson had resolved that the presidential canvass of 1920 should be a "great and solemn referendum" on the Treaty. Upon this issue his party suffered overwhelming defeat. By the mandate of that election, not only was the issue of the League of Nations buried beyond hope of resurrection for at least decades to come, but solemn warning was served that no supergovernment which would involve, even in a remote degree, the derogation of their national sovereignty would be tolerated by the American people. That may again be regarded as an established principle of governmental policy in our foreign relations.

As Viscount Grey came down the gangplank at Southampton after his visit to America, he was greeted with the cry that he might become president of the League of Nations. "I thought that was to be President Wilson's job," he retorted in disclaiming for himself visions of such grandeur and power.

When Clemenceau visited this country in 1923, he expressed to me a good deal of bitterness towards Wilson, and blamed him for everything that had gone wrong at Paris. *Et tu, Brute!*

Venizelos had been spoken of by Wilson as one of the ablest men at the Peace Conference. When I saw the Greek statesman in California in 1922, he had lost whatever admiration he may once have had for Woodrow Wilson. He blamed the failure of America to join the League of Nations on the obstinacy of Wilson in defending his own point of view.

Although the Grey statement had modified the harsh judgments of many European statesmen, the French continued intemperate in their condemnation of the United States for failure to live up to the agreement which Wilson *ultra vires* had made at Versailles.

On Armistice Day, 1923, an admiring throng gathered informally in front of the Wilson residence in Washington. The ex-President appeared before them and imperturbably avowed

"I am not one of those who have the least anxiety about the triumph of the principles I have stood for. I have seen fools resist Providence before, and I have seen their destruction, and it will come upon these again, utter destruction and contempt; that we shall prevail is as sure as that God reigns."

Viewed with the perspective of events since the war, it seems that the World Court idea, because it was less ambitious, was the more practical and possible of realization. A Court, limited wisely in jurisdiction, supplemented by a Council of Conciliation, seemed feasible and had won wide popular support. But the World Court was tied into the Covenant of the League of Nations as inextricably as the Covenant was tied into the Peace Treaty.

President Harding initiated the effort to extricate the Court from the League, so far as our adherence was concerned, by his proposal of February 24, 1923. Secretary of State Charles Evans Hughes devised four conditions for our entrance, and Coolidge, upon his accession to the presidency, urged action along the lines of the Harding-Hughes formula. After numerous modifications, this formula gave way to a Resolution for entrance to which five reservations were attached, and after passing a cloture rule, the Senate finally, on January 27, 1926, voted by a large majority to join the Permanent Court of International Justice.

Article 14 of the Covenant of the League of Nations reads as follows:

The Council shall formulate and submit to the Members of the League for adoption plans for the establishment of a Permanent Court of International Justice. The Court shall be competent to hear and determine any dispute of an international character which the parties thereto submit to it. The Court may also give an advisory opinion upon any dispute or question referred to it by the Council or by the Assembly.

At just this time, the Council convened to consider Germany's application to join the League. From Geneva, Sir Austen Chamberlain made bold to proclaim that the Senate Reservations would require the revision of the Statute under which the League had established the Court. That was discouraging. Presently there came another and more ominous interposition, in the overwhelming defeat for renomination of William B. McKinley in the Illinois primary election. McKinley was the first of the pro-Court senators to go before his constituency after the Senate had voted to enter the Court. The Coolidge administration, taking warning, deftly turned its attention to another undertaking, deriving from Chicago, and soon to be heralded as the Kellogg-Briand Pact to outlaw war. In these circumstances, no question was to be raised about the status of our adherence until after the presidential election of 1928.

Meanwhile, the Council of the League, acting upon the Chamberlain position, named an Advisory Committee of Jurists to revise the Statute of the Court. Elihu Root, who had served on the original committee that had written the Statute in 1921, was again invited to serve. The Council then asked this Advisory Committee also to resolve the problem created by the Senate Reservations, which had been slumbering nearly three years in the archives of the League at Geneva. The Council promptly approved the report of the Committee of Jurists, clarifying the Senate Resolution, which report has come to be known as the "Root Formula." President Hoover thereupon directed our representative at Geneva to sign for the United States the Protocol of membership in the Court, and then urged the Senate to accept the Root Formula. But Mr. Hoover was unable to induce the Senate to take such final action.

Although the Democratic platform of 1932 declared for the Court, the administration of Franklin D. Roosevelt had not moved formally in the matter up to the end of 1934. But on the reassembling of Congress in January, 1935, the thirteen-year-old controversy over the United States entering the Permanent Court of International Justice was reopened on January 9th and the Senate Foreign Relations Committee ordered the World Court protocols favorably reported. It declared once more for the doctrine of the long-disputed Reservation 5 which says the Permanent Court of International Justice "shall not, over an objection of the United States, entertain any request for an advisory opinion touching any dispute or question in which the United States has or claims an interest." This reservation adopted nine years ago by the Senate was rejected by other nations signatory to the Court. Whether these nations will now admit us to the World Court is as yet a matter of doubt. Whether the people of America are eager to join the World Court is in my mind a matter of even greater doubt.

Seemingly ineradicable suspicions, such as that the Court is a "back-door" entrance to the League, that the Court is under the political domination of the League, that war debts and domestic policies of immigration, tariffs, etc., might be subject to its adjudication, continue to militate against final favorable action by the Senate. While it cannot be denied that there has been some ground for suspicion, it is my judgment that the Root Formula adequately protects our domestic interests and concerns but guards against our becoming involved in the League. If we are to join any Court set up by the League, our sense of self-respect should restrain our seeking further protection than the Root Formula attaches to the 1926 Resolution of the Senate.

Were, then, the efforts put into propaganda by our peace societies, particularly the World Court League and the League to Enforce Peace, all pure waste? I think not. At the opening of the century Lord Salisbury predicted of the advocates of arbitration: "Future ages will look with pity and contempt upon those who could have believed in such an expedient for bridling the ferocity of human passions"; and now Spengler grimly warns that "we have entered the age of world wars. It began in the nineteenth century, and will outlast the present, and probably the next."

Notwithstanding the undeniable affirmation which these woeful years give to such pessimism, I cannot give up hope.

There have been gains, even if they do not as yet quite balance the losses. The voluntary efforts of these societies succeeded in making our citizens think in larger terms than before, to see that international problems affected them too. The Ideal of Peace was upheld by the press, the pulpit, the platform, and devoted political leaders. Under the impulses and stresses of war, Woodrow Wilson attempted to carry these aims and ideas to levels to which our nation could not climb; to force them upon peoples whose age-old racial hatreds, deep-seated political animosities, and violent economic antagonisms found them unprepared for such assents among themselves or for submission to sanctions imposed by others. Surely America, in declining to follow paths so precipitous, cannot be charged with disclaiming such honorable part in the world as befits the genius of her people and the traditions of her existence as a nation. On that path my country had never faltered. It has been the bungling statesmanship and not the lofty idealism of Woodrow Wilson that I have criticized. Confessedly, he may some day be remembered as a Messianic prophet. Colonel House still maintains that the League of Nations is Woodrow Wilson's greatest work. It may be so . . . I have my doubts.

CHAPTER THIRTY-TWO

Wilson and Harding, 1914-1923

THE FRIENDSHIP OF WILSON AND HOUSE—POLITICAL
QUARRELS—THE CONVENTION OF 1916—HUGHES IS
DEFEATED—CAMPAIGN PROMISES—THE APPOINT-
MENT OF BAINBRIDGE COLBY—THE BREAK BETWEEN
WILSON AND HOUSE—I SUPPORT GENERAL WOOD IN
1920 CONVENTION—MY TRIP TO JAPAN—THE WASHINGTON DIS-
ARMAMENT CONFERENCE—PRESIDENT HARDING OF-
FERS ME AMBASSADORSHIP TO JAPAN—THE LIVE
WIRE CLUB—THE POST AT THE COURT OF ST. JAMES'S

*W*ith the election of Wilson I lost interest in politics for the time being. I left Washington for New York, and did not return to the Capital until we entered the war in 1917, and then I bought a home there.

In the beginning I was not unfriendly to Wilson. I liked him personally and I told my Democratic friends that I thought the party had put up a surprisingly good candidate. Many of my friends admired Wilson greatly, though I was inclined to regard him as somewhat of a doctrinaire.

When I first met Woodrow Wilson in the winter of 1908-9 he was president of Princeton University. He was in Bermuda convalescing from a recent illness and my wife and I were there for a rest. We were together for several weeks, and Wilson shared our table in the hotel dining room during this interval. We saw him several times a day and greatly enjoyed his society. His discussions with me were invariably concerned with the way political organizations were run. My practical experience in the recent Taft campaign had given me insight into this subject. I remarked to my wife that I thought Wilson had the political bee in his bonnet, though his interest might have been purely academic.

Thereafter not unnaturally I followed Wilson's career with interest.

On February 3, 1906, at a dinner given to Woodrow Wilson at the Lotos Club in New York, George Harvey, the editor and publisher, had "nominated" Wilson for the presidency. He had "discovered" Wilson—though later Harvey declared that Woodrow Wilson had "discovered" himself—at his inauguration as president of Princeton University in 1902.

After the Lotos Club dinner, Harvey, a past master in the promotion of political candidates, gave much thought and publicity to grooming Wilson for the presidency. Through his efforts Wilson became recognized by the Democratic leaders of the country as "presidential timber."

Harvey realized that the election of Woodrow Wilson as governor of New Jersey was an important step to his nomination for the presidency, and it was through his initiative and political skill that Wilson was elected governor in 1910. Also, Harvey recognized the futility of advocating the nomination of Wilson for the presidency in 1908, as Bryan at that time practically dominated the Democratic party and was the inevitable choice as nominee.

Nineteen-twelve was the psychological year: Wilson had made good as governor, and there was the split in the Republican party owing to the Roosevelt-Taft fight. The result was the election of Wilson to the presidency.

Shortly before the nomination of Wilson, Harvey and "Marse Henry" Watterson, editor of the Louisville *Courier-Journal,* who had been his enthusiastic supporters, were discarded by Wilson at the suggestion of other political advisers who asserted that they were too closely connected with Wall Street—an allegation which then as now struck terror to the heart of every office seeker who hoped to obtain the suffrage of the voting public.

660 The Autobiography of John Hays Hammond

Colonel Edward M. House had picked out Wilson when he was governor of New Jersey as the outstanding Democratic presidential possibility. House had been slower to declare his adherence than Harvey, but when the campaign opened he threw himself into it heart and soul. Wilson realized that House had no ax to grind, and turned to the colonel with a trust and affection he showed no other man.

House once said in the course of their ripening friendship, "Isn't it remarkable that we have become so well acquainted in so short a time and have so many views in common?"

To this Wilson replied: "I don't think so. There is no beginning to a friendship such as ours. Our meeting merely gave it expression."

During Wilson's first presidential years, I was in sympathy with many of his domestic measures, particularly the Federal Reserve Act. On the other hand, I disapproved heartily of the Underwood Tariff which in 1914 threatened to bring on a financial panic. This was averted only by the outbreak of the war. I was totally out of sympathy with his policy of unpreparedness, and especially with his treatment of Mexican affairs. He showed no more knowledge of the Mexican problem than he had displayed in our conversation on the train in 1911.

Just before House went abroad at the outbreak of the war, I asked him about the Mexican situation. He said, "Nothing will be done until I get back from Europe."

The Mexican situation became acute during his absence, however. Americans were being murdered, among them some fine young engineers who at one time or another had been in my employ. It was an open season on Americans. Posters were up in Tampico and elsewhere, saying now was the time for all good Mexicans to get rid of Americans. Not a single German, and, up to this time, not a single Englishman had been murdered.

The Mexican government still professed a desire to have mining operations continue, as this was an important source of revenue. A half dozen American engineers returned to the mining districts under a promise of protection by the Mexican government, and with assurance of our own government as to their safety. They were stood up against a wall and shot by "revolutionists" and still no step was taken by the American government. Wilson steadfastly adhered to Bryan's policy of hands off and to an exchange of ineffectual letters of protest.

I could keep silent no longer and made several speeches roundly criticizing Wilson.

When House returned, he said, "I hear you've been attacking the President on his Mexican policy."

"I certainly have," I replied. "I couldn't stand by and say nothing while Wilson permitted open murder of American engineers in Mexico."

From this time on Wilson and I had little to do with each other, although Colonel House and I have remained close friends.

In 1916, I attended the Republican convention at Chicago, again in a private capacity. Though Roosevelt's bolt from the party in 1912 had not been forgotten by the Old Guard, it was my opinion that by concentration on the preparedness issue alone he could heal the break and win strong support. Certainly his vigor would be welcome after Wilson's academic calm.

I found myself practically the only one of the old Taft men who had a favorable word to say for Roosevelt's candidacy. There were many misgivings as to his ability to carry the country. The most important of these was the antagonism roused among the German-Americans by his denunciations of their Fatherland.

My reply to this was: "Oh, well, if Roosevelt were the candidate that would be forgotten in a month or two. He would get out there in the German districts and in no time have Roosevelt-German clubs parading for him."

Those who knew Roosevelt realized the truth of this statement, but I soon found that party bitterness remaining from 1912 was an insurmountable obstacle to his nomination.

When I was convinced that the convention was strongly in favor of Charles Evans Hughes, I advised my friends among the Roosevelt faction to turn their strength to him and stop their talk of secession. I warned the Roosevelt supporters again and again that they were doing great injustice to their leader by trying to push him as candidate for a third party. "If he goes into the fight, he will beat Hughes but he can't be elected. So there will be another term of Wilson."

Roosevelt was reached by long-distance telephone and informed of what was going on. A few days after my return to New York, Mrs. Roosevelt invited my wife and me to Oyster Bay, to have a talk with the colonel. In greeting me he put his arm on my shoulder with his characteristic gesture of friendship, and said, "John Hays, I have to thank you for the good advice you gave my friends at Chicago."

I replied, "Colonel, of course you understand that I was supporting the Roosevelt of 1916, and not the Roosevelt of 1912?"

"Yes," he said, "I understand that. I remember how you denounced me four years ago. But you were then acting as Taft's friend, and I could not have asked your support at that time. Indeed, I respect you for your loyalty to him and for your frankness with me."

At the conclusion of the conversation, Roosevelt told me he intended to support Hughes. This was his first intimation of what he was going to do.

"That's the decision I expected you'd make, Colonel, but none the less it's gratifying to hear it from your own lips."

I at once reported the colonel's decision to Hughes, at the Hotel Astor. He was pleased and relieved.

During the campaign I saw Hughes at frequent intervals, and spent much time at Republican headquarters in New York. Hughes really possessed a charming personality to those who knew him, but this was not apparent in his platform manner or on public occasions.

William R. Willcox was selected to manage Hughes's campaign. Willcox and I resembled each other so closely that our pictures were often interchanged in the newspapers. I was also frequently mistaken for him by heelers, who are always conspicuous at campaign headquarters and whose special interest lies in the anticipation of political favors to be bestowed.

Whenever these spoilsmen caught sight of me they would approach one by one, shake my hand effusively, and say, "You won't forget me, will you, Mr. Willcox?"

"Oh, no," I replied, "I've a good memory. I certainly won't forget you."

After the election, I laughingly told Willcox that perhaps it was better for his peace of mind that Hughes had been defeated and that he could not be called on to keep his "promises" to this hungry mob of political job seekers.

Apropos of promises, I am reminded of a story told me by Senator Stephen B. Elkins, of West Virginia. Once while traveling on a stagecoach in the West, he noted that at every change of horses his driver's friends would remind him not to forget the pup he had promised them. It seems the driver owned a very fine bitch that was about to have a litter. By the time the long journey was ended, the driver had agreed to give a pup to at least a hundred friends.

Elkins said to him, "How on earth can you let every one of those fellows have a pup?"

The old driver grinned and replied, "Well, it's a mighty damned mean fellow who wouldn't 'promise' a friend a pup."

Hughes was defeated for the presidency because of the way he mishandled California. The state had been normally Republican in national elections, but by an inexcusable blunder it went Democratic in 1916, though by a small margin.

Hughes unfortunately visited California while a bitter fight was being waged in the primaries between the rebellious Senator Hiram Johnson and the regular Republican faction. Johnson had controlled state politics for many years through his machine and, in spite of being apostate at times, was fairly certain of renomination.

Hughes was met at the state line by a delegation of Republicans who were leading the campaign against Johnson. Shortsightedly ignoring the significance of the local political situation, Hughes allowed himself to be completely identified with Johnson's enemies, thus inadvertently appearing to take sides against Johnson. During his stay in California he neither met Johnson nor made any overtures towards him.

Johnson won the renomination, and also triumphed at the ensuing election. But his supporters, filled with resentment at the treatment accorded him by the anti-Johnson group, split the Republican vote. This, in turn, lost Hughes the State of California and the presidency.

Another political mistake was the sending of a group of wealthy eastern women to California to urge the women of that state to vote for Hughes. In my absence, my wife had been invited to join this expedition. Using her own good judgment and her knowledge of California affairs, she declined the invitation. She told the committee it was the height of folly for eastern women, who had never been allowed the vote, to presume to instruct the women of California as to how they should exercise the franchise which they had possessed for years.

When I learned this fateful car had started west, I suggested to Willcox that he contrive to lose the ladies somewhere in the wide open spaces until such time as they could do no harm.

This was not considered practicable, and the original program was carried out. The spirit in which the women voters of California received the advice of those from the East amply justified my wife's predictions.

I deplored the defeat of Hughes, not only for partisan reasons but because I was convinced he would have taken measures to prepare our country much more efficiently than Wilson for the war into which I believed we were inevitably drifting.

As a practical man, I had no sympathy with Wilson's effort to avoid issues by phrases, such as "too proud to fight" and "watchful waiting." I did not question his high ideals as to world peace, but I considered them not only unworkable but also unattainable. Moreover, the methods he employed to secure his ends were in my opinion lamentably wrong.

During Wilson's second term I was naturally an outsider so far as administration matters were concerned. But there was one incident in which I had a personal interest. In the winter of 1920, President Wilson sent the name of Bainbridge Colby to the Senate for confirmation as secretary of state in place of Lansing. Colby was a prominent New York lawyer who had originally been a Roosevelt man but had gone over to Wilson in 1916. I had been associated with him in various political and civic activities and therefore knew him well. Our many talks about our foreign policy,

NATALIE HARRIS HAMMOND

WILSON AND HARDING

especially with reference to Russia and Mexico, had given me a high opinion of his knowledge and judgment.

There was considerable opposition to his appointment by the Republican members of the Foreign Relations Committee, due largely to the charge of alleged unprofessional conduct made against Colby by Herbert Parsons, Republican congressman. Although this accusation proved utterly groundless, several of my Republican friends on the committee which was to pass on Colby's fitness for confirmation still hesitated.

I interviewed Knox, now back in the Senate, about Colby's appointment. He said: "Well, it probably won't make much difference who's secretary of state. Wilson intends to run that department himself."

My response was: "From intimate knowledge of Colby's character, I feel sure that not even the President of the United States can use him as a rubber stamp. In politics he has always been hard to drive tandem."

Colby's appointment was confirmed. Immediately afterwards he came to thank me for the influence I had exerted in his behalf.

"Bainbridge," I said, "you have the ability to make a splendid secretary of state for a short time, and to establish an enduring reputation in that office. My fear is that President Wilson will put pressure on you to adopt policies which will not be to your credit if you follow them. Though I realize, of course, that if you try to be independent, you'll run the risk of being dismissed."

"Don't worry about that, Jack," he replied, "I've taken my house for only six months!"

Colby renewed the lease, and in spite of his independence was secretary of state until the end of the Wilson administration. He then formed a legal partnership with Wilson, which was soon terminated by the breakdown of Wilson's health.

It was during the early part of 1914, after I had visited Thomas Nelson Page at Rome, that I first met Lord Northcliffe in Paris. We were staying at the same hotel and occasionally played golf together and spent several pleasant evenings in general political discussions.

I asked Northcliffe why it was that Great Britain had not tied up Italy with the Allies, as Italy's treaty with Germany was soon to expire. I told him that I had found the Italians in government circles very friendly to England. Northcliffe replied that overtures had been made to Italy to prevent Italy tying up again with the Triple Alliance, but without avail. I said that was quite true, but unfortunately, the overtures were made through France, and France and Italy were not altogether friendly because of their disputes about territory in Northern Africa. Besides this, there was no love lost between Italy and Austria. "Irredentism" aggravated this situation. I told Northcliffe that I felt something could be done. Of course, I was not anticipating the war which came so soon afterwards. He said: "I will give you a letter to Sir Edward Grey [at that time foreign secretary of England] and I will write him privately."

I went from Paris to London to spend a few weeks before returning to America. There I had a confidential talk with Grey and found him very much interested in the Italian question.

When I next saw Viscount Grey in Washington in 1919, he said: "Hammond, suppose I had told you when I last saw you in England in 1914, that within six months England would be fighting in France against Germany, and that within three years America would have two million soldiers joined with the armies of England, France, and Italy, what would you have thought?"

"Of course," I said, "I would have replied that the prophecy was absolutely ridiculous."

"That would have been my opinion, and yet," said Grey thoughtfully, "both of these things have come to pass."

I recall a story that Northcliffe told me about Maximilian's invasion of Mexico. He said the most regrettable part of it was that the basis for the invasion was commercial and sordid. It was inspired, he said, by the Duc de Mornay and unscrupulous financiers in Paris, who were interested in being repaid for the Mexican bonds they had purchased.

When Northcliffe came to America in 1917 as representative of the British War Cabinet, he visited me in Gloucester. I asked him whether the World War might not have been prevented if Grey had notified Germany definitively that if she moved into Belgian or French territory, England would join France. Northcliffe was of that opinion. This is also the theory of Lloyd George as related in his memoirs.

I gave a dinner at Gloucester in honor of Lord Northcliffe and invited Calvin Coolidge, then lieutenant governor of Massachusetts, Governor McCall being away at the time. Before dinner was announced, Northcliffe began to question Coolidge insistently but tactfully concerning the opinions of certain influential people in America. All he elicited in return was a succession of monosyllabels. Observing the heavy conversational weather, I cheered Northcliffe by telling him he would be seated next to Mrs. Coolidge at dinner and would be sure to find out all he wanted to know. The result was very gratifying to him.

I recall that at the solicitation of several of Colonel Roosevelt's friends I asked House to suggest Roosevelt's name as the head of the commission the President was sending to Russia at the time the Kerensky government came into power in 1917. Elihu Root had been spoken of in that connection. I was a great admirer of Root but I thought Roosevelt better qualified for the emergency since he would be much more aggressive and forceful. Indeed, I said that he would probably revive the Russian cause by personally leading its troops on the battlefield, whereas Root would talk over the head and understanding of the average Russian. House agreed with me, but when he suggested the appointment of Roosevelt, President Wilson went up in the air. It was not that he failed to recognize the force of my argument; it was because of the pettiness he often showed in treatment of those who had previously offended him.

The Root Commission was a failure.

After the last session of the Paris Conference, June, 1919, House returned to his country place at Manchester. A few days later he lunched with me at my home, Lookout Hill, and told me I would probably be interested to learn why the newspapers were reporting that the friendly relations previously existing between Woodrow Wilson and himself had ended. He began by stating there had never been a serious difference between them nor had they ever exchanged an unpleasant word.

"Probably it would have been better for both President Wilson and you," I remarked, "had there occasionally been heated arguments between you."

"No," he replied, "I know what you have in mind. You think it might have cleared the atmosphere. But I don't agree with you. Had I not minimized and disregarded differences of opinion on certain subjects, I should not have been able to accomplish other measures which we both thought of paramount importance."

To my knowledge there were many instances in which House's views differed from Wilson's and in which subsequent developments proved House the wiser man.

In a previous chapter I have alluded to the advice House gave Wilson as to his and Wilson's participation in the Versailles Conference. Later this advice was urged by those of Wilson's entourage who were unfriendly to House as evidence that House had his own ambitions to serve.

This was not all. An unfortunate article had appeared in the European newspapers the day of Wilson's arrival in Paris on his second trip to the Peace Conference. In it was included the statement that "what Colonel House thinks today, Wilson does tomorrow."

Wilson was led to believe by those jealous of House that this article had been inspired directly by the colonel or by his friends.

This charge was not only untrue, it was entirely foreign to House's attitude towards Wilson, which had always been one of self-subordination. House never had the opportunity to discuss the subject frankly with the President.

Shortly after the appearance of this article, Wilson returned to make his great but losing fight to have the League of Nations ratified by the Senate. He sadly needed the wise counsel of Colonel House during this period. Had House still enjoyed the President's confidence, all his influence would have been exerted towards having the Lodge reservations accepted by Wilson, rather than to risk the utter defeat of the Wilson plan at the hands of the Senate.

The ultimate cause of the break was probably due, as House himself asserts, to the jealousy of a small circle around Wilson which shut him off from his friends.

According to House's statement in the *New York Times,* July 26, 1934: "The bedroom circle kept him apart from me and kept me apart from him. My letters never reached him; no messages were ever sent to me."

In 1920 I was one of General Leonard Wood's active adherents. Since I was an old friend of his family, I felt privileged to state frankly to him my views on matters affecting his candidacy. In the first place, I advised against his coming forward too aggressively; also, I and others cautioned him against extravagant pre-campaign expenditures. He did not follow this advice and, as it later turned out, the reckless use of funds in his campaign was one of the most forceful arguments urged against his nomination at the convention.

While characteristically hesitant about declaring their positions, many of the leading politicians expressed their admiration for Wood. Several said definitely they were for him. I encouraged Wood with this information.

It was shortly after this that the unfortunate selection of Frank H. Hitchcock as his campaign manager became known. I warned Wood that this would estrange many men who would be influential in the coming convention. I referred him to Taft or Hughes if he doubted the wisdom of my advice.

Wood replied: "It's too late. I'm under obligation to make this appointment. The men who are putting up most of the money for my campaign have made it a condition that I choose a practical politician as my campaign manager. They insist Hitchcock fills the requirements. In addition, he can secure the vote of negro delegates from the South, a role in which he specializes."

"You'll lose by it," I told him.

I arrived at Chicago a few days before the convention was scheduled to begin. Since this was my fourth convention, I was well acquainted with the leading politicians. When the Hitchcock appointment was verified a number of them told me plainly they would not support a man who had had the bad judgment to select Hitch-cock as political manager, and thereby had obligated himself to give Hitchcock a Cabinet position.

Alice Longworth, who for some years past had been familiar with Hitchcock's political activities, says in her book, *Crowded Hours:*

> When General Wood got to Washington he told me that King's activities were too secret and devious, and that he had had to get rid of him. [At that time John King of Connecticut was General Wood's political manager.] When I had talked with General Wood in August, Frank Hitchcock's name had come up, and I had warned the General to avoid having much to do with him, as he was just as devious as King, without being in with powers that counted. However, that warning was wasted words, and he proceeded to take Hitchcock as his manager.

Senator Warren G. Harding telephoned me the morning he de-cided to become a candidate and asked for my support. I told him I had not known he was in the field; on the contrary, public state-ments made by him had led me to believe that he was intending to run again for the Senate. I said I had already committed myself to Wood.

He then sent two of his supporters, Harry Daugherty and Mont Reilly, to see me. We agreed that none of the principal candidates —Wood, Lowden, Harding—was likely to go to the convention with a majority of pledged delegates. Daugherty asked me whether, if the proper time came in the convention, Harding could count on Wood's support, provided Harding would throw his sup-port to Wood if the current ran the other way.

I replied that, of course, I had no authority to speak for Wood on this matter, but there was always a possibility of an understanding later should the occasion arise.

George Harvey and I had secured rooms not far apart in the Blackstone Hotel. We were together a good deal during convention week and obtained much inside information as to political doings. On Thursday there had been several ballots for presidential nomination—Governor Frank Lowden, of Illinois, and General Wood were the favorites, with Senator Harding trailing.

On Friday evening Harvey told me there was to be a conference of the leaders of the convention in his suite and invited me to be present. I did not attend the meeting because I had been reliably informed that both Lowden and Wood would be eliminated by those who controlled the political destiny of the candidates. Up to this time Harvey had been friendly to Wood's nomination.

Influential Republicans were threatening to create dissension if Wood should receive the nomination. One of the chief reasons advanced for this was the too-liberal campaign expenditures made by his adherents in securing delegates. There was no insinuation of corruption, but influential party men of Senator William Borah's type thought a heavy outlay of money in selecting the presidential candidate would establish a bad precedent.

Lowden's campaign was criticized because of the charge of political graft on the part of two or three of his delegates. Lowden was absolutely innocent, of course, but it was feared that possible scandal would prevent his election even if he were to receive the nomination.

Harvey came to my room about three in the morning and told me that the leaders had decided to promote the candidacy of Harding and that after two or three perfunctory ballots, purely for appearance' sake, Harding would receive the nomination.

Early next morning I went to Wood's suite. He was there with Mrs. Wood and Nicholas Roosevelt. After telling him of Harvey's plan to nominate Harding on the third ballot, I said, "It's all up."

He replied: "I don't believe it. I've just seen Frank Hitchcock. He says we have the votes."

"I still say I'm right. Don't rely on Hitchcock's estimate of delegates favorable to you."

Wood was troubled, but still confident. He kept repeating: "I can't believe it. You don't mean to tell me that my friends are going to desert me?"

After the third ballot someone from the auditorium telephoned Wood's suite. I answered the phone and a voice came over the wire, "Harding has just been nominated!"

While the news was not unexpected, the necessity for repeating the message to Wood was none the less unpleasant. "General, Harding has been chosen."

Wood said bitterly: "It's another 1912 business. It's the same old thing."

So loath was Wood to accept the fact of his defeat that he hesitated to sign the congratulatory telegram to Harding which Nicholas Roosevelt had prepared. He said he could not understand why certain men, whom he named, had first professed undying loyalty to him and then had betrayed him. His indignation and bitterness were not directed against Harding, but against what he regarded as treachery on the part of some of his own friends.

I told him with some cynicism that the loyalty of the soldier, which leads him to fight to his death in defense of a position assigned to him, need not be looked for in politics; expediency, not loyalty, is the fundamental tenet of the politician's creed.

Immediately upon his return to Washington, Harding came to my house and told me, "If Wood had taken your advice, he would have secured the nomination."

"How do you know what I advised?" I asked.

"I had a good intelligence department," he replied. "You warned Wood against attacking me in Ohio and Lowden in Illinois. Didn't you tell him to get busy elsewhere and let Lowden and me fight it out in our own territories?"

"That's true," I admitted.

"Well, he made a bad mistake in tackling us in our own states. He could hope to win only a few delegates there, while making enemies of the rest."

Although I had been a Wood supporter, I had grown very fond of the Hardings during the years we had been neighbors in Washington. I could not fail to appreciate Mrs. Harding's clever and forceful character. While Harding was acting as temporary chairman of the 1916 convention, my wife and I sat next to Mrs. Harding in her box. During the senator's speech, her lips formed each syllable as he pronounced it. We could not help harboring the suspicion that she had assisted in its composition.

A few months after Harding's inauguration, I started on a long-contemplated trip to study political and economic conditions in the Orient. My first stop was to be Japan. I studiously avoided taking with me letters to government officials or other prominent Japanese. By keeping free of all obligations, governmental or otherwise, I hoped to obtain accurate information for myself rather than to see Japan through the show windows usually provided for official visitors.

Among my first callers was M. Otagawa, a Japanese of high social position and one of the distinguished mining engineers of the country. I had met Otagawa in America several years before and had extended him some professional courtesies. Through him I came in contact with many leading Japanese engineers and businessmen with whom, as a private citizen, I had the opportunity to discuss the economic conditions of Japan and the Orient generally, as well as the political relations between our two countries.

I criticized Japan's excessive expenditure on naval armaments, offering the opinion that this would almost certainly be construed as an unfriendly and perhaps a hostile move against America. There were no other great naval powers against whom Japan might need to prepare. Germany had no navy, Russia had no navy, and the other nations could not endanger her, with the exception of Great Britain, and Great Britain was Japan's ally. I pointed out that the huge sums of money Japan was expending on a navy might much better be diverted to the expansion of her merchant marine.

While in Tokyo, I discussed this subject with Baron Shibusawa, the J. P. Morgan of Japan; he was a gentleman of the old school, a lover of peace, an admirer of the United States. He was a Confucianist and was pleased when I discussed with him the similarity between the Golden Rule of Confucius and that of the Christians.

I also had a talk with Premier Hara, a few days before his assassination. He expressed himself as in full accord with the facts and conclusions I advanced on Japanese-American relations.

It was interesting to ascertain the Japanese attitude towards the Naval Disarmament Conference shortly to be held in Washington, particularly as I knew that our government was apprehensive lest Japan would not be represented.

I wrote in detail to Senator Knox, saying that Japan could not afford to be absent on that occasion. All that would be necessary to ensure her attendance, I said, would be the presence of a mere coolie claiming to represent China, in which case Japan to save her face— a paramount consideration in Oriental politics—would be compelled to send a representative to Washington. No coolie plenipotentiary was needed—Japan attended the conference.

A severe attack of ptomaine poisoning prevented my getting back to Washington, as I had hoped to do, for the conference. It also prevented the continuation of my trip to Korea, Manchuria, and China as planned.

I returned from Japan the latter part of October and decided it was wiser to remain in California for the winter than to risk the Washington climate. When the conference ended in February, I was well enough to be in San Francisco to attend a banquet given the Japanese delegates on their way home. I made an address presenting the views I had previously expressed regarding our relations with Japan.

During the ensuing weeks, I discussed the Japanese question before several of the Chambers of Commerce in California, and stated that Japan's geographical situation, and her progressiveness and energy, entitled her to an important share in the opening up of Manchuria and Eastern Siberia, and that America ought to co-operate with her towards that end. Jealousy, it seemed to me, should not be allowed to appear in our relations with Japan, and it was especially short-sighted to antagonize the country by tactlessness.

I firmly believed in John Hay's open-door policy in China; at the same time, I felt that it ought to be made somewhat more flexible. In respect of Asiatic immigration into America, I thought it should not be allowed, but considered the question ought to be so handled as not to wound the susceptibilities of a country with whom it was essential to be friendly.

I had on several occasions made clear my position on the immigration question to Ambassador Ishii, who was a frequent guest at my house in Washington. Ishii suggested that the problem might be economic and inspired by the labor organizations of California. My reply was that, while this was partly true, Californians themselves were unanimously opposed to immigration of Oriental peoples; they recognized that the races did not assimilate, and dreaded the outcome of possible miscegenation.

In the face of my outspoken sentiments, I have always been regarded by the Japanese press and officials as a true friend of Japan.

When staying in Santa Barbara, California, during this winter of 1921-22, I occupied a cottage in the grounds of the Hotel El Mirasol. The bungalow next to mine was divided for two families. My son Harris and his wife occupied one half of it, and Eleutherios Venizelos and his bride the other half. Both M. and Mme. Venizelos spoke English perfectly and we all enjoyed our association with them. Venizelos had just been run out of Greece by his political enemies, and was awaiting an opportunity to return. He invited us to visit them in Athens, and when I asked, "When do you expect to be there?" Mme. Venizelos replied, "Oh, about May"—and sure enough they were.

One day Venizelos called on my son, saying that he was moving from the bungalow into the main building of the hotel. "I wish to explain," he said, "that it is not because of uncongenial neighbors, but there have been persistent rumors that an attempt will be made to bomb my cottage. It is close to the road and is not therefore as safe as rooms in the other building. I have paid little attention to the rumor, but should the bombing occur you and your wife might become the innocent victims, and it does not seem fair that you should be exposed to a possible calamity of this kind. That is why I am moving to the main building." This, I think, is evidence of the consideration of a real sportsman.

When I returned to Washington in the spring of 1922, I made no secret of my disappointment at the result of the Disarmament Conference. First I told President Harding, and after his death, President Coolidge and other officials that in my opinion we had made a great mistake in sinking a navy *in esse* in exchange for the promise of the British Admiralty to destroy the blueprints of contemplated additions to the fleet. My criticism at that time may not have been popular, but I believe that subsequent developments have shown that, so far as American naval interests were concerned, the

Washington conference must now be regarded as an egregious failure.

Because of my interest in the development of the Orient, and in the political situation in the Far East, President Harding offered me the ambassadorship to Japan. I declined because I wished to remain with my family and friends in my own country.

While I saw but little of Harding socially during his administration, except when my wife and I were guests at White House functions, I was often with him in connection with my duties on the Coal Commission.

In common with people of Washington generally, I, of course, heard allegations reflecting on the President's private life. No doubt, many of these reports were true, though some were probably greatly magnified; the President was doing credit neither to himself nor to his administration. It was soon evident to all except President Harding himself that certain members of his entourage were thoroughly unscrupulous. They were imposing upon his good-nature and abusing his confidence for their own profit. Harding was generous to his friends, but much too easygoing and trustful. The motives of these intimate friends should have been irreproachable, inasmuch as they reflected the attitude of the President on important governmental measures.

Believing as I did in Harding's personal honesty, and that the scandals of the administration were entirely the result of his faith in his friends, I had much sympathy for him, though my admiration naturally was greatly diminished. On several occasions I spoke quite freely to him on this subject, but it was impossible to convince him that he was being betrayed.

I saw Harding a day or two before he left for his Alaskan trip, and he impressed me as being seriously perturbed. What I subsequently learned made me certain that he was beginning to lose confidence in some of his trusted associates. I am sure that if he had lived to return to Washington, there would have been a general housecleaning and the corrupt leaders among his intimates would have been summarily dismissed.

Harding did not have the qualities of greatness but there have been many other presidents lacking in such qualities to whom, nevertheless, the nation has reason to point with satisfaction.

President Harding's good-nature and kindliness are illustrated in a small way by the story of the Live Wire Club. When I called on him one day, he noticed the button in my coat lapel and asked me the meaning of the emblem—a bolt of lightning. "Mr. President," I replied, "that is the emblem of the most exclusive club in the world."

"Tell me about it."

This was the story.

A few months before, I had gone to the Berkshires to call on my friend, Dr. Samuel W. Mixter, a renowned surgeon of Boston who had a beautiful estate on which he raised a herd of pure-blooded Guernseys. The entire village, consisting of some hundred people, was in his employ and looked up to him with pride and some awe. I arrived early and, finding him out, strolled about the grounds and the village. I climbed over the low stone wall of the village grave-yard, read epitaphs for a while, and then sat down against the wall.

While I was enjoying a smoke, I heard boys' voices calling out coaxingly, "Here, Spot! Here, Rover! Here, Sport! Here, Towser!"

I looked over the wall and saw four youngsters eight to ten years of age—but only one dog.

I hailed them. "Hello, fellows. Where are all the dogs?"

"There isn't but one," was the reply.

"But I heard you calling so many different names I thought you had at least four or five."

"No," the biggest lad said, "we only found this dog last night and we don't know his name, so we're calling him all the names we can think of to see which is the right one."

I couldn't help them out but we chatted for some time. During the course of our conversation I asked what they did, to which the spokesman replied that their club was out for a hike.

"Your club must have a name even if the dog hasn't," I said.

"Sure it has."

"Well, what is it?"

"It's the Live Wire Club."

"How many members have you?"

"Just the four of us."

"That's a pretty small club. Why don't you take in those boys?" I asked, pointing to two other youngsters across the street.

"There are only four offices in the club and so we can't take in anyone else," they explained.

I asked who was president, and the youngest spoke up and said he was. The next one was vice-president, and the next secretary.

"Then I suppose the big fellow must be treasurer?" Yes, he was. "And how did he get that office?"

"He wanted to be treasurer, and so we let him have it," said the president.

"How much money have you in the treasury?"

"Two dollars."

"Shh!" I whispered. "Don't talk so loud. Someone might hear you and rob you."

But they were prepared for that possibility. They explained that the treasurer hid the money in a different place every night.

"Well, boys, how about electing me a member of the club?"

They hesitated a little and then the treasurer answered, "But there isn't any office for you."

"That's easy," I said. "Why not make me high private? That's the most important office in a club, and such a club as yours needs a high private."

And so I was duly elected to the Live Wire Club.

It was nearly lunch time, so I asked, "Can you tell me who has the best meals around here?"

Four hands simultaneously pointed to Dr. Mixter's house. "Everyone says that they have grand food there."

"Well," I said, "in that case I believe I'll go over and see if I can't get something to eat."

"But you don't know him," they objected.

"That makes no difference, I'll go and try. Come along and we'll see."

We reached the house, the boys remaining at a respectful distance, and I was admitted much to the amazement of my fellow club members. Dr. Mixter was much amused with the account of my adventure. After lunch, I found the four little fellows again and took them for an automobile ride about the country.

President Harding was greatly interested in the story. "I like those boys," he said. "You'll have to get me elected."

I told him I would take the matter up with the other officers and let him know. In due time I notified him that he had been elected honorary president of the Live Wire Club. He sent the boys an autographed photograph and a friendly letter thanking them for the honor.

In the summer of 1923 President Harding set out for the West and Alaska. He asked my wife and me to accompany him, but my duties as chairman of the Coal Commission prevented.

Before leaving, President Harding informed me that George Harvey was going to resign as ambassador to the Court of St. James's, and he desired to appoint me in his place.

I was highly complimented, and said I would consider it. London was very attractive to me, but the English climate was bad for my wife's health and I should not care to go without her. In any case, nothing could be done until his return from Alaska.

Harding died at San Francisco, August 2nd, on his way back to Washington. After the President's body had been brought to Washington there were special services at the Capitol. Mrs. Harding telephoned and asked me to come to the White House and accompany the mourners from there.

After the burial of the President at Marion, Ohio, Mrs. Harding returned to "Friendship," the home of Mr. and Mrs. Edward B. McLean in Washington. She at once sent word that she would like to see me. I arrived at eleven in the morning, and she related in detail the various incidents of her trip west with the President. She was obviously in great distress of mind, and after luncheon I suggested to the McLeans that I had better leave. But Mrs. Harding begged me not to go, and I stayed with her until late after dinner, hearing again the details she had previously related.

Because of the persistent insinuations that have been uttered against Mrs. Harding by scandalmongers, I should like to say that there can be no possible doubt of her deep and genuine grief over the death of her husband.

CHAPTER THIRTY-THREE

Washington—Coolidge and Hoover, 1923-1932

COOLIDGE THE MAN OF THE HOUR—I AM OFFERED AMBASSADORSHIP TO ITALY—THE UNITED STATES COAL COMMISSION—I REPRESENT PRESIDENT COOLIDGE IN FLORIDA—BRYAN THE REALTOR—LINDBERGH RECEPTION IN WASHINGTON—NATIONAL CIVIC FEDERATION—A BOX OF CIGARS—MY STAND ON LABOR—WASHINGTON SOCIAL LIFE—COOLIDGE AND HIS ADMINISTRATION—HOOVER'S CANDIDACY—BELGIAN RELIEF—THE END OF THE ERA OF PROSPERITY—MY ESTIMATE OF HOOVER

*I*t was most fortunate for the country that a man of Calvin Coolidge's type succeeded to the presidency. He had an estimable record for probity and executive ability during both his Massachusetts governorship and the vice-presidency. Sitting in at Cabinet meetings during the Harding administration had given him special knowledge of national problems.

His slightly rigid personality manifested caution and sanity. His eccentricities were safe ones. There was no derision in the anecdotes that were told of him, and the laughter of the people at hundreds of Coolidgisms only served to increase their belief in him as a wise and forceful leader. After the miasma of suspicion created by the scandals of the Harding administration, the country soon showed implicit confidence in Coolidge.

Shortly after Coolidge became president, Senator Brandegee and George Harvey both told him that Harding had offered me the post of ambassador to England. Dr. Morton Prince, without my knowledge, went to see Senator Lodge, who wrote to Coolidge recommending me as "widely and favorably known" and in a marked degree *persona grata* to England. Since many political favors had already been awarded men of Massachusetts, he added that I, though a resident of that state, was really a western man.

President Coolidge appointed Frank B. Kellogg to that post.

When I returned to Washington from our summer home in Gloucester a few weeks later, the President asked me to dinner. When we went upstairs to smoke, he said he wanted to explain why he had not appointed me.

"No explanation is necessary, Mr. President," I assured him. "You're not bound by acts of your predecessor, and I feel no resentment."

"Yes, I know," he replied, "but Harding offered you the position, and I know you're qualified to fill it properly. Yet if I had given another important post to a Massachusetts man, the politicians in Congress would have raised an outcry. With the President, the speaker of the House, and the majority leader in the Senate, the secretary of war, and the ambassador to Italy, all from Massachusetts, they would be likely to object if the biggest plum in the diplomatic service were to go to that state also. Had the vacancy occurred a few months from now, when I expect to have a stronger grip on the political situation, I should have appointed you notwithstanding."

He then added, "However, there will be other things of importance coming up, and I shall be glad to give you something that will accord with your deserts."

I was somewhat irritated at this method of expression and replied that I had never sought any political reward.

He assured me that political considerations were not in his mind, and the matter was dropped. Later, when there was a vacancy, he offered me the ambassadorship to Italy. I appreciated the honor, but was unable to accept.

I have already explained my feeling about officeholding and presidential appointments. And I do not regret the circumstances that forbade my filling such posts.

The one place, with the exception of the English ambassadorship, that I would have accepted gladly was that of secretary of commerce. I had no private interests which would have made it embarrassing for me to serve in that position, and the whole problem of business and trade, both foreign and domestic, was one that I had been studying for many years. I saw an unusual opportunity to build up a department which at that time was not flourishing. Harding told me that personally he would be glad to offer me the position, but he was advised of the necessity of strengthening his Cabinet by the selection of Herbert Hoover, who had certain political support. The choice was a wise one, as later events proved. Hoover not only brought strength to the party organization, but his conspicuous success in the office was recognized by the country at large.

One of the first important issues to confront Coolidge after Harding's death was the coal crisis. In October, 1922, President Harding, on the authorization of Congress, had appointed a United States Coal Commission composed of the following members: George Otis Smith, director of the United States Geological Survey; Clark Howell, of Georgia; Thomas R. Marshall, former vice-president; Judge Alschuler resigned, and Edward T. Devine was appointed in his stead. The members of the commission made me chairman.

The action of Congress was taken because of the strike of union coal miners in that year, the second since the war. The function of the commission was to discover what could be done to cure the almost continuous crisis in the coal industry. Within the allotted period of a year, we had to assemble our facts and set forth our recommendations in the form of a report, which meant much hard work. The situation in the coal industry was exceedingly complicated and the evidence had to be gathered from many sources.

Our meetings, however, were not taken up exclusively with serious matters. Tom Marshall was a good storyteller, and had a habit of relating humorous anecdotes which, though amusing, threatened to block the transaction of business. I decided that if this flow of wit could be curtailed, we would make better progress, so I purchased a large clock and placed it where both Marshall and I could see it. After that, even when he was fairly launched into a story, one significant look from me at the clock would effectively silence him.

The feeling between mine operators and labor representatives often became tense. When a disputed point threatened an outburst that might embarrass everybody present and retard the proceedings, I would studiously avert my eyes from the timepiece. Marshall, with admirable tact, would then lead us past another difficult corner by telling some apt story at which the miners, operators, and members of the commission would laugh heartily together.

At the conclusion of our labors, the commission presented me with a gold desk clock to commemorate this piece of minor diplomacy.

During the months of intimate association, I came to know Marshall well and to have not only a deep affection but a genuine admiration and regard for him. I considered him one of the most level-headed and upright men in public life.

He was probably the most popular vice-president the country has ever had, more so perhaps than Theodore Roosevelt when he was in that office. Like James Whitcomb Riley, George Ade, and Booth Tarkington, Marshall was a Hoosier and his wit had that pungent quality that seems almost a part of the flat accent of Indianans.

He was quiet, unassuming, and kindly, but once having entered a conversation, he always had something important to say. To bring out points he was making, he drew on his great stock of amusing and original stories; his epigrams were, of course, famous. But he was not a slap-the-back politician. His humor had its roots in deep, fertile soil.

In Washington he had a host of friends and we considered ourselves fortunate in having him and Mrs. Marshall as frequent guests. In my opinion, and to edit one of Marshall's best-known remarks, "What the country needs is more men like Tom Marshall in its government."

The Coal Commission's full report of three thousand pages was printed by the government; a one-volume summary was published in 1925 by Williams and Wilkins under the title, *What the Coal Commission Found*.

We did not solve the coal problem, nor did we expect to. In presenting our report we uttered the warning that the solution of the coal problem could only grow out of a sustained and thoughtful effort over many years by the public, by Congress, by industry, and by students generally. The problem is almost unbelievably complex and there is no easy short-cut to a solution.

This is not the place for an analysis of the report, though two of the principles underlying it may be mentioned. The first of these is that the coal industry is clothed with a public interest, which means that it is not possible for the nation to sit idly by while operators and miners fight each other to a standstill. The government has a right to supervise and to regulate, though fixing of prices and wages was not advised, nor was compulsory arbitration. Furthermore, the collection and publication by the government of data showing costs, profits, and wages, and the airing of the points in dispute in a labor crisis, would, it was thought, bring to bear an enlightened public opinion that neither disputant could afford to flout.

The second principle is in a sense the corollary of the first. We recommended that the responsibility for the smooth running of the industry should lie within the industry itself; we felt that legislative action would tend to diminish efficiency rather than increase it, and that private development, if carried on honestly and as a quasi-public utility, ought to be encouraged. There was in the published figures an implied warning on the monopolistic control of the anthracite fields and the artificially high prices maintained there, particularly for coal used in domestic consumption. The deplorable condition of labor, both union and nonunion, was pointed out in no uncertain terms.

Gifford Pinchot, then governor of Pennsylvania, was eager to gain political prestige by having the difficulties in the coal region adjusted through his intervention. It was, of course, natural that he should be keenly interested, since the scene of the coal trouble was in his state. Interviews had appeared in the press in which he was represented as announcing that he was going to offer the government a solution of the coal problem. When the question was brought before President Coolidge, he agreed with the members of the Coal Commission that the settlement should be effected through the federal government.

When Pinchot approached him for an interview the President immediately notified me by telephone that Pinchot had volunteered his services and wanted to talk the situation over with him. "I've invited him to lunch tomorrow, and since you're better acquainted with the technical and economic problems than I, I'd like you to be present."

"All right, Mr. President," I said, "I'll be glad to come." I then said that Pinchot was an old friend of mine, that I admired him in many respects, but that I did not agree with all his policies.

I added that I was sure Pinchot would bring a plan of his own and suggested that, before Coolidge saw him, he read the Special Report just completed by the commission.

The President not only welcomed this idea, but asked me to bring the report to the White House at once. After reading it, he approved our conclusions and recommendations.

Pinchot and I were the only guests. The conversation during lunch was entirely social. The moment we reached the President's study after lunch, I pulled from my pocket the report Coolidge had already read, and handed it to him, saying: "Mr. President, the commission has studied the conditions in the coal industry with great care, and considers this report covers the situation. After you've examined it, I'm sure Governor Pinchot will wish to read it also."

I had seen Pinchot's hand go towards the pocket where I assumed his own plan reposed. I had beaten him to the draw.

For form's sake, Coolidge glanced briefly over the report and then handed it to Pinchot. As soon as I saw Pinchot had finished, I said, "Don't you agree that this covers the situation?"

The governor had to admit he approved the report, with the result that the coal crisis was met by the Coolidge, and not the Pinchot, plan.

President Coolidge many times referred to this as our "coup."

Pinchot endorsed the commission's report in a statement to the press. At his request, I supplied him with all our data and sent two assistants to Harrisburg to explain technical points.

My next connection with the coal problem was in October, 1923, when I was appointed chairman of the Executive Committee of the New England Governors' Fuel Committee composed of Governors John H. Trumbull, of Connecticut, Ralph O. Brewster, of Maine, Alvan T. Fuller, of Massachusetts, John G. Winant, of New Hampshire, Aram J. Pothier, of Rhode Island, and Franklin S. Billings, of Vermont.

The price of anthracite at the time was excessive and the supply uncertain. We urged that operators and miners in the Pennsylvania fields find some means of furnishing New England with sufficient coal at reasonable prices. We warned them that otherwise New England would turn to oil and bituminous coal. Later figures show that the use of substitute fuels has greatly increased, and Pennsylvania no longer enjoys her fuel monopoly of New England.

The International Conference on Bituminous Coal was held in Pittsburgh in November, 1926, under the auspices of the Carnegie Institute of Technology. Thomas S. Baker, president of the institute, and leading scientists from England, France, and Germany were present. Utilization of coal to provide expanded markets was the primary object of the conference. Considerable discussion was devoted to methods of producing oil and gasoline from coal.

As chairman of this conference, I stressed once more the need for a government study of the economics of the coal industry, and particularly for better protection against the prevalent waste in the mining of bituminous coal. The industry had been for a long time one of the major economic national problems; there was constant overproduction, coupled with intense market competition, and a plethora of miners for whom remunerative employment could not be provided.

In 1924, President Coolidge had asked me to represent him at Tallahassee, on the occasion of the centennial of the first meeting of the Legislative Council of the Territory of Florida. The most interesting part of the assignment was my contact with William Jennings Bryan in the last phase of his extraordinary career.

In my opening speech I extended the good wishes of the President to the people of Florida. Bryan then made a short address in his usual flattering and flowery manner, in which he congratulated the President on having selected me as his representative on this occasion.

"There could be," he said, "no more fitting choice, since Mr. Hammond is known as one of the great Americans who have developed resources in other lands, to the advantage of the people of those lands, as well as of his own country."

Senator Fletcher leaned over to me. "Bryan must have changed his views about Americans being interested in the development of foreign countries. When he was secretary of state, he used to call them all 'unprincipled exploiters.' "

At the termination of the speeches, I accepted Bryan's invitation to lunch. He began at once to regale me with a list of the marvelous opportunities Florida offered as a field for profitable investment.

"In what particular line?" I asked.

"Real estate," he replied.

"But," I said, "is it better in that respect than Los Angeles?"

"Oh, yes," he assured me, "far better. I'll give you an illustration. About ten years ago I bought some land in the Miami section. The other day I sold part of this land for eight times what I paid for the whole."

"That's certainly a good profit," I admitted.

"Oh," he said, "I expect to do much better than that with the rest of the property."

"Well," I replied, "all this seems to resemble what we, in the days of frenzied finance, used to call 'unearned increment.' "

Bryan changed the subject. He knew I had often heard him inveigh against profits made from real estate.

On my return to Washington I related this incident to President Coolidge. His answering smile was equivalent to the laugh of an average human being.

"I think I can cap that story," he said. "Dawes was in here a few days ago and told me he had recently seen Bryan in Florida. The Great Commoner had shown him his property near Miami and told him his investments would return him a profit of several hundred thousand dollars. Dawes then said to Bryan: 'That's a new idea for you. When we were young lawyers in Nebraska, you challenged me to debate on whether any man should be allowed to acquire a fortune of more than a hundred thousand dollars. How does that fit in with your present bank account?'

"Bryan's reply was, 'Circumstances alter cases.' "

Speaking of altered circumstances, my introduction to aviation and the active interest I have since taken in it comes as a far cry to the enthusiasm I felt as a boy, greeting the Pony Express, a contemporary marvel of transportation.

When Charles A. Lindbergh was on his way back to America after his epoch-making flight to Paris in May, 1927, the commissioners of the District of Columbia formed a reception committee to greet him on his arrival at the Capitol. I was asked to become its chairman and take the responsibility, on behalf of the people of Washington, of providing a fitting welcome and entertainment.

My own interest in aviation dated back to the time when, at the Metropolitan Club in Washington, I used to meet S. P. Langley, then head of the Smithsonian Institution. He was full of strange ideas about flying machines. In those days his theories were regarded as too visionary for serious attention, but I used to listen with interest to his lengthy disquisitions and predictions as to what he was going to accomplish in aviation.

When gasoline engines were invented a few years afterwards and the Wright brothers used them as airplane power plants, Langley's ideas were proved sound. I was struck with the difference between the talkativeness of Langley and the taciturnity of the Wright brothers. On the occasion of their receiving from President Taft the medals Congress had voted them, it was with the utmost difficulty that I could induce either of them to utter a word.

On December 15, 1925, I gave a dinner to a group of men actively engaged in promoting commercial air transportation. They had approached me with the idea that I might assist them in getting a measure passed by Congress which would secure government aid in the construction of beacon lights and landing fields for the guidance and convenience of pilots.

I had invited to the dinner those representatives of aviation companies and also government officials whose influence would be of most service in furthering the plan. The dinner was successful and the passage of the bill proved to be a long step in the advancement of commercial aviation.

I like to fly as a passenger. In fact, when a doctor tells me that altitude might dangerously affect my heart, I usually am able to find another who will reverse the decision. With this aviation background, my connection with the welcome accorded Lindbergh proved one of the memorable incidents of my life in Washington.

The haste with which we were forced to complete the reception plans meant strenuous work. But by the day before he was to arrive everything was settled, except the all-important question as to where and how the President and Lindbergh should meet. At the last committee meeting, I asked Postmaster General New, the government's representative on the committee, what the wishes of the President were.

"I don't know," he replied.

"But Lindbergh's going to be here tomorrow."

"The President doesn't want to be bothered with details," New assured me.

Saying I would return in a few moments, I got into my car and drove straight to the White House.

At the executive office, I was told by the staff that the President was not receiving anyone.

"Is anybody with him?"

"No."

I started for the door determinedly, and the executive clerk at once volunteered, "I'll take your card in."

"You won't have to," I responded, and walked into the inner office.

I found the President seated at his desk. I apologized briefly for my intrusion and reminded him that Lindbergh would arrive within twenty-four hours and that it was no longer a question of details but of making the final plans.

Then I asked him where he wanted to receive Lindbergh. He replied, "At the White House." This meant the temporary White House in Dupont Circle, which was serving while the national mansion was undergoing repairs.

"Bring him to lunch," said the President.

This arrangement struck me as unfair to those who would be marching in the parade that had been planned, and also to the thousands of spectators who would be kept waiting in the midday heat while Lindbergh was lunching.

"What will Lindbergh do for lunch then?" asked the President.

I suggested that I might take him one or two sandwiches, which was all he had on his transatlantic flight, or I might send a radio message asking him to have his lunch on the *Memphis* before landing.

"All right. Notify me when he reaches the grandstand, and I'll go there to receive him," said Coolidge.

My answer to this was that courtesy demanded he should be there first to receive Lindbergh. He finally acquiesced.

The weather was extremely hot. I hated to think of this young man, especially with the arduous program ahead of him, being subjected to the discomfort of the stiff and heavy colonel's uniform the army had prepared for him. I knew that one of the St. Louis backers, who had made this flight possible, was going down the river to meet the *Memphis* and was to take the uniform with him. I suggested that he lose it if possible.

The arrangement of the meeting between Lindbergh and his mother, Mrs. Evangeline Lindbergh, was one of my duties. I promised her that if she wished to accompany me to the *Memphis,* there would be no newspaper photographers on board to witness the greeting.

It proved difficult to get through the crowd of officials, congressmen, and others with special passes to the Navy Yard. Only the fact that we were in a White House car enabled us to edge our way finally to the dock. I escorted Mrs. Lindbergh to the captain of the *Memphis* and waited at the foot of the gangplank.

After a few minutes, Lindbergh with the President's aide, followed by Mrs. Lindbergh and the secretaries of war and navy, came down the gangplank amid the deafening uproar of whistles, bells, shouts, and cheers. Colonel Lindbergh, his mother, the President's aide, and I started off in the White House car and joined the long parade.

When Lindbergh appeared in a neat blue business suit, I was not surprised. As we were driving along to the grandstand near the Washington Monument, I asked him why he was not wearing the uniform. He smiled in his disarming manner and said: "Fortunately I couldn't get into it. I don't think I could have survived wearing it in this weather."

Each morning the papers printed his program for the day and, acting on this information, thousands of people would stand patiently for hours hoping to catch a glimpse of him.

As he rode from place to place, without a hat, he remained un-affected so far as anyone could see. He seemed to look on the entire performance as an interesting phenomenon, something apart from himself and having no connection with his astonishing achievement.

At the end of two days, Lindbergh was to fly to New York, where another reception awaited him. Since his arrival at Washington, my telephone had been ringing constantly with personal messages from my friends Grover Whalen and William H. Woodin, heads of the New York committee of reception, imploring me to see to it that he departed on schedule. Having witnessed the mad enthusiasm with which he was being greeted in Washington, I realized even better than they what the New York welcome would be like. Con-sequently, at six o'clock on the morning of his departure, I called at the temporary White House and took him to a breakfast tendered him by members of the different aeronautical associations.

The previous afternoon I had accompanied Lindbergh to Bolling Field while he inspected the *Spirit of St. Louis* and found the plane in perfect condition. That morning, however, he found that through carelessness of those in charge the plane had not been placed in the hangar and during the night a severe storm had rendered it unfit for flight. At the last moment, a plane of a type Lindbergh had never seen or flown before had to be substituted. He had no time to make his customary thorough inspection or even a trial flight.

When Lindbergh left the field, I was standing near Major F. Tru-bee Davison, assistant secretary of war, who, shocked at the angle and speed of the take-off, exclaimed, "My God! What a risk!" and turned his head away. Davison had been in the Yale aviation corps during the war and had had a serious accident.

A few months later the papers told of how Lindbergh started to fly to Portland, Maine, and was caught in such a heavy fog that it had taken him several hours to find a landing place. I knew that he was doing some work at the time for the Guggenheim Founda-tion, and I wrote my friend Harry Guggenheim that Lindbergh had already won his reputation for courage; if anything should happen to him now, aviation would be given a tremendous setback. It would be much better if he were to devote himself to conservative rather than risky flights.

Lindbergh came to see me shortly afterwards in Washington, and told me that Harry Guggenheim had showed him the letter. "I'm going to take your advice," he said.

In February, 1929, when President-elect Hoover was vacationing at Miami for a few weeks, and I was not far away at Palm Beach, he invited me to a luncheon party. One of the first persons I saw there was Lindbergh.

As soon as we had greeted each other, he remarked in some embarrassment: "I'm afraid you've lost confidence in me. You see when I was out in California the army planes were having maneuvers and one of the pilots was killed when flying in formation with two other planes. I felt I had to substitute for him and I may have taken risks, after I told you I wouldn't."

Lindbergh invited Hoover and me to make a flight with him that afternoon. I noticed that Hoover seemed hesitant about accepting, and to keep him from feeling embarrassed, I told him that, as the future President of the United States, he had no right to take chances with his life; that his doing so would be regarded as bravado. He was obviously relieved at my suggeston.

Mrs. Alvin T. Hert, a prominent member of the Republican National Committee, was also a guest. She remarked that Lindbergh was the only person with whom she could be induced to fly and asked whether she might go up with us. When the plane took off there was a full passenger list, including Mrs. Hert, Mrs. Henry Rae, and several other women. Mrs. Hert sat rigid with closed eyes and turned a deaf ear as I endeavored to beguile her with a description of the beauties of Biscayne Bay seen from the air. When we landed, she was the first one out of the plane. I congratulated her on her heroism.

It was not until we were safe on earth again that I related Hoover's account of the famous French aviator who shortly before had made a demonstration flight in Brazil with a party of Brazilian officials. The plane had crashed in landing, and all had met a tragic death. I told her that even Lindbergh had on several occasions been forced to seek safety with a parachute.

She looked at me dubiously and then remarked, "I wouldn't have missed this trip for a million dollars, but it would take a lot more than a million to get me up in a plane again."

In spite of the honors which had come to Lindbergh since the first Washington reception, he had not changed. A characteristic action of his turned my admiration into warm affection for him.

When he made his goodwill trip to Mexico—which not only achieved its purpose but also won him a bride—he had only two days in which to get ready. Inasmuch as I knew he personally supervised all flight preparations, and consequently had his hands full, I was greatly surprised when, at dawn of the day he was to leave, the doorbell of my house in Washington rang and I was told Colonel Lindbergh was downstairs.

Grasping my hand hurriedly, he said, "I'm off in half an hour, and I hadn't a second until now to come and have you wish me good luck."

When later he went to Panama to establish a route for the Pan American Airways, he wired me to join him as a flying companion. Unfortunately, I was at Gloucester and could not reach Miami, the starting point, by the date set for his departure.

Looking back on the Coolidge administration, I find it difficult to estimate either the man or his work. Despite the fact that I saw a great deal of him, I never felt close to him. Few people did. As I have said before, I considered him the man of the hour. And while many people attribute the financial collapse of 1929 in part to some of his policies, I consider the justice of this debatable. I would ask them if these same policies had not been their own.

There is no doubt that in his hour he was one of the most popular presidents we have ever had. And I imagine that part of the resentment which even today is directed towards him is due to the fact that thousands of his former constituents believe that, had he chosen to run again, he would somehow miraculously have saved their personal fortunes and the country from the depression.

To me, as a Westerner who had grown to pride himself on his knowledge of the psychology of that part of the country, one of the most amazing things about Calvin Coolidge was that he came to

694 The Autobiography of John Hays Hammond

supersede even Theodore Roosevelt in the popular affections of the West.

Everything about Roosevelt had been the antithesis of Coolidge: his strenuous activities, his love of exciting adventures, his physical daring, his aggressiveness, and his ebullient manner. It has always seemed phenomenal to me that Coolidge, without any effort on his part, could have won the West. It may perhaps be explained by the fact that the West admired Roosevelt as an *individual* and Coolidge as a *president*.

Those who knew the political game considered Coolidge one of the shrewdest politicians among our presidents. His reluctance to commit himself when it was not necessary, his taciturnity, and his mannerisms help to build up this picture. In my contacts with him I became conscious that these characteristics were real and not legendary.

When he first came into office, I was still chairman of the Coal Commission. Almost daily we would have a smoke and a chat together.

Knowing that Coolidge was a very good judge of cigars, I sent him a box of particularly fine ones with my compliments. I received a note of appreciation. The next time I saw the President, I found him smoking a cigar which had the familiar aroma of my own brand. As I sat down, he opened a drawer of his desk and held out a box of cigars.

I leaned over and eyed it critically. One glance convinced me he must have taken literally Tom Marshall's witticism about the country's need for a five-cent cigar. I smiled, and said, "No, thank you."

Coolidge grinned in response, dipped again into his desk, and brought out my gift box. "Come to think of it, you sent me these. Try one."

I accepted.

The anecdotes about the Coolidge thrift are innumerable. It is said that in his boyhood he could make a worm last longer as fish bait than could any of his companions. About the best of these stories was told me by a newspaper correspondent who was one of three to interview him when he was lieutenant governor of Massachusetts.

It was an exceedingly stormy day. One reporter arrived a few moments ahead of his confreres.

Mrs. Coolidge, always thoughtful and generous, noticed how wet and cold he was, and considerately remarked, "Calvin, I think Bill needs a drink of whisky."

"All right! Give him one," said Coolidge.

Bill had finished his drink by the time the other two reporters arrived. Mrs. Coolidge poured out drinks for them also, and was about to give Bill another when Coolidge interjected hastily, "Oh, no! Bill's already had his."

Coolidge never could be forced to talk. The old story is true of the woman who sat next to him at dinner and wagered that she could get him to converse. "Mr. President," she began, "I have a bet that I can get you to talk to me."

Coolidge hesitated a moment and then replied quietly, "You have lost."

There were evidently times when, like Macaulay, Coolidge had brilliant flashes of silence and yet there were times also when, although he could not be called exactly loquacious, at least he became a most interesting conversationalist. My own experience warrants this statement. Often, after he had finished his work at the executive office and his desk was clear of official data, I dropped in and had most enjoyable talks with him.

He was logical in his theory of the value of silence. As he once remarked to a friend, "Well, after all, you'll have to admit that what I didn't say has never cost me anything."

I remember one illuminating conversation I had with him after the Teapot Dome scandal became public property.

"Mr. President," I said, "you sat in here with Harding's Cabinet. You must have seen a lot of Fall. Did it ever occur to you that he was a scoundrel?"

"Never," was the succinct reply.

"Would you ever have thought he could have been bribed?"

"Never."

"Wouldn't you have thought he was the sort of man who would have been so insulted by an attempt at bribery that he would have knocked the offender downstairs or kicked him out the door?"

"Yes."

At that laconicism I gave up.

Coolidge was exceedingly fortunate in not being in the White House when the storm ultimately broke. He conveyed to me at the time, more or less inarticulately, and he closed his autobiography with this sentiment:

> My election seemed assured. Nevertheless, I felt it was not best for the country that I should succeed myself. A new impulse is likely to be beneficial.
>
> It was therefore my privilege, after seeing my administration so strongly endorsed by the country, to retire voluntarily from the greatest experience that can come to mortal man. In that way, I believed I could best serve the people who have honored me and the country which I love.

In retrospect, I am impressed not so much with Coolidge's lack of foresight as with that which characterized our financial leaders, the bankers. Their judgment proved no better than that of the man in the street, and they failed utterly to realize that the bubble of fictitious prosperity was soon to be pricked. If any voices of protest and warning were raised, they were either inaudible or disregarded.

No doubt most of the justifiable disgust of the people with bankers came from the fact that in investing and losing other people's money (and indeed, to a certain extent, their own) very few of them had direct and accurate knowledge of the things in which they were investing, and in many cases their advisers and agents were both dishonest and incompetent. Even in the best of all possible worlds, it is not always wise to buy and sell goods you have never seen.

Our failure to recover more rapidly from the depression was founded, I believe, on this—and on the fact that our country still has little confidence in its leaders either political or economic. They had been tried and found wanting.

During the years in which my connection with politics was most active, and especially in my work with the Coal Commission, various of my opinions on capital and labor crystallized. But even before

MRS. EVANGELINE LINDBERGH, CHARLES A. LINDBERGH, AND MYSELF

To John Hays Hammond
with Regards
January 1923   Calvin Coolidge

CALVIN COOLIDGE (1872-1933)

this—believing, as I do, that every citizen should take an active part in civic matters—I had always been glad to donate my services where I considered they could be of use.

After the death of Grover Cleveland in 1908, I was asked to join the National Civic Federation as his successor to serve as "representative of the public" on one of the committees. The organization was politically nonpartisan, and included representatives of capital, labor, and the public. Its president at that time was Seth Low, formerly president of Columbia University; later Judge Alton B. Parker served. Ralph M. Easley was its secretary and its moving spirit. Its various committees were active in collecting data concerning many of the problems that affect the citizen, in making a careful study of them, and in advocating reforms. These committees studied and reported on the problems of Americanization, public education, taxation, judicial procedure, uniform state laws, trust regulation, Workmen's Compensation Act, and many purely economic and social questions.

The Women's Welfare Department of the federation, of which my wife was chairman for some time and Miss Gertrude Beeks (later Mrs. Ralph M. Easley) was secretary, was interested not only in women employees but in the welfare of employees in general.

The federation was not reformist in the radical sense. With a membership drawn from all classes of people, it necessarily preserved a balance of common sense and avoided extremes. It was conservative enough to wish to preserve the broad principles underlying Americanism.

It was customary for the officers of the federation to have luncheon meetings once or twice a month at some downtown club in New York. These were attended by many leaders of finance and industry. August Belmont, for example, was conspicuous for the splendid service he rendered up to the time of his death. Samuel Gompers, John Mitchell, and other labor leaders were usually present. The public did not realize that the frank discussions of our committees quietly composed many a difference before it could grow into an open dispute or strike. Gompers once remarked that he found the meetings of great service because they showed him the point of view of the employer, and the employers acknowledged the value of the information about labor matters which they secured from him.

Some of my friends outside took me to task for my association with labor leaders, and once a reactionary coal mine operator reproached me for the sympathy I had expressed for organized labor. In the presence of several prominent industrial leaders, I replied that organized labor was needed to protect the workingman against organized capitalism.

"There must be organization, and you men pursue a mistaken policy in fighting Gompers and Mitchell, who are conservative and patriotic, and are guiding labor with sanity and wisdom. Gompers is not a Socialist, and is energetically opposed to Communism. He has kept organized labor out of the hands of the radicals. Organized labor we will have. You must take your choice between the conservative Sam Gompers and the radical Bill Haywood."

Gompers was the best labor leader we could have found in those days. He stood out against the arbitrary, narrow, and selfish employer, and against the militant radicals in his own party. He used the weapon of the strike only as a last resort and settled many differences before they came to an issue. He broke many an outlaw strike by vigorously and decisively exercising his power as a dominant leader. The regard which the National Civic Federation had for him, a regard which had grown during twenty years' association, was given expression in a memorial meeting held in 1924, in memory of Samuel Gompers and August Belmont, both of whom had recently died.

I remember one occasion when the cigars were passed after dinner. "Try one of these, Sam," I requested.

Gompers picked up one, sniffed it, and a pleased expression spread over his face as he said: "I certainly will. You know I was a cigar roller once. This is one cigar that I hope I'll enjoy. Try one of mine!"

"Well, Sam, you may have been a cigar roller once but you're certainly the best-dressed man here tonight."

He smiled. "If labor didn't think I more than adequately represent it, it would never forgive me."

As a matter of fact, he was always immaculately attired. He met everybody on a plane of equality, with the complete and justified assurance that he was their mental equal. He had an essential humanity which gave him understanding of all, rich or poor, educated or illiterate. His oratory was effective but unaffected, illustrated with homely anecdote and pointed witticisms. He was an artist in playing on the bass string of human experience.

One of my prized possessions is his photograph on which he wrote, "To the most conservative, practical, radically democratic millionaire I ever met, John Hays Hammond, with the compliments of Samuel Gompers."

As Gompers and Mitchell knew, I am a friend of fair labor. I have often said that, were I an employee I would join some labor organization.

I believed in the Railway Brotherhoods and also in the American Federation of Labor under the guidance of such a man as Samuel Gompers. I supported both organizations as valuable parts of our industrial system. On the other hand, I had no use for the radicalism of the I.W.W., of which I had had experience in the Coeur d'Alene and Cripple Creek.

When I later discussed this aspect of the labor question with Samuel Gompers and John Mitchell, both admitted the unusually serious features of the Coeur d'Alene trouble. They confessed they had been wrong in sympathizing with the Western Federation at that time; their subsequent difficulties with Haywood and Orchard disclosed to them the true nature of the situation.

The lesson from labor strikes, as I see it, is that no organization, whether labor or capital, industrial or social, economic or spiritual, can succeed or even continue to exist unless it is founded upon fair intent and is conducted in the main by honest leaders. This truth applies equally to a nation, a trades union, a bank, or a church. If a government does not honestly and speedily enforce the laws made to protect both individuals and corporate bodies against attacks on life and property, it invites disaster upon itself.

My own interest lay primarily in the relations between employer and employee. As a mining engineer I had come in close contact with a type of workman perhaps the most difficult of all to handle because of his independence. I understood the miner, and his problems, and had a good deal of sympathy with his point of view. I was instrumental in securing the passage of legislation for the protection of the miner, and advocated workmen's compensation laws and the minimum wage, and other beneficent measures.

Gompers, curiously enough, was opposed to the movement to set up a minimum wage, fearing it would tend to become a prevailing wage.

I did not fall into the error of class antagonism. The close contact a mining engineer must necessarily have with his men doubtless keeps him democratic. I never lost my liking for cranks and odd characters in general, as they have afforded me amusement and sometimes indeed valuable suggestions.

Though I always kept on friendly terms with workmen, I also understood the point of view of the employer. I early became identified with large corporations and the management of successful companies, and later counted among my friends the great promoters and capitalists of the country. I saw that capital, too, has its rights and minimum wage; that is, the rate of interest necessary as guarantee before the investor can be expected to risk his money in an enterprise.

It is true that capital has often exceeded its rights, and by exercise of its power grasped inequitable rewards. I believe that some method should be devised to prevent such evils as overcapitalization, both in public utility and in private corporation. The recently revealed corruption in some large corporations calls for reform. The public should not be forced to pay for services and products in excess of value received, nor should the credulous investor find that he can hope for no return on his investment unless labor is sweated.

During the Taft, Harding, and Coolidge administrations, my family became more and more intimately involved in the social life of Washington. While we never found it quite so fascinating as the same type of life in London, we felt it was far more interesting than similar aspects of living in any other American city. Washington is, I think, one of the most beautiful cities in the world, especially at Eastertime, with the gorgeous cherry blossoms, Rock Creek Park and the lovely green lawns with beds of multicolored flowers set aside for the public, monuments, buildings, drives along the Potomac, and Georgetown, Arlington, and Mount Vernon only a short distance away.

While the whole make-up of Washington life is complex, it is also in a sense simple, and while, of course, in the days of which I am writing, there was a considerable amount of hospitality on a lavish scale, charming and equally memorable were the simple entertainments given by people of modest means. One of the most admirable characteristics of Washington social life is that money doesn't count as it does in other American cities. In this it resembles London.

The social scene is composed of various groups. Centering in the White House is the administrative and diplomatic life, and on down the line the whole parade of governmental officeholders. I may be prejudiced, but it seemed to me that members of Congress, senators in particular, do not measure up to the intellectual capacity of those who served two or three generations ago. Nevertheless, they are a hard-working class and when one considers Congressional nonentities, one must remember bankers, lawyers, businessmen, and indeed, mining engineers.

The army and the navy add a certain glamour to various dinners and parties. Not only those occupied actively in the army and navy departments are present, but also many men who have served with distinction in one or other of the services and who have, as is their custom, made their residence permanently in Washington.

And there is that other large and select group known, with kindly humor, as the "has-beens," passé politicians, former congressmen and senators, retired diplomats, and more and more people from other parts of the country who come to Washington to spend their later years in a life which offers them contacts both democratic and stimulating.

No description of the character of Washington life would be complete without mention of the "Cave dwellers." They are the real Washingtonians. For many generations their ancestors have lived there, some of them in Georgetown, even before the founding of Washington. Feeling themselves the real aristocrats, they do not seek society, and patronize somewhat the shifting governmental population.

Since the World War, I am glad to observe that American women are becoming "internationally minded"—which must be pleasing to my friend, Nicholas Murray Butler—and the Washington women are particularly fortunate in having the opportunity of acquiring interesting and reliable information about world conditions through the Monday Talks on "Affairs Political and International" of Miss Janet Richards, who is justly known as the Dean of Lecturers on Current Events.

One of the more vital groups in Washington is that composed of the scientific and literary men, many of whom are world famous. During lunch at the Cosmos Club, it is possible to hear conversations dealing with every phase of the world of scholarship and science.

Many of these men are connected with the Smithsonian Institution, Bureau of Standards, Carnegie Institute, the four neighboring universities, the Congressional and Carnegie libraries, the various other branches of science and learning. Unfortunately the members of this group are conspicuous by their absence from most society functions. An innovation that would contribute much to the social and intellectual life of Washington would be dinners given by the President to notable people of the Capital other than high government officials.

President and Mrs. Franklin D. Roosevelt are, to a degree, aware of this and in this respect are following the traditions of Theodore Roosevelt. They have frequently entertained writers, artists, scientists, sculptors, and scholars, and have been subjected to undiscerning criticism. American politicians have always been notoriously afraid of men possessing sound and proved knowledge. In England a procedure such as this has always been taken as a matter of course. On the other hand, in the transaction of the affairs of the government, the designation of power to people, whether intellectuals or politicians, who have not demonstrated their ability and honesty seems to me to be dangerous.

Anyone living in Washington cannot fail to be both irritated and impressed by some of the irksome duties imposed by its custom.

For example, the presidential handshaking seems a great imposition on our Chief Executive—surely an onerous and unnecessary obligation. The right arm of the President, which is sworn to maintain the Constitution of the United States, has often been seriously impaired for efficient service by this senseless business. Witness the case of President Coolidge, who was once forced to carry his arm in a sling for several days from too constant and strenuous handshaking. I understand that at the New Year's Day reception at the White House this has been discontinued. Surely the reception itself clearly shows our democratic spirit, and the handshaking is unnecessary at that time, as well as when the President meets organizations, societies, groups, and committees from all parts of the country.

As all old Washingtonians know, precedence at government functions, and even at conventional private entertainments, is often a matter of considerable embarrassment to the host or hostess. It is probably necessary, however, as its effect dignifies and preserves respect for the custodians of our government. Democratization of governmental functions would perhaps tend to lessen respect for those occupying high positions. On the other hand, an American citizen who holds no official position—though highly important in the life of the nation—may feel himself socially handicapped on these distinguished occasions when he finds himself assigned, perhaps, "below the salt." Only recently I learned that, etymologically, the word "idiot" signifies "a person who is not in the government service."

It must be extremely monotonous for Cabinet officers and their wives to be repeatedly huddled together at the White House, and other places—but the more philosophical "grin and bear it." And if their constant neighbors required by custom prove deadly dull, they get their conversational relaxation elsewhere. At any rate, this is Washington!

I feel quite certain that the men of any family prominent in Washington social life cannot have failed to notice and deplore some of the senseless and irksome duties imposed upon women: for example, the survival of the incessant paying of formal calls, the almost daily task of leaving cards at innumerable front doors—surely a sad waste of time and cardboard, and quite ridiculous as a custom. But I believe that the women of present-day Washington are fast discarding this form of etiquette, which must be a relief to all concerned.

After we came to the Capital to make our home, my wife and I found great pleasure in the dinner parties, the old-fashioned elegance of entertainment, and above all in the fact that we discovered ourselves making new friends, interesting friends, and warm friends.

Emily Beale McLean was one of our close friends; she was a great hostess. Her Sunday luncheons at "Friendship," her semicountry home on the edge of the city, were memorable. Although they were formal and much thought must have been given to their arrangement, they seemed almost impromptu. No fewer than a hundred guests were invited for each occasion, and even at the eleventh hour one might ask the privilege of bringing any number of out-of-town friends. Small tables, at which there was no question fortunately of precedence, seemed to appear as if by magic for a last-moment influx. Delicious food, accompanied by her celebrated mint juleps, was abundant. This hospitality was very gracefully carried on by her daughter-in-law, Evalyn Walsh McLean, for many years.

Among the elaborate dinners at which I was a guest was that given by Colonel Robert M. Thompson several years ago at his home in honor of some members of the Greek royal family who were visiting in Washington. I was asked to take in Lady Sarah Wilson, widow of a British army officer, Colonel Henry Wilson. She was a well-known sportswoman, a great traveler, and a woman of interesting personality. As we sat at table she remarked on the contrast between the luxury of the present appointments and the primitive simplicity of the meal we last had together, nearly thirty years before. The dinner to which she referred was one which she and her husband and I had had when they were visiting Jameson's camp on the veldt, just before the Boer War. Jameson had run short of provisions when I reached his camp after an inspection of some mines, and as I was on my way out to Bulawayo, I divided with him all of the food I had left. So there on the veldt in Jameson's camp we dined that night on game and canned goods.

Another Washington friend of ours, made through old family ties, was Princess Cantacuzene, the granddaughter of President Grant. She naturally had nothing but abhorrence for the violence of the

Bolshevik government, a viewpoint with which I fully agreed, as did most informed Americans with the exception of the rankest ideologists.

On the question of the recognition of the U.S.S.R. I did not agree with Senator Borah. Later I came to see that despite his predilection for the Soviet government he could feel sympathy for the unfortunate sufferers in its terrorist regime. The incident that convinced me occurred at the time the Soviet government had decided to execute a number of Catholic priests. Senator Borah and I were in my study when Judge Alton B. Parker, president of the National Civic Federation, telephoned asking me to be one of a hundred Americans to sign a cablegram of protest against the execution of these priests. I readily consented, of course, and urged the senator likewise to send a cablegram, saying that a protest from him would be more potent than Judge Parker's petition. He flatly refused because the priests had no business taking part in Soviet politics. As he left my home I followed him to the door in an endeavor to appeal to his humanity. I pointed out that he could not rest easy with the thought that innocent priests were suffering when his name might save them. Half an hour later Borah telephoned me from his house saying: "Colonel, you are right. I have sent the cablegram."

William E. Borah, during the Republican administrations, was undoubtedly the outstanding figure in the Senate. His enemies characterized him as one

> Stiff in opinions, always in the wrong,
> [Was] everything by starts and nothing long;

but even his political enemies had to admit that he was a factor to be reckoned with because of his unimpeachable integrity, his political courage, and of the fact that he was an indomitable fighter and an orator with "the applause of listening senates to command." Borah undoubtedly was "the big bad wolf" in the Coolidge and Hoover administrations. He has put Idaho on the map politically and it has never been marked "a windswept plain."

Viscount Grey of Fallodon, my old friend, was in Washington as special ambassador in 1919, and I have told of the luncheon at which we urged him to make a public statement regarding the Lodge reservations to President Wilson's League of Nations. Another time when he was dining with me in Washington, he told a story which he said was the most remarkable example of true sportsmanship he had ever known. Two of the major native tribes in New Zealand were incessantly warring against each other, much to the annoyance of the white residents, and a representative was sent out by the British government to investigate. (My recollection is that Grey himself was the British representative.) Having decided in favor of one of the tribes, he reported that if properly backed by the government it would be able to conquer the other and establish peace. The government sent what it considered a sufficient supply of arms and ammunition to enable its champion to defeat the enemy, who possessed only primitive weapons.

After a few months the government was surprised to receive a request for more guns. They were sent with some reluctance, but when a third request was received for still more guns, the representative was sent out again to investigate. He found the native chief and asked why he needed so many rifles, saying that the great King had at first sent all that were thought necessary. The chief expressed his thanks for the many guns he had received but said that he did not use all of them. Very much surprised, the representative asked him what he had done with the rest. The old warrior replied, "We divided them with our enemy because they did not have any guns." After telling the story, Grey said, "And we call those people uncivilized."

From the time when I first collected stamps as a boy in San Francisco until late in life I did not have the time nor the inclination to indulge in hobbies. But during the years I did develop one other hobby—and that, too, collecting. I collected people, in a sense, people I had met and admired.

It has been my privilege "in the day's work" to meet many of the leading men of my time. On the walls of my study in my Washington home I have what is regarded as a unique collection of autographed photographs, numbering over eight hundred. They represent, so my friends tell me, at least one-half the men of my day who have controlled the destinies of nations.

Charles Coffin, the great genius who was responsible for the development of the General Electric Company, had not been photographed since childhood, but just before his death he was persuaded to have one taken for my collection. He, Myron T. Herrick, and I were a trio bound together by the closest ties of friendship.

In all my collection of famous individuals, the only one I have not known personally was Abraham Lincoln, whose picture was given me by his son, Robert Todd. It is an etching which he declared was the best of all the likenesses of his father.

Bob Lincoln, whose home was one of the most picturesque in Washington, liked to talk of his father, and after our golf at the Chevy Chase Club, he would visit the "nineteenth hole" at my house, and relate stories about him. I remember his telling how his father composed the Gettysburg Address on a sheet of wrapping paper while the train was on its way from Washington. He told me that once when he returned from Harvard to spend his vacation at the White House, certain officials came to him and asked him to complain to his father about Salmon P. Chase, secretary of the treasury. Chase, they said, was considered disloyal to the President, and everyone in the executive office knew it except the President himself. That night when he was studying in his room his father entered and Bob told him what he had heard. The President said, "Well, I have Chase's resignation in my hand." Bob said, "Of course, you will accept it?" The President replied, "Of course, I shall not."

He then asked for writing materials and wrote a note declining to accept Chase's resignation. To Bob's question why he was taking such action, he answered: "He is much safer in my Cabinet than he would be outside." Lincoln's action is known to history. In 1864 he appointed Salmon P. Chase chief justice of the Supreme Court, in which he served creditably until his death in 1873. The story has been told often before but it was interesting to hear the details from Bob Lincoln, as he told me in the presence of Colonel Chase, a descendant of Salmon P. Chase. It had been said that similar considerations—namely, it is safer to have your opponent in the fold than out—largely determined the appointment of William Jennings Bryan to the Cabinet of Woodrow Wilson.

The photograph of Blasco Ibañez recalls to mind an amusing incident which shows that all great men are not recognized generally as such. We had entertained Ibañez at our home for several days, and found him an interesting and brilliant guest. After his visit my wife made a trip to Philadelphia, and remembering that she wished to get some more of his books, went into Wanamaker's Department Store. She asked the young clerk in the book department if he had any Ibañez. Somewhat confused and puzzled, he said: "Madam, you may find them in the underwear department." Evidently something resembling "Ypsilanties" was in his mind.

One of our closest friends in Washington was Senator Frank B. Brandegee of Connecticut, and I have always felt a distinct personal sorrow at his suicide, October 14, 1924. He was a fine, honest man doing real patriotic service. He was one of the outstanding figures in the Senate and was leader of the "irreconcilables" who opposed our joining the League of Nations. Brandegee had invested heavily in real estate near Washington and, although he was losing money currently, later the properties became highly profitable. He was embarrassed by the fact that he had borrowed small sums of money from his friends and could not repay it in the allotted time. Naturally, his friends did not expect or want him to pay until he could do so conveniently, but he became hypersensitive in the matter.

The day before Brandegee committed suicide I called on him. He was a bachelor and lived alone with his servants in a gloomy brick house. He was not in good health and had been deeply affected by the death of his sister a few years earlier. Added to this, he had recently consulted an eminent surgeon in New York who told him that before long it would be necessary to amputate one of his legs. This was enough to break the most resolute spirit. I found Senator Brandegee quite depressed and most difficult to cheer, but before I left we had a good reassuring talk. I asked him to come home with me to dinner, but he declined saying he had an appointment with some real estate men. Then I asked him to come up the next night when George Harvey would be with me; he accepted.

Brandegee did not arrive for dinner, nor did I hear from him. I worried about him. Early the next day as I was getting into my automobile to call on him, William, my chauffeur, said: "Mr. Hammond, I want you to know how sorry I was to hear about Senator Brandegee's suicide." I was shocked. I had not seen the papers and this was the first I had heard of the tragedy.

Brandegee left a note addressed to his butler; this was characteristic of his consideration and affection:

> Dear George: I enclose $100 for you and $100 for Emma and Rufus. I am in the bathroom on the top floor nearest 18th Street; the top floor, the floor above the one I sleep on. If you and Lundy come up there, beware of the gas. Goodbye.

In spite of the fact that the convention of 1920 was my last, I did have an indirect connection with the candidacy of Hoover in 1928. During that winter, Frederic C. Walcott later United States senator from Connecticut, who was prominent in pressing Hoover's candidacy, came to Ormond Beach, Florida, where I was spending the winter. He asked me whether, in my opinion, Hoover should announce his candidacy in the near future or, as had been suggested by some of his political advisers, wait until shortly before the convention.

I thought it was absolutely necessary for Hoover to lose no time; I advised that he make his announcement at the earliest possible moment. When Walcott asked me whether this was not somewhat different advice from that given by me to General Wood, I explained that the circumstances were different. Wood had had many rival candidates while Hoover so far had virtually none. Walcott reported my conversation to Hoover, and my plan was adopted.

A few months before Chief Justice Taft's death, he and Walcott were present at a luncheon I gave in Washington. Walcott told Taft that Hoover and he had just seen General Charles G. Dawes, and Dawes had said that Hoover had had a narrow escape, for if he had not announced his candidacy the very day he did, Dawes himself would have been in the field. Dawes would have been a powerful contestant. Owing to his friendship for Governor Lowden, Dawes had not pressed his own candidacy, but when it began to appear that Lowden would have little chance for the nomination, he found that he could count on Lowden's support. He was then, he told Hoover, on the point of announcing his position and entering on a vigorous campaign for delegates. Sure of Ohio and Illinois and several other states, he would have had a good chance of defeating Hoover.

My first intimate contact with Herbert Hoover was just before we entered the World War, when he was in charge of Belgian Relief. The Rocky Mountain Club gave him a dinner. Funds for the relief work were not being collected in anything like the volume needed, and Hoover was asked to make an appeal to our members, and through them to citizens at large. This appeal was successful in gaining the support of our club. In two months, three million dollars were raised for the Belgian Relief, more than had been secured the previous year. For ten years the club had been collecting a reserve fund to be used in erecting a new building, but this appeal was so cogent that by a unanimous vote the entire fund was to be donated to help feed the starving people of Belgium.

One might think that western men, being used to traveling lone trails, would lose something of gregariousness, but it is not so. The Rocky Mountain Club of twelve hundred members, which maintained an "oasis" in New York for "roundups" and "stampedes," is evidence of the persistent desire even among Westerners to flock with their kind.

Our purpose was to promote good fellowship among our members and to bring about a greater solidarity between eastern and western states. The cosmopolitan nature of our membership list was shown by what happened one evening when a dozen or so mining engineers were talking after one of our banquets was over. These banquets were regarded by all who attended them as among the most enjoyable in New York.

While we were having a last smoke the question came up as to what countries we had all visited. We produced a large atlas and, just as my brother and I used to do with the counties of California, picked out the countries which had been visited by some member of our party. When the checkup was made, we found there wasn't a country on the face of the globe which one member or the other had not set foot on in the course of his professional work.

During the World War the Rocky Mountain Club rendered distinct patriotic service in entertaining and caring for soldiers of regiments raised in the western states, en route to the battlefields of Europe, and in caring for them on their return to New York after the war, before they departed for their homes. The wives of the members formed a committee, of which my wife was chairman, and they worked diligently for the boys.

After this last roundup, the money received from the sale of our real estate holdings was turned over to the American Institute of Mining and Metallurgical Engineers as a gift to be expended under its direction. We considered the institute the most worthy heir of the principles and spirit of the Rocky Mountain Club. The first work of this fund was the publication of a scholarly book, *The Porphyry Coppers,* by A. B. Parsons, secretary of the American Institute of Mining Engineers. In making possible the publication of this book and others to follow, the Rocky Mountain Club continues to live.

Our active members were representative western men living in New York, who were identified with the development of the West; our associate members were the governors of western states, and mostly mining men living in the West whose business brought them frequently to New York. From 1907, when it was founded, to the "last roundup" in 1928, I had the honor of being the club's only president.

The late "Ike" Hoover, of the White House staff, says, "Coolidge perhaps did less work than any president I have known; Herbert Hoover the most work."

Coolidge was not lazy; he had his departments well organized with capable men at their heads. I never saw his desk cluttered with papers, and in that I recognized he was a good executive.

Hoover came into office under far more trying conditions. He had taken his position as a Cabinet officer more conscientiously than is usual, attending strictly to business and not indulging in social life. Indeed, he rarely went out.

He was inducted into the presidency under most adverse conditions. As I told him on one occasion, he had, like Frankenstein, built up a monster, for it is undoubtedly true that the prosperity—whether fundamental or not—developed during Coolidge's administration was in a large measure due to the financial ability of Andrew Mellon and to the commercial ability of Herbert Hoover.

While I saw Hoover occasionally in the executive office as well as at White House social functions, I did not enjoy the intimacy with him that I had enjoyed with his predecessors. As president he was, in many ways, a lonely man. Even Taft, who had been the constant adviser of Coolidge, was never called to the White House by Hoover for conference, nor did Hoover avail himself of the political experience of Calvin Coolidge. It was unfortunate for Hoover that his enthusiastic followers of the younger generation associated with him in his relief work had made him appear to the public as somewhat of a superman—an impossible role to maintain. Then, too, Hoover was handicapped by the fact that he relied too much on "yes, yes" men for advice.

My estimate of Hoover is that he possessed executive ability to an exceptional degree, but lacked the qualities of leadership. This explains in a measure his failure to secure the co-operation of the public, Congress, the politicians, and the press—all essential elements in the successful carrying out of his policies.

The four years of Hoover reminded me of Ovid's remark that "an army of stags led by a lion would be more formidable than one of lions led by a stag."

CHAPTER THIRTY-FOUR

Trekking De Luxe

TRAVEL EQUIPMENT—RENEWING OLD FRIENDSHIPS—
EUROPE'S PREDICAMENT—INEFFECTIVE PEACE
PACTS—FRENCH-GERMAN SITUATION—WE TAKE A
CRUISE TO THE MEDITERRANEAN—MY DAUGHTER
IS BRIDESMAID AT AN EGYPTIAN WEDDING—MUSSO-
LINI AND THE POPE GRANT AUDIENCES—LATIN
AMERICA—THE MONROE DOCTRINE—WE HAVE AUDI-
ENCE WITH THE KING AND QUEEN OF SPAIN—THE PHILIPPINES

During the administrations of which I have written in the preceding chapter, and in view of a life which, to this point, must appear unrestful in its constant motion, it may seem logical that I would settle down in my home in Washington or Gloucester and be content to retire in a definite and fireside manner. Indeed, in thinking about it, it does seem reasonable.

But travel was my busman's holiday and an enthusiasm which my entire family either inherited or acquired. Having in the past journeyed perforce through many countries of the world and having come to know a cosmopolitan and broadly scattered group of peoples, I felt a natural impulse in the years after the war to revisit places I had known, to scrutinize altered political, economic, and social conditions and to find out what had become of old friends.

No doubt, were it still necessary to get about on burros, aboard sailing vessels, in Cape carts, droshkies, buckboards, on snowshoes, and in uncomfortably primitive railroad trains I would have recon-

713

sidered this strong inclination and my zeal would have abated.

To me, traveling on business has always been one thing; traveling without the urgency of business, quite another. I am reminded that my trips to investigate properties and development possibilities were often the despair of my wife. I hated to be encumbered and usually went off with one large valise, or preferably a duffel bag. Coming home ordinarily with more rock specimens in my bag than wearing apparel, and those rocks frequently wrapped in my very best clothes, was an eccentricity that never met with her complete approval.

On the other hand, in recent years when I started out on a recreation trip, I wanted to take along as many as possible of the household. In fact, had it been even remotely possible, I probably also would have taken my entire library and all the movables, and even our lares et penates.

In making such trips I carried with me books relating to the different countries which I was to visit and these I studied assiduously. Comfort was to me the first consideration. In addition to these impedimenta, my family and I had a fixed habit of aggravating our burden with all sorts of objects at each stopping place, and we would often arrive back on shipboard with a number of individual, carefully wrapped purchases, and the prized autographed photographs. All of these things brought about perpetual confusion among the servants. And I can say with some assurance that the family is remembered in one way or another in a number of distant ports and railroad stations. In later years, my secretary, Griffin, added final touches to traveling de luxe. I relied on him in the purchase of tickets and securing comfortable accommodations on steamers as on trains, and to keep an eye on all trunks, valises, holdalls, suitcases, bags, and boxes.

He justly prides himself on never having lost an article.

Attached to my entourage were a maid and a valet to complete the vicious circle, not for swank, but as indispensable to the Sybaritic mode of travel into which we had gradually drifted.

Speaking of traveling de luxe: a few years ago when lunching with the officers of the British South Africa Company in London I was urged by them to revisit Rhodesia to see the wonderful progress that had been made in the development of the country. In a casual way

I inquired as to the comforts of hotel accommodations there. This provoked considerable amusement among my friends who remembered the hardships I had uncomplainingly experienced in the pioneer days. It must have occurred to them that I was getting very soft—which was indeed the case. Alas!

The spring, summer, and part of the fall of 1924, I spent in Europe, accompanied by my wife and my daughter Natalie. In spite of the depression abroad, it proved to be an enlivening trip, particularly since we met such a wide range of interesting personalities. We stayed in London several weeks meeting old friends. Natalie was presented at the first Drawing Room held that year by King George and Queen Mary, who entertained us also at luncheon at the Ascot races. And, on a gala occasion, the Duke of Connaught took us to the Wembley Exposition. One particularly interesting event I recall is when I was a guest at the magnificent banquet given to Ras Taffari by Lord Granard in the name of the British government.

Ras Taffari was then the reigning prince of Ethiopia (Abyssinia). He has since ascended the Gold Throne of David as Emperor Haile Selassie I, King of Kings of Ethiopia, Elect of God, Conquering Lion of Judah, and Light of Ethiopia. He claims royal descent from King Solomon and the Queen of Sheba, without benefit of clergy.

In recent years this sovereign, who seemed a quiet, unpretentious gentleman when I met him, has been affording the press opportunities for amused comment through his grandiose styles of entertainment and his quixotic statesmanship.

Through an interpreter I managed to tell Ras Taffari—and he seemed much interested—of the reopening of the great mines of his ancestor, King Solomon, in Rhodesia and of the immense wealth being taken from the ancient workings.

For several years I used to broadcast a graduating address to the high school and college classes throughout the United States on "Essentials of a Successful Career," and generally ended my address with the quotation about the plucky cowboy:

> Life ain't in Holding
> A good Hand
> But in Pla-ing
> A Pore Hand Well.

While in London I was asked to broadcast a similar address to the youth of the British Isles. It happened that my broadcast was to take place on a Sunday evening. When I submitted in advance copy of my address to those in charge of the program, I was told that I could not use that motto as the pious audience in Scotland would be scandalized at a reference on *Sunday* to card playing.

On this trip we visited Berlin. There we again saw the British ambassador to Germany, Lord D'Abernon, and his beautiful and charming wife. I had the opportunity to meet interesting German statesmen and economists, among them Secretary of Foreign Affairs Stresemann and Dr. Hjalmar Schacht, the eminent German financier. I also met the members of the Dawes Commission who were working on the Dawes Plan.

A most interesting luncheon was given us by Count and Countess von Schoen. Count von Schoen was at that time in the Foreign Office. Countess von Schoen and her sisters, Mrs. Harold Walker and Mrs. E. R. Finkenstaedt, of Washington, were noted southern beauties. This occasion was also my first meeting with Baron Ago Maltzan. The countess told me privately that Baron Maltzan, one of the undersecretaries of foreign affairs, had been offered the ambassadorship to the United States, but was hesitating about accepting.

I brought up the subject as tactfully as possible in my talk with him. He admitted that he was considering the post but was disinclined to accept, as he believed it was too soon after the war for a German ambassador to be favorably received in Washington. He asked my opinion. I told him that I thought he was wrong; if he would go to Washington in the proper frame of mind, I was convinced he would be given a cordial reception. I urged him then and on subsequent occasions to accept, and he finally did. He proved to be democratic, that is, a good mixer, making friends particularly with the newspapermen. This quality made him a popular ambassador. I had the pleasure of giving the first large dinner in his honor in Washington, and later help him to find a place for his summer embassy at Magnolia, on the North Shore of Massachusetts. Our acquaintance developed into a most pleasant friendship.

He came to see me just before he sailed to spend the summer at home. He planned to visit many parts of Germany in the short time at his disposal. When I asked how he could possibly cover so much territory, he said: "Of coure, by airplane," and added that aviation was so far advanced that flying was perfectly safe, and no one had ever been killed in a plane of the company he was to use. Unfortunately, the first exception was his own case: he and the best pilot of the company met their death on one of these flights. So my farewell "auf Wiedersehen" was not to be realized.

In visits to the capitals of England, France, Switzerland, and Germany and in discussions with men of authority in different governmental and private capacities I was beginning to get a clearer picture of the current political situation in Europe and to reaffirm ideas I had held during the years when I devoted much of my time to international peace work—ideas which later events have developed into more or less definite convictions.

When I entered Freiberg in 1876, Bismarck was at the height of his power. It was his policy to let England and France fight it out for territory, while Germany intensified her internal industrial development.

It was not until the latter part of the eighties that Germany became territory-conscious and overzealous in her aim to secure a place in the sun. As a consequence of this policy she felt compelled to build a navy and a merchant marine on a parity with other great powers. This naval ambition created political unfriendliness between herself and England, and this was accentuated when Germany declined the invitation of Winston Churchill on behalf of England for a naval holiday.

In my former visits to Berlin over a period of years, I had observed the increasing hostility growing out of this rivalry. The sudden presence of a militant Germany among the contenders for territorial expansion inevitably led to clashes and tariff wars with England and France, which in turn brought about other disputes and accentuated national hatred, and finally to the World War.

I talked with statesmen in France, and later with Stresemann in Germany, of Briand and Stresemann's aim to establish an economic accord among the European nations by the creation of a United States of Europe. When Briand asked Stresemann for his offhand comment on this plan, Stresemann said: "Start from the one inevi-

718 The Autobiography of John Hays Hammond

table manifestation of European unity, I mean Industry . . . It is obviously the only escape from the chaotic and impossible industrial relations of today—from the artificial segregation by customs barriers of forces that are striving to combine."

Briand brought his proposal for a United States of Europe before the council tables of practical statesmanship and won for it approval in principle from all the nations of Europe that are members of the League. Since 1930 the Committee for a European Union set up by the League has met regularly to formulate plans, the details and scope of which are common knowledge.

Foremost among the economic measures to bind these nations together would be the leveling of tariff barriers among themselves and the removal of quotas, embargoes, and other strictures now bewildering producers and paralyzing the commerce of Europe. Thus there would be created a great zollverein providing a free internal market comparable to the domestic market upon which the prosperity of the United States of America has been built. Commerce on such a scale would call for a unified system of money and the stabilization of banks of issue. This should mean an end to periods of false prosperity such as recently afflicted both Europe and America, prosperity which consisted largely in buying and selling money, or more exactly in the creation and selling of credit, which ultimately took on the nature of counterfeiting on a colossal scale. Finance could then again be surbordinated to and made to serve the needs of production and distribution.

By such a plan racial jealousies would become less acute in the realization of a community of economic interests. It would do much towards the economic stabilization of the world and building up a prosperous economic entity that ultimately would prove of advantage to the United States, Great Britain, and other great commercial nations in that eventually it would afford a market within its own boundaries which does not obtain at present owing to the lack of purchasing power and the low standard of living of the industrial and agricultural population. By developing an important trade from other countries it would help to create markets; it would, by increasing their purchasing power, benefit the nations outside of the United States of Europe. There certainly would be no opposition to such a plan on the part of the United States or Great Britain. We have established a high tariff policy in our own country, and Great Britain, at the Ottawa conference, gave to her dominions and colonies a preferential tariff which in many items becomes a prohibitive tariff against other nations.

It would seem to me reasonable to hope that the nations that would be members of this contemplated United States of Europe would be willing to make extreme concessions of their political and economic interests in order to establish such a zollverein, or trade league.

The League of Nations, Locarno, and the Kellogg-Briand Pact, admittedly, have not proved sufficient to reassure the world as to peace, although they have greatly contributed to peace-psychology which has tended to restrain overt acts of hostility.

And yet, in view of the recent developments in Europe, it seems incredible that practical statesmen have been considering and working chiefly towards this objective, knowing how hopelessly improbable its accomplishment is.

By the stipulations of Locarno both Germany and France have bound themselves to respect and to preserve the boundary line drawn at Versailles between Germany and France, and Great Britain and Italy have engaged to go to the defense of either nation should that boundary, a rampart of hatred for thousands of years, be violated by the other.

The keeping of this faith, already strained, nevertheless remains the supreme test of the civilization of the French and German people. It is a key to the peace of the world. Whether so precious a heritage shall be preserved rests now with the wisdom of French and German statesmanship.

As to the French-Italian situation, I am still of the opinion expressed to Lord Northcliffe and to Viscount Grey in the early part of 1914: it is unfortunate that better understanding does not exist between those two countries.

It seems obvious that the quandary in Continental Europe today is that there can be no economic recovery until political controversies are adjusted, and political controversies cannot be adjusted until economic conditions improve. This is the vicious circle. I feel that no solution of this problem has been effected through the League of

Nations nor by the various financial and political expedients. The Dawes Plan and the Young Plan, heralded by Europe and the world as instruments to bring about economic recovery, have both failed in the realization of their objectives. D'Abernon, Dawes, Schacht, Young, and countless others have been tireless in their efforts to repair the springs of economic difficulty. They and their various plans and accomplishments were the best expedients at the moment and at least helped to postpone the crises of 1924 and 1929.

There is less security for the world today than there has been at any time since the Armistice. If war is to be avoided, some effective economic plan must be worked out and followed. To me and to most thinking men, war as a policy is insanity. While it is impossible for anyone to predict what is going to happen to Europe or, as the days go by, confidently to hope for the maintenance of peace, nevertheless the present outlook is more reassuring.

We had returned to the United States by way of London in time for me to take an active part in connection with the election of President Coolidge. But in the spring of 1926, my wife, my daughter, and I again had a touch of wanderlust and started out on another trip. This time we went through the countries on the Mediterranean, including Spain, Algiers, the ruins of Carthage—"*delenda est Carthago*"—in Northern Africa, Greece, Turkey, Palestine, and Egypt. Major and Mrs. Burnham joined us at Gibraltar from their trip around the world and went with us to Egypt, our first visit to that country.

We made a trip to Luxor and arrived on the first rainy day there had been for many decades. We spent several days in the Valley of the Kings, visiting the tomb of Tutankhamen, which was just being excavated, and other points of interest.

I have many friends in the diplomatic corps of foreign countries, among them Yousry Pasha and Samy Pasha, successively Egyptian minister at Washington. Loutfia Yousry, daughter of the former, went to school with Natalie and came often to our house. When we started on our trip to Egypt, Samy Pasha, then minister to Washington, gave me a letter to Hassanein Bey, a writer and explorer of note and the son of the sheik of a powerful Bedouin tribe.

I found Hassanein Bey an attractive and highly cultured man. He had been educated at Oxford, and spoke English with a decided Oxford accent. Major Burnham was with me at the time I presented my letter of introduction and the three of us discussed the gold ornaments in the Cairo Museum, and particularly those from the recently discovered tomb of Tutankhamen. We also talked of the possible location of the gold fields from which the ancient world derived its gold supply, and I became more than ever convinced that much of the gold had been brought to Egypt from Rhodesia.

By arrangement, I was presented to King Fuad I and enjoyed my talk with him about conditions in Egypt and the development of the country. He was democratic and jovial and given to making "wisecracks," but he showed that he could be serious when discussing the future of his country. He was greatly impressed with the possibilities of railroad development in North Africa which would connect up with Cairo, and also the improvement in aviation which would bring Egypt nearer to the nations of Europe and easier of access for tourists.

Several years later at a garden party given by King George V in London, I saw King Fuad again; he reaffirmed his optimism as to the future importance of Cairo as a resort for foreign visitors.

After my audience with King Fuad, Hassanein Bey expressed his regret that he could not show me more attention during the next few days, but told me with some diffidence as befits a prospective husband that he was to be married, and that the young lady—the party of the first part—was the daughter of a former Egyptian minister to Washington. I asked the name and was delighted to find that it was Loutfia Yousry. Hassanein Bey, who saw his fiancée almost immediately after I had taken my leave, told her of my daughter's presence in Cairo. That same afternoon Natalie received a letter from Miss Yousry, welcoming her to Egypt, and asking her to call and see her without delay, as she was for the moment confined to her harem.

My daughter telephoned her and then went to have dinner and spend the evening with her. When she had not returned at a late hour I became anxious and went to the palace to call for her. I must say that it took courage, but of a different sort from more harrowing adventures I have had in mining camps. At the entrance I was stopped by two imposing eunuchs, and by others, again, at the door. Finally, I was admitted just in time to see a bevy of charming young women scampering up the broad stairs on which they had been sitting talking, when my sudden appearance startled them. However, I succeeded in finding Natalie.

She was asked to be a bridesmaid at the wedding, and since an American girl is seldom present at a marriage ceremony of that kind, I think her description will be of interest.

The marriage in Egypt is complete after the act of marriage has been signed. The husband and wife could, if they wished, immediately assume marital relations; yet, it is often the custom that they live apart for a month or more while their furniture and trousseau are arranged. After that period and without any new formality, the couple assume the relations of husband and wife. It is on this occasion, however, that the festivities are generally given.

The civil ceremony was performed one Sunday evening at the palace of Princess Omar Hallim. The house, a free translation of Italian and Arabic architecture, opened on to a large palm-bordered garden, across which one saw against the stillness of the desert the Pyramids of Gizeh.

I had been asked to appear at Loutfia's apartment in the palace punctually at nine, and to wear a green evening gown. When I arrived she was being dressed by two Sudanese women. She wore a lace coif, and a medieval tiara of sapphires and diamonds. Her eyes were outlined with kohl. Three of her four cousins also wore green evening dresses. Later I learned that I had replaced the fourth, in the wedding ceremony. We descended a curving flight of alabaster stairs. In the hall below were the women of the diplomatic corps, and of the Egyptian court. No men were present. The hall which we crossed was lighted by flares held by nautchgirls in magenta skirts and vermilion boleros. We stood at the side while Loutfia mounted a low dais at the end of the room. On the dais were two massive chairs inlaid with ebony and gold. On one of these she sat. Faintly and at a distance one heard a native stringed orchestra.

Hassanein Bey entered, after a minute's interval, with Yousry Pasha. He wore "tails" and a fez. He advanced to the dais, kissed first the back of her wrist, then her forehead, and seated himself beside her in the second chair. No other ceremony took place. They rose and left the hall, scattering tiny gold pieces to the crowd. Hassanein Bey and Yousry Pasha rejoined the men in another part of the palace, while the women danced together till the buffet supper was served in the garden.

Later I had tea several times in the harem with Loutfia and her cousins, Wahid and Gina. For my benefit they spoke French, though together they conversed in Arabic. Most days were spent in the pleasant loggias of the palace, a special hour being reserved for the visits of Hassanein Bey. At half-hour intervals Turkish coffee was served, and they smoked incessantly. With a few exceptions their only outings were at a Cairo night-club, which was put at the disposal of the women of the court one day a week. On these afternoons they danced together, eagerly learning the latest European steps. What other excursions they wedged into their routine existence I could not say. But there was a court fortune teller who appealed greatly to their superstitions.

Loutfia's grandmother had two hundred slave girls in her harem, and lived in strictest seclusion. Footmen and chauffeurs are always eunuchs, and the royal automobile is a long vermilion affair, with two of these gorgeously caparisoned Sudanese on the box.

The reader will not blame me for envying my daughter her glimpse of the life that goes on behind the mysterious walls of the East.

From Egypt we went to Sicily, then to Italy. In Rome I was granted an audience by Mussolini. After being passed through several anterooms, I was admitted into a long room at the end of which sat the Great Dictator on a dais. As I approached him he fixed his eyes on me in the penetrating way peculiar to him.

It is said that this slow approach is arranged not so much for his physical protection, as for the purpose of disconcerting the interviewer. During his progress up the length of the room, the visitor forgets the set speech he has prepared and is likely to say something closer to his real thoughts. And, of course, the setting is arranged to make Il Duce very impressive indeed.

When I reached the dais Mussolini gave me the Fascist salute. I thanked him. He then asked me with surprise if I did not recognize it. I said that I did but could not understand why I was accorded the honor. Smilingly he said that he had been informed that I, on a certain occasion (referring to the Jameson Raid), had had the courage to go to jail for my political convictions. That was true, I replied, but in this respect he had me at a disadvantage, since he had gone to jail on several occasions for the same reason. He laughed at that and asked me if this was my first visit to Rome. I told him that I had been to Rome several times before but that, having just returned from seeing something of the wonders of the ancient world, the Pharos of Alexandria, the Sphinx, and the Pyramids of Egypt, I was anxious to see one of the wonders of the modern world, which he personified.

He seemed pleased at this; being encouraged, I told him that I considered his action in establishing the Fascisti comparable to the deed of the famous Dutch boy who inserted his arm in the hole of the dike to prevent inundation of the country; that his heroic action had prevented the inundation of Italy, France, and other European countries by the wave of Communism already started by the Bolsheviks.

I asked if any provision had been made for the maintenance of the Fascisti should Italy be unfortunately deprived of his beneficent dictatorship. Mussolini informed me that one of my Italian friends, who had spent many years in America, would call on me at my hotel that evening and give me a clear understanding of this subject.

My friend assured me that after Mussolini there would be no deluge. I was not entirely convinced, however, that the optimism expressed by him was justified, for I believed it was Mussolini's great personality that enabled him to carry out his Fascist movement. The Celtic people are deeply impressed, I believe, by the personality of their leaders whose influence transcends the inherent importance of the principles they represent. In contradistinction, Anglo-Saxons are more imbued with the principles underlying any reform movement. With them leaders may come and leaders may go, but the spirit lives on and there is a persistent determination to carry out the movement initiated by the leaders.

Mussolini gave me a signed photograph of himself for my collection. I have not seen him since but have kept directly in touch with him through my son, Jack, who installed for him a selective system of radio which he uses in communicating with his representatives in Italy and Africa. For this service my son was decorated by Mussolini with the order of a Grand Officer of the Crown, an exceptionally high honor.

My wife, my daughter, and I were granted a private audience with Pope Pius XI, the third pope my wife and I had met. My friend, Taft, had written Cardinal Gasparri, the all-powerful papal secretary. Through him and Cardinal Bonzano, with whom I first became acquainted when he came to Washington as papal legate, they had made the arrangements for our audience. Bonzano had been a missionary priest in India and China and possessed a remarkably deep and fine religious sense. He had great intelligence and breadth of mind, and was a most accomplished gentleman. As cardinal, he successfully presided over the Eucharistic Congress in Chicago. Though he was in poor health at that time, his spiritual energy never faltered. He was on the way, it is said, to the very highest office in the church, when he died.

From Rome we went to the French Riviera and while at Cannes I met King Gustaf V of Sweden, one of the most democratic of the reigning monarchs of Europe. He told me that his son, the crown prince, was soon to visit America and he would be greatly obliged if I would see that he received a "rousing good welcome for which the

Americans are noted." I promised King Gustaf that I should see that his wishes were carried out.

When Crown Prince Gustaf Adolf arrived in Washington, shortly after we returned from our trip, I gave an afternoon reception at my home in his honor, and invited the leading newspaper correspondents, assigned to duty in Washington, to meet him.

In showing the crown prince through my gallery of autographed photographs he commented on the remarkable collection of famous men. I asked him if he would kindly give me a photograph of himself to be placed with those of other royalty, which he had already seen in our drawing room. He demurred at my suggestion at first, and then said that if I considered him qualified he would much prefer to have his photograph on the walls of my study among the men of "real achievement" rather than with royalty. The newspaper correspondents heard his remarks and were so impressed with his democratic spirit that immediately after the reception they telegraphed his conversation with me to their papers throughout the United States. They all agreed that the crown prince was a "real fellow" and his photograph now hangs among the "men of achievement" where it rightly belongs.

My last trip of importance was to South America with my wife in December, 1929. From there we went to Portugal and Spain.

I was particularly interested in the study of the economic conditions of Brazil and Argentina, countries which I had not visited. This was to supplement my knowledge of Latin America. Besides this I was desirous of obtaining firsthand information regarding the iron deposits in the state of Minas Geraes, in one of the companies of which I have a substantial interest. The Minas Geraes deposits are probably the most extensive of high-grade iron in the world but at present cannot be developed economically on a large scale This is due to the lack of coke and of an adequate supply of charcoal for treatment locally. Added to this economic obstacle, there is no market for iron in Brazil. For these reasons it is necessary to transport the crude ore to the United States or to Europe for treatment. The inaccessibility of the iron deposits precludes shipment of the ore to meet the present competition of other countries.

The area of Latin America (South America, Central America, Mexico, and the Caribbean islands) is approximately that of continental United States and Canada combined, with a population nearly equal that of the United States.

At first glance, because of the size of its population and great extent of undeveloped territory, one is favorably impressed with the potential markets in Latin America. But a closer study shows that of this large population not over ten per cent possesses purchasing power of any significance and that a large part of the territory is valueless for both agriculture and mining.

Indians and negroes constitute the mass of the population. The Indians live in the interior under conditions bordering on destitution. The negroes, originally slaves from Africa, are confined to the Caribbean islands and the coast of Central and South America. Their wants are few and their means scant even for the bare necessities of life.

The general opinion prevailing abroad is that Latin-American countries have unbounded natural resources, development of which would add greatly to the purchasing power of their peoples and in that way open up important markets for the rest of the world. I do not concur in this opinion as I regard the outlook as pessimistic, and find confirmation of my viewpoint in Frank Tannenbaum's recently published *Whither Latin America?*

> Broadly speaking, the west coast of South America exports minerals, mainly copper, nitrates, tin and, in an increasing degree, petroleum; Central America and the Caribbean mainly bananas, coffee and sugar; and Mexico, silver and oil. The east coast of South America exports mainly coffee from Brazil, and cereal and meat products from the Argentine and Uruguay. This regional specialization can best be illustrated by citing the commonly known facts of the Latin American foreign trade. In six of the countries coffee constitutes more than 50 per cent of the total export. These countries are Brazil, 65 per cent; Colombia, 65 per cent; Costa Rica, 63 per cent; Guatemala, 79 per cent; Salvador, 93 per cent; and Haiti, some 80 per cent. . . .

Excessive dependence upon unitary export items is not confined to agricultural products but also holds for mineral exports. Bolivia depends for 72 per cent of its total export upon tin, and 74 per cent of Venezuela's exports is crude petroleum.

Thus, at least 15 countries are dependent for the major part of their export trade upon some single item. . . .

Since these countries have no monopoly of any of these items their export trade is obviously precarious, and without a favorable trade balance there can be no import trade of importance.

In its agricultural exports Latin America meets with severe competition from many other countries. Besides this, since the World War, European countries that formerly constituted an important market for agricultural products have been developing in an important measure their own agricultural resources to supply their domestic needs.

There does not seem any likelihood that Latin-American countries will be able to expand their home markets to the extent of justifying any considerable agricultural or industrial development. This, because it is impossible adequately to increase the purchasing power of local consumers. There will, however, be a tendency to develop home industries on a small scale to supply the urgent needs of commodities they will be unable to import as their export trade balance diminishes. And in pursuance of the policy of economic nationalism which they have recently adopted an import trade will be further restricted.

While there is the possibility of an interchange of goods with adjacent states, unfortunately physiographic conditions make transportation difficult, putting this trade under a severe economic handicap.

I agree with H. F. Bain and T. R. Read in the opinions expressed in their recent publication, *Ores and Industry in South America*, that the potential mineral resources of South America have been greatly overestimated.

The nitrate industry, hitherto the backbone of the fiscal system of

Chile, is becoming less important owing to synthetic processes now employed elsewhere in the production of nitrogen.

The development of new deposits of copper or other minerals is not probable, in the near future at least, as a result of keen competition resulting from overproduction of these commodities in other parts of the world.

There is, of course, the likelihood of the development of new oil fields in certain parts of South America which would increase the export trade, but in that case, too, there would be formidable competition for markets by other fields more favorably situated.

In the development of the mineral industry of South America as well as that of other parts of Latin America, most of the capital required has thus far been supplied by investors from the United States. For the most part these investments have not proved sufficiently remunerative to attract new capital. Nor do the political conditions of South America in general provide an incentive for investors.

The Pan American Union in Washington has done much to promote friendly understanding between the United States and the sister republics of Latin America, yet there is an abiding lack of wholehearted confidence on the part of Latin America in our integrity of purpose. The sister republics are both jealous and suspicious of our power and wealth. They do not comprehend the Monroe Doctrine and its implications. In spite of the fact that by virtue of the Monroe Doctrine our nation has at various times rendered inestimable service to Latin America in frustrating the aggression of European powers, the doctrine has not been favorably regarded by those countries. Our threatened intervention in behalf of Mexico, which prevented Maximilian from establishing a monarchy, has not earned for us the gratitude of that country.

Again, we rendered a service by our intervention in behalf of Venezuela against what President Cleveland regarded as aggressive action by Great Britain. This friendly act, too, was soon forgotten. These are but a few of many instances of the kind. Nations have short memories for favors received. We cannot blink the fact that Americans of North America are not popular with South Americans and Central Americans. South Americans in particular object to the citizens of the United States referring to themselves as "Americans" and not as Americanos del Norte.   Much of the antipathy is to be ascribed to the insidious propaganda of our commercial rivals who have stigmatized the Yankees' activities as imperialistic, imputing ulterior political motives.

Latin Americans are a peculiarly sensitive people, with a highly developed racial and national pride.   I have had many discussions of the Monroe Doctrine with leading statesmen of Latin America and am convinced that its modification would eliminate much misunderstanding.   Within the past few years there has been what is practically a repudiation of our former policy regarding our rights and duties under the Monroe Doctrine.   In this we may have gone too far.   In one respect it certainly will not be to the advantage of Latin America as it will, in a large measure, prevent future investments of American capital in the development of those countries.   Furthermore, I believe that later it may result in considerable embarrassment to our government in that we cannot consistently intervene for the protection of the lives and vested interests of other nationals who have hitherto relied upon our government under the implication of the Monroe Doctrine to perform this service.

We left Buenos Aires and arrived in Portugal in February, 1930, where I had the opportunity to get firsthand information regarding operations of a tin dredging company in which I was interested. After several days' motoring through Portugal we went to Seville to see the Ibero-Americano Exposition.   The American representative at the exposition was none other than my old friend, Thomas E. Campbell, former governor of Arizona, and a most capable representative he was.   He, with Mrs. Campbell and Richard Ford, the American consul, met us on arrival and contributed greatly to the interest and pleasure of our visit.

To me the most interesting exhibits of the exposition were the documents of Columbus, with the original contract between him and Ferdinand and Isabella in their handwriting.   In this contract Columbus stipulated that he should be full admiral in the Spanish Navy, governor general in the newly discovered world, and that he should receive one-tenth of all the findings.   His first expedition was successful in the discovery of the New World and he became a hero, and received as a reward, it is said, the sum of about three hundred and twenty dollars. From his third voyage he was returned in chains; after his fourth, having opened a new empire to Spain, he died poor and neglected at Valladolid.

All this early historical data about Columbus made me interested in getting other information about the expedition from the original documents which are stored in the Casa Municipal ó del Ayuntamiento (City Hall). During several hours I spent at the Ayuntamiento I was shown many interesting documents dealing with the discovery of America and was informed by the custodian that the actual money expended for fitting out the first voyage would be equivalent to about three thousand dollars of American money today. Of course, much of the labor was donated, as well as food and supplies. The custodian assured me that there was no foundation for the story that Isabella had pawned her jewels to outfit the expedition, for as he said, her jewels had already been pawned for other purposes.

After several weeks in Seville and vicinity, we went to Madrid where we were entertained by our friends, Ambassador Irwin B. Laughlin and Mrs. Laughlin, and Mr. and Mrs. Walter Schoellkopf. Mr. Schoellkopf was first secretary at the American Embassy. Through the ambassador we had the opportunity of meeting many interesting Spanish people, prominent socially and politically.

While we were in Spain the king and queen granted my wife and me a private audience; we were shown into the queen's personal reception room. We had known her father and mother and other members of her family and had many intimate mutual friends in England. My wife and I stayed a long time, as it was in the forenoon and we were the only visitors. Suddenly realizing this, I said: "Your Majesty, I am afraid that we are keeping you longer than our appointed time. You must have other engagements?"

My wife smiled: "Your Majesty, my husband has probably forgotten the etiquette for occasions of this kind."

The queen replied laughingly: "He is quite right, but I still have plenty of time and I will serve notice when I must go."

After "notice was served" we were escorted to an audience with King Alfonso. It is well known that he is unusually democratic and absolutely free from all conventionality. He asked me if I had been to Seville to which I replied: "Quien no ha visto a Sevilla no ha visto maravilla."

Alfonso told me that his royal position was very irksome; it was impossible for him to play polo, his favorite game. It seems the court objected to his taking such risks, and this he highly resented. But he said: "Perhaps they are right. I have broken every bone in my body, and some of them several times, at polo or other dangerous sports. They regard it as not only perilous, but beneath the dignity of a king to play any more." I believe he was sincere in his feeling of the arduous nature of kingship and in his distaste for its unpleasant royal inhibitions.

Later at the Escorial, where each royal coffin is placed in a white marble vault or sarcophagus, I noticed particularly that there was no space provided for future kings and queens of Spain, with the exception of Alfonso XIII and his queen. I remember the passing thought that perhaps this was an omen that at some future date Spain might be a republic. The king's popularity was great up to the time of the revolution; in fact, it was said that, should Spain become a republic, the king would be its first president. Unfortunately this did not prove true; when revolution did occur, shortly after my visit, Alfonso was compelled to abdicate in order to avert bloodshed, and to join the ranks of other royal exiles.

Sidney Franklin, the young Brooklynite who achieved a reputation as a matador in the bullrings of Mexico and Spain, and later in the motion pictures, was in Madrid at the time of my visit. A number of businessmen of the American colony gave a lunch in my honor at which Franklin was present. After lunch some of the newspapermen introduced him to me. I was surprised to see a youth with a face "unusually kind." Being reassured on the part of the newspapermen that this was really the great American bullfighter, I said: "You do not seem to me like a man who would enjoy killing a bull. You have a very kindly look on your face and might well be taken for an official of the Society for the Prevention of Cruelty to Animals." "Well, sir," he replied: "I'm looking at *you*, but you should see my face when looking at an infuriated bull." He spoke feelingly, for he had recently been seriously gored in the bullring.

The minister for foreign affairs at this time was the Duke of Alba, the descendant of a long line of Spanish noblemen and the foremost grandee of Spain. He was wealthy, highly cultured, a world traveler, a great sportsman, and thoroughly familiar with America, where we had many friends in common. He invited me to luncheon and showed me over his beautiful palace in Madrid, with its treasured documents of Columbus, Cortez, and other makers of Spanish history. The duke told me that he had been drafted for his position very much against his wish; that he had no experience in state affairs as his whole life had been devoted to sports. He hoped to be able to "muddle through," but also hoped the king would not find him satisfactory and would soon "fire" him.

I expressed surprise that Americans receive such cordial treatment in Spain.

"Of course," he replied, "you have in mind the late unpleasantness between our countries?"

"Yes," I said, "the Spanish War."

He went on: "The Spanish people are philosophical. They lost the war, but after thinking it over, they came to the conclusion that it was a blessing in disguise.

"It had been a very heavy drain on the mother country to administer the Philippines and Cuba, not only in money but in soldiers, and the people of Spain were tired of having their sons drafted to suppress revolutions in those countries. Realizing this, they feel grateful to the Americans for having relieved them of this burden."

The pertinence of this idea for America is becoming obvious in its sponsorship of the Philippines.

Many of us have changed our former views about the Philippines. Some years ago I had alluring visions of America as an economic empire and regarded the Philippines as the stepping stone to the development of Oriental trade; today this does not fit the American spirit, which holds such retention as undesirable and autocratic. The maintenance of benevolent relations with the Philippines is regarded by many as a duty we assumed in accepting the islands as a protectorate after the Spanish-American War, but they feel that aside from this our policy should be to accede to the request of the Filipinos for complete autonomy.

That the Philippines are as yet wholly unfit for independence was recognized by General Wood, Henry L. Stimson, Nicholas Roosevelt, and other authorities "whether from the viewpoint of instructed public opinion, preparedness for defense, or a common language."

In his report to the secretary of war, General Wood stated that "To turn these islands over to self-government would mean the betrayal of our trust and would plunge twelve million people into dire disorder and strife. For it would result at once in serious clash between the Moros and the Christian Filipinos. Such a step would, in short, defeat true independence both economic and political."

Nevertheless, American public opinion strongly inclines to the granting of complete independence to the Filipinos. If this is done, there should be a distinct understanding that when we withdraw we absolve ourselves from all further responsibility and in no wise commit ourselves to protect the Filipinos from aggression by any other nation or to intervene in their internal affairs.

In view of the increasing conflict of interest with Japan, the Philippines are to be considered as the heel of Achilles in the maintenance of our military position in the Pacific. This is undoubtedly a scuttling policy, but in the circumstances seems inevitable. We should now concentrate on making Hawaii a Gibraltar as the basis of naval operations to ensure the protection of our Pacific Coast states against an invading enemy.

CHAPTER THIRTY-FIVE

Spreading Interests

RECLAMATION OF THE SAN JOAQUIN VALLEY—IRRI-
GATION BY ELECTRIC POWER—DIVERTING THE PITT
RIVER—ASSURING SAN FRANCISCO OF AN ADEQUATE
WATER SUPPLY—DEVELOPING THE YAQUI VALLEY—
SECRET OF PERPETUAL YOUTH—YAQUI INDIANS ON
WARPATH—DEUS EX MACHINA—MEXICAN REVOLU-
TIONS—BLACK GOLD—PRESIDENT OBREGON PERMITS
US TO ARM—THE MEXICAN SEABOARD OIL COMPANY

Our machine civilization has been wrought by the engineer, who contrives its apparatus, utilizes and harnesses the physical and chemical forces of nature, and exploits the resources of the earth. All that he designs and invents and exploits redounds in the end to the public benefit.

My business career began as a mining engineer. But when I had reached a certain proficiency and standing in my profession, I was tempted to branch out in other fields of engineering activities. The technical knowledge for carrying out these new ventures was at my command through the services of younger men. My experience guided and tempered their enthusiasm.

The science of engineering covers not only mining for metals but the production of all other forms of wealth from the earth. Those portions of the globe which for eons had remained comparatively barren and useless now are being transformed into a blessing to man.

The idea of irrigation and reclamation, later so publicized by Theodore Roosevelt, had taken possession of my brother William's imagination as early as 1891. He had established himself in the pleasant little town of Visalia, California, in the semi-arid San Joaquin Valley which stretches for miles between the Sierra Nevadas and the Coast Range. He believed that, if water could be delivered to the farms of the valley at reasonable rates, it would bring about an agricultural revolution. In association with A. G. Wishon, his partner in the local water company, and Ben M. Maddox, the owner-editor of the Visalia *Times,* he worked to bring his theory to realization.

It was no simple matter to obtain water in the San Joaquin. There was in the valley no sufficiently large or dependable river from which a supply could be brought by canals. Wells had to be driven sixty to a hundred feet below ground to find the water table. The soil was rich, but rainfall was irregular and occurred only during the winter. Grain was about the only crop that could be raised, and the profits from this were small and uncertain.

My brother had seen what Captain A. J. Hutchinson, pioneer farmer, had done to his arid acres at Lindsay in the foothills not far from Visalia by attaching a six-horsepower engine to a pump. Hutchinson was raising oranges, lemons, olives, grapes, and all sorts of vegetables. It seemed to my brother that an abundant water supply would transform the entire countryside into a paradise.

Bill tried to interest San Francisco and Oakland capital in building a power dam on the Kaweah River and bringing electricity by long-distance transmission line from Mount Whitney to operate irrigation pumps in the San Joaquin Valley. They listened to him with interest, and said they did not care to invest at the moment; apparently they were too polite to call him visionary for entertaining such an idea. Having failed in America to obtain the funds necessary to launch the project, Bill as a last resort came to see me in London in 1898.

The idea of going into the public utility business had never occurred to me but I could see that my brother's scheme had possibilities. I had known the valley since boyhood and the fact that another brother, Richard, had done the surveying gave me added assurance.

"Jack," urged Bill, "we already have options on the water sites and

A STRIKE. THE DISCOVERY WELL IN THE KETTLEMAN OIL FIELDS,
MARCH 21, 1927

White gas that precedes the gush of crude oil

THE DISCOVERY WELL, NORTH DOME, KETTLEMAN HILLS

The oil production of this field from the time of its discovery, March 21, 1927, to December 31, 1934, was approximately 19,590,000 barrels, and the gas production within the same period was approximately 660,000,000,000 cubic feet, from which 18,300,000 barrels of casing-head gasoline were extracted

the rights of way. As you know, we have a soil and climate that will grow anything. Whenever we drill a well we strike water, and all we need is the power to pump it. Gasoline and steam engines work, but they're too expensive and can serve only a few acres each. With cheap electric power available, thousands of acres will go into cultivation."

"But can you send electricity as far as that?" I asked. "It's never been done before for irrigating purposes, has it?"

"No, but we have an engineer who guarantees it can be done," he replied. "Robert Doble. He'll build the power house at Mount Whitney and bring the current the necessary thirty-five miles. This will put all of Tulare County within reach of our feeder lines."

"How about customers?" I queried again. "There are practically none in the valley."

"We'll have to build ahead of them and take a chance," he told me frankly. "Once the electricity is there for delivery, the settlers will follow."

On the night Bill arrived in London, Leopold Hirsch dined at my house. During the dinner he and my brother talked about American affairs and California. Hirsch was so impressed by this conversation that he took me aside after dinner and asked me all about Bill. I assured him that my brother had earned such a reputation for honesty and sound judgment that throughout the San Joaquin Valley many bitter disputes were taken to him for arbitrament rather than to the law courts.

I told him about the Mount Whitney project, which Bill and I had agreed should be financed by private capital and not offered to the public. Hirsch expressed great interest and, when I informed him I was thinking of putting money into it, said he would like to discuss the matter a little further with my brother. He might even want to have an interest in it himself.

The next day I told Bill I would supply half the funds required and would assist him in raising the balance among my friends in London. Naturally, I had Hirsch in mind.

I made an appointment for the two to meet again, and the banker agreed to underwrite the other half of the funds required. So simply was the Mount Whitney Power Company launched.

Bill strongly recommended that both Hirsch and I buy land in the valley. He felt sure that it would greatly increase in value and that we could realize more quickly on this investment than on the hydro-electric plant.

Shortly after my return to America I purchased the Hirsch interest in the Mount Whitney project and became its sole backer. This put a heavy financial burden on me and I was unable to make the land purchases urged by my brother.

Before I bought Hirsch's interest, Bill had given us another opportunity, to make an investment in an oil region that was being developed in Kern County not far from Visalia. We were so favorably impressed that we authorized my brother to secure options on possible oil-bearing land in the district, which at that time could be acquired on very reasonable terms.

After the options had been secured, Hirsch and I sent an English oil expert to examine the territory. Unfortunately the expert made an adverse report and we abandoned the project. Not long after, however, one of the large oil fields in California was opened up by local capital, encouraged by quick and enormous profits from recent oil strikes.

The construction of the Mount Whitney powerhouse and transmission line went steadily forward. On June 26, 1899, the motors began to hum at the Lindsay substation, the first time electric power had ever been used for irrigation purposes in California. Until this moment only our own little group had been convinced that the idea was financially sound or technically feasible. As the switch was thrown and the water began to flow, one of the skeptical spectators exclaimed, "By God, it does do it, don't it?"

At Lindsay, our first outlet, ten growers made contracts at once, the entire load aggregating only one hundred and seventy-five horsepower. But within the next few years thousands of acres of idle land were brought under cultivation. In 1914 fifty thousand acres were irrigated by power from our lines. In a district where even in successful seasons wheat had brought a profit of no more than fifteen dollars an acre, orange, lemon, walnut, and olive groves now flourished, splendid vineyards covered the hillsides, and peach and prune orchards were coming into bearing. Some of these crops were giving a profit of a thousand dollars an acre; undeveloped land, selling in the nineties at ten to fifteen dollars, now brought several hundred dollars an acre. From 1893 to 1900 there had been a loss of $600,000 in assessed valuation of Tulare County property. This loss was turned into a gain of $30,000,000 by 1914.

Abundant wealth was being created from the soil by cheap power. Money was pouring into the valley. Lindsay, which, in 1899, consisted of a small railroad station, a schoolhouse, and the home of Captain Hutchinson, had grown to be a prosperous community of four thousand inhabitants. Visalia, the county seat, had tripled its former population of twenty-five hundred. Through my representations to E. H. Harriman, the Southern Pacific Railroad had built an electric spur line from Visalia to Lemon Cove, one of the pioneer towns of the citrus fruit development, and had thereby greatly improved transportation facilities.

A dozen years passed before other electric companies followed our lead. They realized that profits would be slow and did not foresee the large amounts of current which must ultimately be used by this type of enterprise.

In 1916, the Southern California Edison Company desired to obtain a market for the electric power it had developed in the upper Sierras. Its offer for the Mount Whitney Company was so attractive that we decided to accept. When the transaction was made public, we were gratified at the receipt of a telegram from the head of the Railroad Commission of California, which has jurisdiction over all public utilities in the state, that our company was the best operated in California.

Through association with the Mount Whitney Company, I became interested in developing the Pitt River hydroelectric supply, and I personally financed this work. The Pitt River had previously flowed over a circuitous course around a mountain. Our plan was to tunnel a passage near the top of the mountain, and divert the flow of the river to a point on the opposite side several hundred feet above the old bed. From this end of the tunnel the water would be conducted by huge pipes to a powerhouse below.

The engineering difficulty in building the tunnel was the presence of thermal springs which, if encountered, might at any moment

740 The Autobiography of John Hays Hammond

flood our workings. From surface indications it was evident that the ground might prove so porous that difficulty would be found in making the walls of the tunnel stand up.

We took the risk, drove the tunnel through some thousand feet of rock, and proved that the undertaking was practicable.

This flow of water was capable of developing from one to two hundred thousand horsepower, and was destined to be one of the cheapest producers of electric current in California. It was a magnificent project. My chief difficulty came from the fact that it was located on government land. Though no one else had seen fit to undertake this work, the Department of the Interior insisted that it be done at such a rate that I could not afford to comply with government specifications. I was forced to sell out to the Pacific Gas and Electric Company of San Francisco, a company which uses it now as one of the most important sources of hydroelectric power for San Francisco.

Among other electrical engineering enterprises in which I had a large interest was the Yosemite Power Company, which furnished electric current to the farmers of various irrigation districts. This company owned some old and valuable water rights, and was eventually sold at a good price.

In 1908 I bought Lake Eleanor in the Sierras with a view to developing its potential one hundred thousand horsepower. When San Francisco launched the Hetch-Hetchy project to bring water from the Sierras a hundred and sixty-seven miles distant, Mayor McCarthy came to see me and said that Lake Eleanor was indispensable to their plan. He urged me, as a civic duty, to sell at a fair valuation. I agreed to let Lake Eleanor be embodied in the Hetch-Hetchy plan.

Looking back upon these early enterprises in the public utility field, it is interesting to see how their original promise has been fulfilled under the management of those to whom I sold. Today they form most important integral parts in the great network of public utilities in California.

The trail-blazing work on the Mount Whitney project was purely of an engineering nature. In an irrigation venture in Mexico we had to meet pioneer problems more typical of the frontier.

In 1909, Major Burnham said to me: "Mr. Hammond, I have something that'll interest you. I've picked up an option on the water rights of the Yaqui River and some three hundred thousand acres of land from my friend, Davis Richardson, of Los Angeles. The soil is sixty feet deep and there's not a pebble in it. Once this valley is irrigated, it'll be one of the garden spots of the world."

Curiously enough, the potential value of the Yaqui Valley had been pointed out to me many years before by my father-in-law, Judge Harris, who had owned a large plantation in Mississippi before the Civil War. He had passed through a part of the valley in 1882 on the trip from Guaymas to join our family at Alamos, and had recognized its agricultural possibilities.

The delta of the Yaqui River consists of two thousand square miles of rich alluvial soil, brought down through the ages from the surrounding mountains. The Yaqui Valley itself is enclosed on one side by the Bacotete Mountains and on the other by a sixty-mile coast line on the Gulf of California. Through this valley runs the Yaqui River, hundreds of feet wide when the snows were melting on the mountains but shrunken to a trickle during the summer. If the water could be impounded in a storage dam somewhere in the upper courses, it could be released gradually for irrigation purposes.

Along the river, and generally on its northern side, lie the eight Yaqui pueblos of four square leagues each, or about one hundred and eighty-five thousand acres in all. The portions of these pueblos watered by the overflow of the river were being cultivated after a fashion by the peaceable Indians who owned them. These Indians were called Mansos to distinguish them from the fighting tribes of the nation, the Bronchos. The rest of this inherently rich valley was covered with chaparral and cactus.

Knowing that Burnham was not likely to be overoptimistic, I immediately started preliminary investigations. His claims proved conservative. I then went to Harry Payne Whitney, outlined the proposition to him, and as usual found him a ready listener. Together we took up the option on this acreage.

A. P. Davis, whose work in Russia has already been described, was sent to determine the engineering problem. He made a highly favorable report. An ideal site for a storage dam was found about one hundred miles from the northern borders of our concession. It would make a lake several miles wide and sixty miles long, lying between the pine-clad slopes of the Sierra Madre Mountains. In addition to a supply of water sufficient to irrigate the entire valley, this would furnish fifty thousand horsepower, enough power and light for the whole district and the neighboring mines. So beautiful was the country around the proposed site of the lake that we had visions of its becoming a pleasure resort where the settlers in the Yaqui could spend the hot summer months. It was but a few hours' trip from the valley by motor.

According to the Davis plan the river bed would serve as a canal until it reached our property. At this point we could build a diversion dam to check the flow of the water and send it into the headgates of our canal system. Then, because of unusually favorable topographical conditions, the water would flow by gravity south and west over practically the entire Yaqui Valley.

We lost no time in buying an additional nine hundred thousand acres of land contiguous to that already acquired and in every respect equal to it. This also would come under the proposed water system.

When we had completed the purchase, our acreage covered an area the size of Rhode Island. None of this property was obtained by free land grant; all was purchased from the Mexican government or from private owners. None of it lay within the eight Indian pueblos.

We estimated twelve million dollars as the cost of building the entire system. Before making any attempt to raise this money, we used our private funds to construct a temporary diversion dam and some hundreds of miles of canals and laterals. Seventy thousand acres were ultimately brought under cultivation. The amazing diversity and abundance of the crops convinced us that this agricultural area equaled or even surpassed the world-famous Imperial Valley of California.

The climate of the Yaqui was incontrovertibly better than that of the Imperial Valley. There were no rains during the winter. The days were warm; the nights were cool but without frost. Fruits and vegetables invariably ripened some weeks earlier than did similar crops in Southern California.

Under W. W. Mackie, who was recognized by the government as an authority in the agricultural development of the arid regions of the West, we established a thousand-acre experimental station. Here we grew oranges, grapefruit, cotton, rice, alfalfa, and garvanza beans.

At first everything seemed to favor us. While our plans were yet maturing, the Southern Pacific Railroad, passing along the northern boundary of our property, completed its line to Mexico City. We would not only have this terminal as a ready market for dairy and farm products, but freight rates to the large American cities were identical with those from Southern California, an important advantage to the Yaqui settler. We also located ports within our own territory from which the products of the valley could be shipped to foreign countries by way of the Panama Canal.

One of the most alluring aspects of this venture was the water rights to the Yaqui River. Our concession gave us the right in perpetuity to charge fifty cents per acre foot on all water furnished for irrigation purposes. Since on the average each acre used from four to five acre feet a year, this would have assured a handsome return to us at an unusually low cost to the settler.

Whitney and I were so impressed with the attractions of the Yaqui Valley that we bought many thousands of acres with the idea of forming a winter colony of our friends. There Whitney also planned to raise polo ponies and race horses.

The valley offered many inducements to sportsmen. Nowhere had I seen wild game in such abundance. There were duck, dove, and quail. In the mountains and foothills were bear, deer, peccary, and puma. According to the famous sportsman, Professor Holden, the Gulf of California was an angler's paradise—better than Catalina. Mighty Nimrods and Izaak Waltons could shoot without let and fish without hindrance. There were oysters, delicious bivalves, in abundance, and, believe it or not, they grew on trees.

Over the savannas beautiful wild stallions and mares galloped up to neigh at the intruders. From the great caves of the Bacotete Mountains, filled with countless tons of guano, millions of bats poured out like black smoke from a chimney.

When my son Harris made his first visit to the valley, he found a reception committee which had been camped in the dust and heat for hours. In its midst was an old gentleman in a frock coat, green with age. Battle-scarred from innumerable Indian raids, Don Tomas Sexton's lean weather-beaten frame was still erect in spite of his sixty-odd years.

He had heard that Mr. Hammond was coming to inspect the valley.

All that afternoon Don Tomas followed Harris around like a hungry dog until the latter became restive under the intent gaze. Finally the old man buttonholed him and whispered mysteriously, "You have a secret I want to know."

Harris replied mildly, "I haven't any secret."

"Yes, you have!" Sexton insisted.

"No, I haven't! I don't know what you're talking about!"

"But you must have! I remember you as a young mining engineer at Alamos in 1881. You're not a day older than you were then."

Don Tomas believed I had drunk at the fountain of perpetual youth. At the time of this trip to Mexico, Harris was just about the same age I had been at the time of my meeting with Don Tomas so many years before.

When Harris said he was my son, Don Tomas was at first incredulous. Then a little shadow of disappointment clouded his countenance, but he took the news like the soldier he was.

By 1912, just as we had reached the point where we felt justified in going into the money market to secure capital for completing the project, the long series of Mexican revolutions began. The first serious effect upon us was the uprising of the valley Indians who had hitherto been an excellent source of labor supply. Inspired by the Bronchos, and by false promises of local Mexican revolutionary leaders, they formed bands and began to raid our settlers.

Annoyed by the inability of the Mexican government to control the Yaqui, I suggested to the government that Major Burnham and I go into the Bacotete Mountains and bring out every hostile entrenched there. My plan was to give each family a plot of land in fee and supply water to irrigate it. There was a change in government, however, and my offer was not accepted. These Indians would have provided a constant and efficient supply of farm labor.

The Bronchos had been supplied with arms by both sides in the

WELLS AT THE DOMINGUEZ FIELD

The Burnham Exploration Company have drilled 137 wells in this field

BULOLO DREDGE, NEW GUINEA—AN EXAMPLE
OF MODERN MINING TECHNIQUE

*This and three other dredges have been brought in from the seacoast 100 miles distant
and over a mountain range more than 5000 feet high by this fleet of three airplanes*

Mexican revolution, but had refused to fight for either. From the seventy-foot watchtower at Esperanza, our headquarters, the lookout could see the dusty war trail running down the center of the valley. One spring day a mounted band of Yaqui were observed moving rapidly towards the barricade. Waldo Sheldon and Cappy Jones, the two young Yale graduates who were in charge of the Hammond ranch, served out rifles to the peons and warned the outlying districts by telephone. The fighting lasted a few hours and several settlers were killed. When they found they could not make any impression in our defenses, the Yaqui withdrew, abandoning their dead and wounded.

Less than a month later they were again on the warpath. This time we were prepared. But they had learned their lesson, and detoured around the ranch in going down the valley.

Although on each occasion the pioneers succeeded in clearing the valley of Indians, crops were ruined, cattle stolen, and the experimental station buildings burned. The destruction of seven years' statistics on seeds and plants gathered from all corners of the world was an irreparable loss.

Johnny George and Bill Franke, two of Harris's associates, were running a store at the town of Yaqui. The constant raids taught them caution. Late one oppressively hot August night, Johnny was sitting alone in the store going over his books. Suddenly he heard what he thought was the report of a 30-30. He dropped instantly to the floor and crawled halfway under the desk. He waited and waited but nothing happened. Finally the torture of this cramped position became worse than the anticipation of what might occur if he showed himself. With infinite caution he rose, glancing warily around. At his feet was a little rivulet. His eyes followed it to the shelf, and there lay the shattered remains of a soda water bottle which had been exploded by the heat.

These young storekeepers were constantly called upon to meet emergencies. One afternoon a group of thirty or forty Yaqui came around the corner of the corral. Since the Yaqui never wore distinctive signs when on the warpath, the two boys had no way of telling whether their intentions were friendly or otherwise. But, from their taciturn and sullen manner, there was every reason to fear they were looking for trouble. The Indians crowded into the store. The odds against the boys would have been too great even if they had been able to reach their guns.

Johnny, who had a charming personality, spoke to them pleasantly in Spanish. For fifteen minutes the Indians milled around indecisively, and then one of them approached the counter, threw down a coin, and said, "Cigarettes."

Johnny placed a package on the counter before the Indian, and picked up the coin. He pressed the keys of the cash register, the numbers flew up, the drawer opened, and the bell rang.

The Yaqui, startled out of his impassivity, pointed and asked, "Que es este?"

Johnny explained that it told how much money went into the drawer, how much the article cost, and how a little record was made of the transaction.

The Indian was doubtful but interested. After a moment's thought, he threw down another coin, and, without picking up the first package of cigarettes, ordered another.

Again the numbers flew up, the drawer opened, and the bell rang.

The Indian beckoned to his companions and they swarmed about the machine, fascinated. All of them began to make purchases, watching each movement of the register with unblinking curiosity. They bought sixty dollars' worth of goods, and then, excited and happy, left with the promise to come back again soon.

Years afterwards I told this story to John R. Patterson, president of the National Cash Register Company. He was so delighted with it that he promptly used it in the company advertising. In his opinion there could be no more impressive testimonial from the poor Indian "whose untutor'd mind" beheld in this handiwork from Dayton, Ohio, a veritable deus ex machina.

We could have coped with the Indian menace, but the instability of the various Mexican governments made it impossible to protect our settlers. With the whole country disintegrating, and lawless desperadoes roaming about in search of plunder, any attempt to interest American or foreign capital in our enterprise was hopeless, and the Mexicans themselves had none to offer.

The final blow fell in 1917 when President Carranza passed the agrarian laws prohibiting the sale of land to foreigners. From that moment the colonization plan became inoperative. We carried the property until 1930, when it was sold to the Mexican government.

To Mexico the project would have meant the employment of labor in great numbers, warranted the collection of high taxes sorely needed by the republic, and the development without expense to her of an agricultural project on a scale unparalleled in any other part of the North American continent. Although we were much disappointed at being prevented from carrying out an enterprise of such inestimable value, we wish every success to the present Mexican government which is about to start development of the Yaqui Valley along the original plans.

Mining for metals and mining for oil involve different specialized sciences. The name "black gold" applied to oil means only that the flow of riches derived from the wells is comparable to that secured from the gold mines. My own training and experience as a mining engineer caused me to take a lively interest in oil development.

In the winter of 1910 I was about to go to Mexico City when Harris suggested that I look into the oil developments in the Tampico region on the east coast. That district offered excellent opportunities, he said. After leaving Mexico City, I got in touch with Ricardo A. Mestres, who for some years had been consulting expert for Lord Cowdray's famous Aguila Oil Company in Tampico.

Mestres was half English and half Spanish. His father died when the boy was only fourteen, and Ricardo had begun to support his mother and sisters by taking charge of the billiard tables in one of the Tampico saloons. Being exceptionally intelligent and energetic, thoroughly honest and brave, he had ultimately risen to an important position in the oil industry.

Mestres offered me an option covering 167,000 acres, scattered in large tracts from the Panuco River to the Tuxpam. We took over his entire acreage and made him general manager and gave him a substantial interest. We then went to the Consolidated Gold Fields of South Africa for capital; this company purchased ten thousand of our acres in the Panuco district. Mestres assumed full charge of the exploitation and development of its Transcontinenal Oil Company. Our company was called International Petroleum. For several years little was done except to keep our properties intact.

In 1916, just as we were about to begin developing our holdings, we received news of Mestres' death. This was a great personal, as well as business, loss to all who knew him.

Harris, who had managed the Mount Whitney Power Company from 1914 to its sale in 1916, was now free to devote all his time to our oil venture. I formed a million-dollar syndicate to carry on active exploration work, and in the beginning of 1917 put Harris in charge.

Prior to the Carranza regime it was the custom for oil companies to buy land outright at low prices and pay no royalty on oil production. After talking things over, we had agreed to reword all our previous purchase agreements by inserting royalty clauses. In this way the former Mexican owner would enjoy considerable profit whenever we struck oil. As a result, there were few potential oil properties in Mexico that were not offered to us in preference to any other company. This was our reward for treating owners justly when we were under no legal obligations to do so.

One day the oil companies in the Tampico field received notice from Pelaez, a bandit leader, that the monthly government royalty on oil production would be collected by him. His troops were in control of the district in which we were operating. The oil companies knew the Mexican government would not credit us with this illegal tribute on account as taxes, but we also knew that the wells would be burned by the bandits if we did not pay. We all made a virtue of necessity and the first month turned many thousands of dollars over to Pelaez. As expected, the Mexican government promptly notified us that it did not consider our obligations discharged. When nothing was paid to Pelaez the second month, he gave all the companies seven days to pay, announcing that at the end of this period he would act against any company he might catch operating.

Our company had used Mexican labor in the oil fields wherever possible, and when Mexicans proved their ability we had promoted them. This seemed to us good policy as it allayed any ill feeling against us as foreigners and gained us their loyal support.

Many of our head drillers, camp bosses, and other workers were stockholders in the company. We wired them from New York to use their own judgment as to what they should do, and enclosed a copy of Pelaez' proclamation. All the companies prudently closed down, except the Mexican Seaboard Oil Company—as International Petroleum was now called. When Pelaez rode in with his men, he found the Seaboard doing business as usual.

He demanded of the Mexican who met him, "Let me see your camp boss at once."

"I'm the camp boss," was the reply.

"You are? I never heard of a Mexican being in charge of a mine before!" exclaimed Pelaez in surprise. "Well, didn't you get my orders?"

"Yes," admitted the camp boss, "but many of the Mexicans here are stockholders, though we are men of modest means. We could not believe that this order included us. Moreover, we have instructions to feed you and your men and make you welcome."

Pelaez could not afford to antagonize the Mexican element, from whom his followers were recruited, so he allowed the Seaboard to continue operations.

During the enforced absence of the other companies from the field, we drew from the common pool two and one half million barrels of oil that were sold at $1.10 a barrel. This was a handsome profit on the stock we had given the men.

At Chereras we had a great loading rack that could fill three Standard Oil tankers at one time. A pipe line connected it with the storage tanks on land, which had a capacity of a million barrels.

From Chereras to the camp we had built a twenty-one-mile narrow-gauge railroad which was used to transport materials and gold coin for payrolls. José and Pedro, two Mexican brothers who had charge of the payroll train, had handled several million pesos for us without losing a centavo.

It was the custom to notify the camp by telephone the moment the train left Chereras. If it was a few minutes late, a car of armed men would be sent to meet it. One day in 1921 the usual message came that the train had started. When it was five minutes overdue, our manager tried to call Chereras and found the telephone line had been cut. Within a few moments the manager, accompanied by guards and the camp doctor, was on the way down the line. In twenty minutes the relief came upon the twisted, splintered wreckage of the light train. It had been literally blown to pieces by dynamite. Of the crew of seven men only José showed signs of life. He was badly broken by the explosion and shot through the chest.

The doctor reported that José's wounds must prove fatal, but that an injection of adrenalin might bring him back to temporary consciousness. The drug was administered.

In a few moments the doctor leaned over him to inquire: "Can you tell us who they were? Were they masked?"

"One was El Diablo," came the dying man's whisper. "He put his foot on my chest to shoot me. I saw the patch on the bottom of his shoe. It was three-cornered."

The manager knew that El Diablo had been hanging around the camp and would naturally have been observed carefully by anyone as conscientious as José.

In their wanton brutality and their desire to kill and leave no witnesses, the bandits had prepared so heavy a charge of dynamite as to defeat their own purpose. The gold coin had been so twisted and scattered by the violence of the explosion that little had been recovered in the few minutes before the arrival of the camp guards.

At the time of the dynamiting, Harris was in California with me. After a hasty discussion, we agreed that he should see President Obregon at once to ask whether the law against the carrying of arms could not be modified so that we might clean the bandits out of the district.

Harris described the outrage to Obregon and then added firmly, "We can't expose our men to this sort of thing, and we want to get the bandits no matter whether they're American, English, French, German, or Mexican."

Obregon replied, "You're the first man who has ever admitted to me that a bandit could be anything but Mexican."

He thereupon gave the company permission to arm its employees and also the right to call on the local garrison for help.

Acting on this authorization, we procured the services of seventeen men who had spent years with the Texas Rangers and similar bodies in hunting down criminals. They had been trained to act on the command, "Get your man, dead or alive."

After drifting around for two or three months at the bandit hideouts in Tampico and Zacamixtl, they began to pick up information here and there as to El Diablo's whereabouts. One day there came a tip that El Diablo was in a Tampico saloon. Our man suspected a trap, but he entered. As the door swung shut behind him, El Diablo and the two men with him opened fire from their table at the side of the room. When the smoke cleared the Texan walked out unharmed; the three bandits were dead.

This started real war.

The bandits were eventually tracked to their retreat in the mountains, where they had a supply of dynamite, rifles, and ammunition. With the explosives cached there, the Texans blew up the whole place.

After the death of El Diablo, a fine-looking young American assumed leadership of the gang. Lacking the necessities of life and war, the leader came in the night to the camp of one of the Panuco oil companies. Pounding on the door of the superintendent's shack, he called out, "If you don't open the door, we'll shoot it down." He was answered by a burst of gunfire which killed him and scattered his men. For several days the bandit leader's bullet-riddled body was exhibited in Tampico as a warning to evildoers.

By the end of two years our men had killed thirty or forty bandits. The spirit of the rest was broken and they wandered off. Life and property in our district were once more safe.

After discovering and developing the famous Toteco pool, the Mexican Seaboard extended its operations to California and to the equally famous Kettleman Hills field in Kern County, near Bakersfield. The geological formation there indicated oil, although the drilling of several dry holes seemed to disprove its presence. Even at a depth of six thousand feet, no traces of petroleum had appeared and drilling had been abandoned.

In a *Popular Science Magazine* article, Ray Lyman Wilbur, former secretary of the interior, said: "So finally came Harris Hammond, son of John Hays Hammond, who decided to plunge for the fluid gold where others had failed. He drove a well 7000 feet deep, at a cost of $250,000, and found incomparably greater wealth than his father had in South Africa." The secretary of the interior particularly approved of the manner in which the gas was conserved. The Mexican Seaboard Company had not only brought in the richest oil field in the world, but had supplied Northern California with natural gas.

When the Mexican revolution of 1923 broke out, Obregon had no money to pay his soldiers and could obtain no arms because of the United States embargo on the shipment of munitions into Mexico. We heard that Obregon had tried to borrow money from other oil companies. Finally one of his emissaries came to see Harris, who at once telephoned me in Washington.

I told him that if he could advance the money I would go at once to Secretary of War Weeks and explain that Obregon had been legally elected president and had been recognized by our government. Unless he could at once secure arms from the United States, anarchy would once more be let loose in Mexico. Moreover, if de la Huerta should win, relations between the United States and Mexico would be imperiled because of the rebel's well-known unfriendliness to our government.

Upon learning that the administration had already turned down de la Huerta's request for guns, I urged Secretary Weeks to send down airplanes or anything else in the way of fighting equipment that might help Obregon to win.

Weeks assured me of his sympathy with my views. I then called upon President Coolidge and told him: "We'll be the laughingstock of the world if we don't send guns to Mexico. Look what happened when Wilson refused to support Huerta. If we allow Obregon to be overthrown, we shall be put in a ridiculous position as we have already rendered him some aid and are committed to his cause. We've simply got to keep Obregon and Calles in power in spite of the revolution!"

Coolidge assured me of his determination to support Obregon to the full extent of his power.

The money was supplied and the embargo was lifted.

When the fighting was about to begin, we received a telegram to the effect that "General Obregon was taking the field to defend President Obregon." We were sure President Obregon could have no better defender than himself in the role of general. The money was paid back in full by rebating the taxes due the government by the company, and Obregon was successful in putting down the rebellion.

My second venture into oil took place in 1919 through the Burnham Exploration Company. Major Burnham, who was visiting me in New York, had been deploring the inactivity of the Yaqui project.

"Major," said Harris, "since you have so much time on your hands, why don't you try scouting for oil? You were a scout before most of the oil prospectors were born, and if you'll have a try at it, we could likely get hold of a profitable field to develop."

The idea of action appealed to Major Burnham, and the syndicate was formed, with Harris as president and Burnham as field manager.

In the course of two years Major Burnham examined properties in several states and took options in various sections of California. After a personal examination of these, Harris selected one property in the heart of the producing area of the Los Angeles basin. According to all geological indications, it seemed the most promising. As in the case of Kettleman, the field had already been tried and abandoned. The Union Oil Company had given up its options, and the Standard Oil of California had done the same after drilling two unsuccessful wells.

Major Burnham's son Roderick, "Rick" Templeton, and other geologists familiar with the structure recommended it strongly and were satisfied that the Standard Oil drillings had been no fair test of the field. Finally E. A. McKenna, the consulting geologist of Seaboard, made an exhaustive examination which resulted in thorough approval and recommendation of the structure. Harris and I then put up part of the money necessary to acquire the property, and, by telegraph, obtained the rest from Ogden Mills and Harry Payne Whitney.

While we were negotiating for the land, our intentions leaked out and we found ourselves bidding against Dutch Shell Oil and Union Oil, both of which companies wanted a footing in the field. A tripartite arrangement was accordingly made. We and the Union were to have a one-half undivided interest each, and the Dutch Shell a certain specified area for itself.

The first well, put down jointly by the Union Oil Company and ourselves in this Dominguez Hill field, came in at the rate of fifteen hundred barrels a day. Ever since then, the property has been one of the most highly valued fields in California.

The Mexican Seaboard Oil Company and the Burnham Exploration Company were exceedingly successful and are still earning. The Seaboard, between 1920 and 1930, paid off all its bonds and their interest, the value of the bonds being $10,700,000, and paid over $11,500,000 in dividends. The Burnham company, from 1923, its first year of operation, to 1933 inclusive, paid off its $1,000,000 worth of preferred stock with a bonus of ten points and during this ten-year period paid $10,240,000 in dividends.

It is estimated that the available oil still underground in the Dominguez Hill field runs from two hundred to four hundred million barrels.

One of the interesting features of the acquisition of this property was the fact that Major Burnham, who had been all over the world seeking his fortune, returned to find wealth in the very place where as a small boy he used to graze cattle, and shoot game which he sold to the neighboring mining districts to support his widowed mother and infant brother.

There are phases of development work in the Dominguez Hill field that are worth mentioning because of their bearing on oil recovery the world over. For a number of years, in various oil fields of the United States (exclusive of California), processes had been devised with a view to increasing oil production by the injection into the field of gas, compressed air, or water. Each field presented a problem in itself and several different processes were used successfully in Ohio and Oklahoma.

In the early part of 1925 the officers of the Burnham Exploration Company sent their engineer to consult with the Union Oil Company as to the possible application of the injection process in the Dominguez field. As a result of several conferences and many tests, we adopted a process which I believe had never been used in the state of California. This is the process of gas injection. The gas is taken from the well, the gasoline extracted, and the gas then driven by huge compressors into the oil-producing formation. There it again absorbs the oil locked in the sands and conveys another load to the surface. This invention has made possible the recovery of many millions of barrels of oil that otherwise never could be recovered.

CHAPTER THIRTY-SIX

In Retrospect

FAMILY LIFE—MY YOUNG PALS—A SHIP OF THE
DESERT—THE "UNDERPRIVILEGED" BOY—MY
WIFE'S CIVIC AND PHILANTHROPIC WORK—THE
TITANIC MEMORIAL—OUR SUMMER HOME AT
GLOUCESTER—JACK AND HARRIS TRY AN EXPERI-
MENT—FRIENDS ON THE NORTH SHORE—JUSTICE
HOLMES'S "RED-LETTER" DAY — GOLF — CAPTAIN BLACK-
BURN—SWAPPING YARNS WITH OLD GLOUCESTER FISHERMEN

*A*s I look back over these eighty years, it seems to me that I have been fortunate, most fortunate, perhaps, in the family into which I was born, the family I helped to found, and the friendships I have formed.

In two other things I was fortunate: that I was able to choose during college the life course I wanted to pursue and that I married early and had the responsibility of a family.

I have had more than a fair amount of success according to the world's standards, but I hope this has not been at the cost of sacrific-ing the finer quality of life. Even in my later years I have been busy and it seems to me that most of my leisure hours were occu-pied with things other than dolce far niente. Now and then, of course, I was able to sandwich in relaxation between business and other activities, but I have not often enjoyed a real vacation as is the habit of most businessmen of today.

In contemplating the writing of this book and, after a great deal of hesitation, in undertaking it, I have come to realize that perhaps because my life has been so active, retrospect is not particularly natural to me.

The world into which I was born was one where driving power and physical energy were essential to survival. Frontiers were being extended on every hand. On many of these I lived and encountered adventure. This seemed but part of the day's work. I recognized adventure, of course, when it came, but whatever elements of romance may now seem to surround those episodes are due to my seeing them as a whole, rather than as a disconnected series of events. And in later years I was not insensible to the drama that was coming into business and political affairs. I lived in it while it was unfolding; when it was over I did not forget it, but the conscious memory was displaced by the immediacy of other things to be seen and accomplished.

I have led such an active life that I have had literally no time and no desire to keep a diary wherein I might jot down the facts which the average traveler observes automatically. One may be a guest at a dinner where the conversation proves so enthralling as to make one oblivious of the food. One may travel through the countryside and be so absorbed in a problem as not to know whether the road is rough or smooth. It is possible to have one's attention so fixed on a definite goal that it overshadows everything else.

The reader may feel that in telling this story I have left out certain human values. This may be true. The momentum of events has carried me along and I have detailed incidents as they came to mind. In looking back on my life I realize that my truly happy hours of recreation seem always to have been spent with my wife and children.

I have talked little of home or homes. And yet, to men who are forced to spend a large part of their lives in out-of-the-way places, family life is of far greater importance than to others.

In this respect I was particularly fortunate. My wife possessed the gift, with sometimes but few facilities at her command, of creating the background essential to our family life. She never allowed the unsettled character of my activities or her own various interests to interfere and she made a real home for us in many parts of the world. She had feminine methods of accomplishing this and one of the cleverest was her ability to appeal to our appetites. She was not only a good cook herself, she could teach others how to cook. In kitchens the world around she provided the favorite dishes of the family. In Mexico we would find awaiting us at dinner Maryland beaten biscuits; in Johannesburg, spoon bread—real delicacies to one of southern rearing.

In every mining community there are many young engineers, married and unmarried, and in our various homes they found welcome. Under my wife's sympathetic guidance they soon forgot any shyness and talked at length of other days, the theater, music, their homes and families. As a result, they felt less lonely and not quite so far from things dear to them.

Our third abode in Washington—this time really our own—delightfully situated on Kalorama Road was purchased in 1917. Here we spent many busy and interesting winters (until my wife's death in 1931). My own children had by this time grown up and I became friends with those in my neighborhood as I was conscious of missing the cheerful society of the very young.

I owned some vacant lots across the street from our house where children of the neighborhood used to congregate. I made it into a sort of community playground for them. I fenced in sand piles and put up swings for the smaller ones, and benches for their nurses. To the older boys I gave baseball bats and gloves with the strict proviso that they should not use them until the "kids," as they scornfully called them, had gone home. I spent many delightful and refreshing hours in the companionship of these children—we became real pals.

One day when walking near our house I saw a small boy lying flat on the sidewalk, screaming at the top of his lungs, while his nurse with soothing words vainly endeavored to induce him to move. Having many times heard the same sort of cry from my own children I knew that he was not hurt; he was merely indulging in a fit of temper.

"What's his name?" I asked the distracted nurse.

"John."

"John, did you see that big black bear run across the street!" I exclaimed.

The crying suddenly ceased, and John's face was lifted from the sidewalk as he asked, "Where?"

"It's too bad you've been making such a noise. You must have scared him away. There he goes around the corner! Come on, maybe we can catch up to him."

Hand in hand we started after the bear, but we never caught up with him. But John had forgotten his troubles and, after we bade each other a cordial farewell, he allowed his nurse to take him peaceably home.

The next day I received a letter from Mrs. Franklin D. Roosevelt, thanking me for the service I had rendered her family. From that time on young John Roosevelt and I were friends. He and an older brother often visited me at my house. Before an expected call, I would bury a few pennies and nickels in the back yard. They would come armed with buckets and shovels, and, under my instruction, would start digging like true miners. Great was their excitement and elation when they came upon the bonanza.

The three of us once went on a pleasant expedition to the zoo. After gazing for some time into bear pits and monkey cages, I asked John, "Have you ever seen a ship of the desert?"

"No," replied John thoughtfully.

"You don't mean to tell me you've never seen a ship of the desert? And your father is assistant secretary of the navy?"

They were indignant at their father's failure to keep them up to date on nautical matters.

"Well, come on with me then."

I led them to the camel yard, explained to them why these animals were called ships of the desert, and told them stories of camels I had seen in my travels.

"We're going right home and ask father if he's ever seen a ship of the desert," John declared.

Following up my affection for children and my delight in their society, it was not unnatural that I should undertake some work in behalf of the boys of the country.

I believe that some of the most valuable supplements to the system

760 The Autobiography of John Hays Hammond

of public education, and the upbuilding of character, are in the Y. M. C. A., the Boy Scout movement, and the Boys' Clubs of America. The latter organization—until recently called the Boys' Club Federation—was founded in 1906 and for many years has had my friend William E. Hall as its president; it has been my privilege to serve under him as vice-president for about fifteen years. Nearly two-thirds of the boys in our country have been classed as "underprivileged." They are born in humble homes where family life is unattractive and sometimes pernicious; they are able to take advantage of educational opportunities to only a limited extent; they are often handicapped by prejudice of race or religion; and they make up the sad army of juvenile delinquents. Yet, if I were to select a team to compete in the battle of life, I should unhesitatingly select boys of this class. They are intelligent, self-reliant, and used to hardships. They are not "bad boys," but good boys doing the wrong things, and have never had a fair chance in life. I have often said this when talking to them. Ninety per cent of the criminal class is drawn from this great two-thirds of America's boyhood—this undernourished, undefended majority. We really cannot pretend to be amazed at crime waves and the degeneracy of which newspapers make a daily chronicle. The cause is not obscure nor difficult to locate.

An appalling and pitiable fact in the crime situation is not that hordes of bandits and gangs of racketeers swarm the city and defy suppression, but that the *offender is often only a boy*—a boy who has been denied the opportunity of developing good character in proper environment.

Former Police Commissioner Whalen, of New York City, recently said: "One of the tragedies of the crime problem of today is the extreme youth of the criminal. Of all persons arrested last year 44 per cent were under the age of twenty, and 60 per cent of all holdups were committed by youths between the ages of sixteen and twenty."

It was to offset this menace that the Boys' Clubs of America was founded. Branches have been established in 134 American cities with a membership of 240,000 divided among 260 clubs. The average club numbers 940 boys. Its aim is to provide the poorer, more congested districts with clubhouses which will offer wholesome mental and physical activities.

CAPTAIN HOWARD BLACKBURN (1863-1932)

GLOUCESTER HARBOR FROM LOOKOUT HILL

The enormous success of the clubs in dealing with these boys may
be attributed to the fact that they have shrewdly capitalized the gang
interest which is strong in every boy. Youth, after all, learns largely
from youth. It will not learn voluntarily from moral precept, but
once arouse in a group of youngsters interest in their grown-up contacts with young men, who will sanely embody a boy's admiration
for daring and adventure, and the youthful pack is headed in the
right direction. Hero worship is an inherent part of a boy's life.
The man chosen by a boy as a type of hero exerts a vast influence on
his life. We must counteract the evil influence of the racketeer and
the bandit. If no other associations with elders are granted them, can
they be blamed if they emulate these men?

Lewis E. Lawes, warden of Sing Sing Prison, says: "Boys' Clubs
cost $15.00 per capita per year, whereas it costs $400.00 to maintain
an inmate at Sing Sing for that period."

These clubs have made an amazing record in reducing juvenile
delinquency.

I feel no disgrace in having been involved in the following episode
as reported in *Fortune:*

JOHN HAYS HAMMOND TAKES THE COUNT

An unusual pugilistic upset was recorded when John
Hays Hammond, vice-president of the Boys' Club Federation, was knocked out by Walter Brady, eight year
old champion pugilist of the Boys' Club of Washington,
during the first round of a challenge bout at the formal
opening of the new sixty thousand dollar gymnasium of
the Washington Boys' Club on Tuesday evening, November 9th. The vanquished boxer admitted that he
was beaten in a fair fight with the exception that young
Brady assured him before the fight that he would not
"hit him hard."

In reviewing our lives at this period I remember that my wife was
continually engaged in work of civic and philanthropic nature. Her
charity list was not long. She would find something worth remedy-

ing, raise the money needed, and administer it personally. She never stopped in the middle of an undertaking.

If her interest was a hospital or a charitable home, she would frequently drop in and talk to the doctors, to the directors, and to the inmates so that there was always the direct personal touch.

During her term as chairman of the Women's Welfare Department of the National Civic Federation she was active in a move to improve the living conditions in the federal prisons, and particularly in the one first called to her attention in Washington and known as the "D. C. Jail." She interested her friend George W. Wickersham, the attorney general, and took him to visit that notorious prison. They found that the gallows stood at the end of the dining room, covered with a scant curtain. On the days of execution the prisoners ate their breakfast in the corridor. The men lived in tiny cells that had no running water; there was no outdoor exercise for women. The prisoners were fed like animals, and were grossly maltreated. As a result of her efforts, conditions were radically improved.

She established and was for five years president of the Women's Evening Clinic in Washington, which was free to the poorest and charged fees from ten cents to a dollar for workingwomen. In 1914, through her influence, the first woman interne was appointed in Garfield Hospital. It was at that time a very difficult matter to gain recognition of this kind for the woman physician.

As was natural, her thought was often directed to the welfare of children. The War Children's Christmas Fund owed its success to her ability as an organizer. The result of her efforts, aided by a corps of volunteer workers, was the shipment to Europe before the Christmas of 1915 of a large quantity of clothing, food, and toys, which was distributed without racial distinction among the children of all the warring nations.

My wife then undertook the direction of the Militia of Mercy which devoted itself to caring for poor children of Boston and New York who had been crippled by the infantile paralysis epidemic of 1916. These are only a few of the philanthropic interests that occupied her time and energy.

In 1912 my wife organized the movement to erect the Titanic

Memorial, to commemorate the bravery of the men who sacrificed their lives "that women and children might be saved."

The response to the appeals of the Woman's Titanic Memorial Association was remarkable.

Benefit performances of various kinds, given in different places, added substantial sums. Of these the most notable was a benefit that took place in December, 1912, at the Century Theatre, in New York. My sister expressed its spirit in these words which appeared on the outside of the program:

> GREATER THAN SELF, STRONGER THAN FATE,
> HEROIC SOULS ASK OF US NO TRIBUTE BUT REMEMBRANCE.

Over three hundred of the leading actors and actresses gave their services with the usual warm-hearted, generous response of that profession to all appeals for charity. The organization of the benefit was in the capable hands of Daniel Frohman. He suggested to my wife that it would be advisable for her personally to enlist the interest of Charles Frohman, as he felt sure that many of the artists then under his brother's direction would gladly appear if Charles were willing.

My wife then called on Charles Frohman and was received with the utmost courtesy. He was in a jocular mood, and her glowing praise of the heroism of the men who had gone down on the *Titanic* was met by a facetiously expressed doubt as to their being entitled to the honor of a monument.

I am inclined to think that Mr. Frohman was favorably impressed as he continued to rally her in regard to her warmly expressed admiration for the bravery of men in general, in order, I suspect, to draw her out.

Finally he remarked: "Well, personally, I should have shoved my way to a lifeboat and got into it." But, he soon ceased to joke, and gave his promise to aid the benefit—a promise generously fulfilled in his contribution of talent.

A few years later, as everyone remembers, Charles Frohman intrepidly faced death on the sinking of the *Lusitania*. His last words have been widely quoted: "Why fear death? It is the most beautiful adventure in life."

With the co-operation of Major U. S. Grant III, in charge of public grounds and buildings, Congress finally appropriated a site in Potomac Park in Washington, and in 1931 the beautiful monument designed by Mrs. Harry Payne Whitney was unveiled. The President, the secretary of state, many officials and statesmen were present, with a great crowd of representative citizens. Mrs. Taft unveiled the monument. On one side are inscribed the following words:

TO THE BRAVE MEN WHO PERISHED IN THE WRECK OF THE TITANIC, APRIL 15, 1912. THEY GAVE THEIR LIVES THAT WOMEN AND CHILDREN MIGHT BE SAVED. ERECTED BY THE WOMEN OF AMERICA.

There is every year an exodus from Washington, New York, and other large cities, of all who are not bound by their official duties to remain and swelter in the unpleasant heat. My wife and I were anxious to find a place where the children could spend their long vacations. In the summer of 1903 we chartered a boat and cruised along the coast from Long Island to Bar Harbor, looking at various sites, always anxious to avoid such enervating routine as one finds in Newport and other fashionable resorts. Finally, we decided on Gloucester, Massachusetts, because it was a town of fishermen—men whose rugged character reminded us of communities we had known and loved in the Far West. We built a home, and called it "Lookout Hill."

Even in the midst of affairs of business, which did not entirely cease with the summer, I was able to spend more and more time with my wife and youthful family. On many long walks through the woods, I taught Natalie woodcraft, and we spent many afternoons swimming, sailing, and fishing, pleasant and healthful diversions for both of us. When she was six she had already begun to be interested in drawing, and we always encouraged her. At the age of eight she wrote an ambitious romance entitled *The Adventures of Sir John Hammond* and illustrated it profusely. The unconscious humor of both text and pictures put a severe strain on the polite seriousness of her family readers. Since then her work has been shown and sold in many art exhibitions both here and abroad, and her designs for theatrical sets and costumes have been used by Nazimova and for special performances at the Guild Theatre.

Harris, Jack, and Dick spent most of their time sailing around the harbor in their boat, the *Swallow*. Three times they won the Massachusetts championship for boats in that class.

Dick became a skilled sailor and, at the beginning of the World War, turned naturally to the navy. He and three college friends were commissioned by the government to do night patrol work on the Cape Ann coast, where German submarines were getting their fuel supply. Dick knew every channel and rock in this section and could navigate without lights.

The boys were so conscientious in the discharge of their duty that they would board any suspicious-looking vessel they encountered and, unless the skipper could prove to their entire satisfaction that his business was harmless, they would order him summarily in to the port authority at Boston. More often than otherwise the irate captains were able to prove complete innocence of intent. But the boys continued to do their duty as they saw it.

I fitted up a laboratory for Jack on the Gloucester grounds. There he used to carry on experiments in boat control by radio, alarming and mystifying both natives and summer people who observed his boat careering around the harbor without anyone on board.

My summers would probably not have been so peaceful had I known all that was going on at the laboratory.

There was in the cove an old fisherman called Joe Adams, who had been more or less adopted by the boys. In his declining years, he used to place lobster pots a few yards from the shore. Usually, before starting out, he took a few drinks. From the terrace the boys would watch him make his uncertain rounds during which he sometimes pulled up the same pot several times within the hour.

Jack and Harris one day laid a homemade mine about a hundred yards offshore, which Jack was going to try to explode by wireless. They didn't know much about explosives then, and put in far too big a charge. Harris was to be stationed at the door of the laboratory to sound a warning should any boat approach too near the mine. After pulling the switch a dozen times without anything happening, Jack buried himself in the complicated wiring, and called Harris inside to help. Finally Jack said: "I have all the connections made. This time the infernal thing is sure to go off. I'll pull the switch when you get outside, and then I'll run out to see the fun."

When Harris returned to his post, he saw old Joe calmly pulling up a lobster pot directly over the mine. Just as Harris yelled to Jack, "Hold everything," there was a terrific detonation. Joe and his boat rose fifty feet on a trumpet of water, capsized, and came down in a shower of lobster pots, boulders, seaweed, rocks, and fish.

In three jumps Harris reached the rowboat at the foot of the little cliff and battled his way out among the waves to rescue Joe who was splashing about in a half-drowned condition. Harris hauled him in, thankful to see he was not hurt.

When Joe had partially caught his breath, he gasped, "God-amighty, did you see what happened to me? I went up right top of a big wave."

"Nonsense, Joe," Harris said. "We've been watching you for the last quarter of an hour. I saw you lean over to pull in that lobster pot and you fell in."

"But I felt it," Joe insisted. "My boat's all broke up! As I went up, I could see right over the top of the house."

"You're crazy," Harris insisted, this time with some show of justice, since the top of the house was a hundred feet above the water line. "You must have kicked the boat as you fell. I think you've had a few too many drinks."

The people of Gloucester heard the noise of the explosion but thought it was probably blasting in the near-by Rockport quarries. The boys comforted Joe and bought him a new rowboat.

To his dying day Joe thought he had been the victim of a hallucination. But once in a while he would mutter to himself, "I know damn well the ocean blew up."

In 1913, Jack explained his ideas about remote control by radio to the secretary of war, Lindley M. Garrison, and to the chief of coast artillery, General Weaver. The general promised to come to Gloucester when Jack was ready.

Two years later the first demonstration took place. With no one on board, a motorboat was run across the harbor to the breakwater and around the spar and back, a course of three miles. The experiment was perfectly successful. Eventually the potential range of control was increased to thirty miles.

Later the government's interest lay in the application of remote control of torpedoes. Jack was using his boat as a theoretical torpedo, which, of course, could run only on the surface. By further development he was able to control the U.S.S. *Iowa* without anyone on board, at a distance of several miles. The *Iowa,* discarded as a warship, was used in this instance for target practice.

Our cautious government refused to accept his invention until he perfected his methods so that torpedoes could be directed at the standard depth, though this was not contemplated (indeed, not regarded as possible) in his original agreement with the government. These inventions now constitute an important part of our naval equipment.

In connection with his radio researches Jack obtained most important patents for receiving and broadcasting and these he sold to the Radio Corporation of America and became its consulting engineer.

There were two fishing boats in Gloucester which interested my family very much. Both were owned by Captain Lemuel Spinney. One of them had been named the *John Hays Hammond* and the other the *Natalie Hammond.* There was great rivalry between my daughter and myself as to which would return first from the Grand Banks and which would have the larger catch. With the telescope we would watch the boats making harbor and then telephone to the pier to find out which had won. I jokingly accused Captain Spinney of knowing we had bets up on the result, and therefore of unduly favoring the *Natalie Hammond.* These boats were regarded as "lucky" boats, but in reality Captain Spinney was the best fisherman in Gloucester. He had picked crews who would not return until their cargoes were complete, although many other vessels in the fleet would come back with half a load. My namesake was torpedoed in the North Sea by the Germans, when it was used by the Allies in the World War.

Among the residents of the North Shore were people I had known in Washington and elsewhere. A few of my Massachusetts friends occasionally assumed an attitude of friendly superiority towards me, because of my western birth. The chief offender was the late Major

Augustus P. Gardner, congressman from my district. "Gussie" and I often used to speak on the same political platform. At times he would point to the fact that every drop of his blood was Puritanic blue. He was trying to make me feel a rank outsider in the Bay State, although it had been my legal residence since 1903.

On one occasion Gussie went too far. When I spoke, following him, I said that in my opinion my distinguished friend was not entitled to special commendation for having been born in Massachusetts. That event was merely an accident of birth. On the other hand, I had been born in California, lived in many parts of the world, and after attaining an age of discretion and mature judgment, had of my own volition chosen Massachusetts for my permanent residence. Gussie appreciated the point.

I had really enjoyed sailing and fishing with the children. Later when I bought a yacht, the *Atreus,* for longer trips it seemed that every time my wife and I took a cruise something happened to shorten our trip. Even when we took the smaller children with us on the *Atreus* for an extended cruise, invariably their nurses were seasick. I began to feel that yachts were fools' paradises, but I used the *Atreus* advantageously for business purposes. When compelled to be within reach of my office in New York, I would take members of my staff with me, spending the evening on the boat working out engineering problems.

During one of our cruises we anchored off Coney Island. Among the guests were Baron Rosen, Dr. Morton Prince, R. D. Evans, Finley Peter Dunne (*Mr. Dooley*), and Major Burnham.

Baron Rosen was the Russian ambassador and accompanied me on many trips on the yacht. He was an excellent raconteur, and a man of extensive diplomatic experience. Of all the diplomats I have met, I consider that he was best qualified to comment on international questions. We were somewhat shocked when he ridiculed the open-door policy of John Hay which we had unquestioningly accepted as one of the Ten Commandments of international relations. Rosen claimed that it had not settled the Japanese question in any way. He prophesied, however, that the Japanese would unobtrusively creep up inch by inch until they had taken possession of all the Asiatic coast opposite their islands. With the recent establishment of Manchukuo his prophecy has come true.

Dunne was an occasional visitor at Lookout Hill and I came to know something of the rigors of the newspaper "copy date." He could never finish his material on time. I have often sat up late with him, urging him on by various methods, then sent off his material by automobile to Boston to make a late train to his New York publishers.

Dr. Morton Prince of Boston, charming and well-informed gentleman as well as great psychiatrist, was a very dear friend of the family. One of the chief ambitions of Dr. Prince's life was to beat Charles Francis Adams at sailing. They both owned boats made by the same firm and of an identical type. They raced constantly but, so far as I can learn, Prince never once took a race from Skipper Adams.

One of the visitors who always received a hearty welcome at Lookout Hill was Moreton Frewen of London, noted bimetallist and an intimate friend of Justice Oliver Wendell Holmes. On our way to the Myopia Club for lunch one day Frewen and I stopped to invite Holmes to join us.

He regretfully declined, saying, "I have to prepare an opinion immediately, and much as I should enjoy being with you I cannot spare the time."

Frewen, with his extraordinary persuasive powers, finally induced Holmes to accompany us. But Mrs. Holmes said, "Oliver shouldn't be going, but, since he is, I want you to promise you'll get him back here sharp at three o'clock."

We were so engrossed in enjoyable conversation that our promise to Mrs. Holmes entirely slipped our minds. After tarrying long over lunch we motored to the Eastern Yacht Club at Marblehead for further refreshments. About six o'clock we boarded my boat and sailed to Lookout Hill, arriving just in time for dinner. It seemed quite natural that the justice should remain.

We had not been long seated at the table when I was called to the telephone. It was Mrs. Holmes, who indignantly upbraided me for having failed to return her husband at the promised hour. She said she had been telephoning all up and down the North Shore trying to locate him.

We guiltily bolted our food and hurried to his home. I had not the courage to face Mrs. Holmes, so I abandoned the justice on the door-step and beat a hasty retreat. The only notice she would take of me for a long time thereafter was a formal and reproachful nod.

Holmes was unrepentant, and professed never to have forgotten his truancy. Whenever we meet he refers to it as "that red-letter day."

My first lessons in golf were received in England under the tutelage of Lord Lorne, later Duke of Argyll. When I came to America, I was told that I should have to forget all I had learned abroad and begin over again. The professional at the Myopia Club told me patroniz-ingly that I would never make a good golfer. Disappointed, I asked why he had not told me so before giving me lessons.

To console me, he replied: "President Taft is no better than you are."

"That's a comfort, anyhow," said I. "How do you explain our inability to master this difficult sport?"

"The reason is," he explained, "that the brains of both of you are always working on so many things that you can't concentrate on the game."

Taft used to carry a score book with him, which I, in an unguarded moment, had presented to him. Whenever I boasted of some par-ticularly fine record I had made, he would pull out this book and check me up.

Our favorite playing ground was the golf links at the Myopia Club. The name of this club was selected because several of the leading incorporators had been myopes. Among the many people who ques-tioned the origin of the name was a certain party of New Yorkers who were being driven out from Boston. They were asking each other what the derivation of "Myopia" might be.

Amid a chorus of "Search me" and "Darned if I know," the driver interpolated, "Beg your pardon, sirs, but the word myopia is derived from the Greek *myein,* to close, and *ops,* meaning eye, hence near-sightedness."

"You get inside, and I'll drive," retorted one of the New Yorkers, who possessed a sense of the fitness of things.

There was one hole on the Myopia course which used to give Taft particular difficulty. I dubbed it the President's bunker, because it had been devised, so the story goes, by Herbert Leeds, chairman of the golf course committee, especially to vex the President and vex him it did. Leeds was an alumnus of Harvard and up to the time of his death had no use for a Yale man, not even if he was President of the United States.

Taft was bent on getting around under one hundred. All the club members had bets on his score, offering odds against him. As Myopia golfers will attest, ninety-eight on their course is fully as good as ninety on any ordinary links. I shall never forget one particular day when Taft came to lunch at Lookout Hill. When I met him at the door, he was bubbling with good-humor and was chuckling so merrily that I was sure he had some joke on me.

"Well, Jack," he announced jubilantly, "I've gone around at Myopia in less than one hundred. My score this morning was ninety-eight."

Major Archibald Butt's famous *Letters* make me out more of a duffer at golf than I am willing to admit. Even so, I regarded Archie as one of the most tactful men I have ever known. No one not possessing that quality could have retained the friendship of both the Tafts and the Roosevelts during the trying years of their estrangement.

As to the revelations which came out in his book, they are more valuable for small incidents and sidelights on character than for any knowledge imparted as to serious matters. Butt used to gather up the scraps of conversation which fell his way and report them without a full understanding of the background. This makes them somewhat misleading to the credulous reader. Charles D. Hilles, who succeeded Charles D. Norton as secretary to President Taft, wrote me recently that he "considers the inaccuracies to be innumerable and inexcusable." Butt's comments are, to say the least, indiscreet, distorted, and often far from kind.

When the news first came of the sinking of the *Titanic,* on which Archie was taking a long overdue vacation, I telephoned Taft to ask whether there was any reason to hope that Butt had been saved.

"Not the slightest chance," he replied. "Archie would be the last man to leave the ship."

Golf was a great pleasure to me so long as my health allowed me to play. I was sorry when I had to give it up, although I never played more than an average game. Arthur T. Hadley, for example, was not particularly enthusiastic about my golfing abilities. Once when I ignominiously missed a drive, he burst forth in rhyme:

> I thought I saw a friendly soul
> Whose face beamed mirth and jollity.
> I looked again: He'd missed the ball
> And only hit the tee.
> "Now how," said I, "could anyone . . ."
> "You go to hell," said he.

In the fall of 1913, I was in the midst of an extended tournament with Thomas Nelson Page when his appointment as ambassador to Italy threatened to cut it short.

Page at once declared: "We mustn't let the unkind intervention of affairs of state interfere with our golf. Let's settle this matter in Italy. I could then prove to you once and for all that I could beat you."

This was a challenge not lightly to be disregarded. I went to Rome for the winter. Since it must be admitted that this pretext for a vacation was somewhat flimsy, I ostentatiously left my own golf kit at home. I knew that I could borrow clubs from Colonel Dunn of the American Embassy, and the true nature of the trip would then be less apparent; certainly less embarrassing to me in case of defeat.

In the end I was able to satisfy Page that his advantage over me was not so great as he had assumed.

It was at the Myopia Club that George Harvey brought about a reconciliation between Senator Beveridge and me after we had fallen out several years before during Taft's administration owing to political differences. Harvey, who was visiting me at Gloucester, told me that Beveridge was anxious to make up. This pleased me greatly, and I enjoyed the renewed friendship up to the untimely death of this remarkable man.

But Beveridge never made up his quarrel with Tom Marshall, whose sense of humor sometimes carried him further than he had intended. For example, once when Senator Beveridge, up for re-election, was covering Indiana in a whirlwind campaign of eloquence, he declared that if the voters would send him back to the Senate, he would put Indiana on the map.

Marshall could not resist this opening. He commented: "I agree with Beveridge. If he were elected, he would put Indiana on the map, but the area would then be marked 'windswept plain.'"

Beveridge never forgave him.

The country at large did not agree with Marshall's characterization of Beveridge: it recognized that he was a brilliant, upright, and courageous statesman, and a historian of marked ability.

Albert Beveridge's direct and serious nature sometimes prevented the exercise of his sense of humor. Once, after an after-dinner conversation, there was some discussion of his *Life of John Marshall,* which had just appeared.

Aware of the antipathy of Beveridge for Tom Marshall, I said, "Albert, I think the writing of the life of Marshall was magnanimous on your part."

He looked at me in his characteristic way to search for my meaning, then he exclaimed: "Why, Jack! What do you mean? You don't really think I wrote the life of Tom Marshall, do you?"

At my look of pretended bewilderment, Beveridge, obviously annoyed, stalked into another room. The others appreciated the joke, and one of them followed Beveridge to remind him that I had already read much of the manuscript before publication and naturally was well aware that his hero was John, not Tom.

The last time I saw Beveridge, shortly before his death, he brought to my home some chapters of the biography of Lincoln which he was then writing. We spent the afternoon discussing the book. I remember vividly his telling me that he had greatly changed his views about the South. He admitted that, although he had been raised in an abolitionist atmosphere, a close study of the conditions preceding the Civil War convinced him that the South had had much right on its side, and that, in many respects, the North had been too intolerant.

The harbor life of Gloucester added to my love of the place. I enjoyed chatting with the old sailors as much as I did with my other friends. I used to go to Captain Blackburn's store on Main Street and get him to tell about his extraordinary life. In 1883, at the age of twenty, his dory was separated from its schooner in an icy norther off the Grand Banks. He was forced to sit four days looking at his dead dory mate frozen on the seat in front of him. When he realized that his own hands were freezing, he curved them around the oar handles so that he could continue to row after the hands themselves became immovable. Ultimately he came safe to land but lost his fingers and one foot.

Despite this crippled condition, he never gave up his life as a sailor and continued to complete daring and incredible voyages. Some years later, in a small schooner, with a limited crew, he sailed around the Horn to the Klondike to prospect for gold, but was forced to give up the undertaking because of his health. In 1899 he sailed alone in a thirty-foot sloop from Gloucester in New England to Gloucester in Old England. He was one of the most undaunted sailors America has ever had and I have seldom enjoyed exchanging yarns with anybody so much. I was proud to be one of the honorary pallbearers at his funeral, with Captain Bob Bartlett, Commander Donald B. MacMillan, Sir Wilfred Grenfell, Charles Francis Adams, and others.

I look back with the greatest pleasure on the hours I have spent with other old Gloucester fishermen. In the winter of 1910 several of these old fellows appeared before the district court and pleaded guilty to vagrancy. Without other means of gaining food or shelter, they were seeking some sort of sustenance in the poorhouse for the winter. In Washington, I read about this in the papers and got in touch with Judge York, Dr. Dickswell, Fred Shackelford, and others who were interested. We established a home to provide for these old fishermen. I learned to appreciate the fine traits of these men who were given refuge there. Often it was exceedingly difficult to persuade them that they were too old to stand the hardships of deep-sea fishing. Their truck garden faced the sea, and from there they could watch with their telescopes for the fishing vessels as they left and entered the harbor.

Sailors, like miners, are notoriously spendthrifts and these of Gloucester were no exception. They would arrive at the Home in a destitute condition. Because they no longer went to sea, and there was no chance of their reaching the traditional sailors' grave, they had a great dread of potter's field. For that reason I provided a cemetery near Gloucester where all could be assured of decent burial. Above the gate is inscribed:

AND HERE REST, BRAVE TOILER OF THE SEA,

SLEEP UNDISTURBED.

GOD'S PEACE BE WITH THEE.

Many of the inmates were choosey about the location of their graves. There were two in particular, bunkies since boyhood, who quarreled daily and, I fear, nightly, but who exacted from me a promise that they might be buried side by side.

Like the old prospectors of the West, they were given to enlarging upon their experiences. I used to slip them a little grog and a pipe of tobacco and then start them off spinning yarns. Each of the yarns would grow somewhat better than the one just told. But when they overstepped the bounds and the yarn became too fantastic, the size of the fish too large, or the description of some strange sea serpent or "queer doings" in foreign lands became utterly preposterous, I would raise my hand in protest and say: "Wait a minute, boys! Not quite so fast! Remember, I can tell some 'tall' stories myself."

ACKNOWLEDGMENTS

The stanza from Kipling's "The Burial" is reprinted by kind permission of Mr. Kipling.

"Ghost Town," from Let Us Dream *by Don Blanding, copyright, 1933, by Don Blanding, is used by permission of the publishers, Dodd, Mead & Company, Inc.*

Bibliography

BOOKS COVERING THE PERIOD

BAKER, HERBERT, *Cecil Rhodes, by his architect.* London: Oxford University Press, 1934.

BLAKE, WILLIAM P., *Tombstone and Its Mines.* New York: Cheltenham Press, 1902.

BRYCE, JAMES, *Impressions of South Africa.* New York: The Century Co., 1897.

BURNS, WALTER NOBLE, *Tombstone, an Iliad of the Southwest.* Garden City, N. Y.: Doubleday, Page & Co., 1927.

California State Mining Report. Ninth Annual Report.

CANFIELD, CHAUNCEY L., *The Diary of a 49r.* San Francisco: M. Shepard Co., 1906.

CURLE, J. H., *The Gold Mines of the World.* New York: Engineering and Mining Journal, Inc., 1902.

DEWAAL, D. C., *With Rhodes in Mashonaland.* Cape Town: J. C. Jusa & Co., 1896.

Economic Geology (Magazine), May, 1930.

GARRETT, F. E., *The Story of an African Crisis.* Westminster: A. Constable & Co., 1897.

HALL, R. N., *Great Zimbabwe.* London: Methuen & Co., 1905.

———, *Pre-historic Rhodesia.* London: T. F. Unwin, 1909.

———, and NEAL, W. G., *The Ancient Ruins of Rhodesia.* London: Methuen & Co., 1904.

HATCH, F. H., and CHALMERS, J. A., *The Gold Mines of the Rand.* London: Macmillan & Co., Ltd., 1895.

HOLE, HUGH MARSHALL, *The Making of Rhodesia.* London: Macmillan & Co., Ltd., 1926.

IMPERIALIST (Dr. Jameson), *Cecil Rhodes, a biography and appreciation.* London: Chapman & Hall, 1897.

IRELAND, ALLEYNE, *The Anglo-Boer Conflict.* Boston: Small, Maynard & Co., 1900.

KEANE, AUGUSTUS HENRY, *The Gold of Ophir.* London: E. Stanford, 1901.

KRUGER, PAUL, *The Memoirs of Paul Kruger.* New York: The Century Co., 1902.

LAKE, STUART N., *Wyatt Earp, Frontier Marshal.* Boston: Houghton Mifflin & Co., 1931.

LYMAN, GEORGE D., *The Saga of the Comstock Lode.* New York: Charles Scribner's Sons, 1934.

McDONALD, J. G., *Rhodes, A Life.* London: P. Allan & Co., 1927.

MACLAREN, J. M., *Gold.* London: The Mining Journal, 1908.

MITCHELL, SIR LEWIS, *The Life of the Rt. Hon. Cecil J. Rhodes.* London: E. Arnold & Co., 1910.

NEVILLE, MRS. AMELIA R., *The Fantastic City.* Boston: Houghton Mifflin & Co., 1932.

O'MEARA, JAMES, *Pioneer Senators.*

PHILLIPS, SIR LIONEL, *Some Reminiscences.* London: Hutchinson & Co., 1924.

———, *Transvaal Problems.* London: J. Murray, 1905.

Pioneer Miner and the Pack Mule Express, The. California Historical Society.

Report of the Select Committee on the Jameson Raid in the Territory of South African Republic. Printed by order of the House of Assembly, July, 1896. Cape Town: W. A. Richards & Sons, Government Printers.

RICKARD, T. A. (editor), *Economics of Mining.* New York: Hill Publishing Co., 1907.

SLOCUM, CAPT. JOSHUA, *Sailing Alone Around the World.* New York: The Century Co., 1900.

TRUSCOTT, SAMUEL J., *The Witwatersrand Goldfields Banket and Mining Practice.* London: Macmillan & Co., Ltd., 1898.

WILLIAMS, GATENBY, *William Guggenheim.* New York: Lone Voice Publishing Co., 1934.

BOOKS AND PERIODICALS MENTIONED IN TEXT

Almanach de Gotha.

BAIN, H. F., and READ, T. R., *Ores and Industries in South America.* New York: Harper & Brothers, 1934.

BENT, JAMES THEODORE, *The Ruined Cities of Mashonaland.* London: Longman, Green & Co., 1892.

BEVERIDGE, ALBERT J., *Life of John Marshall.* Boston, New York: Houghton Mifflin Co., 1919.

Bible.

BURNHAM, FREDERICK R., *Scouting on Two Continents.* Garden City, N. Y.: Doubleday, Page & Co., 1926.

BUTT, ARCHIBALD W., *Letters of Archie Butt.* Garden City, N. Y.: Doubleday, Page & Co., 1924.

CHURCHILL, LORD RANDOLPH, *Men, Mines, and Animals in South Africa.* London: S. Low, Marston & Co., Ltd., 1897.

COLVIN, IAN, *The Life of Jameson.* London: E. Arnold & Co., 1922.

CORNING, FREDERICK G., *A Student Reverie.* New York: The De Vinne Press, 1920.

DAVIS, RICHARD HARDING, *Soldiers of Fortune*. New York: Charles Scribner's Sons, 1902.

D'ABERNON, LORD, *An Ambassador of Peace*. London: 1929-1931.

FITZPATRICK, PERCY, *The Transvaal from Within*. New York: Frederick A. Stokes Co., 1899.

HAMMOND, NATALIE HARRIS, *A Woman's Part in a Revolution*. New York, London: Longmans, Green & Co., 1897.

History of the Texas Rangers.

HOBBS, WILLIAM H., *Leonard Wood*. New York, London: G. P. Putnam's Sons, 1920.

HOUSE, EDWARD M., *Intimate Papers of Colonel House*. Arranged as narrative by Charles Seymour. Boston: Houghton Mifflin & Co., 1926-1928.

John Hays Hammond's Report.

KESSLER, CAMILLUS, *At the Bottom of the Ladder*. Philadelphia, London: J. B. Lippincott Co., 1926.

LONGWORTH, ALICE ROOSEVELT, *Crowded Hours*. New York: Charles Scribner's Sons, 1933.

MARBURG, THEODORE, *Development of the League of Nations Idea*. New York: The Macmillan Co., 1932.

MARVEL, IK, *Reveries of a Bachelor*. Philadelphia: D. McKay, 1850.

MILLIN, SARAH GERTRUDE, *Rhodes*. London: Chatto & Windus, 1933.

PARSONS, A. B., *The Porphyry Coppers*. New York: Published by the American Institute of Mining and Metallurgical Engineers, sponsored by Rocky Mountain fund, 1933.

POTTER, ELIZABETH, and GRAY, M. T., *The Lure of San Francisco*. San Francisco: P. Elder & Co., 1915.

PRESCOTT, WILLIAM HICKLING, *History of the Conquest of Mexico*. New York: Harper & Brothers, 1843.

RANDALL-MACIVER, DAVID, *Mediaeval Rhodesia*. London: Macmillan & Co., Ltd., 1906.

RICKARD, T. A., *Man and Metals*. New York: Whittlesey House, McGraw-Hill Book Co., 1932.

SCHREINER, OLIVE, *The Story of an African Farm*. London: Hutchinson & Co., 1910.

———, *Trooper Peter Halket of Mashonaland*. Boston: Roberts Brothers, 1897.

SIRINGO, CHARLES A., *A Cowboy Detective*. New York: J. S. Ogilvie Publishing Co., 1912.

———, *History of "Billy the Kid."* Sante Fe, N. M.: The Author, 1920.

STEAD, W. T., *Americanisation of the World*. New York, London: H. Markley, 1902.

———, *If Christ Came to Chicago!* Chicago: Laird & Lee, 1894.

STEAD, W. T., *Letters from Julia.* New York: John Lane Co., 1907.

SULLIVAN, MARK, *Our Times, The United States 1900-1925.* New York: Charles Scribner's Sons, 1928-1929.

TANNENBAUM, FRANK, *Whither Latin America?* New York: Thomas Y. Crowell Co., 1934.

United States Army Register.

What the Coal Commission Found. Report of commission appointed by President Coolidge.

WILLIAMS, BASIL, *Cecil Rhodes.* London: Constable & Co., 1921.

Fortune; Forum; Independent; National Geographic Magazine; Pall Mall Gazette; Popular Science Magazine; Review of Reviews; Saturday Evening Post; South Africa; World Court Magazine; Yale Literary Magazine. *Courier-Journal,* Louisville, Ky.; *Daily Mail,* London; *Globe,* New York; *Herald,* New York; *Standard and Diggers News,* Johannesburg; *Star,* Johannesburg; *Sun,* New York; *Times,* Johannesburg; *Times,* London; *Times,* New York; *Times,* Visalia, Calif.; *Tombstone Epitaph,* Tombstone, Ariz.; *Volksstem* (Boer newspaper).

Index

Index

Index 787

55

Blake, W. P., 149
Blanding, Don, 89
Blasco Ibañez, Vicente, **707**
Blick, John, 267-269, **272**
Blick, Judd, 272
Bliss, Tasker H., 640
Blood River, 245
Blythe estate, 144
Boardman, Mabel T., **623**
Bodie, Calif., 86, 489
Body, W. S., 86
Boer government, 215; policy toward Uitlanders, 308, 312; factions in, 308, 309; Volksraad, 308, 315; liberals in, 309; expenditures, 309; courts not fair, 315; taxation of Uitlanders, 317, 320; drifts closed, 318; propaganda, 320; suspicious of Uitlander plans, 334; demands on, 335; threaten to arrest Reform leaders, 352; Raadzaal, 370; preliminary trial of Reform leaders, 370; choice of law in trying Reformers, 379, 381, 382; court procedure, 379; sentenced Reform leaders, 383, 389; demonstrations against, 391; petitioned for Reform leaders, 392, 401, 403; bill rendered British South Africa Co., 418; preparing for war, 421; entente with Germany, 422; *see also* Boers *and* Kruger
Boers, love of Rhodes, 227; settling of South Africa, 243; treatment of blacks, 245; defeat of Zulu, 245; fighting the Matabele, 246; defense methods, 251; language, 314; Christmas festival, 333; treatment of Reform leaders, 355; in World War, 427; *see also* Boer government *and* Kruger
Boer War, 308, 422, 424, 444
Bolivar, Simon, 152
Bolivia, 728
Bonzano, Cardinal, **725**
Booth, E. H., 406
Booth, Edwin, 435
Borah, William, 671, **705**
Boswell, James, 432
Botha, Louis, 308, 392, **427-429**
Bourn, William B., 178
Bourn, Mrs. W. B., 179
Bourne, Jonathan, 585
Bours, Tomas, 114
Boxing, learning and use, 49, 58
Boys' Clubs of America, 760-762
Braden Copper Co., 519
Bradley, Frederick W., 482, 495, 510
Brady, Walter, 761

Brandegee, Frank B., 552, 649, 680, **708**
Brewer, William H., 40, 45
Brewer, Mount, 45
Brewster, Ralph O., 685
Briand, Aristide, 717
British Empire, Rhodes's ideas for enlarging, 221; territory added by Rhodes, 228; expansion, 455; *see also* England
British South Africa Company (Chartered), 414, 575, 714; founding of, 214; territory controlled by, 228; mining laws, 241; formed, 247; charter confirmed, 248; land grants issued, 248; police, 249; lands of Lobengula given to, 254; in Rhodesia, 286; control of railways, 288; London shareholders, 293
Brock, John W., 491
Broden, Dominick, 161
Broderick, David C., 11
Broiderick, Mrs. J. P., 144
Brooks, Phillips, 220
Brown, American in Transvaal, **315**
Brown, Page, 481
Brown, T. B., 341, 342
Browne, Ross E., 377, 511
Brownell, George L., 55
Browning, Robert, 146
Bryan, William Jennings, 127, 536, **686**
Bryce, James, Viscount, 328, 624, 638
Buckingham Palace, 593
Budapest, 608
Buenaventura, Colombia, 152, 154
Bulawayo, 233, 246, 249, 251, 274, 287, 704; native attack on, 256
Bull Moose party, 553, 583
Buller, General, 445
Bunker Hill and Sullivan mine, 88, 116, 181, 186, 495, 510, 533; production, 187; discovery, 187; labor troubles, 188-196
Burdett, Sir Francis, 439
Burdett-Coutts, Baroness, 416, 438-440, 590
Burdett-Coutts, Mr., 439, 589, 590, 592, 602
Burger, Schalk, 392, 420
Burke, Edmund, 432
Burke, Jack, 533
Burlingame, Calif., 481
Burnham, Frederick Russell, 267, 768; scouting in Africa, 252; killing of the 'Mlimo, 256; land grant to, 272; looking for coal, 272; finds copper fields, 273; protecting two presidents, 565; Mediterranean cruise, 720; irrigation plans, 741, 744; oil ventures, 753

798 Index

804 Index